PRESIDENT AND CONGRESS

**Executive Hegemony
at the Crossroads
of American Government**

PRESIDENT AND CONGRESS

Executive Hegemony at the Crossroads of American Government

ROBERT J. SPITZER

Temple University Press
Philadelphia

To Peggy
I'd love to kiss you,
but I just washed my hair—

Temple University Press, Philadelphia 19122

ISBN 1-56639-016-8

Library of Congress Cataloging-in-Publication Data

Spitzer, Robert.
    President and Congress: executive hegemony at the crossroads of
American Government / Robert Spitzer.
        p.   cm.
    Includes bibliographical references.
    ISBN 1-56639-016-8 (cloth: alk. paper)
    1. Presidents—United States.   2. United States.   Congress.
3. Separation of powers—United States.   I. Title.
JK585.S654   1993
320.473—dc20   92-14781

About the Author

ROBERT J. SPITZER is professor of political science at the State University of New York, College at Cortland. He received a Ph.D. in government from Cornell University in 1980. His books include *The Presidency and Public Policy, The Right to Life Movement and Third Party Politics, The Presidential Veto,* and *Media and Public Policy* (as editor). Professor Spitzer has also contributed articles to a variety of journals and edited books, and has testified before Congress on matters relating to the separation of powers. He served as a member of the New York State Commission on the Bicentennial of the U.S. Constitution from 1986 to 1990 and served as chair of the political science department at the College at Cortland from 1983 to 1989.

Contents

TABLES

FIGURES

BOXES

Preface

This book is designed to address two related purposes. The first is to serve as a lively, informative, and readable text for class use. Too much of political science literature has neglected its roots in law, history, and politics in favor of narrow, empirical approaches that seem more concerned with what can be proved than with what is important. Much of this empirical work is confusing for students because of its narrow scope and apparent detachment from larger political questions. By no means does this book ignore important empirical work; on the contrary, such work is given important attention. That and other research, however, is discussed in the context of the broader questions and debates that have shaped the interaction of the legislative and executive branches, including the trends that have led to the rise of the modern strong presidency, the apparent decline of Congress, and the implications of these trends for the constitutional separation of powers.

In addition, the book gives careful attention to such specific and important topics as the budget process, leadership, war powers, and treaty-making. From Civil War financing to Gramm-Rudman-Hollings, from St. Clair's Defeat in 1791 to the 1991 war with Iraq, the presidential-congressional relationship animates American politics. Numerous examples and cases are sprinkled throughout the book to enliven the reading and illustrate important principles. While this book focuses on only one of three interbranch relations, I argue that, as the book's subtitle says, this interaction is quite literally the "crossroads of American government." Students who understand this relationship will understand a great deal about American politics.

The second purpose and need this book addresses is that of the scholar who is interested in the important and controversial questions that surround these two key national institutions. I argue that the interbranch balance has shifted toward the executive branch, yielding a situation where the executive has in effect become the first branch of government. The consciously provocative heading I apply to this is "executive hegemony."

In addition, I take issue with most of the near-avalanche of criticism surrounding the traditional separation of powers. The prevailing criticisms of the presidential-congressional relationship argue either that Congress has become an ineffectual roadblock to effective presidential government, or that Congress has become imperial by sapping the President's proper powers. These criticisms share the same two flaws: first, they assume that presidential dominance is a natural or inevitable outgrowth of the constitutional structure, an assertion that is demonstrably false; and second, they reject an accommodation between President and Congress under the separation of powers.

In order to provide student and scholar with appropriate context, Chapters 1 and 2 summarize and analyze the constitutional and historical bases of the presidential-congressional relationship, incorporating specific discussions, such as those of the historic First and contentious Twenty-seventh Congresses. Chapters 3 and 4 focus on the domestic realm, summarizing the modern presidential-congressional balance and offering several explanations for this interbranch relationship founded in the book's analytic perspective. Chapters 5 and 6 give careful and parallel attention to foreign affairs, following the same style of analysis and argument. Chapter 7 addresses the normative questions arising from the rest of the book. Two appendixes at the end of the book offer general information about President and Congress for the reader seeking to supplement basic knowledge.

Robert J. Spitzer

Acknowledgments

This book is dedicated to the proposition that teaching and scholarship are two sides of the same coin. I share the experience of many of my colleagues who find that a dynamic balance between classroom and research activities enhances one's ability to develop and express important ideas and interesting facts in a clearheaded way. This book is the consequence of the convergence of teaching and research. In turn, I hope that it will be useful in both realms.

Fred Friendly tells a story of a conversation he once had with Carl Sandburg, who told Friendly that writing is easy: "You write down one word and then another." Friendly's verdict on this sage advice was, "It's not that simple." I would split the difference by saying that writing is easy, but not simple, at least insofar as written work needs, and benefits from, the good efforts of many other individuals. I would like to extend my sincere thanks to the many reviewers who read part or all of the manuscript, including James Best, Kent State University; Jeffrey E. Cohen, University of Houston; Byron Daynes, Brigham Young University; Louis Fisher; Susan Hammond, American University; John R. Johannes, Marquette University; Loch Johnson, University of Georgia; G. Calvin MacKenzie, Colby College;

J. Keith Melville, Brigham Young University; David M. Olson, University of North Carolina–Greensboro; Laurellen Porter, Indiana State University; L. Earl Shaw, Northern Arizona University; Sally Jo Vasicko; and Cheryl D. Young, University of Arkansas. I also wish to thank Lori Padavona for her assistance in this and numerous other projects.

I again take much pleasure in recognizing my parents, Bill and Jinny Spitzer. As Seneca said, "He who receives a benefit with gratitude repays the first installment on his debt."

Finally, I need hardly add that any faults or omissions in this work are entirely the responsibility of Jim Pfiffner's tiny gremlins.

Robert J. Spitzer

Introduction

The framers of the Constitution sought to construct a system in which no branch of the national government could make important decisions alone. To be sure, the last 200 years of history include many examples of autonomous actions taken by one branch despite the wishes of the rest of the government. Nevertheless, the fabric of national politics consists of a system of "separated institutions sharing powers."[1]

For this reason, the course of national politics cannot be understood without an appreciation of the relationships between the branches. This book will examine only one of the three interbranch relationships—that between the executive and the legislative. This relationship merits special attention for several reasons.

First, the executive and legislative branches engage in regular, affirmative governance. The third branch—the judiciary—does not.[2] The primary means by which this governance takes place is through

---

[1] Richard E. Neustadt, *Presidential Power and the Modern Presidents* (New York: Free Press, 1990), p. 29.

[2] This is not to say that the courts are less important than the rest of the government but rather to acknowledge that the courts' impact on national politics and policy-making is sporadic. Unlike Congress and the executive branch, the courts are passive institutions in that they must wait for cases to come before them. No court ruling can occur without a court challenge. When they do arise, however, court cases may dramatically change the nature of governing, as in the areas of abortion and civil rights.

lawmaking, a process that can occur only through joint presidential-congressional action (leaving aside the process of administrative rule making, which itself springs from prior legislative enactments).

The Constitution divides these responsibilities. Even though Congress is granted "all legislative powers" in Article I, any proposed legislation enacted by both houses of Congress must cross the President's desk for a signature or veto. Any vetoed bill, excluding bills which the President cannot return to Congress (the conditions for a pocket veto), must go back to Congress for reconsideration. The President is charged with recommending to Congress "necessary and expedient" measures. The President may also call Congress into session when circumstances warrant.

To be sure, the contemporary political relationship between the two branches extends well beyond this formal framework. Presidential administrations put their own distinctive mark on the legislative process by influencing every phase of that process from bill drafting to implementation, yet the President's politically strong hand in legislative affairs could have come about only within a constitutional structure that shared these responsibilities in the first place. As constitutional scholar Louis Fisher notes, "To study one branch of government in isolation from the others is usually an exercise in make-believe."[3]

Second, the presidency and Congress are elective and therefore popularly based institutions. This simple but crucial fact means that policy-making and governing extend well beyond the mechanics of formulating and carrying out laws. It means that presidents and members of Congress must be prepared to gauge public opinion when it is likely to be a factor and more often be adept at influencing and molding public opinion. One key reason presidents have tended to dominate legislative affairs in the twentieth century is because of their built-in advantages over Congress when it comes to rallying national sentiment. After all, the President is the only national leader whose district consists of the entire country. Moreover, the President is widely expected to be both the administrative and the symbolic head of the government.

Third, the political fortunes of each branch are affected by its relations with the other. A President who is considered skillful at deal-

---

[3]Louis Fisher, *The Politics of Shared Power* (Washington, D.C.: C Q Press, 1987), p. ix.

ing with Congress and who succeeds in realizing the enactment of important parts of a legislative program will be considered effective. By contrast, a President whose relations with Congress are confrontational, belligerent, and negative (as shown, for example, by heavy veto use) will probably not be considered either successful or effective. Similarly, a Congress caught up with policy and power struggles with the President is likely to be criticized for excessive partisanship and an inability to deal with substantive problems and concerns.

Congress faces a double standard in the public's evaluation of its performance. It is alternatively criticized for being too submissive to presidential wishes, as during the early days of the Franklin Roosevelt and Lyndon Johnson presidencies, and for behaving too aggressively toward the President, as during the later years of the Nixon and Reagan administrations. Political life for presidents is less contradictory in that weak or unambitious presidents are typically scorned for their weakness, whereas stronger, assertive presidents are rarely condemned in the long run for their assertiveness.[4] In fact, presidential success is frequently determined by the extent to which presidents expand the limits of their office and powers.

Fourth, anyone who understands and appreciates the presidential-congressional relationship can also claim a considerable knowledge of American politics. Those who follow national news know that reporting on national affairs is invariably laced with stories about presidential-congressional dealings. Whether a confirmation hearing, haggling over the size and impact of the national debt, the future of farm subsidies, or a quarrel over a national security leak, presidential-congressional relations provide the news media with endless political grist. What a stormy marriage between celebrities is for the supermarket tabloids, the presidential-congressional "marriage" is for national political news hounds.

✧ ✧ ✧

[4] An exception to this statement might be the case of the Franklin Roosevelt administration and the Twenty-second Amendment. Roosevelt's popularity carried him through four successful elections. After his death, the Twenty-second Amendment was added to the Constitution, barring presidents from being elected more than twice. On its face, this action limits presidential power by limiting access to the office. Yet whether this amendment actually has the effect of inhibiting the President's power while in office is open to debate. See Earl Spangler, *Presidential Tenure and Constitutional Limitation* (Washington, D.C.: University Press of America, 1977); Thomas E. Cronin, *The State of the Presidency* (Boston: Little, Brown, 1980), pp. 46-49.

This book will advance two broad arguments and a related analytic perspective. The first is didactic in that it is aimed primarily at those who seek to acquire a basic understanding of our national institutions and is inspired by the Constitution itself. When the Constitution's framers constructed a three-branch system, they considered Congress the first branch and indicated this preference by devoting the Constitution's first article to it. This "significant" fact reflects the framers' desire for " 'a government of laws and not of men,' and they expected Congress, except in times of war or emergency, to be the central and directing organ of the government."[5] But if the Constitution were to be rewritten today, an honest appraisal would recognize that the executive branch has in effect become the first branch. This is not to suggest that Congress is any less empowered to enact law than it was two centuries ago. It is, rather, a commentary on how much the relationship between these two branches has changed, especially in the twentieth century. It is for this reason that the title of this book lists the presidency first. What was designed as a congressionally centered system has evolved into a presidentially centered, or "executive-hegemonic," system. I rely on the straightforward dictionary definition of *hegemony,* derived from description of the city-states of ancient Greece, meaning here a presidentially predominant system. This does not mean that the executive usually or even often succeeds in political endeavors with respect to the legislature but rather that the President establishes most of the assumptions, tone, style, and nature of national political discourse between the two branches.[6] In short, we have undergone "a polar shift in how the constitutional system operates."[7]

This observation is old news to most analysts of American politics (although some may disagree over the degree of the shift), yet it is a plain fact that has been set aside or even challenged by two divergent but intersecting schools of thought. The first includes those who applaud the return of the post-Watergate strong presidency as a rem-

[5] J. W. Peltason, *Understanding the Constitution* (New York: Holt, Rinehart & Winston, 1988), p. 36. See also Alfred DeGrazia, ed., *Congress: The First Branch of Government* (New York: Anchor, 1967).

[6] According to the *Oxford English Dictionary,* the Greek city-state of Athens, for example, was considered hegemonic when it dominated the other city-states of the peninsula in ancient times. The analogue for the presidency might be labeled the sphere of influence. This concept is discussed in more detail in Chapter 7.

[7] Donald L. Robinson, *Government for the Third American Century* (Boulder, Colo.: Westview, 1989), p. ix.

edy for the alleged obstructionism and anachronistic nature of Congress. Most of these critics see the growth of the modern presidency as being well within the constitutional framework of 200 years ago. The second school of thought incorporates those who criticize Congress for its "imperial" behavior since the Watergate era, arguing that it is Congress rather than the presidency which has principally overstepped its constitutional boundaries and that Congress has been responsible for improperly restricting presidential governance. For both educational and argumentative reasons, the first argument merits careful attention.

As a corollary to this argument, I propose that the presidential-congressional intersection quite literally forms the crux of national governing. In imagery and form it is, as this book's subtitle says, the "crossroads of American government."

The second argument I will advance addresses a fundamental critique of modern governing. The prevailing contemporary critique of presidential-congressional relations posits that our national system is infused with the disease of paralysis. Variously characterized as stalemate, decay, deadlock, or gridlock, this problem causes our governing institutions to be ever less able to govern successfully—that is, lacking in speed, efficiency, and responsiveness. As early as 1963 historian James MacGregor Burns warned of the "cycle of deadlock and drift." [8] These concerns were echoed and amplified in the 1970s and especially the 1980s and indeed have become a prevailing critique of relations between the President and Congress.[9] Pertinent to this book, the stalemate argument serves as the centerpiece of a recent important study of the President and Congress by political scientist Michael Mezey, who observes an "inability to produce good public policy [that] is rooted in our constitutional arrangement of separate political institutions sharing power and in our political cul-

[8] James MacGregor Burns, *The Deadlock of Democracy* (Englewood Cliffs, N.J.: Prentice-Hall, 1963), p. 2. The concern over deadlock and drift actually predates Burns's analysis, as seen, for example, in repeated calls for more "responsible" political parties as a means to add coherence and vigor to national governing. See Austin Ranney, *The Doctrine of Responsible party Government* (Urbana: University of Illinois Press, 1954).

[9] See, for example, Donald L. Robinson, ed., *Reforming American Government* (Boulder, Colo.: Westview, 1985); James L. Sundquist, *Constitutional Reform and Effective Governance* (Washington, D.C.: Brookings Institution, 1986); Donald L. Robinson, *To the Best of My Ability* (New York: Norton, 1987); Report and Recommendations of the Committee on the Constitutional System, *A Bicentennial Analysis of the American Political Structure*, January 1987 (Washington, D.C.: Committee on the Constitutional System).

ture. . . ."[10] These critics offer much insightful analysis about the
problems of contemporary government. I will argue, however, that
contemporary governing problems have been in part misdiagnosed;
that traditional separation of powers is a source of strength, not of
weakness for modern governing, its alleged and actual inefficiencies
notwithstanding; that separation of powers invigorates rather than
enervates national governing; and that much of our self-described national malaise can be traced to our abandonment of the principles of
separation of powers rather than continued adherence to them. This
argument is addressed specifically in Chapter 7.

Aside from sustaining these two arguments, this book also applies
an analytic perspective to the study of the presidency and Congress
that is summarized by presidential scholar Michael Nelson, who offered this comment in a review essay on the presidency: "Political science, traditionally the intellectual bedfellow of history and law, has
become distressingly ahistorical since World War II in its haste to im-
itate, in rapid succession, sociology, various branches of psychology,
economics, even biology."[11] I do not propose to reject nontraditional
analytic or methodological perspectives pertaining to the study of the
President and Congress. I do, however, share Nelson's distress at the
sometimes narrow and arcane vision of those who would study these
two institutions. Therefore, this book will lean heavily on historical,
legal, and structural perspectives pertaining to political relations insofar as history, law, and political structures are central to explaining
the evolution and behavior of the executive and legislative branches
of government. In addition, careful and detailed attention will be
given to foreign policy, because (1) this realm of interaction has been
central in shaping relations between the branches[12] and (2) the literature on the presidency and Congress tends to focus on either domestic or foreign policy but not both in the same work.[13]

[10] Michael Mezey, *Congress, the President, and Public Policy* (Boulder, Colo.: Westview, 1989), p. xiii.

[11] Michael Nelson, "Is There a Postmodern Presidency?" *Congress and the Presidency,*
16 (Autumn 1989): 155.

[12] This argument has been made by, among others, Arthur Schlesinger, Jr., *The Imperial Presidency* (Boston: Houghton Mifflin, 1973).

[13] For example, foreign policy receives little or no attention in such studies of presidential-congressional relations as Rowland Egger and Joseph P. Harris, *President and
Congress* (New York: McGraw-Hill, 1963); Louis W. Koenig, *Congress and the President* (Chicago: Scott, Foresman, 1965); Nelson W. Polsby, *Congress and the
Presidency* (Englewood Cliffs, N.J.: Prentice-Hall, 1986); Fisher, *The Politics of*

To this end, Chapters 1 and 2 summarize and analyze the constitutional and historical basis of the presidential-congressional relationship, setting the stage for the evolution of executive hegemony. Chapter 3 discusses the ways in which executive hegemony plays itself out in domestic executive-legislative processes. Chapter 4 offers several explanations for presidential-congressional behavior that are grounded in the book's analytic perspective. Chapters 5 and 6 pay careful attention to foreign affairs, and Chapter 7 draws on information and conclusions arising from the previous chapters to return to the normative questions raised in this introduction. I will argue that executive hegemony is certainly inevitable, probably necessary, and possibly desirable, but I will also argue that it is acceptable only in the context of a renewal of separation of powers in which Congress can continue to play a vigorous and active role.

Finally, two extended appendixes follow Chapter 7 to provide basic information about the President and Congress for readers not fully acquainted with the political forces that serve as the context for the two branches. This basic descriptive information is placed at the end of the book so as not to disrupt the book's arguments. Readers are invited to refer to these appendixes as appropriate.

Shared Power; Mezey, *Congress, the President, and Public Policy.* By contrast, foreign policy is the sole focus in such books as Cecil V. Crabb, Jr., and Pat M. Holt, *Invitation to Struggle: Congress, the President, and Foreign Policy* (Washington, D.C.: CQ Press, 1989); Thomas E. Mann, ed., *A Question of Balance: The President, the Congress,* and *Foreign Policy* (Washington, D.C.: Brookings Institution, 1990).

Chapter 1

Foundations of the Presidential-Congressional Relationship

In a republican government, the legislative authority necessarily predominates.

JAMES MADISON, *FEDERALIST* NO. 51

Our long tradition of veneration for the U.S. Constitution has helped perpetuate the myth that there was something inevitable about the political system that emerged at the conclusion of the federal convention in 1787. To be sure, the Constitution's founders had an intimate acquaintance with such concepts as separation of powers, a three-branch governmental system, and a two-house legislature. Indeed, these features were an integral part of most state governmental systems.

But even a casual look at colonial history, the country's experience under the Articles of Confederation, and the founders' deliberations reveals wide disagreement over the appropriate configuration of the new national government. It also reveals the antecedents of the struggles and ambiguities surrounding executive-legislative relations. More specifically, it reveals how this relationship lay at the very core of the constitutional system.

ANTECEDENTS

Early American experiences with governing were of two types: governing forms and rulers imposed by Great Britain and indigenous

1

governing institutions. Dissatisfaction with British rule was of course a principal cause of the revolution. Many Americans came to resent the laws and procedures dictated by the British monarch, the colonial governors, and Parliament.

Nowhere are these complaints more loudly articulated than in the Declaration of Independence, which purports to detail "a long train of abuses and usurpations." Of George III (and by extension "his [colonial] Governors"), the Declaration charged that "the history of the present King of Great Britain is a history of repeated injuries and usurpations" whose actions resulted in the "establishment of an absolute tyranny over these States." The Declaration goes on to provide a laundry list of complaints, most of which pertain to fundamental matters of governing, including the making of law, individual rights, and the administration of justice.

While the king is the primary target of criticism, Parliament also comes under fire for "attempts . . . to extend an unwarrantable jurisdiction over us" and for being "deaf to the voice of justice." James Wilson noted during debate at the federal convention of 1787 that Americans "did not oppose the British King but the parliament—the opposition was not agt. an Unity but a corrupt multitude." While Wilson's argument understates the actual antipathy toward the British monarch during the revolutionary period, his comments underscore the ire that was also directed toward Parliament.[1]

The American revolutionary leaders sought autonomy from the arbitrary and oppressive features of British rule, but they were also British descendants who embraced the Magna Carta, the British Bill of Rights, and other landmarks of the British constitutional tradition. The outgrowth of this dilemma was the weak governing structure embodied in this country's first constitution, the Articles of Confederation. It called for a single governing structure—a national single-chamber Congress—that would exercise executive and judicial as well as legislative powers. Unquestionably, the country's leaders were reacting in this document to distasteful experiences with strong centralized governmental authority in general and strong executives in particular.

Under the Articles, administrative responsibilities came to be assumed by congressional committees. These committees resembled

[1] Max Farrand, *The Records of the Federal Convention of 1787*, 4 vols. (New Haven, Conn.: Yale University Press, 1966), I, p. 71.

modern legislative committees in form, but in substance they attempted to fulfill the purpose later served by the cabinet departments. Burgeoning size and responsibilities forced Congress to establish separate administrative boards that eventually came to be headed by single executives. Responsibilities over such areas as the treasury, the military, foreign affairs, commerce, and taxation were given by Congress to boards and individuals who remained dependent on Congress for authority and direction. The executives were usually chosen from outside Congress. As often happens with committees, most of the work fell on the shoulders of the appointees, who often requested added powers from Congress commensurate with their responsibilities. In 1781, for example, Congress agreed to grant overall administrative direction to a secretary for foreign affairs. The first man to occupy the post, Robert Livingston, quit the job after a year out of frustration. Without administrative centralization and adequate independent authority, the need for administrative reform became increasingly evident, and the problems with this jerry-built system of legislative committees exercising executive powers became exacerbated with the end of the Revolutionary War and war-related pressures (the war was a key factor in establishing stronger executive authority in the national government).[2]

In short, the governing of the country in the postrevolutionary United States under the weak one-branch national system was an administrative nightmare. Dissatisfaction with this system's administrative inefficiency was a central factor leading to the convening of a special convention organized to examine the government's evident problems.[3]

THE FOUNDERS' FEARS

Three important facts can help us understand the difficulties of constructing this new system of governing. First, the founders had real difficulty grappling with the definition, nature, extent, and limits of legislative, executive, and judicial power (while such offices had long existed, this by no means resolved the more complex question of the

---

[2] See Louis Fisher, *President and Congress* (New York: Free Press, 1972), pp. 6–14.

[3] J. W. Peltason, *Understanding the Constitution* (New York: Holt, Rinehart & Winston, 1988), pp. 8–11.

powers of the offices). Americans today take these concepts for granted, although they are subject to continual interpretation and evolution. However, for the founders, "the conceptual content of these terms was inchoate."[4] This ambiguity was much in evidence in the definition and operations of early state governments, and it contributed to the observed abuses of legislative powers.

Second, "the chief structural problem of the Constitutional Convention," according to Wilfred Binkley, was "a solution of the old problem of the relation of the Executive to the legislature."[5] The difficulty of resolving the relationship between the legislative and executive branches in the eighteenth century foreshadowed similar contemporary political problems.

Third, the construction of the legislative and executive branches that emerged in the Constitution was influenced by both theoretical and practical concerns. We know that the founders were well read and sophisticated in their understanding of theories of governance. Principal among influential works was Montesquieu's treatise *The Spirit of the Laws,* published in 1748. In this work Montesquieu articulated the notion of separation of powers as an essential means for limiting governmental power and protecting individual liberty from governmental usurpations.[6]

However, the theoretical formulations of Montesquieu and others probably played a less vital role than did the practical considerations and experiences that the founders brought with them.[7] For example, of the fifty-five delegates who attended the 1787 convention twenty had participated in the writing of state constitutions, thirty were serving as members of their state legislatures, and more than

---

[4] Wilfred E. Binkley, *President and Congress* (New York: Vintage, 1962), p. 27.

[5] Binkley, *President and Congress,* p. 12.

[6] For more on the intellectual tradition behind the Constitution, see Donald L. Robinson, *"To the Best of My Ability": The Presidency and the Constitution* (New York: Norton, 1987), chap. 2.

[7] Fisher makes this argument in *President and Congress,* pp. 3–4. Binkley said that "the vogue of Montesquieu in America . . . provided the formula with which Americans could rationalize their political experience." *President and Congress,* p. 19. References to the political thought of Montesquieu and others can be found in the records of the debate at the federal convention and in the *Federalist Papers.* See Farrand, *Records of the Federal Convention;* and *Federalist Papers* (New York: New American Library, 1961). For example, Madison discusses Montesquieu in *Federalist* No. 43 and No. 47, as does Hamilton in No. 9 and No. 78.

three-fourths had also served in the national Congress under the Articles.[8] These experiences converged in the debate and bargaining that composed the Philadelphia convention.

Nowhere was this exploration and tinkering more evident than in the various plans, proposals, and counterproposals that provided the basis for discussion and debate at the federal convention. Delegates from Virginia took advantage of initial delays at the start of the convention to caucus and produce a package of fifteen resolutions that came to be known as the Virginia Plan. Formally offered by the Virginia delegate and governor, Edmund Randolph, but masterminded by James Madison, the plan proposed a tripartite system of government, yet the legislative branch was clearly to be the center of this three-member solar system. The lower house was to be popularly elected, with more representatives apportioned to the more populous states. The upper house was to be elected by the lower house. The executive was to be chosen by Congress and could serve only a single term, the length of which was not initially specified. The President was to exercise a qualified veto, but only as a member of a "council of revision" composed of the executive and "a convenient number of the national judiciary." Among other powers, the legislature was to have the power to veto state laws, without recourse to override.[9]

The leading alternative constitutional scheme, the New Jersey Plan, was promoted by representatives of smaller states that feared a system dominated by the larger states. This proposal was composed of nine resolutions that were really amendments to the existing Articles of Confederation. This plan proposed to keep a single-house Congress organized with equal representation from each state, but with enhanced powers. There would be an executive, but it was to be a plural executive (the actual number was not specified) rather than a single individual. This collective group would have powers and limits similar to those spelled out in the Virginia Plan, except for the veto power. A federal court ("supreme Tribunal") was to be appointed by the executive alone.[10]

[8] Kenneth Prewitt, Sidney Verba, and Robert H. Salisbury, *An Introduction to American Government* (New York: Harper & Row, 1987), p. 31.

[9] See Max Farrand, *The Framing of the Constitution of the United States* (New Haven, Conn.: Yale University Press, 1913), chap. V and app. II.

[10] Farrand, *The Framing of the Constitution,* chap. VI and. app. III.

Fear of a Strong Executive

Adverse colonial experiences with British monarchs and their appointed governors provoked a strong backlash to executive authority. Speaking as a delegate to the 1787 convention, Ben Franklin related a story of how the king's appointed governor of Pennsylvania had used his absolute veto powers over colonial legislation to "extort money. No good law whatever could be passed without a private bargain with him." Such bargains, according to Franklin, usually involved salary increases or other direct monetary benefits in exchange for the governor's assent.[11] These and similar experiences helped fuel indignation against executive authority.

As a result, the independent state governments established in the 1770s were structured to sharply limit executive powers in that they encouraged "the tendency to make the governor as far as possible dependent upon and subordinate to the legislature."[12] This tendency is clearly seen in early state constitutions. The state constitution of Virginia, for example, said that its governor could "exercise the executive powers of government, according to the laws of this Commonwealth." The thrust of this kind of language was to allow legislatures to subject executive actions to final legislative approval.[13] Legislative intervention in state executive affairs extended to such areas as appointment and removal of administrative officials, the granting of pardons and reprieves to citizens, and the convening and adjournment of state legislatures.[14] In fact, some states abandoned the idea of governors altogether, in favor of state commissions. And until the New York State Constitution of 1777, no state granted its governor permanent veto power over legislation.[15]

Antiexecutive sentiment was expressed by many at the federal convention. This sentiment usually took the form of cautions against

[11] Farrand, *Records of the Federal Convention*, I, p. 99.

[12] Quoted in William M. Goldsmith, *The Growth of Presidential Power*, 3 vols. (New York: Chelsea House, 1983), I, p. 15.

[13] Charles C. Thach, Jr., *The Creation of the Presidency, 1775–1789* (New York: Da Capo, 1969), p. 29. This study was first published in 1922.

[14] Stephen J. Wayne, *The Legislative Presidency* (New York: Harper & Row, 1978), p. 3.

[15] New York was the last state to complete its constitution and the first to include a permanent veto. South Carolina experimented with a gubernatorial veto in its constitution of 1776. When its governor, John Rutledge, actually used the power, the resulting outcry forced him to resign; in its revised constitution of 1778, South Carolina eliminated the veto.

the development of an American monarchy. While some favored the idea, it did not garner public support. Edmund Randolph cautioned that a single executive would be "the foetus of monarchy." Franklin spoke at length, articulating his apprehension that the new American government would eventually evolve into a monarchy. John Dickinson proposed that the executive be removable by vote of the Congress as a means of placing limits on an executive that he considered otherwise inconsistent with a republican form of government. Pierce Butler observed, perhaps with foresight but certainly with concern, that executive power seemed to be on the rise in countries around the world. George Mason feared that an elective executive would pose an even more dangerous threat to liberty than would a hereditary monarch. James Madison stated as an axiom that if the new constitution created a single executive with appreciable powers, that executive would inexorably become a monarchy. John Rutledge figured that any effort to create a single executive would be interpreted by the people as an attempt to create a monarchy. Hugh Williamson viewed the proposals to limit the executive to a single term and to establish a plural executive as vital checks on monarchy. Luther Martin urged circumspection on the convention, lest the rest of the country fear that the convention intended to impose a monarchy.[16]

The sentiment to construct a more "parliamentary" system, as seen in the legislature-centered Virginia Plan, was reflected in its provision that the executive be elected by Congress. The convention voted on five separate occasions in support of this method of selecting the President. Independent selection of the President by an electoral college was proposed as early as mid-July, but the idea gained support and ultimate acceptance relatively late in the convention's deliberations. Its inclusion was the product of a small committee organized to iron out persisting difficulties in the draft document (called the Committee of Eleven, it was dominated by delegates who favored a stronger executive).[17]

---

[16] Farrand, *Records of the Federal Convention*, I, pp. 66, 83, 86–87, 100, 101, 113, 119; II, pp. 100–101; IV, p. 27.

[17] James Wilson was a strong proponent of using the Electoral College as a method of selecting the President, but the idea was defeated in a vote on July 17. Hamilton proposed the idea on June 18, but no vote was taken. For more on the politics at the convention relating to choosing a presidential selection method, see William H. Riker, "The Heresthetics of Constitution-Making," *American Political Science Review,* 78 (March 1984): 1–16.

Fear of a Strong Legislature

For all the concerns expressed about the dangers of strong executives, most agree that the founders and other early leaders shared an even greater concern about domineering legislatures. This concern received strong impetus from state experiences in the time preceding the 1787 convention and from the shortcomings of an executiveless national government under the Articles. As Charles Thach concluded in his important study, "the political psychology of the men who framed the Federal Constitution was by no means characterized by that jealousy of the executive which was so prevalent in 1776 . . . indeed, the pendulum of conservative opinion had swung so far in the opposite direction that the 'people's representatives' had become the chief object of its dislike. . . ."[18] Historian Gordon Wood concluded that state legislatures in the postrevolutionary period were susceptible to corruption and were the object of much pressure by various special-interest groups. The result, according to Wood, was the enactment of many laws considered "unjust" in such areas as debtor relief, paper money, and property rights. Thus, "state assemblies were abusing their extraordinary powers."[19]

These suspicions of legislative-dominated systems are readily seen in the Constitution itself. Article I, the longest in the document, details numerous specific congressional powers, but also specific limits on those powers. Limits also appear in the Bill of Rights, which was added in 1791. By enumerating powers with such specificity, the founders were codifying the legislature's importance, but they were also seeking to impose clearly defined boundaries.

Article II, by contrast, is much more brief and vague in its description of executive powers. The importance of vagueness in law lies in the fact that it bestows discretion; that is, it affords an opportunity to interpret powers as one sees fit. The founders were well aware of this fact and sought to give the President this discretion so that the executive would have greater room to maneuver in dealings with Congress (although the vagueness of Article II also resulted from the founders' inability to come to a more precise agreement about the

[18] Thach, *The Creation of the Presidency,* p. 76. See also Fisher, *President and Congress,* pp. 21–22.

[19] Gordon S. Wood, "Democracy and the Constitution," in *How Democratic Is the Constitution?,* ed. by Robert A. Goldwin and William A. Schambra (Washington, D.C.: American Enterprise Institute, 1980), p. 8.

appropriate nature and shape of the executive; the founders labored throughout the convention over appropriate wording and powers for the President). Judicial scholar Robert Scigliano goes so far as to argue that the three-branch system was not designed to be equal among the three branches but was rather a two-on-one arrangement; that is, the executive and judicial branches were fortified with defensive powers against the legislative branch, which was expected to be more aggrandizing and aggressive.[20]

The framers' fears of an aggrandizing legislature prone to domination of the executive are illustrated by the debate over the veto power. Much discussion at the convention was devoted to the veto. A central theme of that discussion was the necessity of the veto as a method for presidents to defend themselves against legislative encroachment. This lesson emerged directly from state experiences. The first two governors to be given permanent veto powers were those of New York (in 1777) and Massachusetts (in 1780), and both states were cited as places where executives had functioned effectively, in contrast to the experiences of the other states. The need for a veto power as a defensive weapon for the President is also articulated in several of the *Federalist Papers*.[21] Interestingly, despite ambiguity and uncertainty at the convention over the scope and nature of executive power—not to mention resentment at the way the king and his colonial governors had used and abused their veto power—no serious disagreement arose over granting the executive some kind of veto power.

As with other political problems of the time, delegates to the federal convention had much to say about the problems of legislative domination. Elbridge Gerry observed that contemporary governing problems flowed from what he called "the excess of democracy"— that is, legislatures. Edmund Randolph argued in favor of a Senate not directly elected by the people so that such a body could serve as a check on the popularly elected House, a body prone, he said, to turbulence and folly. James McClurg thought an open-ended presidential term lasting as long as the President exhibited "good behavior"

[20] Robert Scigliano, *The Supreme Court and the Presidency* (New York: Free Press, 1971).

[21] For more on the veto power, see Robert J. Spitzer, *The Presidential Veto: Touchstone of the American Presidency* (Albany: State University of New York Press, 1988), pp. 15–16 and passim. The *Federalist Papers* in which the veto power is discussed are No. 51, No. 66, and No. 73.

was necessary to prevent tyrannies committed in the name of republican (representative) government. Gouverneur Morris proposed that
the legislature would "continually seek to aggrandize & perpetuate
themselves" and that the executive had to serve as the people's
guardian against legislative tyranny. John Mercer saw the judicial
branch to be in a similar position as that of the executive, that is,
needing to defend itself against legislative excesses and oppressive
practices. James Wilson said that the natural tendency of legislatures
was to devour executives. Wilson's ally, Alexander Hamilton, spent
six hours detailing his plan for an executive-centered constitutional
system predicated on the premise that a congressional-centered system is incompatible with good government. Hamilton's vision incorporated sweeping executive powers, including a national executive
selected by electors chosen by electors, to serve for life; an absolute
veto; sole power to appoint cabinet secretaries; presidential impeachment by the Supreme Court; and broad war-making powers. Hamilton's plan for an executive-centered national system was not accepted
by the convention.[22] As the delegate Dr. William Johnson noted,
Hamilton "has been praised by every body" but "supported by
none."[23] But the provisions of Article II that emerged in September
reflected Hamilton's influence and some of his ideas. Of greatest importance was the decision to leave executive power and organization
relatively vague and undefined in order to leave open the possibility
of a more Hamiltonian executive.[24]

Perhaps more than any founder, James Madison agonized over
the appropriate structure and nature of executive authority. While he
cautioned the convention about executive excesses, he also observed
"a tendency in our governments to throw all power into the Legislative vortex. The Executives of the States are in general little more
than Cyphers; the legislatures omnipotent."[25] Madison's analysis underscored the difficult lessons learned from the state governments

[22] Farrand, *Records of the Federal Convention,* I, pp. 48, 51, 107, 282–293; II, pp. 36,
52, 298; III, pp. 617–630. No actual vote was taken on the plan Hamilton introduced
on June 18. Several versions of Hamilton's plan survived, and disputes continue as to
whether these discrepancies represent changes in Hamilton's thinking or recording er-
rors.

[23] Farrand, *Records of the Federal Conventions,* I, p. 363.

[24] See Forrest McDonald, *Alexander Hamilton: A Biography* (New York: Norton, 1979),
pp. 95–107.

[25] Farrand, *Records of the Federal Convention,* II, p. 35. Madison offered similar comments in *Federalist* No. 48 and No. 49.

and also the intractable problem of balancing effective, energetic government with responsible government mindful of individual rights.[26]

Finally, it is important to point out an obvious but often overlooked fact about the founders and their fear of legislatures. The men attending the 1787 convention represented the cream of society, which is to say they were America's political and social elite. Many of these men were frankly suspicious of any mechanism that facilitated direct popular control of the government because they considered the citizenry unqualified to make direct governing choices and feared that the citizenry might rise up and deprive the wealthy of their property and other holdings. Founders such as Hamilton, Madison, and Gerry all expressed their mistrust of direct links between governing institutions and the people. This concern is directly seen in the Constitution, where of the four national governing institutions—the House, Senate, presidency, and judiciary—only the House was directly elected (the Senate was to be elected by the state legislatures, the President by the Electoral College, and the members of the federal court by the President and the Senate only).

Fear of Concentrated Power

The particular concerns about executive and legislative excesses are more clearly understood in the larger context of apprehension about governments. The very idea that the legislative and executive branches would share responsibility over such matters as control of the military and the appointment of ambassadors stems from an abiding suspicion of too much governmental power concentrated in too few hands. Whether referring to the excesses of King George III or to those of the early state legislatures, their collective sin was also one held in common, that is, the abuse of governmental powers resulting from power concentrated in the hands of one branch or body. Similarly, the idea that executive, legislative, and judicial powers ought to be exercised by distinct bodies was also a means of limiting the concentration of power, as was the principle of legislative bicameralism.

These two principles—known familiarly as checks and balances and separation of powers—aroused no little controversy in the eighteenth century and were vigorously defended in the *Federalist Pa-*

[26] For more on the design of the executive and the evolution of Madison's thought on the subject, see Jeffrey Leigh Sedgwick, "James Madison & the Problem of Executive Character," *Polity*, XXI (Fall 1988): 5–23.

pers. James Madison spoke directly to this arrangement of powers in the context of this nation's adverse governing experiences when he observed in *Federalist* No. 51 that

> the great security against a gradual concentration of the several powers in the same department consists in giving to those who administer each department the necessary constitutional means and personal motives to resist encroachments of the others. The provision for defense must in this, as in all other cases, be made commensurate to the danger of attack. Ambition must be made to counteract ambition.[27]

This principle was central to Madison's resolution of the dilemma facing the executive branch, that is, how to construct an energetic executive without also encouraging executive tyranny. Madison's resolution—and that of the Constitution—was to rely on separation of powers as a means of grounding executive energy in the constitutional document.[28]

Another provision of the Constitution that was considered vital to maintaining proper separation of the executive and legislative branches was that which barred a member of Congress from simultaneously holding any other governmental office. Concern for such dual office holding was long-standing in the British system (although it is now an integral part of the contemporary British Parliament, where members of Parliament also serve as cabinet secretaries). On several occasions in the late seventeenth century Parliament enacted such a ban on dual service as a means to limit the monarch's influence in Parliament, only to have such measures vetoed by the king.

Fear of Governmental Paralysis

Much emphasis has been placed on the founders' desire to construct a governing system that was slow, deliberate, and multicentered, yet it is also important to remember that if the founders had really wanted governmental sloth, they could have kept the Articles of Confederation. Without question, they were also seeking greater governmental efficiency and effectiveness. Unless the nation created a more effective governing apparatus, it could not hope to ward off the intrusions of hostile nations, improve economic conditions, or conduct the

---

[27] *Federalist Papers*, pp. 321–322.
[28] See Sedgwick, "James Madison & the Problem of Executive Character," p. 22.

business of the country.[29] As Madison noted in *Federalist* No. 45, "If the new Constitution be examined with accuracy and candor, it will be found that the change which it proposes consists much less in the addition of *new powers* to the Union than in the invigoration of its *original powers.*"[30] In other words, the new government was to be given greater powers to do what the Articles had failed to do.

In *Federalist* No. 9 Hamilton argued similarly that "A Firm Union will be of the utmost moment to the peace and liberty of the States as a barrier against domestic faction and insurrection."[31] An early and shrewd constitutional scholar, Joseph Story, summarized the problem, suggesting that "feeble executive implies a feeble execution of the government. A feeble execution is but another phrase for a bad execution; and a government ill executed, whatever may be its theory, must, in practice, be a bad government."[32]

THE CONSTITUTIONAL FRAMEWORK

The plain words and composition of the Constitution reveal much about the basic relationship between the legislative and executive branches. It is no accident, for example, that Article I is devoted to the legislative branch. As John Locke wrote, "In all cases whilst the government subsists, the legislative is the supreme power . . . and all other powers in any members or parts of the society [are] derived from and subordinate to it."[33] As a result, Congress was to be the first branch, the cornerstone of the republican system.

In Article I, "Congress is granted a breathtaking array of powers . . . the bulk of governmental authority as the Founders understood it."[34] This sweeping collection of powers begins with the first sentence

[29] See Fisher, *President and Congress,* esp. p. 3.

[30] *Federalist Papers,* p. 292.

[31] *Federalist Papers,* p. 71. Hamilton made a similar point during the federal convention when he discussed the weakness of confederated systems of government. Farrand, *The Records of the Federal Convention,* I, p. 285.

[32] Joseph Story, *Commentaries on the Constitution of the United States* (Durham, N.C.: Carolina Academic Press, 1987), p. 517. Story's *Commentaries* were first published in 1833.

[33] John Locke, *Of Civil Government* (Chicago: Regnery, 1955), p. 125.

[34] Roger Davidson, "'Invitation to Struggle': An Overview of Legislative-Executive Relations," *Annals of the American Academy of Political and Social Science,* 499 (September 1988): 11.

of Article I, which vests "All legislative powers herein granted" in the two houses of Congress. Primarily in Section 8, Congress is given authority in three broad, inclusive areas: economic affairs, other domestic affairs, and foreign affairs.

Congress's economic powers include the power to "lay and collect taxes," deal with indebtedness and bankruptcy, impose duties, borrow and coin money, and otherwise control the nation's purse strings. Its other domestic responsibilities include the charge to "provide for the common defense and general welfare," regulate interstate commerce, undertake public works, acquire and control federal lands, promote science and "useful arts" (this pertains mostly to patents and copyrights), and regulate the militia.

In foreign (including military) affairs, Congress was given the power to deal with piracy, regulate foreign commerce, declare war and make rules pertaining to land and water captures, and raise and regulate the armed forces and military installations. The Senate was given the power to approve treaties (by a two-thirds vote) and approve the appointment of ambassadors.

Capping these powers is a provision charging Congress to make laws "which shall be necessary and proper for carrying into execution the foregoing powers, and all other powers vested by this Constitution in the Government of the United States, or in any department or officer thereof." This latter phrase is known as the elastic clause.

Presidential powers, by contrast, are both relatively brief and vague. They begin with the first sentence of Article II, which vests "the executive power" in the President. Note in comparison that Congress's powers consist of those "herein granted," a more limiting phrase referring only to what is listed in Article I; the absence of the "herein granted" tag for executive powers is usually taken as a grant of executive-type powers not necessarily limited to those specifically listed in Article II.

Pertaining to legislative activities, the President is to inform Congress of the state of the union, make recommendations to Congress deemed "necessary and expedient," convene special sessions of Congress (as well as adjourn under some circumstances), and exercise the veto power. The President is also designated as the commander in chief of the military forces and may grant reprieves and pardons, make treaties in conjunction with the Senate, offer nominations to the Senate, receive ambassadors from other nations, and

President
- "Executive power"
- Approval or veto of bills
- Commander in chief of military
- Make treaties
- Bicameralism of legislature
- Independent election of President
- Offer nominations to Senate
- Appoint "inferior officers" alone
- Recommend "necessary and expedient" measures to Congress
- Convene special congressional sessions
- Grant pardons
- Execute law

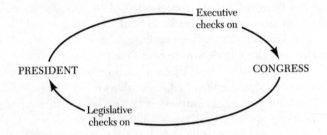

Congress
- Legislative powers "herein granted"
- Power of purse
- Declare war
- National defense and welfare
- Regulate military
- Regulate commerce
- Impeachment
- No simultaneous service in legislative and executive branches
- Ratify treaties (Senate only)
- Approve executive appointments (Senate only)
- Elastic clause
- Propose constitutional amendments

Figure 1.1   The Constitutional Balance, President and Congress: Expressly Granted Powers and Checks

"take care that the laws be faithfully executed." The reciprocal nature of these powers is summarized in Figure 1.1.

In accordance with a strict reading of these powers, the President's ability to lead in legislative affairs was, according to historian James S. Young, "as bare as Mother Hubbard's kitchen." How, then, have presidents become so central to legislative matters? Young concluded that it was "through the exercise of political skill, of statecraft."[35] While this is not a complete answer, presidential skill has been of central importance.

CONCLUSION

As I have argued, it is impossible to appraise presidential-congressional relations without an appreciation of the sequence of events leading up to, and the thought behind, the creation of the two branches. Without doubt, the constitutional framework contains ambiguities, and the founders were by no means of one mind on much of anything. However, the constitutional framework did establish (1) a government stronger than that under the Articles of Confederation but (2) still a limited government with divided and shared powers. The headings used in this chapter outline the respective "fears" of the founders as they pertained to legislative and executive powers. The organizing concept of fear explains the product of 1787 but also the modern governing dilemma of the two branches—how to act quickly, efficiently, and in unity within a structure that is designed to resist these very qualities. The Constitution sets the legislature against the executive but also sets the legislature against itself by creating two houses with different election methods and constituencies. Much of the interaction between the first and second branches of government has been nothing less than an ongoing attempt to redeal the cards dealt by the framers. It is to these changes that we now turn.

[35] James S. Young, *The Washington Community* (New York: Columbia University Press, 1966), pp. 158–159.

Chapter 2

The Evolving Relationship

Energy in the executive is a leading character in the definition of good government.

ALEXANDER HAMILTON, *FEDERALIST* NO. 70

The typical image of presidential-congressional relations is that of a seesaw; that is, when the power or influence of one rises, the power of the other declines proportionately. But such an image is too simplistic. First, there have been times in history when both branches worked vigorously and harmoniously to achieve important goals, as during the Eighty-ninth Congress (1965–1966) and the presidency of Lyndon Johnson. While this period is often cited as one of presidential dominance, it was also a period when Congress played a creative and active role in pursuing a vigorous national agenda.[1]

Second, there have also been times when both branches faced mutual deadlock or gridlock. Critics have noted the presence of gridlock during periods of the Ford, Carter, and Reagan presidencies when neither branch seemed to be able to provide leadership or direction.[2] Third, the principle of shared powers between the branches incorporates the assumption, if not the hope, that the two branches

---

[1] See Gary Orfield, *Congressional Power: Congress and Social Change* (New York: Harcourt Brace Jovanovich, 1975).

[2] This criticism is discussed in James L. Sundquist, *Constitutional Reform and Effective Government* (Washington, D.C.: Brookings Institution, 1986); Committee on the Constitutional System, *A Bicentennial Analysis of the American Political Structure*, January 1987 (Washington, D.C.: Committee on the Constitutional System). See also Hedrick Smith, *The Power Game* (New York: Ballantine, 1988), pp. 640–643.

can operate successfully without one branch consistently dominating the other. Despite these qualifications, however, a quick scan of the past 200 years makes it clear that both branches have experienced periods of dominance. Yet the prevailing pattern during this time has been the rise of the strong institutional presidency. The reasons for this trend are several, including the vague definition of executive powers in Article II of the Constitution, the dynamism of forceful Presidents who have exploited that vagueness through precedent-setting actions, the tendency to seek presidential leadership during times of crisis, and the periodic willingness of Congress to surrender authority to the executive. The impact of these factors emerges not only in this chapter but throughout the book.

The following account of the development of executive-legislative relations takes two forms. The first is a descriptive overview of the evolving relationship between the two branches; the second is a specific focus on two Congresses—the First and the Twenty-seventh. The First Congress is important because it was first, because it will demonstrate how quickly many of the executive-legislative patterns we recognize today developed, and because it represents much of the texture of early governing. The Twenty-seventh Congress is examined because it represented the point that was constitutionally furthest from the contemporary legislative-executive relationship. Subsequent periods, notably the post–Civil War period, are often cited as instances of equivalent or greater congressional dominance. But at no time in our history was a *constitutional* argument as widely advanced proclaiming the subordination of the executive to the legislature.

To assist in the evaluation of these two Congresses, we will consider two traits: (1) policy initiation, or which branch seems to be the main source of the ideas, plans, expertise, and proposals that compose the substance of lawmaking and which branch is able to claim policy credit, and (2) political initiative, or which branch assumes political offense and defense and whose ox is gored in the process. In regard to the second point, we will examine how each branch fares when political disputes arise and whether disputes are infrequent or common. These traits do not preclude mutual gain or loss or constructive engagement between the branches, but they provide a convenient yardstick. Assessment sections will appear after these cases and sporadically throughout the rest of the book to zero in on key points and conclusions.

CASE I: THE FIRST CONGRESS, 1789–1791

No less than in later centuries the First Congress was abidingly concerned with the relationship between it and the executive. The members of the new government knew that they would be setting precedent in interbranch relations. This fact was keenly felt, as "no one could state where legislative power as such left off and executive power began."[3] Much of this relationship centered on matters unique to the establishment of a new government, but the underlying concerns and political patterns are no less pertinent for modern analysis.

Politics as Usual

The First Congress immediately became a focal point for specialized interests from around the country. The fact that the term *lobbyist* had not been invented was no deterrent to efforts by specialized interests to extract narrow concessions from Congress. Manufacturers from Baltimore sought the imposition of duties on British imports, openly requesting "a just and decided preference to the labors of the petitioners." Artisans from New York presented Congress with a list of products for which they sought protection from imports. Philadelphia mustard producers sought duties on imported mustard, and coachmakers from the same city requested that no tax be imposed on American-made carriages. By contrast, shippers in Boston and New York sought congressional help to increase international trade and tobacco and snuff manufacturers requested that no export duties be placed on their outgoing shipments. Citizens from New York's Westchester County requested that Congress reimburse them for quantities of oats, hay, corn, rye, wheat, cattle, hogs, and sheep which had been appropriated for use by the military during the Revolutionary War. These and numerous other requests consumed much of Congress's time, and many in Congress were professionally and financially enmeshed in these business matters as well.[4]

[3] Leonard D. White, *The Federalists* (New York: Macmillan, 1948), p. 52.
[4] Margaret C. S. Christman, *The First Federal Congress, 1789–1791* (Washington, D.C.: Smithsonian Institution Press, 1989), pp. 151–154.

What's in a Name?

Among the first signs of the concern over interbranch relations was the dispute over what to call the President. This seemingly trivial matter assumed considerable importance, given the long-standing fear of executive excesses and the more immediate worry, expressed by Representative Thomas Tucker (S.C.), of a "most intolerable Rage for Monarchy" among the people of 1789.[5]

Members of the upper house, the Senate, sought an exalted title for the President such as "His Highness the President of the United States, and Protector of the Rights of the Same." Vice President John Adams felt that proper dignity and respect would not be accorded the new government without such titles and that titles for the President and Vice President were necessary as a means to command respect and enhance stability for an office he considered too weak, although Adams was also something of a stuffed shirt. The House, by contrast, believed that such titles were inconsistent with the republican nature of the government. With the blessing of Washington, the Senate yielded after "extensive and repetitive debate," and Congress settled simply on "Mr. President." Other, similar ceremonial matters, such as the treatment of the members of each house by the other, the receipt and transmission of messages between the houses, and how the President was to be received when he came to Congress to deliver messages, all consumed considerable time during the first several weeks of the first session.[6] The underlying importance of this matter was summarized by historian Forrest McDonald, who noted that it was "deadly serious jockeying for power."[7]

Congress and the President dealt with a wide array of issues during these first two years, but the two issues that President Washington, among others, considered to be paramount were the selection of a permanent site for the nation's capital and the debt issue.

---

[5] Quoted in Charlene Bangs Bickford and Kenneth R. Bowling, *Birth of the Nation: The First Federal Congress, 1789–1791* (New York: First Federal Congress Project, 1989), p. 23.

[6] Bickford and Bowling, *Birth of the Nation*, pp. 26–28; Joel H. Silbey, "'Our Successors Will Have an Easier Task': The First Congress under the Constitution, 1789–1791," *This Constitution*, 17 (Winter 1987): 6–7.

[7] Quoted in Alvin M. Josephy, Jr., *On the Hill* (New York: Simon & Schuster, 1979), p. 49.

The Government Seat

The national government had struggled over the matter of where to locate a national capital for several years. Northern states favored a site in New Jersey or Pennsylvania, whereas southern states preferred that the capital be located on the Potomac River, closer to the south. The location of the capital was important for more than symbolic reasons: The political and economic importance of the capital would be a boon to the chosen area. New Yorkers wanted to keep the capital in their city; others favored moving the site to Philadelphia until a permanent location could be found.

Discussion on location of the capital was delayed until the end of the First Congress's first session. By that time several towns in Pennsylvania, Maryland, and New Jersey had launched vigorous campaigns to win the location site. Support in Congress grew for a location in Pennsylvania, but Rep. James Madison (Va.) managed to sway some key New Yorkers to support a move to postpone the issue until the second session. The delay did nothing to calm tensions between northern and southern states, which split on both the capital's location and debt assumption. The debt issue received the most attention, but the capital issue continued to emerge. By June no resolution had been achieved, and threats of dissolution of the union and civil war were heard openly for the first time. President Washington was reluctant to intercede. He was known to favor the Potomac location but did not want his preferences to compromise his position. (Even after a compromise was reached, Washington was criticized harshly by northerners for signing the bill.) Clearly, some compromise had to be found.

In mid-June Hamilton and Secretary of State Thomas Jefferson chanced to meet outside the President's residence and agreed to get together with Madison to try to resolve the stalemate. Over dinner, Madison agreed to line up southern votes in favor of debt assumption; in return, Hamilton agreed to influence New England representatives to support the Potomac capital site. This agreement, labeled the Compromise of 1790, materially aided in the successful resolution of both issues the following month. Madison was able to sway several southern representatives; Hamilton probably helped undermine northern opposition to the Potomac location.[8]

[8] See Bickford and Bowling, *Birth of the Nation*, pp. 55–59, 69–71; Josephy, *On the Hill*, pp. 72–74.

Debt Funding and Assumption

The most immediate and pressing economic concern of the new nation was the handling of the country's large debt, both foreign and domestic, accrued from the Revolutionary War. The country needed to address the debt issue immediately in order to win the confidence of American citizens and state and foreign governments, stimulate economic growth, and establish sound public credit. The nation's financial condition was a matter about which everyone had opinions but few had facts. As Representative Aedanus Burke (S.C.) ruefully noted, "I know of no man in either house, who is not totally at a Loss on this important subject."[9]

Congress turned to President Washington's newly appointed secretary of the treasury, Alexander Hamilton. In September 1789 he was charged to prepare a report that would aid Congress in clarifying the nation's chaotic financial picture. The following January Hamilton delivered his *First Report on the Public Credit*.[10] In the plan he proposed to pay off the entire national and foreign debt by issuing new government stock, for which the government would guarantee minimum payments. In addition, he proposed that the federal government assume the states' war debts, which would involve the establishment of an excise tax and the creation of a national bank. The plan was hailed for its brilliance, but the proposal to assume state debts sparked fierce controversy. Hamilton's plan was introduced as legislation; the proposal for national debt was quickly adopted, and assumption of state debt was finally adopted in July, after a deal was struck to place the nation's permanent capital in the south in exchange for southern votes in support of assumption.

The political importance of Hamilton's plan extended beyond its content. Unlike the legislation that created the other cabinet posts, the bill that created the position of secretary of the treasury required that the secretary work directly with Congress. The purpose was to limit executive power in the realm of financial affairs in order to secure congressional control of taxing and spending. However, the unintended consequence of this action was to pave the way for a strong

[9] Quoted in Bickford and Bowling, *Birth of the Nation*, p. 61.

[10] This report was the first of several by Hamilton dealing with the nation's financial situation. His most well-known report was the *Report on Manufactures*, which laid out a series of proposals for internal improvements and industrial policies that presaged future American development.

treasury secretary to co-opt the congressional agenda by providing the means by which the secretary could "ram his own measures through Congress with the support of a loyal majority."[11] In his diary, Senator William Maclay (Pa.) referred to Hamilton's congressional followers as "the Crew of the Hamilton Galley."[12] In the case of Hamilton's credit report, Congress was getting far more than just information; it was getting a treasury secretary who was initiating legislation. During his six years in Washington's cabinet Hamilton became the administration's chief spokesperson and policy advocate. He directed and coordinated congressional supporters, proposed legislation, influenced committee assignments, made enemies, and won important political victories. According to Wilfred E. Binkley, Hamilton "was influenced by the example of Pitt who was the [British] prime minister at the same time that he was first lord of the treasury and chancellor of the exchequer."[13] President Washington took no active part in this politicking, but he did propose legislation to Congress, starting with his State of the Union address in 1790. His proposals were more in the nature of suggestions for consideration, however, than specific legislative blueprints. Congress was anything but quick to respond to them.[14]

Assessment

As this account reveals, policy initiative was to be found in both branches of the government. In the case of the location of the capital, policy alternatives and ultimate resolution occurred primarily within the halls of Congress. The involvement of Hamilton and Jefferson was important, but policy options were developed, weighed, and debated primarily within Congress.[15] In the case of debt assumption,

---

[11] Josephy, *On the Hill*, p. 65.

[12] Kenneth R. Bowling and Helen E. Veit, eds., *The Diary of William Maclay and Other Notes on Senate Debates* (Baltimore: Johns Hopkins University Press, 1988), p. 214.

[13] Wilfred E. Binkley, *President and Congress* (New York: Vintage, 1962), p. 46. Hamilton "went so far as to ask his friends to speak of him as the first lord of the treasury."

[14] Binkley, *President and Congress*, pp. 67–92; Forrest McDonald, *Alexander Hamilton: A Biography* (New York: Norton, 1979), pp. 211–243; White, *The Federalists*, pp. 54–55.

[15] Executive-legislative interaction during this early period was certainly facilitated by the simple but important fact that the President, the cabinet, and Congress all worked in the same building. Without established party structures and separate institutional cultures, the possibilities for interaction were far greater.

Hamilton was clearly the key initiator; this initiative and his subsequent exercise of political influence in Congress on this and other issues resulted from the unintended consequences of Congress's actions toward the treasury secretary. Hamilton then exploited his opportunity and expertise to become the active player in legislative politics that he believed was appropriate to the executive. In 1794, Hamilton wrote that there ought to be some "Executive impulse. . . . Many persons look to the President for the suggestion of measures corresponding with the exigency of affairs."[16] After his departure from the Washington administration, Hamilton's "Executive impulse" would not emerge for another century.

In terms of political initiative, Congress was the decisive political actor on the capital's location. The role of Hamilton and Jefferson was important insofar as they provided timely interdiction. However, a sense was also emerging in Congress that a compromise had to be achieved, and this matter had been a primary legislative concern as far back as 1783. For the debt question, Hamilton's policy expertise and forceful politicking made him a pivotal figure and precipitated the formation of political parties. It also prodded Congress to form committees to develop rival expertise. His behavior foreshadowed the political dynamics of twentieth-century executive leaders. Yet the vigor and will of Hamilton's opponents in Congress made them formidable, indicating their equivalent political force. Anti-Hamilton sentiment grew in Congress to the point where Washington began his second term with opposition Democratic-Republicans in control of the House. Congressional critics eventually pushed Hamilton out, although he continued to play a behind-the-scenes role during the balance of the Washington and Adams administrations. The precedent-setting nature of Hamilton's efforts for nineteenth-century presidencies was undercut by the fact that Washington remained generally aloof and detached from the political fray. Still, he did set important precedents as the nation's first President, such as voluntarily imposing a two-term limit on presidential service (a practice followed by every succeeding president until the four-term administration of Franklin Roosevelt) and using the presidential veto on two occasions.

[16] Quoted in White, *The Federalists*, p. 54.

THE EVOLVING RELATIONSHIP[17]

John Adams's presidency was marked by escalating belligerence between the branches, as the opposition Democratic-Republican party gained political strength. Adams continued Washington's practice of avoiding direct presidential involvement in legislative matters, and no member of Adams's cabinet adopted Hamiltonian aggressiveness toward Congress. Thomas Jefferson relied heavily on personal persuasion and social events to mold the congressional agenda. Adopting a Hamiltonian approach, the President and his cabinet secretaries worked closely, if informally, with congressional leaders, and important legislative proposals were sometimes drafted in the executive branch. Jefferson was kept apprised of developments in Congress through sympathetic members who secretly passed information to him, and he wined and dined key congressional leaders almost daily at the White House when Congress was in session. Such informality and secrecy were important at a time when active presidential involvement in legislative affairs was by no means accepted.[18]

He was also the first President to use effectively his role as leader of the Democratic-Republican party (which now held majorities in both houses) to influence and direct congressional affairs. Jefferson's skills and success in dealing with Congress were especially impressive because they exceeded the accomplishments of any other nineteenth-century president. Only in the twentieth century did an activist role for the President in legislative affairs become the norm.

Jefferson's three competent but less politically adroit successors—James Madison, James Monroe, and John Quincy Adams—were far less actively involved in legislative matters owing to several developments. One was the development of congressional committees, which served to disperse congressional power; another was the growth of the power of the speaker of the House; a third was the growth of executive departments, which made presidential management more difficult and cumbersome; a fourth was the development

---

[17] Much of the following historical account is taken from James L. Sundquist, *The Decline and Resurgence of Congress* (Washington, D.C.: Brookings Institution, 1981), pp. 21–36; and Stephen J. Wayne, *The Legislative Presidency* (New York: Harper & Row, 1978), pp. 8–22.

[18] See James S. Young, *The Washington Community* (New York: Columbia University Press, 1966), pp. 16, 162.

of rifts within the dominant Democratic-Republican party; a fifth was that from 1800 to 1824 presidential nominations came from congressional caucuses, which meant that Presidents were beholden to those who nominated them (Jefferson created this system and was therefore not subservient to it, as were his successors); a sixth was philosophical sympathy for the principle of legislative dominance.[19]

For example, pressure from the so-called congressional War Hawks, led by the young Speaker of the House Henry Clay (Ky.), was the primary impetus that pushed the United States and a reluctant Madison into the War of 1812. President Monroe's administration coincided with an era of near one-party domination, and this precluded many routine partisan struggles between the branches. Yet despite the relative harmony of the Monroe years, congressional leaders made it clear that Presidents were not to meddle in legislative matters. The power of the Speaker during Monroe's administration was such that Clay was able to enact a series of measures despite presidential opposition. In his two terms Monroe vetoed only one bill. Prior to the veto, Monroe had made it clear in an early message to Congress that he would use his veto against congressional efforts to finance internal improvements such as roads and canals. This veto threat was interpreted by leading members of Congress as a grave intrusion on the legislative prerogative in that "the Presidential veto would acquire a force unknown to the Constitution, and the legislative body would be shorn of its powers from a want of confidence in its strength."[20] Obviously, such a view would garner little support today.

The Jacksonian Era

The Monroe dispute was dwarfed by the furious struggle that ensued between Andrew Jackson and his congressional opponents. Jackson was swept into office in 1828 on a wave of popular enthusiasm, and he used his electoral mandate to promote his own policy agenda vigorously. Foremost among his goals was opposition to the Second Bank of the United States. Jackson's 1832 veto of a bank bill prompted an intense outcry in Congress and was a central issue in

---

[19] See Leonard D. White, *The Jeffersonians* (New York: Macmillan, 1951), pp. 54–56.

[20] Quoted in Robert J. Spitzer, *The Presidential Veto* (Albany: State University of New York Press, 1988), p. 32.

that year's elections. Two years later the Senate voted to censure Jackson for his "assertion of a power which was greater than that possessed by any king in Europe."[21]

Jackson's ground-breaking actions, including advocacy of his own legislative agenda, the application of twelve vetoes (more than all six previous Presidents combined) against bills with which he disagreed, and his use of the popular mandate to promote his views, presaged the twentieth-century legislative presidency. However, they also helped galvanize his political opponents, who formed the Whig party. The Whigs elected two Presidents—William Henry Harrison (1840) and Zachary Taylor (1848)—who espoused as a matter of principle the view that the President should not take an active role in legislative matters. Whigs urged such measures of executive restraint as infrequent and restricted use of the veto power, the limitation of presidential service to a single term, and the avoidance of public comment on legislative proposals by Presidents so as not to unduly influence the legislature during its deliberations. In this sense, the Whig party was the conservative party of its day.

CASE II: THE TWENTY-SEVENTH CONGRESS, 1841–1843

The Whig philosophy concerning presidential-congressional relations was at no time more prevalent than during the presidency of John Tyler. Elected Vice President as Harrison's running mate, in 1841 Tyler became the first man to become President through the death of a President. Despite his Whig ties, Tyler progressively enraged supporters and opponents in Congress by assuming full presidential duties instead of acting merely as a caretaker, breaking with members of his party in Congress over the national bank issue, and using his veto power ten times. These actions fed the flames of what historian Carlton Jackson called "perhaps the most bitter assembly in American history."[22]

---

[21] Spitzer, *The Presidential Veto,* p. 37. Most in the Senate would have preferred to impeach Jackson, but they realized that they could never muster the necessary votes in the House, where Jackson was more popular and from where motions to impeach must originate.

[22] Carlton Jackson, *Presidential Vetoes, 1792–1945* (Athens: University of Georgia Press, 1967), p. 75.

Tyler's Whig party had been a strong advocate of a national bank. Tyler himself was an unknown quantity to most in Congress, but when he assumed the presidency after the death of William Henry Harrison in 1841, he stated in his inaugural address that he would "promptly give my sanction to any constitutional measure which . . . shall have for its object the restoration of a sound circulating medium."[23]

Senate Whig leader Henry Clay immediately set about to implement his party's doctrine of legislative supremacy by introducing a series of resolutions, drawn up in a Whig legislative caucus, which he assumed would be accepted by Tyler and the Whig majority in Congress as a party program. Heading the list was a bill to reestablish a national bank, an effort that had been frustrated by President Andrew Jackson. Yet on August 16, 1841, Tyler shocked Congress by vetoing the bank bill, claiming that it was unconstitutional. Particularly objectionable to Tyler was the provision giving the federal government the power to establish branch banks in the states without their permission.[24]

The veto shocked the Whigs, but, hoping to reach an accommodation after the failure of an override attempt, they sent a representative to meet with Tyler. The President gave every indication that he was amenable to a compromise bill, exclaiming to the representative, "Stuart! if you can be instrumental in passing this bill through Congress, I will esteem you the best friend I have on earth."[25]

A new bill was passed, but on September 9 Tyler again vetoed it. The reaction was unrestrained fury. With the exception of Secretary of State Daniel Webster, Tyler's entire cabinet resigned. Whigs railed against Tyler and revived the effort to reduce the veto override to a simple majority. Representative John Minor Botts (Va.) accused the President of "perfidy and treachery." Effigies of Tyler were burned by the thousands around the country, and the White House received thousands of letters threatening the President with death.[26]

These two vetoes sparked an intense, lengthy debate during Congress's second session in 1842 about the extent and scope of

[23] *Messages and Papers of the Presidents* (Washington, D.C.: Bureau of National Literature, 1913), III, p. 1892.

[24] Josephy, *On the Hill*, p. 185.

[25] Oliver Chitwood, *John Tyler* (New York: Russell and Russell, 1964), p. 239.

[26] Binkley, *President and Congress*, p. 116.

presidential powers, particularly the veto. Most speakers argued that vigorous use of the veto represented an improper, even unconstitutional intrusion by the President into the legislative realm. The Constitution, of course, places no limits on either the numbers or types of bills subject to a veto, yet this debate reflected the widespread view of the time that the President should be subordinate to the legislature and that presidential powers should be narrowly construed. The vehemence of this argument was also fanned by Tyler's inept handing of the bank matter.[27]

Tyler proceeded to veto two more bills in 1842. Both were tariff bills, and both vetoes further fanned anti-Tyler sentiment. After the third veto a Whig newspaper called Tyler a "corrupt fool and knave who pretends to act as President" and who "ought to be shot down in his tracks, as he walks along."[28] In congressional debate Tyler was accused of acting under a "strange delusion," called a "stupid yet perfidious devil," and compared to "Judas Iscariot, who sold his Master for thirty pieces of silver. He was both a traitor and an ingrate. Thus the parallel between him and the President starts fair; but to assert that it continues throughout, would be doing injustice to the memory of Judas, who repented, returned the money, and hung himself."[29] This was incredibly venomous rhetoric to be directed against a President whose sin was the exercise of three lawful vetoes!

Anti-Tyler sentiment climaxed during Congress's third session, when on January 10, 1843, Representative Botts introduced a nine-count impeachment charge against the President. The charges centered on Tyler's veto use, which was characterized as "an arbitrary, despotic and corrupt abuse of the veto power." After some debate, the motion was defeated, 83–127.

Assessment

Policy initiative undeniably lay with Congress in the Twenty-seventh Congress. Tyler offered proposals to Congress during his term, and

[27] Spitzer, *The Presidential Veto,* pp. 44–46. Tyler could have blunted the fury of his critics by at least providing some warning before the fact and by cultivating congressional leaders. Leonard D. White noted that Tyler "destroyed his influence over either Congress or his own party by his vetoes. . . ." *The Jacksonians* (New York: Macmillan, 1954), p. 20.

[28] Jackson, *Presidential Vetoes, 1792–1945,* p. 66.

[29] Congressional Globe, July 1, August 4, 1842, app., pp. 769, 803, 867.

some matters were enacted without acrimony. In the two key policy areas of the bank and the tariff, however, the congressional Whigs clearly set the agenda. That they were frustrated by Tyler and unable to marshal sufficient votes to override his vetoes speaks primarily to the ability of the President to block and oppose legislation success-fully as long as the executive can hold a sustaining minority of one-third plus one in one house. Political initiative also favored Congress. The ascendancy of Whig philosophy was a built-in constraint to a more aggressive, assertive, positive presidential approach, especially because it was the President's party that held this perspective. Still, the President was able to use his veto to thwart a congressional ma-jority's highest priorities. As political scientist Richard Pious noted, Tyler "had demonstrated conclusively that a president without a shred of popular or party support could wield prerogative power and by doing so reduce his congressional opponents to complete ineffec-tiveness."[30] The most important observation derived from this case is the simple fact that a sitting President was nearly impeached and was repeatedly threatened with assassination simply for exercising the veto power.

Tyler's successor, James K. Polk, demonstrated greater skill and ambition than his predecessor by proposing and enacting a legislative program, defending his use of the veto, and pushing the nation into war with Mexico. Except for Jackson, the stature and influence of Presidents during this period was overshadowed to a great extent by such distinguished congressional leaders as Henry Clay, John C. Cal-houn (S.C.), Daniel Webster (Mass.), and Thomas Hart Benton (Mo.). Their preeminence, along with the Whiggish predilections of many during the period from the 1830s to 1850s, contributed to a presidency that "was being drawn into a role subordinate to Congress. . . ."[31]

THE ROAD TO A STRONGER PRESIDENCY

If the 1840s was the heyday of the Whig philosophy, it was also the beginning of the end for a view of the presidency that precluded an

[30] Richard M. Pious, *The American Presidency* (New York: Basic Books, 1979), p. 64.

[31] This argument is developed by Theodore J. Lowi, *The Personal President* (Ithaca, N.Y.: Cornell University Press, 1985), p. 32. Lowi goes so far as to suggest that the American system during the early part of the nineteenth century was a quasi-parlia-mentary system.

active legislative role. Even Presidents who stood almost alone against Congress would not have to face a prevailing constitutional argument that denied their full use of their constitutional powers.

The Civil War–Reconstruction Era

The pre–Civil War presidencies of Fillmore, Pierce, and Buchanan largely followed the Whig approach of their immediate predecessors, although only Fillmore was a member of the Whig party (Fillmore became President with the death of Taylor). Two important issues underscored the state of presidential-congressional relations during this period.

Slavery emerged in the 1850s as a national issue, one, in fact, that played prominently in presidential elections. Yet the Presidents of this period found themselves impotent, by virtue of their political philosophy and the nature of the times, to move meaningfully to defuse or resolve the matter (presuming, of course, that the Civil War was not an inevitable outcome). The important efforts to deal with slavery, including the Compromise of 1850 and the Kansas-Nebraska Act of 1854, were principally the result of legislative initiative and leadership. Thus, Congress assumed the primary burden of attempting to resolve this all-consuming national problem.

The other key issue involved public works and internal improvements. Responding to an era of rapid commercial expansion, Congress pressed ahead with a variety of measures aimed, for example, at improving land and water navigation and the postal service. Presidents Pierce and Buchanan, however, continued to argue that many of these measures were unconstitutional. Similar arguments had been made by past Presidents. However, this position suffered from two fatal flaws. First, the constitutional argument was suspect on its merits, and many past Presidents who had advanced this proposition had applied the doctrine selectively, supporting some public works bills and vetoing others. Second, public sentiment increasingly favored such efforts, and by the 1850s Pierce and Buchanan were clearly out of step with the times. All sixteen bills vetoed by these two Presidents dealt with internal improvements or private claims. Presidents so poorly attuned to public sentiment could hardly expect to bridle Congress. Presidential conservatism toward internal improvements was capped in 1860 by Buchanan's veto of the popular Homestead bill, which was later signed into law by Lincoln. This veto did much to drive northern workers and farmers away from the Democratic party and into the arms of the new Republican party, paving the way for Lincoln's election later that year.

Abraham Lincoln's presidency is usually cited as a watershed administration. Renowned and revered for his strong leadership during the Civil War, Lincoln took unprecedented steps to confront this threat to the union. However, two central conditions played a crucial role in molding Lincoln's opportunities and actions.

The first was his electoral mandate in the election of 1860. In the nationwide popular vote, Lincoln won only 39.8 percent of the popular vote running against three other candidates. But he received almost 60 percent of the Electoral College vote; more to the point, he won every northern and western state except New Jersey, which he split with Stephen A. Douglas, and the border states of Maryland and Delaware. In the House, Republicans won 105 of 178 seats; in the Senate, they took control for the first time, winning 31 of 49 seats. In short, outside the south Lincoln and the Republican party received an electoral mandate to keep slavery out of the territories. Lincoln's political background had helped sensitize him to shifts in popular sentiment, and the secession of seven southern states before his inauguration hardened northern sentiment and therefore Lincoln's mandate to act decisively. Second, the Civil War represented the most dire crisis facing the nation since the American Revolution, and it is a truism of presidential behavior that Congress and the country are far more likely to tolerate and even expect bold presidential action during crises than at other times.[32]

These two conditions provided an opportunity for Lincoln to expand the size of the military beyond the limits set by Congress, call up the militia, suspend the writ of habeas corpus, commit governmental credit to a substantial loan, censor the mails, and then call Congress into special session after he had taken those actions. Without question, Lincoln exceeded legal and constitutional limits, yet Congress acquiesced by endorsing his actions after the fact. Still, congressional leaders did not abandon their views of congressional dominance in war making and other areas, and in the final years of the Lincoln presidency members of Congress became progressively more outspoken against Lincoln's efforts to influence legislation, appoint military governors, and oversee the prosecution of the war. As

[32] See, for example, Arthur Schlesinger, Jr., *The Imperial Presidency* (Boston: Houghton Mifflin, 1973).

Senator Lyman Trumbull (R-Ill.) insisted on the Senate floor, "He [the President] is just as much subject to our control as if we appointed him, except that we cannot remove him and appoint another in his place."[33]

Lincoln's hapless successor, Andrew Johnson, sustained the fury of the congressional backlash that followed the end of the war. This congressional reassertion of power culminated in the nearly successful effort to remove Johnson from office for what were essentially trumped-up political charges. Congressional contempt for Johnson was such that Congress overrode most of his vetoes (fifteen of his twenty-one regular vetoes), a higher proportion than for any other President before or since. By the end of Johnson's term Congress was overriding his vetoes without debate and literally within minutes of their return to Congress.[34] Johnson's successor, Ulysses Grant, was happy to leave postwar matters to Congress.

The Presidents of the latter part of the century—Hayes, Garfield, Arthur, Cleveland, Harrison, and McKinley—are usually considered a relatively undistinguished lot who fought a domineering Congress over such matters as pension bills but played a relatively minor role in setting and directing national policy. This judgment is echoed not only in current analyses but in accounts of the time. Perhaps the most well known of these came from the eminent British analyst James Bryce, who included a chapter in his 1888 study of the American political system entitled "Why Great Men are not chosen Presidents."[35] Another distinguished analyst, Woodrow Wilson, observed in 1885 that the American government was actually "congressional government."[36]

These assessments of the late-nineteenth-century presidents are both overly simple and inadequately sensitive to the prevailing view of presidential power. Rutherford B. Hayes, for example, fought vigorously with Congress over appropriations and used the veto effectively to force Congress to eliminate special-interest provisions tacked on to spending bills. Grover Cleveland forced the repeal of

---

[33] Quoted in Binkley, *President and Congress*, p. 143. Trumbull echoed the sentiments of many in Congress who came to be known as Radical Republicans and who dominated national politics in the postwar years.

[34] Spitzer, *The Presidential Veto*, p. 59.

[35] James Bryce, *The American Commonwealth*, 2 vols. (New York: Macmillan, 1891), vol. I, chap. VIII.

[36] Woodrow Wilson, *Congressional Government* (Cleveland, Ohio: Meridian, 1956).

the Tenure of Office Act, enacted over Andrew Johnson's veto, which required Senate approval before Presidents could remove executive officials. He also vetoed twice as many bills in his first term (414) as had all his predecessors combined. Most of these bills were highly questionable private pension bills. Cleveland's prolific veto use helped persuade the American people that the President was more trustworthy with public funds than Congress was. Yet the Presidents who fought most vigorously with Congress, including Hayes and Cleveland, were reacting to congressional initiatives and paid a heavy political price for doing so. Hayes was not renominated by his party, and Cleveland was defeated in his first reelection bid. Thus, both political and policy initiative lay with Congress. As Henry Adams wrote in 1870, "So far as the President's initiative was concerned, the President and his Cabinet might equally well have departed separately or together to distant lands. Their recommendations were uniformly disregarded."[37]

Still, these Presidents were for the most part laboring to have a greater impact on national policy than had their pre–Civil War predecessors, and these legislative-executive struggles did have a cumulative effect. Writing about presidential-congressional relations during the last thirty years of the century, Leonard D. White concluded that this relationship "involved a series of hard fought battles between Presidents and Congress, the net result of which was to restore in part the constitutional, political, and administrative balance between the two branches of government."[38]

Nevertheless, this period was not a time of great change in presidential-congressional relations. As in the earlier part of the century, Congress could rightfully claim to be the dominant national institution. As Senator John Sherman (R-Ohio) noted, "The executive department of a republic like ours should be subordinate to the legislative department."[39] Leaders of the House, such as Speakers James G. Blaine (R-Maine), Thomas Reed (R-Maine) and Joe Cannon (R-Ill.), who served as Speaker in the early twentieth century, provided forceful leadership that relied heavily on party organization, loyalty, and the substantial powers of the Speaker's position. The Senate, however, underwent something of a character change. Instead of attract-

[37] Henry Adams, "The Session," *North American Review*, CXI (1870): 41.

[38] Leonard D. White, *The Republican Era* (New York: Macmillan, 1958), p. 20.

[39] Quoted in Binkley, *President and Congress*, p. 184.

ing great statesmen of the like of Webster and Calhoun, toward the end of the century the Senate increasingly attracted undistinguished men who sought the Senate as a capstone to their state political careers. Senate seats were often purchased outright through bribery of state legislators. As a consequence, the Senate suffered a loss of public esteem which led many states to opt for direct election of their senators. These changes in many states combined with reformist zeal of the progressive era to produce the Seventeenth Amendment to the Constitution in 1913, calling for the direct election of senators.[40]

The Ascendancy of the Modern Strong Presidency

Relationships between the branches began to change dramatically with the first President elected in the new century, Theodore Roosevelt. Roosevelt's contribution to presidential ascendancy was primarily symbolic. His actual legislative requests were both relatively few and modest, and the "big stick" approach he applied in foreign affairs was left in the closet when he dealt with Congress. Roosevelt did use executive powers aggressively in such areas as the creation of national forests and antitrust actions. But more important, this young President stirred the public imagination, in part by his masterful courting of the national press, which he literally brought in from the cold by giving it office space in the White House, using a vigorous, aggressively positive style that was capped by his great election victory in 1904. He also articulated a philosophy of the presidency in which he compared himself to Lincoln and Jackson, arguing that the President had the right to take any action he deemed necessary in the public interest as long as such action was not explicitly barred by the Constitution. This "stewardship" view of presidential power was exceptional up to this time; afterward, it became the norm.[41]

Roosevelt's successor, William H. Taft, assumed an approach that was by philosophy more restrained. Despite the fact that Taft actually accomplished more than Roosevelt did in some areas (for example, Taft instigated more antitrust actions than did the great trust-

---

[40] For more on the evolution of Congress, see *Origins and Development of Congress* (Washington, D.C.: Congressional Quarterly, 1976).

[41] See Theodore Roosevelt, *The Autobiography of Theodore Roosevelt* (New York: Scribner's, 1958), pp. 197–200.

buster Roosevelt), Taft's Whiggish approach and perceived inactivity in the legislative realm hurt him in the eyes of the public.[42] One analyst writing at the end of the Taft administration echoed sentiments often heard today when he wrote: "The public expects the President to manage Congress. If he does not do this he is not considered a successful President. A failure to dominate Congress was Mr. Taft's chief shortcoming in the public mind."[43] The irony of this criticism lies in its contrast of Taft to the Presidents of the previous century, who were harshly criticized for meddling in congressional affairs.

Taft's successor, Woodrow Wilson, was eager to pick up where Roosevelt had left off. Buttressed by a more sympathetic Congress, Wilson promoted and used party discipline and cohesion to vigorously promote an ample legislative agenda. Despite the political humiliation he suffered at the hands of the Senate in the defeat of his cherished League of Nations proposal at the end of his second term, Wilson rode the twin tides of political progressivism and World War I to legitimize a regular, active presidential role in legislative affairs.

Presidents Harding, Coolidge, and Hoover were three Republicans who retreated from Wilsonian activism but did not seek to return to nineteenth-century Whiggery. Instead, they steered a middle course by presenting some legislative measures to Congress, lobbying on occasion, and using the veto. While this approach generally sufficed in terms of public expectation and congressional preference, it proved to be political poison when the country entered the crisis years of the great depression during Hoover's administration. Hoover's efforts to cope with the depression went beyond the philosophy and actions of his two predecessors, but his philosophy and reticence to deal more frankly and boldly with the nation's crisis sealed his defeat to Franklin D. Roosevelt, the epitome of the activist President. Eagerly sought by Congress and the country, Roosevelt's leadership of the legislative branch was a cornerstone of his presidency. In fact, the FDR years are virtually defined by his legislative program, the New Deal. The two great crises of his four-term presidency, the depression and World War II, combined with FDR's activist style to usher in an institutionalized activist presidency.

Roosevelt would become the yardstick by which every future

[42] Taft expanded on his restrained view of presidential power in *The President and His Powers* (New York: Columbia University Press, 1967). The volume was first published in 1916.

[43] Quoted in Sundquist, *The Decline and Resurgence of Congress*, p. 32.

president would be measured. From Roosevelt's time to the present, for example, every President would submit to Congress an annual, detailed legislative agenda. In the one instance when a president did not do so (in 1953, President Eisenhower's first year), the President would be roundly criticized by members of both parties in Congress for what had by then been defined as an obligation of the office. As succeeding chapters will detail, an elaborate and complex administrative machinery now exists to facilitate and formalize the President's role in legislative matters.

Since Roosevelt's time Presidents have assumed added obligations. Two presidencies—those of Nixon and Reagan—would be rocked by scandals suggesting that the presidential-congressional balance had tipped too far in favor of the President. Congress would make several important efforts during the 1970s and 1980s to redress the imbalance. The immediate successors to Nixon and Reagan would make conscious efforts to curtail their predecessors' excesses. Yet despite these new twists, the Rooseveltian model of aggressive, institutionalized presidential leadership of Congress would be accepted as proper for the President *as though the Constitution itself specifically mandated these activities.*[44] While we might (or might not) agree with the desirability of this dramatic change, it is vitally important to understand at the outset how much the institutional relationship between the President and Congress has changed in the last two centuries.

CONCLUSION: EXPLAINING THE CHANGING RELATIONSHIP

Without question, strong Presidents of the Jefferson-Jackson-Lincoln ilk have emerged throughout our history. But the idea of a strong in-

---

[44]Theodore J. Lowi asserts that since the New Deal era, the relationship between the branches of government has changed so dramatically that we have in effect an entirely new governing system characterized by a presidentially centered, partyless system in which traditional separation of powers no longer applies. He dubs this system the Second Republic. See *The Personal President*. Richard Rose picks up on this theme by arguing that we have had three successive kinds of presidencies: a traditional President who was minimally involved in governing, a modern President dating from Franklin Roosevelt who was more activist, and a postmodern President dating from the 1970s who finds himself overwhelmed by responsibilities. See *The Postmodern President* (Chatham, N.J.: Chatham House, 1991).

stitutional presidency as a natural and inevitable counterpart to the legislature is a phenomenon of the twentieth century. Several factors help explain this phenomenon.

First, the relative vagueness of Article II of the Constitution opened the door to presidents who sought constitutional justification for broader use of power. Both the stewardship-activist and Whiggish interpretations of presidential power fit within the constitutional framework. Aside from actions judged to be plainly illegal, however, the stewardship role has provided an umbrella to protect activist Presidents from criticisms that they exceeded constitutional authority. And even if such arguments prevailed during an activist presidency (such as during the Jacksonian era), the actions themselves provided a precedent for future Presidents.

Second, the dynamism and imagination of forceful Presidents operated within the loose constitutional framework to extend preexisting limits. History is filled with examples of leaders who achieved and held power through despotic means—Julius Caesar, Napoleon, and Mao Tse-tung, for example—but who also possessed and cultivated enormous popularity. The point is that even an executive despot can rally the people. As elected executives in a republican system, American Presidents have sought and captured the public's imagination in a way that no assemblage of several hundred members of Congress ever could.[45] Even Presidents who were considered bad leaders or whose administrations were considered unsuccessful contributed to this progression. The presidencies of John Tyler and Andrew Johnson, for example, helped erode the view that there were or ought to be limits on the President's use of the veto. Popular dissatisfaction with Taft's image as a Whiggish president fed Wilson's mandate to be an activist. Similarly, the more restrained and less imperial post-Watergate presidencies of Ford and Carter only whetted the public's appetite for a more ceremonial and activist presidency. Much of Reagan's enduring popularity stemmed precisely from his embrace of activism and the grandly ceremonial trappings of the office.

Third, both Congress and the country as a whole historically look

---

[45] Congress has attempted to catch up to the President's built-in media advantage. See Michael J. Robinson, "Three Faces of Congressional Media," in *The New Congress*, ed. by Thomas E. Mann and Norman J. Ornstein (Washington, D.C.: American Enterprise Institute, 1981); Smith, *The Power Game*, pp. 35–39, 132–145; Timothy E. Cook, "The Evolution of Congressional Press Operations," in *Congressional Politics*, ed. by Christopher J. Deering (Chicago: Dorsey, 1989).

to the President for leadership in times of crisis. The threats of war and economic dislocation provide the clearest examples of periods when Presidents extend the limits of their powers. In theory, presidential authority reverts back to its "normal" dimensions when crises subside. In practice, however, precedents set during crises may be applied to future crises, whether those crises are actual or imaginary, and enhance the image of the President as omniscient parent figure to whom the country runs when troubles arise. The continuation of a perpetual crisis mentality in the post–World War II era, from the start of the cold war, has figured directly in the postwar strong presidency. As political scientist Louis Fisher notes, the usual flow of powers back to Congress after times of emergency did not occur after Franklin Roosevelt, as it had in the past.[46]

Fourth, as several examples in succeeding chapters will make clear, Congress has willingly surrendered authority to the executive in areas such as budgeting and war powers. Presidential scholar Edward Corwin noted many years ago that "a vast proportion of the great powers which the President nowadays exercises are the immediate donation of Congress."[47] As the previous account also mentioned, Congress has suffered from a checkered if not tarnished reputation over the years in comparison to the presidency, and this has fueled the broad feeling that the presidency is more capable of handling national problems.

These reasons for the shift in presidential-congressional relations raise a final question: Might we ever return to the kind of congressional-dominant system of the last century? Many have ruminated on this in recent years.[48] The likelihood of a new era of congressional dominance seems extremely remote, but this does not preclude future changes in the relationship between the two branches. The possibilities for change will be discussed more fully in Chapter 7.

[46] Louis Fisher, "War Powers: The Need for Collective Judgment," in *Divided Democracy*, ed. by James A. Thurber (Washington, D.C.: CQ Press, 1991), pp. 199–218. See also Bill Moyers, *The Secret Government* (Cabin John, Md.: Seven Locks, 1988).

[47] Edward S. Corwin, *Constitutional Revolution, Ltd.* (Claremont, Calif.: Claremont Colleges, 1941), p. 104.

[48] Some have gone so far as to propose that Congress has in fact come to dominate or "fetter" the presidency. See L. Gordon Crovitz and Jeremy Rabkins, eds., *The Fettered Presidency* (Washington, D.C.: American Enterprise Institute, 1989). This unusual view will be discussed at greater length in Chapter 7 of this book.

Chapter 3

The Domestic Realm I: The Legislative Presidency

REPORTER: I'd like to continue with this kinder-gentler theme for a moment. You tried this with Congress for the entire six months you've been in office, yet your crime bill has failed, your defense bill appears to have been savaged, your nominee for the civil rights post, whom you say is qualified, is being given the rough ride, to say the least, and the S&L [savings and loan] bill, you have great concerns about. How would you rate your own legislative success in your first six months?

PRESIDENT BUSH: I'd be rating the Congress, wouldn't I, if I rated the legislative success and I wouldn't give it very high marks. . . . I would not give Congress very high marks on doing what I want done on legislation. . . .

REPORTER: Do you think this is just a harbinger of things to come, a Republican President working with this Democratic Congress . . . ?

PRESIDENT BUSH: Nobody ever said it would be easy.

PRESIDENTIAL PRESS CONFERENCE

PRINTED IN *THE NEW YORK TIMES,* JULY 29, 1989

George Bush might have owed his successful 1988 presidential bid to the political legacy of his predecessor, Ronald Reagan, but from the start of the Bush administration it was clear that he would not duplicate the early legislative triumphs of the Reagan years. Hardened by the harsh turbulence of much of the Reagan administration, Republicans and Democrats alike welcomed Bush's professed "kinder, gentler" approach—a theme first developed in the 1988 campaign—to governing and politics. Yet as the inquiring reporter quoted above observed, Bush's softer sell seemingly found little success in Congress during the crucial first six months of his administration. Bush revealed the wisdom of an experienced political insider when he noted that Congress shares much of the responsibility for the fate of any President's program, that he was of course unhappy with Congress's lack of responsiveness to some of his proposals, and that success for any President is no easy or simple goal. But more important than these observations is a larger, looming fact: The ebb and flow of legislative politics is usually defined by the President's priorities.

In this chapter we continue to examine the modern President's role as coordinator of the legislative process. It is a responsibility that has followed a path emerging from constitutional structure, history, and modern institutional traits. The President's coordinative role has been cultivated by ambitious Presidents and expectant Congresses; it is also institutionalized, affecting every important step in the legislative process. This fact is reflected in the chapter's subtitle.[1] Yet this presidential presence guarantees only the opportunity for presidential involvement; it does not guarantee presidential domination or success. The matter of how success is measured is discussed at the end of the chapter.

CHIEF LEGISLATOR

As the discussion of history in Chapter 2 revealed, the executive and legislative branches share powers by design. It is therefore all but inevitable that each branch will have a hand in the actions of the other. In addition, our previous discussion makes it clear that Presidents in the twentieth century play a far more dominating role in legislative affairs than did their nineteenth-century predecessors. Despite holding few formal legislative powers, modern Presidents are typically considered the chief legislator—a term popularized by presidential scholar Clinton Rossiter.[2]

---

[1] The subtitle is taken from Stephen J. Wayne, *The Legislative Presidency* (New York: Harper & Row, 1978).

[2] See Clinton Rossiter, *The American Presidency* (New York: New American Library, 1960), p. 26. Rossiter's book was first published in 1956. The term *chief legislator* was apparently first applied to the President in Howard L. McBain, *The Living Constitution* (New York: Macmillan, 1927).

One of the important facts about the president's vigorous role in legislative affairs is that it is expected and even welcomed by Congress. This holds true even if Congress is controlled by the President's political opponents.

An area where presidential involvement is considered essential is in the presentation of an annual legislative program to Congress. This presidential laundry list spells out the President's primary legislative priorities, urging favorable congressional consideration.[3] The last time a President failed to present such an agenda to Congress was in 1953, the first year of the Eisenhower presidency. Following on the heels of presidential activists Franklin D. Roosevelt and Harry S. Truman, the more conservative Eisenhower sought "adherence to 'proper' principles of 'balance' between [the] branches."[4] Yet this presidential restraint provoked sharp criticism from both parties in Congress. A fellow Republican in the House of Representatives admonished the Eisenhower administration when he said, "Don't expect us to start from scratch on what you people want. That's not the way we do things here—*you* draft the bills and *we* work them over."[5]

WHY A LEGISLATIVE PRESIDENT?

Presidential involvement in legislative affairs rests with practice and precedent set by Presidents who worked vigorously to extend their influence over national policy-making. The list of so-called activist Presidents, such as Theodore Roosevelt, Woodrow Wilson, Franklin D. Roosevelt, John F. Kennedy, and Lyndon Johnson, is also a list of Presidents who labored to dominate the legislative process in order to realize their ambitious national programs.[6] The very labels that

---

[3] Jeffrey E. Cohen has traced the rise of this function as reflected in State of the Union addresses since 1861 in "The Impact of the Modern Presidency on Presidential Success in the U.S. Congress," *Legislative Studies Quarterly,* 7 (November 1982): 515–532.

[4] Richard E. Neustadt, "Presidency and Legislation: Planning the President's Program," in *The Presidency,* ed. by Aaron Wildavsky (Boston: Little, Brown, 1969), p. 562.

[5] Quoted in Neustadt, "Presidency and Legislation," p. 594. The President's favored legislative proposals are usually highlighted in the annual State of the Union address and Economic Message to Congress.

[6] For more on the rise of the modern activist presidency, see James W. Davis, *The American Presidency* (New York: Harper & Row, 1987), pp. 18–33. An excellent, balanced treatment of presidential legislative programs can be found in Mark A. Peterson, *Legislating Together: The White House and Capitol Hill from Eisenhower to Reagan* (Cambridge, Mass.: Harvard University Press, 1990).

came to be identified with these presidents, such as FDR's New Deal, Kennedy's New Frontier, and Johnson's Great Society, all embodied ambitious legislative agendas.

Ambitious Presidents do not, however, provide the only explanation for the President's expanded role in legislative matters. This pattern also stems from concerted efforts by Congress to delegate some of its authority by statute to the President and other executive officials, efforts that predate the twentieth century. Several factors have encouraged this willing transfer of power by Congress. First, until this century, Congress typically held session for only a few months of the year. Congress thus found it necessary to delegate certain of its powers to the executive to ensure the smooth functioning of governmental programs when it was not in session.

Second, the need for flexibility in the timing of legislative policy has often resulted in delegation. For example, Congress voted to renew commercial restrictions against France in 1799 but gave the President the option of ending them "if he shall deem it expedient and consistent with the interest of the United States."[7] Third, delegation of power to the President occurred as a result of the long tradition of Presidents acting as channels for communication with foreign nations. For example, an 1822 law barred British West Indies ports from shipping to the United States unless the President received information that American ships could enter British ports.

Fourth, the President has long been considered the singular representative of the American people. As a consequence, many powers have been delegated to the executive by Congress in an attempt to avoid the political fragmentation and controversy that often attend congressional decision making. This was seen, for example, in several attempts to delegate tariff powers to the executive early in the twentieth century.

Fifth, executive responsibility to engage in fact-finding and coordination has also encouraged delegation. This is seen especially in the area of intervention in the economy, where measures designed to stimulate or otherwise direct the economy are directly dependent on the quality and timeliness of the information available. Since the executive gathers and generates much of this information, it has often proved to be the logical source of timely action. For example, the Federal Pay Comparability Act of 1970 was enacted to ensure that

---

[7] Quoted in Louis Fisher, *President and Congress* (New York: Free Press, 1972), p. 60.

federal pay levels remained roughly comparable with those of similar jobs in the private sector. Such assessments depended on data supplied by several federal bureaus. Based on the data, the President made appropriate recommendations to Congress, although Presidents have generally recommended pay levels for federal employees substantially below those of comparable jobs in the private sector.[8]

Finally, national emergencies have been an important basis for delegating power to the President. During times of war and economic crisis, the desire for speed and flexibility, respect for presidential expertise, and the innate tendency to seek answers from a benevolent national father figure all contribute to a congressional willingness to give broad powers to the President.[9]

The delegation of congressional powers to the executive is a practice that extends back to the beginning of the country. For example, in a challenge to the Judiciary Act of 1789, Chief Justice John Marshall observed that Congress could in fact delegate certain powers to either of the other two branches.[10] Over the last two centuries Congress has delegated authority in hundreds, perhaps even thousands of instances.

To select one example, in 1934 Congress surrendered to the executive considerable authority over an area that dominated more of its time than had any other issue from the Civil War up to that time—the tariff. Congress's preoccupation with the tariff was based on the importance of the revenues it generated for the government, especially before the enactment of the income tax in 1913, and on its profound impact on agriculture, manufacturing, and other sectors of the national economy. A policy of free trade (few or no tariffs imposed on imported goods) rather than protectionism (substantial fees on imports) could please domestic consumers and foreign manufacturers but enrage domestic producers and produce worker layoffs,

[8] From correspondence with Louis Fisher. This small example illustrates how presidential discretion can defeat legislative intent.

[9] An excellent discussion of delegation of power is found in Fisher, *President and Congress*, chap. 3. See also Richard M. Pious, *The American Presidency* (New York: Basic Books, 1979), pp. 213–217. The tendency of Presidents to use wartime and other emergencies to enhance the power of the office is discussed in Arthur Schlesinger, Jr., *The Imperial Presidency* (Boston: Houghton Mifflin, 1973). For more on the tendency to view the President as a benevolent, omniscient father figure, see Thomas E. Cronin, *The State of the Presidency* (Boston: Little, Brown, 1980), chap. 3 (aptly titled "The Textbook and Prime-Time Presidency").

[10] The case, of course, was *Marbury v. Madison* (1803).

whereas a policy of protectionism could reverse the fortunes of each of these groups. Yet by the 1930s Congress came to realize that it could no longer devote legislative time to setting thousands of tariff schedules, a complex and high-pressure task that could easily consume an entire legislative session. With the passage of the Reciprocal Trade Agreements Act of 1934, Congress empowered the President to unilaterally raise or lower duties by as much as 50 percent in exchange for similar concessions from other nations. Congress granted this sweeping authority for a period of three years, but it has been regularly renewed,with virtually no suggestion from Congress that the power should return to the legislature.[11] Congress does, however, continue to enact legislation on trade matters.

To pick another, more recent example, concern over rising unemployment during the summer of 1991 prompted Congress to pass a bill to extend unemployment benefits past the standard twenty-six weeks of benefits for up to an additional twenty weeks. President Bush opposed the benefits extension, arguing that the government could not afford the $5.3 billion cost and that the nation was already climbing out of its recession. Despite threats of a veto, Congress enacted the measure on August 2, and Bush signed the bill shortly thereafter. However, the language of the bill was such that the President could ignore its purpose without actually vetoing it.

According to the bill, the benefits would be distributed only if the President, after signing the bill into law, declared an emergency. In his signing statement, Bush announced that he would not declare an emergency but would sign the bill anyway because "it at least demonstrates I am concerned."[12] Congressional leaders were fully aware of Bush's intentions but passed the bill because it would buttress Democratic claims that Republicans were unsympathetic to the plight of the jobless.[13] For our purposes, this bill typifies the congressional granting of discretion which often undercuts that institution's

[11] See James L. Sundquist, *The Decline and Resurgence of Congress* (Washington, D.C.: Brookings Institution, 1981), pp. 99–103; Congressional Quarterly, *Guide to Congress* (Washington, D.C.: Congressional Quarterly, 1971), pp. 175–179; and Raymond A. Bauer, Ithiel de Sola Pool, and Lewis Anthony Dexter, *American Business and Public Policy* (Chicago: Aldine-Atherton, 1972).

[12] Adam Clymer, "President to Sign Jobless Measure but Block Money," *New York Times,* August 17, 1991.

[13] Jill Zuckman, "Congress Clears Benefits Bills, but Funding Is Unlikely," *CQ Weekly Report,* August 3, 1991, pp. 2164–2164. A worsening economic picture eventually prompted Bush to sign and implement a bill to extend benefits in November 1991.

power; that is, Congress won the battle by enacting a jobs bill but lost the war by giving the President complete discretion to decide on his own whether to actually provide benefits.

Another area where the President has acquired broad legislative authority is as a legislative policy planner. Since the end of World War II Congress has granted to the President specific policy-formulating responsibilities. In 1946, for example, Congress passed the Employment Act, which requires the President to continually monitor the economy, provide Congress with annual reports (the president's Annual Economic Message/Report), and recommend appropriate government action to resolve economic problems such as inflation and recession. Congress by no means foreclosed its role in economic planning, and it has even moved to enhance its capabilities in this area in recent years, such as through the enactment of the Budget and Impoundment Control Act of 1974,[14] but the President's hand in economic policy-making was substantially increased. Similar responsibilities were granted to the President over planning labor policy in the Manpower Development and Training Act of 1962, over housing in the Housing and Urban Development Act of 1968, over urban growth policy in the Housing and Urban Development Act of 1970, and in other areas, including the environment and national security. Subsequent Presidents have not taken an equivalent interest in all these areas; nevertheless, Congress established a pattern of granting responsibility for long-range policy formulation and coordination to the President by statute instead of assuming for itself the primary policy-formulation role. In the process, Congress's own proclivities for policy initiation have to some extent atrophied.[15] In Chapter 4 we will examine the evolution of the budgetary process as another example of how congressional delegation has led to greater presidential influence in legislative affairs.

AN ADMINISTRATIVE CONGRESS?

If the President has had a greater hand in legislative matters, has the reverse also occurred, namely, greater congressional involvement in

[14] See John W. Ellwood and James A. Thurber, "The Politics of the Congressional Budget Process Re-examined," in *Congress Reconsidered,* ed. by Lawrence C. Dodd and Bruce I. Oppenheimer (Washington, D.C.: CQ Press, 1981), pp. 246–274.

[15] See Sundquist, *The Decline and Resurgence of Congress,* pp. 66–68.

presidential/executive affairs? The simple answer is yes. In a system of shared powers, it should come as no surprise that Congress has a "legitimate stake and interest . . . in administrative matters."[16] The federal administrative apparatus that exists today—the myriad federal agencies, offices, departments, and programs that compose the executive branch—was created by legislative enactment and is funded by dollars appropriated by Congress. Congress also retains a keen interest in the expenditure of those dollars, and it devotes much of its effort to overseeing the administrative process. Congressional oversight investigations of presidential and administrative activities have often been responsible for bringing to light cases of fraud, waste, mismanagement, and abuse. Such investigations have a long history. In 1792 the House of Representatives voted to investigate the most disastrous military defeat ever suffered by the U.S. Army at the hands of Native Americans, dwarfing even the massacre of General Custer's forces at Little Big Horn a century later. Known as St. Clair's defeat, the military disaster decimated the small U.S. Army. Bowing to a congressional request, President George Washington directed his secretaries of war and the treasury to turn over copies of pertinent records to the congressional investigative committee.[17]

In comparing the involvement of each branch in the other's affairs, it is important to note three facts. First, congressional involvement in executive affairs has been contested by Presidents and others far more than the reverse, a fact generally indicative of the President's greater relative rise in power and accompanying acceptance of that change. As one study concluded, "It is both ironic and inconsistent . . . that the evolution of a legislative presidency has taken place smoothly and with relatively little controversy in response to changing systemic needs, while efforts by Congress to control administration have been attacked as unconstitutional."[18]

Second, presidential/executive resources for influencing the legislative process are generally far greater, given the sheer size—almost

---

[16] Louis Fisher, *The Politics of Shared Powers* (Washington, D.C.: CQ Press, 1987), p. 112.

[17] This and other important congressional investigations are discussed in Arthur M. Schlesinger, Jr., and Roger Bruns, eds., *Congress Investigates: A Documented History, 1792–1974*, 5 vols. (New York: Chelsea House, 1983).

[18] William F. West and Joseph Cooper, "Legislative Influence v. Presidential Dominance: Competing Models of Bureaucratic Control," *Political Science Quarterly*, 104 (Winter 1989–90): 606.

3 million employees—and level of resources as well as the more hierarchical structure of the executive branch, than are those of the legislative branch (which centers on 535 semiautonomous congressional
offices and far more limited resources; in toto, Congress is composed
of about 25,000 people, about the size of one of the smaller cabinet
departments).[19] Third, both presidential involvement in legislative
matters and congressional involvement in executive affairs play themselves out largely through, within, or from the legislative process. As
a consequence, we will study these interactions primarily from the
perspective of the legislative process.[20]

In the following section we will examine the resources and capabilities that Presidents bring to bear on the legislative process.
Whether conservative Republican or liberal Democrat, the modern
President brings to the legislative realm a wide array of formal and
informal powers that essentially define that process today. Except for
international crises, no other realm more closely defines the relative
success of a presidency than executive interaction in legislative matters.

SETTING THE AGENDA

Many have studied the question of who bears the primary responsibility for the formulation and initiation of legislation and have argued
that Congress has not received the credit it deserves. Even though
Congress waits on the President's annual legislative program, many
of the ideas and suggestions found in the President's program may
come from Congress or elsewhere, such as private-interest groups.

The first important study of legislative initiative examined ninety
major pieces of legislation passed by Congress from 1870 to 1940.
The study reported that presidential influence predominated for

---

[19] For more detailed information on the size and organization of congressional staff and
offices, see Norman J. Ornstein, Thomas E. Mann, and Michael J. Malbin, *Vital Statistics on Congress, 1989–1990* (Washington, D.C.: CQ Press, 1990), chap. 5. For similar
information about the executive branch, see Gary King and Lyn Ragsdale, *The Elusive
Executive* (Washington, D.C.: CQ Press, 1988), chap. 4.

[20] For more on congressional involvement in administrative affairs, see Fisher, *The Poli-
tics of Shared Powers*, chap. 3; R. Douglas Arnold, *Congress and the Bureaucracy*
(New Haven, Conn.: Yale University Press, 1979); Lawrence C. Dodd and Richard L.
Schott, *Congress and the Administrative State* (New York: Wiley, 1979); and West and
Cooper, "Legislative Influence v. Presidential Dominance."

nineteen of the bills, congressional influence dominated in thirty-five cases, joint influence was important in twenty-nine cases, and pressure-group influence was decisive in seven cases. The study's principal conclusion was "not that the president is less important than generally supposed, but that Congress is more important."[21]

A follow-up study applied similar methods to sixty-three major pieces of legislation enacted into law from 1945 to 1964. This study concluded that "the President has indeed become a major partner in the legislative process, and . . . very little significant legislation is now passed that either does not emanate from the executive branch, or is not significantly influenced by executive action at some stage of its legislative history."[22] Another analyst, writing at the height of the Johnson era, concluded that the President "now determines the legislative agenda of Congress almost as thoroughly as the British Cabinet sets the legislative agenda of Parliament."[23]

These conclusions have been challenged by several scholars who argue that the role of Congress has been undervalued. One studied the period 1940–1967 and found many areas where the Congress played a decisive role, including the economy, transportation, agriculture, urban policy, and technology. Its conclusion was that "Congress continues to be an active innovator and very much in the legislative business."[24] Other studies have explored what many view

[21] See Lawrence Chamberlain, *The President, Congress, and Legislation* (New York: Columbia University Press, 1946); and Lawrence Chamberlain, "The President, Congress, and Legislation," in *The President: Roles and Powers,* ed. by David Haight and Larry Johnson (Chicago: Rand McNally, 1965), p. 304. While the Chamberlain and other studies cited in this section include legislation in both the domestic and foreign realms, the great majority of legislation considered is domestic. Indeed, Chamberlain did not include a category for foreign policy.

[22] William Goldsmith, *The Growth of Presidential Power,* 3 vols. (New York: Chelsea House, 1983), 3, p. 22.

[23] Samuel Huntington, "Congressional Responses to the Twentieth Century," in *The Congress and America's Future,* ed. by David Truman (Englewood Cliffs, N.J.: Prentice-Hall, 1965), p. 23. Huntington goes on to propose that lawmaking ought to be left to the President and that Congress ought to devote its energies to constituent work and bureaucratic oversight.

[24] Ronald C. Moe and Steven C. Teel, "Congress as Policy-Maker: A Necessary Reappraisal," *Political Science Quarterly,* 85 (September 1970): 468. Of Moe and Teel's twelve policy categories, one incorporated foreign policy. The inclusion of a foreign policy category did not skew the results in the President's favor. See also Hugh Gallagher, "Presidents, Congress, and the Legislative Functions," in *The Presidency Reappraised,* ed. by Rexford Tugwell and Thomas Cronin (New York: Praeger, 1974), esp. pp. 232–233.

as Congress's undervalued role in legislative initiation and enactment.[25]

These apparent contradictions can be resolved if one recognizes several facts. First, it is often impossible to identify the original source of legislation, and credit is frequently shared. For example, many of the Great Society initiatives enacted during Lyndon Johnson's presidency were actually adapted from proposals worked up in the 1950s by Democratic representatives. Those members of Congress deserve recognition for their initial work; however, Johnson also deserves credit for putting the weight of the presidency behind those proposals and seeing them through to enactment. President Kennedy received credit for enacting the Area Redevelopment Act of 1961 despite the fact that several Democratic senators had advanced this idea in the late 1950s, when it was successfully blocked by President Eisenhower. Although the idea did not originate with Kennedy, he made it part of his program and saw it through to enactment.

Second, studies such as those mentioned above are often inspired by reactions to prevailing wisdom shaped by contemporary politics. The Roosevelt and Johnson eras, for example, were periods of relative presidential dominance. But Congress's role during the Eisenhower era was more assertive, and it was even more so during the 1970s. Studies that had the mid-1960s as their end point would almost certainly come to a different conclusion about presidential-congressional relations than would studies completed during the mid-1970s, for example.

Third, a reordering of data from different studies often uncovers greater consistencies. For example, the data from the first two studies mentioned above were reordered in Table 3.1. The table illustrates clearly that over time the President's influence has progressively increased while that of Congress has progressively declined, with joint responsibility also on the rise.

CENTRAL CLEARANCE

Concomitant with the expansion of the President's legislative role, the growth of the federal bureaucracy, and need for greater fiscal

[25] See, for example, John R. Johannes, "The President Proposes and Congress Disposes—But Not Always: Legislative Initiative on Capitol Hill," *Review of Politics*, 36 (July 1974): 356–370.

Table 3.1   Responsibility for Passage of Major Legislative Proposals

	President	Congress	Joint	Pressure Group	Totals
1870–1910	17% (5)	53% (16)	20% (6)	10% (3)	100% (30)
1911–1930	12 (4)	48 (16)	27 (9)	12 (4)	99 (33)
1931–1940	37 (10)	11 (3)	52 (14)	0 —	100 (27)
1945–1954	33 (12)	17 (16)	44 (16)	6 (2)	100 (36)
1955–1964	56 (15)	4 (1)	41 (11)	0 —	100 (27)

NOTE: Variations from 100 percent are due to rounding error. Data taken and readjusted from Lawrence Chamberlain, "The President, Congress, and Legislation," reprinted in *The President: Roles and Powers,* ed. David Haight and Larry Johnson (Chicago: Rand McNally, 1965), pp. 301–303, and William Goldsmith, *The Growth of Presidential Powers* (New York: Chelsea House, 1974), 3, 1398–1399. Goldsmith claimed to use the same evaluation standards and techniques as Chamberlain. Data from 1870 to 1940 from Chamberlain study. Data from 1945 to 1964 from Goldsmith study.

SOURCE: Robert J. Spitzer, *The Presidency and Public Policy* (University: University of Alabama Press, 1983), p. 92. Reprinted by permission.

economy, budgetary authority was delegated to the President starting in 1921 with the enactment of the Budget and Accounting Act. This act stated that any agency or department planning to request legislation for the expenditure of funds would first have to obtain approval from the newly created Bureau of the Budget (BOB). In the 1930s this "central clearance" process was extended to all requests for legislation from the executive branch. The BOB would then determine if the requests were consistent with the President's legislative priorities. By 1939 the BOB was handling department reports on 2,448 pending bills and 438 drafts of proposed bills emanating from executive branch agencies.[26] This degree of White House control was eventually extended beyond legislative proposals to include the political activities of agencies. Any agency seeking to take a public stand on issues would first have to clear its views with the budget office. As political scientist Theodore J. Lowi noted, "the process of legislative clearance has a long tradition as the foundation of the development

[26] See Goldsmith, *The Growth of Presidential Power,* 3, 124. Roosevelt first handled legislative clearance through his National Emergency Council. With its demise, BOB assumed this responsibility after the publication of the Brownlow Report in 1937.

of the president's program . . . and the theory that all presidents have to be strong presidents."[27]

At the other end of the legislative process, the BOB also assessed all "enrolled bills" (those passed by Congress but not yet signed by the President). These bills were forwarded by the BOB to any agencies affected by the legislation, and they would submit a response to the BOB as to whether the bill should be signed or vetoed by the President. The BOB would then send its final recommendation to the President. Communication between the President and the BOB was made easier in 1939, when the office was moved from the Treasury Department to the newly created Executive Office of the President. According to one expert, clearance and enrolled bill processes "lie at the core of the legislative presidency."[28]

From the Franklin Roosevelt period to about 1965, the BOB tried to avoid overt political considerations in its recommendations, concerning itself more directly with budgetary limitations and the objective merits of bills. Primary responsibility for these activities fell to the Legislative Reference Division within the BOB. Because of the volume of legislation, BOB recommendations carried considerable weight, as did those of the career civil servants within the bureau who assumed the brunt of the work. Toward the end of his term, however, President Johnson created a new political-level position at the bureau. This appointment marked the beginning of a process of greater politicization in the BOB.

In addition, the Johnson White House began to take a more active role in determining political and policy priorities and their relationship to the President's broader agenda. Items of special interest to the President were given higher priority and were often handled by White House aides. This greater White House interest was accompanied by an expansion of Johnson's domestic policy staff.

Under Nixon, the BOB was reconstituted as the Office of Management and Budget (OMB). The agency was given greater managerial responsibility, and four politically appointed associate director positions were created to assume key responsibilities. As a consequence, central clearance and the assessment of enrolled bills came

[27] Theodore J. Lowi, *The Personal President* (Ithaca, N.Y.: Cornell University Press, 1985), p. 138. See also Allen Schick, "The Budget as an Instrument of Presidential Policy," in *Governance: The Reagan Era and Beyond*, ed. by Lester Salamon (Washington, D.C.: Urban Institute, 1985), pp. 91–122.

[28] Wayne, *The Legislative Presidency*, p. 72.

under the purview of political appointees rather than civil servants. The outgrowth of these changes was that the OMB was less receptive to the suggestions and recommendations of civil servants and federal agencies. Instead, the OMB has increasingly served as an instrument for extending White House policy preferences into federal agencies. During the latter part of the Nixon administration the OMB was derisively labeled TOMB—The Office of Meddling and Bumbling—because of its interference in departmental and agency management.[29] Despite such criticism, the process of politicizing the OMB accelerated under the Reagan administration, especially in the areas of budgetary control and regulatory review.[30]

LIAISON

Presidents have always maintained informal connections with congressional leaders. Woodrow Wilson was the first President in this century to engage in personal lobbying on Capitol Hill. Franklin Roosevelt sent his top aides directly to the Capitol to push for his proposals. But it was President Truman who first established a White House office to maintain regularized ties between the President and Congress. The office was enlarged and reorganized under Eisenhower and grew to maturity under the guidance of Lawrence O'Brien, special assistant for congressional affairs to Presidents Kennedy and Johnson. O'Brien's office served as a focal point for the liaison activities of executive agencies and departments. He and his staff also spent much time roaming the halls of Congress, seeking information and reinforcing congressional contacts. The liaison office prepared weekly reports for the President and made projections about the week to come. Johnson, a former Senate majority leader, also played an active role in building support in Congress for his programs and proposals.[31]

[29] Larry Berman, *The Office of Management and Budget and the Presidency, 1921–1979* (Princeton, N.J.: Princeton University Press, 1979), p. ix.

[30] See Peter M. Benda and Charles H. Levine, "Reagan and the Bureaucracy," in *The Reagan Legacy*, ed. by Charles O. Jones (Chatham, N.J.: Chatham House, 1988), pp. 112–120. See also Wayne, *The Legislative Presidency*, chap. 3; Stephen J. Wayne and James F. C. Hyde, Jr., "Presidential Decision-Making on Enrolled Bills," *Presidential Studies Quarterly*, 8 (Summer 1978): 284–296. For more on the evolution of the OMB, see Berman, *The Office of Management and Budget and the Presidency.*

[31] Davis, *The American Presidency*, p. 159.

President Nixon constructed what was considered a strong liaison staff, but it found its judgments and operations preempted by Nixon's top assistants, including H. R. Haldeman and John Ehrlichman. After two frustrating years Nixon's liaison head, Bryce Harlow, resigned. Harlow's successors were similarly frustrated by administration broadside attacks against Congress. By 1973 the liaison office had lost its effectiveness, and such efforts were left to a few top Nixon aides. When Gerald Ford became President, the former House minority leader sought to rebuild liaison efforts, and he was credited by members of both parties with doing much to repair the damage of the Nixon years. Despite this, Ford found his weak political standing to be an impediment that forced him to rely mostly on vetoes as a means of molding legislation, a strategy that eroded more positive presidential-congressional relations.[32]

President Carter took office with high expectations, but those expectations were soon dashed by his mishandling of legislative liaison. Carter's choice to head the Office of Congressional Liaison was Frank Moore, who had been Carter's liaison with the legislature when Carter served as governor of Georgia. But Moore had no Washington experience, and he and his staff neglected the early construction of solid relations with an initially receptive, if more assertive Democratic Congress. In particular, Moore was noted for failing to return the phone calls of representatives, not informing members of Congress when federal appointments were made in their districts, and "an uncanny ability of failing to consult with Speaker O'Neill."[33] Aside from this, the liaison office was organized by issue categories rather than by regional blocks, a structure that deemphasized the needs and perspectives of individual members of Congress. These problems combined with a flood of initial legislation forwarded to Congress from the administration that overwhelmed and confused Carter's Democratic legislative allies to produce poor and relatively unproductive relations between the branches (in contrast, Johnson sent important bills to Congress one at a time).

President Reagan's initial liaison efforts were more successful despite the fact that the Republicans controlled only the Senate. At the start of his administration some of Reagan's staff people conducted a

---

[32] See Wayne, *The Legislative Presidency,* chap. 5.

[33] Larry Berman, *The New American Presidency* (Boston: Little, Brown, 1987), p. 121.

study of the first three months of presidencies dating back to Franklin Roosevelt. They concluded that their best chance of success lay in working hard and early on a few key proposals. Reagan selected an experienced Washington hand, Max Friedersdorf, to head liaison efforts (Friedersdorf had been Ford's liaison head). Reagan was also careful to extend personal favors and courtesies to key congressional leaders of both parties.[34] In one often repeated example, Reagan sent Speaker of the House Tip O'Neill (D-Mass.) an ample supply of inauguration tickets, a fact that made Washington tongues wag not only because O'Neill was a member of the opposition party but also because Carter had denied O'Neill tickets four years earlier.[35] As a result of these efforts, Reagan achieved some important early successes, including the enactment of his major legislative proposal, a comprehensive package that included a 25 percent tax cut over three years.

The Bush administration sought to emulate its predecessor's skill at dealing with Congress, as seen in its recruitment of Washington insiders for congressional liaison. Bush's choice for liaison head was Frederick D. McClure, a Washingtonian with work experience in several congressional offices, including service as a member of Senator John Tower's (R-Tex.) staff.

At the same time, the Bush administration sought to distance itself from the Reagan administration's ideological stridency. Bush's efforts to emphasize low-key conciliation and personal involvement were buttressed not only by his experience as a longtime Washington insider but also by the reality that his party failed to win more seats in either house in the 1988 election, leaving the Democrats in control of both houses despite Bush's decisive win over Democrat Michael Dukakis. Congressional Democratic leaders openly praised Bush at the start of the administration for everything from the conciliatory tone of his inaugural address to his willingness to return phone calls. Despite early bruising battles over such issues as the savings and loan bailout crisis and Bush's unsuccessful attempt to name former Texas Senator Tower as secretary of defense, Bush's personal hands-on ap-

---

[34] Harold M. Barger, *The Impossible Presidency* (Glenview, Ill.: Scott, Foresman, 1984), pp. 128–130. For more on legislative liaison, see Abraham Holtzman, *Legislative Liaison* (Chicago: Rand McNally, 1970).

[35] Davis, *The American Presidency*, p. 160.

proach was characterized by one reporter as "a triumph of blue-blood manners and old-boy schmoozing."[36] According to liaison head McClure, within the first nine months of his presidency Bush had met at the White House with virtually every member of the Senate and 300 House members.[37]

Yet despite some early praise, Bush's personal approach seemed to produce its own problems. The White House came under increasing criticism from both Capitol Hill and some of his own staff for by-passing his liaison office (leaving them, in Washington jargon, "out of the loop"), relying instead on personal contacts and on his chief of staff, John Sununu, and his budget director, Richard Darman, to negotiate with important lawmakers. This approach led to criticism from one Republican strategist that Bush's efforts at times seemed "amateurish."[38] By the end of his first term, Bush came under heavy criticism from members of his own party for allowing Sununu, Darman, and White House counsel C. Boyden Gray free rein to define administration priorities while ignoring congressional Republicans.[39]

LOBBYING FROM THE WHITE HOUSE

An extensive and effective lobbying effort by the White House might seem to be of only secondary importance, considering the many other ways in which the executive branch is now a part of the law-making process. Yet no President seeking to maximize influence can afford to neglect either liaison or other lobbying efforts.

Executive lobbying begins but does not end with the White House. Its legislative liaison office is relatively small. Under the Reagan administration, for example, it consisted of ten people: five who covered the House, four who covered the Senate, and the liaison head. In addition, extensive liaison work was and is conducted by the

---

[36] Robin Toner, "Congress Still Purring as Bush Applies the Right Strokes," *New York Times*, January 31, 1989. See also "For Bush and Congress, Some Spirited Battles but No Full-Scale War," *New York Times*, August 9, 1989; Maureen Dowd, "Kindness Is Foundation as Bush Builds Bridges," *New York Times*, February 6, 1989; and Richard E. Cohen, "The Gloves Are Off," *National Journal*, October 14, 1989, pp. 2508–2512.

[37] Cohen, "The Gloves Are Off," p. 2510.

[38] Andrew Rosenthal, "Bush's Ties to Congress Show Strain," *New York Times*, October 16, 1989.

[39] Maureen Dowd, "White House Isolation," *New York Times*, November 22, 1991.

OMB and, in particular, its Office of Legislative Reference. The latter's job is to keep track of all bills of any interest to the executive, whether substantial or minor. In addition, each executive department devotes some of its own staff to legislative matters, as agencies have a direct stake in policy and appropriation actions taken in Congress. The Department of Defense alone has over 200 staff members assigned to liaison. By at least one estimate, the executive branch has as many as 1,500 employees assigned to liaison. Both the White House and the OMB staff act to coordinate departmental liaison activites.[40]

Much executive lobbying consists of routine information gathering. This task is important because it dovetails with the two-pronged nature of lobbying. Lobbyists, whether executive or otherwise, use information to press their case for or against legislation, but members of the legislature also rely on lobbyists for information when they are formulating their own views. Although lobbying by its nature involves presenting a one-sided argument rather than a balanced view, lobbyists are also often experts whose opinions are valued by sympathetic members of Congress. This principle applies to executive lobbyists because they possess not only expertise but the added legitimacy of being part of the government.

Liaison officials must be sensitive to the preferences and leanings of key legislators. For example, the Carter administration generally opposed the use of tax credits as a means of providing incentives. But according to Dan Tate, Senate liaison chief for Carter, the administration was prepared to accommodate the preference for tax credits among influential senators, such as the chair of the Finance Committee, understanding that sensitivity to senatorial preferences could later provide political dividends for the administration.

The Carter administration also employed a procedure known as the troublesome bills process. Early in the legislative session, the OMB would compile a list of bills that were likely to encounter difficulty in Congress. The list would be regularly reviewed by the OMB, the domestic policy staff, and liaison personnel to determine what positive steps might be taken to advance those bills. The maintenance of such a list also minimized the likelihood of unwelcome surprises.

Much lobbying effort is focused on predicting the preferences of legislators on administration-favored bills. In both the Carter and

---

[40] John H. Kessel, *Presidential Parties* (Homewood, Ill.: Dorsey, 1984), p. 138.

Reagan White Houses, liaison staff members categorized legislators into those supporting the administration on given bills, those opposed, and those undecided. Executive lobbyists then concentrated on the undecideds and those whose commitments were less than firm. The President is often brought in at key moments to apply his prestige and personal skills to sway wavering legislators. In June 1981 President Reagan contacted undecided legislators to marshal the support necessary to ensure the enactment of his budget and tax package. Even during this first year of the Reagan presidency the liaison staff had little difficulty identifying the key legislators.

Liaison staff members not only lobby but also actually engage in policy-making. When involved in face-to-face bargaining, they often need to make promises and commitments that constitute policy agreements. For example, President Kennedy's liaison head, Lawrence O'Brien, found himself agreeing to a level and amount of coverage of the new proposed minimum wage in a 1961 meeting with congressional leaders without consulting the White House. The occurrence of such situations means that liaison staff members must be well informed and have the trust of the President.

Liaison staff members are often incorporated into other White House policy forums. One of Reagan's liaison chiefs, Ken Duberstein (who succeeded Friedersdorf), participated in four decision forums in the White House, including morning senior staff meetings, cabinet council meetings, weekly luncheon meetings with the President, and the Legislative Strategy Group.

Liaison is often most effective when it does not directly involve the liaison staff. If the liaison staff can succeed in involving key decision makers with each other directly, a favorable and expeditious resolution may be more likely. Similarly, if a key member of Congress adopts and is willing to aggressively promote the President's position, the result is more likely to be favorable to the President. Acting as an institutional insider, a committee chair, for example, can deal effectively with his or her fellow chamber members. The Reagan administration found that the House minority leader, Robert Michel (R-Ill.), and the minority whip, Trent Lott (R-Miss.), were effective congressional point men for key administration initiatives. Still, any President who ignores the liaison staff does so at the risk of crippling the process of influencing Congress.

As was mentioned earlier, the inclusion of personal presidential persuasion may be a decisive lobbying force. President Carter disliked personal lobbying but applied it effectively in a few instances. The Reagan administration used the "Great Communicator" more frequently, and Reagan's personal efforts often provided a key nudge.

In one instance, conservative Senator James McClure (R-Idaho) had championed a bill dealing with standby petroleum allocations. The Reagan administration had registered its opposition to the bill, but it passed both houses early in 1982. The administration considered a veto but promised McClure that he would have the opportunity to present his case for the bill to the President before the decision was made. After he did so, Reagan vetoed the bill. After the veto, the Senate Republican leader and McClure were both contacted by Reagan, who explained the justification for the veto. On March 24, 1982, the Senate sustained the veto. Despite the defeat for a bill important to McClure, hard feelings were minimized by regular communications and presidential involvement.[41] President Bush also vigorously applied personal pressure to sway members of Congress on key votes.

THE PRESIDENT'S FULL-COURT PRESS

Presidential politicking in Congress as it has been described to this point is not very different from the techniques employed by private lobbying organizations that seek to influence government decisions. Despite the President's formal role in the legislative process, the chief executive comes to Congress as an outsider seeking to sway the decisions of legislators. However, certain entrenched political relationships provide the President with added levers that greatly enhance presidential ability to promote a program in Congress and make it stick. To state this another way, Presidents cannot expect anything resembling a guarantee of success, but through political party ties, patronage, and appeals to the public, the opportunities leading to success are far more numerous.

---

[41] Kessel, *Presidential Parties*, pp. 137–144. See also Wayne, *The Legislative Presidency*, chap. 5; Holtzman, *Legislative Liaison*.

Party Leadership

A President whose political party controls both houses of Congress begins with an immediate political advantage.[42] Presidents who have had the greatest success with Congress, including Thomas Jefferson, Theodore Roosevelt, Woodrow Wilson, Franklin Roosevelt, and Lyndon Johnson, have used party ties to chamber and committee leaders to cement support for important programs. Sometimes, however, Presidents run afoul of their own party leaders, as President Kennedy did when southern conservative Democrats who held influential positions in Congress blocked many of his programs because of ideological differences.

President Carter encountered difficulties with members of his own party in Congress because of his lack of experience and that of his staff. Carter would treat each important proposal as a stern test of loyalty to his administration. At the start of his administration, bills dealing with nuclear arms negotiations, human rights, tax reform, energy, the Panama Canal, welfare, national health insurance, and urban assistance were all pressed as equally vital. In all likelihood, no President could have succeeded in realizing the enactment of all these measures. Carter's mistake was that he made no allowance for failure, and so every failure became a blow to his prestige and further evidence to the Carter team that congressional Democrats were somehow insufficiently loyal. The administration attempted to adjust to these early shocks but never succeeded in shaking the impression, whether justified or not, that they were amateurish outsiders.[43]

Even Presidents who find the opposition party in control of Congress may find ways of dealing with partisan differences. President Reagan amassed a series of major successes in his first year in office by relying on the Republican majority in the Senate and a working House majority composed of minority Republicans and about thirty "boll weevil" Democrats, that is, southern conservative Democrats who were sympathetic to many of Reagan's objectives. The centerpiece of Reagan's efforts was a controversial three-year tax cut plan, which was enacted only a few months after its introduction. Reagan also won passage in 1981 of major shifts in budget priorities,

---

[42] For more on how Presidents Kennedy and Johnson mobilized core supporters in Congress, see Cary R. Covington, "Mobilizing Congressional Support for the President: Insights from the 1960s," *Legislative Studies Quarterly,* 12 (February 1987): 77–95.

[43] Berman, *The New American Presidency,* pp. 315–317.

including significant cuts in domestic social programs and a major increase in defense spending.[44]

Although party ties can provide an important advantage to Presidents, it is also clear from political patterns since the 1960s that a President lacking partisan majorities in Congress may still be able to log important victories. During the thirty-six-year period from 1932 to 1968 the President's party controlled both houses of Congress for all but eight years. But during the twenty-four-year period from 1968 to 1992 the President's party controlled both houses for only four years. Clearly, recent Presidents have been forced to accept divided party control as the norm rather than the exception. The urge in both parties to avoid legislative stalemate, combined with long-standing deference to the President's preferences regardless of party, have helped minimize the initial handicap of Presidents who lack partisan congressional majorities.[45]

Presidents have sought and will continue to seek their first allies within their own parties, but under contemporary conditions of partisan division, party cannot be expected to play the same role. Yet even given the potential unifying force of political party, its limitations were nicely summarized by presidential scholar Richard Neustadt: "What the Constitution separates our political parties do not combine."[46]

Patronage

Presidents readily rely on patronage as a means of winning support. They may, for example, grant favors through their power of appointment. Although civil service limits the extent to which positions may be filled by presidential appointment, the President nevertheless has

---

[44] For more on the relationship between Presidents and parties, see Kessel, *Presidential Parties;* Alan R. Gitelson, M. Margaret Conway, and Frank B. Feigert, *American Political Parties* (Boston: Houghton Mifflin, 1984), chap. 12; and the voluminous literature on political parties.

[45] The idea that divided party control between the President and Congress no longer constitutes a serious impediment to positive and productive interbranch relations is discussed in Roger H. Davidson, "The Presidency and the Three Eras of the Modern Congress," in *Divided Democracy,* ed. by James A. Thurber (Washington, D.C.: CQ Press, 1991), pp. 61–78; and David R. Mayhew, *Divided We Govern* (New Haven, Conn.: Yale University Press, 1991).

[46] Richard E. Neustadt, *Presidential Power and the Modern Presidents* (New York: Free Press, 1990), p. 29.

the authority to fill thousands of federal positions, including judge-ships, positions for federal marshals and attorneys, customs collec-tors, and selective service (draft) boards. Such appointments can be used to curry favor among members of Congress.

Presidents also have an important amount of personal patronage that they can use, such as making campaign trips to the home district of a representative, extending special White House invitations to members of Congress, and even providing tickets to the President's box at the Kennedy Center. Such personal favors can have an effect on those of either party whom the President wishes to win over.[47]

In addition, Presidents have great influence over another kind of patronage: that found in "distributive" (also often called patronage or pork barrel) policies. Presidents may reward friends and punish ene-mies by throwing their support to or withholding it from distributive policies such as public works projects, construction projects, defense contracts, river and harbor work, and agricultural subsidies. Federal programs that bring tax dollars into a state or congressional district provide direct economic benefits (jobs and other spin-off spending) that may boost a local economy and for which a local representative is likely to claim credit. President Carter incurred the ire of many in Congress when he attempted to eliminate nineteen water resource projects in 1978. While the proposed cuts might have been justified, Carter paid a high political price because of the proposal and his fail-ure to cushion the blow. In Carter's words, the fight over these pro-jects "caused the deepest breach between me and the Democratic leadership."[48] Congress ultimately defeated his efforts.[49]

In contrast to Carter, Reagan encouraged water development. Similarly, he overrode the recommendations of his budget director, David Stockman, and continued to support price supports for to-bacco growers during the major effort in 1981 to reduce elements of the federal budget. In the case of the water projects, Reagan lent his support to programs that benefited the western states, which had

---

[47] See, for example, Cary R. Covington, " 'Guess Who's Coming to Dinner': The Distri-bution of White House Social Invitations and Their Effects on Congressional Support," *American Politics Quarterly*, 16 (July 1988): 243–265.

[48] Jimmy Carter, *Keeping Faith* (New York: Bantam, 1982), p. 79.

[49] See Paul E. Scheele, "President Carter and the Water Projects," *Presidential Studies Quarterly*, 8 (Fall 1978): 348–364; and Charles O. Jones, "Keeping Faith and Losing Congress: The Carter Experience in Washington," *Presidential Studies Quarterly*, 14 (Summer 1984): 438.

provided him with key support during the election. Tobacco support was of great political and economic importance to key southern states, including North Carolina and Virginia, despite the obvious contradiction that the federal government was supporting tobacco growers on the one hand and crusading against smoking as a serious public health problem on the other.[50]

To cite another example, Reagan provided specific concessions to key House members in exchange for their support of his 1981 tax package. At a picnic held at the presidential retreat Camp David, Reagan won the vote of first-term Democrat Charles Hatcher in exchange for an administration pledge to reverse its opposition to peanut subsidies, a key issue for the Georgia representative. The support of Representative Bill Goodling (R-Pa.) was won with an administration promise to keep an important military base in his district open and to support a bill to clean up the Three Mile Island nuclear power plant. Other representatives were similarly persuaded.[51]

Another side to the President's support for pork barrel projects can be seen in a study of presidential proposals to Congress from 1954 to 1974. The results of the study demonstrated that Presidents propose more distributive policies to Congress during presidential election years than at any other time in the four-year term, clearly suggesting that Presidents are likely to gear policy-making to those policies most likely to be beneficial to their reelection.[52]

Rallying Public Support

One of the President's most important bases of political strength is public support. Abraham Lincoln once stated, "Public sentiment is everything. With public sentiment nothing can fail, without it nothing can succeed."[53] Political scientist Bruce Buchanan referred to public support as the President's "core resource."[54]

[50] See David Stockman, *The Triumph of Politics* (New York: Harper & Row, 1987).

[51] Benjamin I. Page and Mark P. Petracca, *The American Presidency* (New York: McGraw-Hill, 1983), p. 249.

[52] See Robert J. Spitzer, *The Presidency and Public Policy* (University: University of Alabama Press, 1983), pp. 98–100. See also Peggy A. James and Kathleen Pritchard, "Presidential Influence on Congress: The Use and Impact of Favors," a paper presented at the Annual Meeting of the American Political Science Association, Washington, D.C., August 28–31, 1986.

[53] Quoted in Davis, *The American Presidency*, p. 163.

[54] Bruce Buchanan, *The Citizen's Presidency* (Washington, D.C.: CQ Press, 1987), p. 7.

An important empirical study of the relationship between the President's public standing and presidential support in Congress concluded that the two are inextricably linked. Presidents who manage to satisfy public expectations are rewarded by high and stable public support. In turn, public support translates directly into success for the President in Congress. According to the data analysis of political scientists Charles Ostrom, Jr., and Dennis Simon, "the cumulative rate of roll-call victories [for the President in Congress] will decline by three points for every ten-point drop in [public] approval."[55] In turn, "presidential effectiveness in the legislative arena is an important component in maintaining public support."[56] Naturally, many of the factors that influence the President's standing are beyond direct control, such as the onset of a sharp economic downturn at the start of an administration. But Ostrom and Simon conclude that a shrewd President can influence public support and that the typical long-term decline in a President's public standing is by no means inevitable.

Presidents have long recognized the value (and evanescence) of popular support.[57] Lyndon Johnson often quoted poll results to demonstrate the depth of public support for his programs in the early days of his presidency. Later, as public support for his conduct of the Vietnam war and his social programs faded, so too did his success in Congress. Richard Nixon found that the Watergate revelations eroded his popular support after his landslide reelection in 1972. As his popular support eroded, so too did his political strength and support for policy initiatives in Congress.

A remarkable jump in the polls early in Reagan's first term had a key impact on the passage of his economic program. After initially favorable poll ratings during his first few weeks in office (about two to one in his favor), Reagan's public standing began to slump in February and March. Then on March 30, 1981, John Hinckley attempted to assassinate the President. Reagan was hit with a single bullet to the chest but recovered. According to White House assistant Richard

[55] Charles W. Ostrom, Jr., and Dennis M. Simon, "Promise and Performance: A Dynamic Model of Presidential Popularity," *American Political Science Review*, 79 (June 1985): 349. Another empirical study found that each 1 percent increase in the President's public support translated into a 1 percent increase in the President's approval rating in Congress. See Douglas Rivers and Nancy L. Rose, "Passing the President's Program: Public Opinion and Presidential Influence in Congress," *American Journal of Political Science*, 29 (May 1985): 183–196.

[56] Ostrom and Simon, "Promise and Performance," p. 350.

[57] See Peterson, *Legislating Together*, pp. 135–139.

Beal, "It [the assassination] did a lot to endear the President to the people. . . . His personal attributes might never have come across without the assassination attempt." People admired Reagan's courage, calmness, and humor. After the attempt, Reagan's standing in the polls shot up to a three-to-one favorable rating.[58] Reagan aides met after the assassination attempt to decide how best to capitalize on this new reservoir of good feeling. According to the White House communications director, David Gergen, the attempt on Reagan's life "gave us a second life, a second honeymoon. . . . We had new [political] capital."[59] Their conclusion was that the immediate push should be to enact his economic program, and Reagan's first public speech after the assassination dealt with that subject. The postassassination burst of euphoria for Reagan was central to his victories in Congress during the summer of 1981.

Three observations about the relationship between Presidents and the people warrant mention here. First, the link between the President's public standing and the President's influence in Congress is indisputably important but also more complex than the above examples suggest. When the President's standing is high, members of Congress are likely to interpret this positive support as either direct or indirect evidence of a popular mandate for the President. Fearing a popular backlash, Congress is less likely to buck presidential preferences under these conditions. Moreover, some members of Congress accept as a matter of principle that Presidents with a popular mandate are entitled, by virtue of that mandate, to have their programs enacted. Continued public approval is a sign of success (or, to be more precise, perceived success); declining public approval signals an ebbing mandate.[60]

Related to this is the simple fact that presidential popularity may

---

[58] See Sidney Blumenthal, "Marketing the President," *New York Times Magazine,* September 13, 1981, p. 112.

[59] Quoted in Mark Hertsgaard, *On Bended Knee: The Press and the Reagan Presidency* (New York: Farrar, Straus & Giroux, 1988), p. 116.

[60] For more on this, see George C. Edwards III, *The Public Presidency* (New York: St. Martin's, 1983); Samuel Kernell, *Going Public* (Washington, D.C.: CQ Press, 1986); and Buchanan, *The Citizen's Presidency.* Doubts about the link between public opinion and presidential influence in Congress are cast in Harvey G. Zeidenstein, "Varying Relationships between Presidents' Popularity and Their Legislative Success," *Presidential Studies Quarterly,* 13 (1983): 530–550; and Jon R. Bond and Richard Fleisher, "Presidential Popularity and Congressional Voting," *Western Political Quarterly,* 37 (June 1984): 291–306.

be unrelated to the actions of the President. During his first year, for example, George Bush enjoyed popularity levels higher than those of his predecessors, including Reagan. Yet many political observers concluded that this high popularity was primarily a result of positive changes in world events for which Bush bore no responsibility, such as reforms instituted by Soviet Premier Mikhail Gorbachev, the democracy movement in eastern Europe, the dismantling of the Berlin wall, and the freeing of Nelson Mandela in South Africa after twenty-seven years' imprisonment. As *The New York Times* noted, "The President seems to be on a roll, though it may simply be the times."[61]

The second lesson of the president's standing in the eyes of the public is that, as Figure 3.1 illustrates, it is at its greatest immediately after the President's election. Presidential resources and opportunities are thus greatest at this time.

President Johnson was keenly aware of this fact in the aftermath of his overwhelming election victory in 1964. He moved ahead quickly to enact major legislation, including the highly controversial Voting Rights Act of 1965. Johnson ignored warnings that the landmark civil rights bill was too explosive and that he ought to bide his time more carefully, knowing from his years of experience as Senate majority leader that Presidents need to strike quickly to enact important programs while their popularity stands high.

However, presidential administrations often lack the experience and skill necessary to take full advantage of the honeymoon period. Later in the term, when skills and experience are greater, the President invariably stands lower in the polls and thus possesses less of a mandate to act. The inexorable decline in presidential popularity means that a President is best off acting quickly early in the term to enact important programs in order to realize benefits from high popularity.[62]

The third lesson is that Presidents enjoy a far greater ability to rally support through intensive media coverage, whether it be against Congress or for other purposes, than does Congress. George Bush's 1989 clean air proposals received extensive and relatively uncritical

---

[61] R. W. Apple, Jr., "Good or Just Lucky?" *New York Times,* February 18, 1990.

[62] For more on the importance of popularity or "public prestige," see Neustadt, *Presidential Power,* chap. 5; George C. Edwards III, *Presidential Influence in Congress* (San Francisco: Freeman, 1980), chap. 4; and Paul C. Light, *The President's Agenda* (Baltimore: Johns Hopkins University Press, 1982).

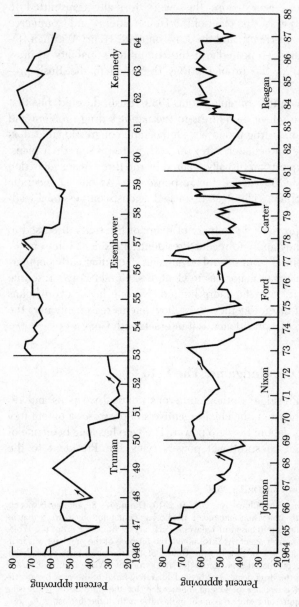

Figure 3.1 Presidential Performance Ratings from Truman to Reagan. Nationwide responses to the question: "Do you approve of the way the President is handling his job?"

NOTE: Arrows indicate pre-election upswings.

SOURCE: Data from Gallup Poll and the Harris Survey through regular press releases. Courtesy of the Gallup Organization and Louis Harris & Associates. From Theodore Lowi and Benjamin Ginsberg, *American Government* (New York: Norton, 1990), p. 289. Reprinted by permission.

media attention even before they were formally transmitted to Congress. In contrast, the chair of the House Energy and Commerce Subcommittee on Health and the Environment, Henry Waxman (D-Calif.), complained repeatedly of the committee's inability to draw press attention to the problems they discerned in the Bush proposal.[63]

To take another example from 1989, Bush devoted his first prime-time live television address to the nation's drug problem and to his forthcoming drug proposals. Democratic congressional leaders sought air time immediately after the address to present their plans. While such requests are usually granted by the three major television networks, only CBS carried the response live. As one Democratic aide noted ruefully, "The deck is stacked against congressional leaders."[64]

Table 3.2 provides a summary of many of the traits discussed to this point as they apply to recent Presidents. President Johnson, for example, benefited from several advantages, including early popularity and large partisan majorities in Congress. Gerald Ford's resource base, by contrast, was far more limited. No one factor overwhelms the others, but taken together, they allow one to reasonably map the likely direction of a presidency as it interacts with Congress.

Controlling the Endgame: The Veto

After all the President's other numerous political weapons and resources are exhausted, the chief executive still possesses a potent tool for shaping legislation: the veto power. The veto has long been one of the cornerstone constitutional powers tying the President to the

---

[63] Cohen, "The Gloves Are Off," p. 2511.

[64] Quoted in Cohen, "The Gloves Are Off," p. 2510. During his September 5 speech, Bush held up to the television audience a plastic bag containing illicit drugs that he claimed had just been purchased in Lafayette Park, across the street from the White House, by an undercover agent. As Bush noted, the purpose of the purchase was to illustrate the omnipresence of drugs in the United States, the point in this case being that they could be purchased even across the street from the White House. It turned out, however, that the drug dealer had been deliberately lured to the park by government agents from a distance of several miles solely for the purpose of buttressing Bush's claim. Despite some embarrassment in the aftermath of the disclosure, the revelation received little press attention.

Presidents	Congressional Experience	Domestic Policy Objectives	Involvement in Lobbying	Partisan Support in Congress	Initial Electoral Support	Subsequent Public Support
Eisenhower (1)	None	Limited	Moderate	Narrow to no majority	Landslide	Steady and high
Eisenhower (2)	None	Limited	Moderate	No majority	Landslide	Steady and high
Kennedy	Moderate	Moderate	Moderate	Large	Narrow	Steady and high
Johnson	Extensive	Large-scale	Active	Large (moderate in House, 1967)	Landslide	Variable—high to low
Nixon (1)	Moderate	Limited	Restricted	No majority (but increase in seats)	Narrow	Steady and moderate
Nixon (2)	Moderate	Limited	Restricted	No majority	Landslide	Variable—low to lower
Ford	Extensive	Limited	Active	No majority	None	Variable—high to low
Carter	None	Moderate to ambitious	On call	Large	Narrow	Variable—high to low
Reagan (1)°	None	Large-scale	Moderate	Narrow to no majority	Moderately large	Variable—high to moderate
Reagan (2)	None	Moderate	Moderate	No majority (1987–1988)	Landslide	Variable—high to moderate
Bush (1)	Limited	Moderate	Moderate	No majority	Moderately large	Variable—high to moderate

KEY:

Congressional experience
Extensive (including leadership posts)
Moderate
Limited
No experience

Domestic policy objectives
Large-scale program
Moderate program
Limited or no major initiatives
Cut back existing programs

Involvement in lobbying
Active and personal
Moderate personal
On call
Restricted

Partisan support in Congress
Large majorities
Moderate majorities
Narrow majorities
Partly in the minority

Initial electoral support
Landslide
Moderately large
Narrow victory
None

Subsequent public support (measured by polls)
Steady and high (over 60%)
Steady and moderate (over 50%)
Steady and low (below 50%)
Variable from high to low
Variable from low to lower

°Reagan and Bush evaluations added by author.

SOURCE: Charles O. Jones, *The Trusteeship Presidency* (Baton Rouge: Louisiana State University Press, 1988), pp. 73–75. Copyright ©1988 by Louisiana State University Press. Reprinted by permission.

legislative process, and its historical use has paralleled the expansion of the President's involvement in legislative matters.[65]

The first six presidents used the veto sparingly—a total of only ten times. President Andrew Jackson drew heavy political fire for using the veto twelve times in eight years for plainly political reasons that infuriated his opponents. President John Tyler used the veto ten times in his single term of office and was even subject to a vote of impeachment in the House for one of his vetoes (see Chapter 2). The loud congressional outcry that followed those early vetoes was founded partly in political opposition but also in the belief that the veto should be used only against bills of questionable constitutionality, although the Constitution places no restrictions on veto use. Also, many felt that frequent veto use was simply inappropriate and reminiscent of the abuses of British monarchs. By the mid-nineteenth century, however, these objections had subsided. Table 3.3 reveals the dramatic rise of veto use in the nineteenth century and Presidents' relative reliance on the veto since then.

Veto use did not occur frequently until after the Civil War, with the significant increase attributable to greater presidential involvement in legislative affairs and a flood of private pension bills, many of questionable justification, stemming from war-related claims. The veto provided a key way for presidents to exert greater influence over the legislative process in the nineteenth century, first through the veto itself, then through the presidential threat to use the veto, and finally through congressional anticipation of the President's legislative preferences as a means of avoiding the veto.

The veto continues to be a key presidential weapon in dealing with Congress. Its potency is evident in the fact that about 93 percent of all vetoes subject to override have been sustained. When broken down by public and private bills, presidential vetoes of public bills are upheld about 81 percent of the time and vetoes of private bills are upheld over 99 percent of the time.[66]

Several factors help explain why Presidents veto or are likely to

---

[65] This argument is made in Robert J. Spitzer, *The Presidential Veto: Touchstone of the American Presidency* (Albany: State University of New York Press, 1988). See also Edward C. Mason, *The Veto Power* (Boston: Ginn, 1890); and Carlton Jackson, *Presidential Vetoes 1792–1945* (Athens: University of Georgia Press, 1967).

[66] See Spitzer, *The Presidential Veto,* pp. 81–83. For more on private bills generally, see Congressional Quarterly, *Guide to the Congress* (Washington, D.C.: Congressional Quarterly, 1971), pp. 329–352.

Table 3.3   Summary of Bills Vetoed, 1789–1991°

President	Total Vetoes	Regular Vetoes	Pocket Vetoes	Vetoes per Year[†]	Vetoes Over-ridden
George Washington	2	2	—	.2	—
John Adams	0	—	—	—	—
Thomas Jefferson	0	—	—	—	—
James Madison	7	5	2	.9	—
James Monroe	1	1	—	.1	—
John Q. Adams	0	—	—	—	—
Andrew Jackson	12	5	7	1.5	—
Martin Van Buren	1	—	1	.2	—
W. H. Harrison	0	—	—	—	—
John Tyler	10	6	4	2.5	1
James K. Polk	3	2	1	.7	—
Zachary Taylor	0	—	—	—	—
Millard Fillmore	0	—	—	—	—
Franklin Pierce	9	9	—	2.2	5
James Buchanan	7	4	3	1.7	—
Abraham Lincoln	7	2	5	1.7	—
Andrew Johnson	29	21	8	7.2	15
Ulysses S. Grant	93	45	48	11.6	4
Rutherford B. Hayes	13	12	1	3.2	1
James A. Garfield	0	—	—	—	—
Chester A. Arthur	12	4	8	3.0	1
Grover Cleveland	414	304	110	103.5	2
Benjamin Harrison	44	19	25	11.0	1
Grover Cleveland	170	42	128	42.5	5
William McKinley	42	6	36	10.5	—
Theodore Roosevelt	82	42	40	10.2	1
William H. Taft	39	30	9	9.7	1
Woodrow Wilson	44	33	11	5.5	6
Warren G. Harding	6	5	1	3.0	—
Calvin Coolidge	50	20	30	8.3	4
Herbert Hoover	37	21	16	9.2	3
Franklin D. Roosevelt	635	372	263	52.9	9
Harry S. Truman	250	180	70	31.2	12
Dwight D. Eisenhower	181	73	108	22.6	2
John F. Kennedy	21	12	9	10.5	—
Lyndon B. Johnson	30	16	14	5.0	—
Richard M. Nixon	43	26	17	7.8	7
Gerald R. Ford	66	48	18	26.4	12
Jimmy Carter	31	13	18	7.7	2
Ronald Reagan	78	38	40	9.7	9
George Bush(1988–1991)	25	18	7	8.3	—
Total	2,494	1,436	1,058	—	103

°Data drawn from *Presidential Vetoes, 1789–1976, 1977–1984,* and update from U.S. Senate Library.

†Rounded to the nearest tenth. For those Presidents who did not serve full years, their years in office were rounded to match the nearest complete Congress, since voetes can be exercised only when Congress is in session.

SOURCE: Robert J. Spitzer, *The Presidential Veto* (Albany: State University of New York Press, 1988). Copyright © 1988 by State University of New York. Reprinted with permission. Update by author.

veto legislation. First, presidential vetoes are more likely when the presidency and Congress are controlled by different political parties. Second, they are more likely when the President has little or no prior service in Congress, since such Presidents are less likely to be sensitive to the congressional resentment that may ensue from vetoes. Third, vetoes are more likely when Presidents are serving in the second and fourth years of a term (because of greater congressional independence during election years), when the role of government expands (expanding governmental output results in more veto possibilities), and when there is a sag in public support for the President (an instance when Congress is more likely to confront the President). Congress is more likely to override a veto when party control is split between the branches, when the President's political standing is low, and in times of economic crisis, because these are all instances when presidential prestige is diminished.[67] As any boxer knows, the time to step up one's attack is when the opponent weakens.

The veto poses a key paradox for Presidents who contemplate its use. With the exception of vetoes of private bills in the twentieth century, frequent veto use by Presidents tends to erode their reservoir of political resources. This occurs because Congress invariably becomes more resentful and confrontational when its measures are rejected too frequently.

In addition, despite the fact that the founders viewed the veto as a creative, positive tool (it was often called the "revisionary power") that could be used to mold better legislation in concert with Congress, the predominant modern impression of the veto is that it is simply a negative power used by Presidents to frustrate and block. A President who acquires a negative image stemming from heavy veto use faces a significant political obstacle in dealing with Congress.

Indeed, when the veto is used often, it usually means that the President has not succeeded in establishing a pattern of positive leadership based on the presidential legislative program. Presidents who establish such leadership are usually able to avoid numerous vetoes

[67] See Jong R. Lee, "Presidential Vetoes from Washington to Nixon," *Journal of Politics*, 37 (May 1975): 522–546; Gary Copeland, "When Congress and the President Collide: Why Presidents Veto Legislation," *Journal of Politics*, 45 (August 1983): 696–710; David Rohde and Dennis M. Simon, "Presidential Vetoes and Congressional Response: A Study of Institutional Conflict," *American Journal of Political Science*, 29 (August 1985): 397–427.

by winning passage of their important programs or obtaining a favorable compromise with congressional leaders. Thus, Presidents who most need the veto are those who lack other power resources. The Presidents with least need of the veto are those who exert greater influence over Congress and who have more ample power resources, such as a high standing in the eyes of the public.[68]

One President known for his strong legislative leadership but one who also vetoed many bills was Franklin D. Roosevelt, yet his administration is an exception that proves the rule. While FDR vetoed more bills annually than did any other President except Cleveland, the vast majority of his vetoes were of private bills or other matters that garnered little attention and less interest. He almost never needed the veto to block an important bill. In addition, he openly urged Congress at times to send him a bill he could veto as a way of demonstrating his willingness to use all the tools at his disposal in his dealings with Congress.[69]

The recent presidencies of Ford, Carter, Reagan, and Bush illustrate both pertinent characteristics of the veto power and its continued importance to executive-legislative relations.

Ford.   The veto power was a vital tool in the brief administration of Gerald Ford. Ford's political position was weak from the start by virtue of the process by which he became President (he was appointed Vice President by a President who later resigned). Moreover, he had little opportunity to formulate his own legislative program after becoming President. This left the Republican Ford few options beyond reacting to the initiatives of the Democratic-controlled Congress. As the first post-Watergate president, he faced a strong anti-Republican, anti–imperial President backlash. Ford hoped to gain the initiative by winning election in his own right in 1976 but was defeated by Jimmy Carter. During his two-and-a-half-year term Ford vetoed 66 bills; of these, 54 were sustained. Insofar as the veto was a cornerstone of his legislative relations, Ford's presidency was the only one in this century to adopt a true veto strategy. Ford's aides recognized the adverse effects of the numerous vetoes but believed that they had few other options.

---

[68] See Spitzer, *The Presidential Veto,* chaps. 2 and 3.

[69] See James MacGregor Burns, *Roosevelt: The Lion and the Fox* (New York: Harcourt Brace Jovanovich, 1956), pp. 186–190.

Carter.   Jimmy Carter's administration saw a return to veto use on a par with that of the Kennedy and Johnson years, when control of both branches was in Democratic hands. Despite Carter's reputed difficulties with the Democratic-controlled Congress, Carter had relatively little need to resort to the veto. Unlike Ford, Carter established a substantial legislative agenda from the start of his presidency, which impelled Congress to react to him, rather than the reverse. Most of Carter's thirty-one vetoes aroused little interest in Congress.

Reagan.   The presidential veto played an important role in the administration of Ronald Reagan, but not in the way it had for Ford. In his eight years, Reagan averaged fewer than ten vetoes per year, with most involving relatively uncontroversial measures. This is explained partly by his legislative successes, despite the fact that the Republican party never controlled the House and controlled the Senate for only six years during his presidency. Yet veto rhetoric played a large role in Reagan's administration. He often challenged Congress to defy his wishes by sending him bills that exceeded his spending guidelines, even using a line from a movie in daring Congress to "make my day." He persistently advocated that he be granted item veto powers, and he issued numerous veto threats. Despite these public statements, many conservatives continued to urge Reagan to use the veto more often as a brake on federal spending.[70]

Bush.   The veto has been a major tool for shaping the course of legislation in the Bush presidency. Elected with about 54 percent of the vote in 1988 and facing a Congress firmly under Democratic control, Bush found the veto to be a key instrument for blocking such major pieces of legislation as a civil rights bill, a parental leave measure, an orphan drug measure, crime legislation, and several appropriations bills that included funding for abortion. Bush's success with this approach was reflected in the fact that all of his twenty-one vetoes during 1989–1991 were sustained, a fact that encouraged Democratic leaders to give greater attention to Bush's preferences. In addition, Bush often used the threat of the veto and renewed the call for a presidential item veto. Bush's reliance on this tool yielded claims that

[70] For more on the veto and these presidencies, see Spitzer, *The Presidential Veto*, chaps. 3 and 5.

he was "governing by veto" and was the "veto president."[71] Thus, while Bush has used the veto power shrewdly, his reliance on this tool has severely limited his ability to promote his own legislative alternatives in Congress.

The Veto Threat.   For as long as the veto power has existed, so too has the veto threat. Writing in *Federalist* No. 73, Alexander Hamilton noted that the veto would often have "a silent and unperceived, though forcible, operation" that might give pause to those seeking to challenge the President.[72]

The veto threat's special value is as a tool to shape, alter, or deter legislation before it reaches the President's desk. Like the veto itself, a threat applied too often loses its potency, and a threat not considered credible is not a threat at all.

Veto threats have been important tools for modern Presidents. For example, a legislative coordinator during the Nixon-Ford years estimated that the veto threat resulted in legislative alterations favorable to the President in twenty to thirty cases.[73] President Carter's threat to veto any bill containing tuition tax credits prompted Congress to remove such a program from its 1978 education bill.

One study examined the number of publicly announced veto threats from the Kennedy through Reagan administrations. Four possible actions can occur in the aftermath of a veto threat. Congress may back down as a concession to the President's threat; a compromise bill can be constructed, leading to the passage of a modified bill; the President may back down; or neither side may back down, in which case the bill is passed and is vetoed. As Table 3.4 shows, the public veto threat was not used by Kennedy and Johnson. Although threats were used by Carter, the greatest amount of confrontation over the threat occurred for the three Republican presidents (Nixon,

---

[71] David Lauter, "Under Bush, Veto Is Potent Tool for Battling Congress," *Los Angeles Times*, June 14, 1990; Nathaniel C. Nash, "Governing By Veto: Who Is in Control?" *New York Times*, September 29, 1990; Ruti Teitel, "Bush, the Veto President," *New York Times*, December 12, 1990. See also Robert J. Spitzer, "Presidential Prerogative Power: The Case of the Bush Administration and Legislative Powers," *PS: Political Science and Politics*, 24 (March 1991), 38–42.

[72] The first known veto threat came from President Washington, who voiced displeasure over a tonnage bill that Congress passed four months into his first term. It was too late for Congress to take back or alter the original bill, so in response, Congress allowed the first bill to die and passed another bill more to Washington's liking.

[73] Wayne, *The Legislative Presidency*, p. 159.

Table 3.4 Fate of Veto-Threatened Bills

President	Total Threatened Bills	Congress Backs Down; Bill Dies	Compromise	President Backs Down; Bill Enacted	Bill Passed as Is and Vetoed	Vetoes Overridden
Kennedy	0	0	0	0	0	0
Johnson	0	0	0	0	0	0
Nixon	5	0	0	0	5	1
Ford	10	2	0	0	8	1
Carter	12	3	5	2	2	1
Reagan	48	9	19	4	16	5

SOURCE: *New York Times Annual Index, 1961–1986.* The numbers of veto threats listed above are not considered definitive. Threats may have been delivered by Presidents Kennedy and Johnson, for example, but were not reported in the newspapers; however, there is no doubt that Presidents with larger numbers of threats used them more, as their potency is dependent in large part on the extent to which they are widely known. Adapted from Robert J. Spitzer, *The Presidential Veto* (Albany: State University of New York Press, 1988). Copyright © 1988 by State University of New York. Reprinted by permission of the State University of New York Press. Update by author.

Ford, and Reagan) who faced Congresses controlled partially or entirely by the opposition party.

Presidential Success: Measuring the President's Batting Average

Taken together, these elements of presidential influence—what I have labeled the president's full-court press—constitute a considerable array of political friction points for presidential influence of the legislative process. Yet Presidents apply pressure with varying degrees of success. We know that a number of factors are related to the President's success in dealing with Congress, including the President's personal leadership skills, public standing, party, ideology, policy type, and term cycle.[74] These and related explanations will be explored in Chapter 4.

For the moment, however, it is important to remind ourselves how far the President's influence in legislative affairs has evolved. The very concept of presidential success in Congress—one almost universally accepted as a measuring stick for assessing presidential-congressional relations—today defines congressional accomplishment by the degree to which it accedes to the President's agenda. To appreciate how dramatically the President's role has expanded in size and importance, note the following assessment of the President's influence on policy-making, which was written in 1891 by one of that century's foremost political analysts, James Bryce: "The expression of his [the President's] wishes conveyed in a message has not necessarily any more effect on Congress than an article in a prominent party newspaper. No duty lies on Congress to take up a subject to which he has called attention as needing legislation; and, *in fact, the suggestions which he makes, year after year, are usually neglected,* even when his party has a majority in both Houses. . . ."[75] It is almost inconceivable that this assessment could apply to a modern President.

Beyond general statements about presidential success or failure in Congress, several scores have been used to measure the President's track record in Congress. One such measure is the presidential

[74] For a detailed discussion of the interplay of factors related to presidential success in Congress, see Jon R. Bond and Richard Fleisher, *The President in the Legislative Arena* (Chicago: University of Chicago Press, 1990), chap. 3.

[75] James Bryce, *The American Commonwealth,* 2 vols. (New York: Macmillan, 1891), I, 206. Emphasis added.

box score. From 1954 to 1975 *Congressional Quarterly* kept track of the proposals that composed the President's annual legislative program (excluding proposals emanating from the executive branch but not specifically endorsed by the President and those endorsed by the President but not specifically included in his program). The box score provided a ready means for comparing numbers of proposals and percentages of success, but the score also had limitations. It took no account of less or more important bills; it included a large number of foreign policy proposals, where the President was more likely to gain congressional approval; it took no account of measures favored by the President but not included in his formal proposal list because of overwhelming congressional opposition; it did not account for measures included solely because the President anticipated that they would be enacted anyway; and finally, there is reason to believe that the rate of enactment of presidential initiatives is probably greater than the box score numbers indicate.[76]

Despite these limitations, the box score has provided a source of information for those interested in comparing the track records of presidents, variations in their success rates, and the kinds of proposals they have selected for inclusion in their legislative menus (Table 3.5). Problems with use of the data arise when the summary percentages are used as sole indicators of a President's success. Another measure kept by *Congressional Quarterly* is presidential support scores. This measure, collected annually since 1953, summarizes all public statements and messages of the President to determine the President's position on pending roll call votes in the House and Senate. These votes may or may not involve presidential proposals. Support scores address the question of how often Congress supports the President's position.

This measure also has limitations. It takes no account of the reasons for the President's positions on legislation, major versus minor proposals, party, or ideological balance in Congress, nor does it indicate which bills are more important to the President. Still, support

---

[76] The presidential box score is discussed critically in Wayne, *The Legislative Presidency*, pp. 168–171; Cronin, *The State of the Presidency*, pp. 169–173; Spitzer, *The Presidency and Public Policy*, pp. 93–94; George C. Edwards III, *At the Margins* (New Haven, Conn.: Yale University Press, 1989), pp. 17–19; Bond and Fleisher, *The President in the Legislative Arena*, pp. 55–60; and Peterson, *Legislating Together*, pp. 302–308.

Table 3.5   Presidential Boxscore: The President's Proposals and Congressional Approval, 1954–1975

Year	Proposals Submitted	Approved by Congress	Percent Approved
1954	232	150	65
1955	207	96	46
1956	225	103	46
1957	206	76	37
1958	234	110	47
1959	228	93	41
1960	183	56	31
1961	355	172	48
1962	298	133	45
1963	401	109	27
1964	217	125	58
1965	469	323	69
1966	371	207	56
1967	431	205	48
1968	414	231	56
1969	171	55	32
1970	210	97	46
1971	202	40	20
1972	116	51	44
1973	183	57	31
1974 (Nixon)	97	33	34
1974 (Ford)	64	23	36
1975˙	110	30	27

˙ *Congressional Quarterly* ceased tabulation of these scores after 1975.
SOURCE: *Congress and the Nation,* vol. II (Washington, D.C.: Congressional Quarterly, 1969), p. 625, as updated in the *Congressional Almanac.* Reprinted by permission of Congressional Quarterly, Inc.

scores do provide a basis for comparison.[77] As Figure 3.2 reveals, presidential rates of support are higher than Presidents' box score percentages. Support scores are also usually highest at the start of a presidential term, especially during what is termed the honeymoon period.

[77] For more on the problems with support scores, see Rivers and Rose, "Passing the President's Program," and Peterson, *Legislating Together,* pp. 302–308.

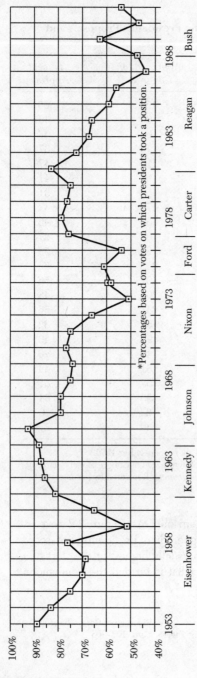

Figure 3.2 Presidential Support in Congress, 1953–1991

Eisenhower		Kennedy		Johnson		Nixon		Ford		Carter		Reagan		Bush	
1953	89.0	1961	81.0	1964	88.0	1969	74.0	1974	58.2	1977	75.4	1981	82.4	1989	63.0
1954	82.8	1962	85.4	1965	93.0	1970	77.0	1975	61.0	1978	78.3	1982	72.4	1990	46.8
1955	75.0	1963	87.1	1966	79.0	1971	75.0	1976	53.8	1979	76.8	1983	67.1	1991	54.0
1956	70.0			1967	79.0	1972	66.0			1980	75.1	1984	65.8		
1957	68.0			1968	75.0	1973	50.6					1985	59.9		
1958	76.0					1974	59.6					1986	56.1		
1959	52.0											1987	43.5		
1960	65.0											1988	47.4		

NOTE: Percentages based on votes on which Presidents took a clear position.

SOURCE: *Congressional Quarterly Weekly Report*, November 19, 1988, 3324–3330; *CQ Almanac 1989*, p. 22-B; update by Congressional Quarterly. Reprinted with permission.

*Percentages based on votes on which presidents took a position.

A third measure kept by *Congressional Quarterly* is key votes. Studies of key votes focus on a few pivotal issues of great importance to Congress and the President. In order to be judged a key vote, a roll call vote must involve a major controversy, be an important test of political power, or involve a decision that will have a great impact on the country. The intent is to weed out less important legislative efforts to discern the priorities and interests of both branches when the political stakes are high.

An important study using key votes found that Presidents did well on key votes from 1957 to 1972 but not as well during the period 1973–1978. Dividing support on key votes by party, the study reported that support from the President's party in Congress remained about the same throughout the period from 1957 to 1978. A major drop occurred, however, among opposition party members after 1973. The drop was especially great in opposition party support for the President in foreign policy matters.[78]

Key votes do not focus solely on issues of concern to the President, but not surprisingly, the President takes a position on a majority of such votes.[79] The usefulness of this measure is limited by the fact that relatively few bills are included in the key votes score each year. For example, in 1957 only five House and five Senate roll call votes were included in the key votes scale. In 1965, during the height of the Johnson administration, eighteen roll calls from each chamber were included.

Political scientist Paul Light has formulated perhaps the shrewdest empirical measure of presidential success by focusing on a box score listing of bills that is composed of bills deemed by the President (as opposed to the executive branch) to be centrally important to the President's legislative agenda. Light's list is drawn from the intersection of two lists: bills stamped "in accord" with the President's wishes by the OMB and bills that are also mentioned in at least one

---

[78] Lee Sigelman, "A Reassessment of the 'Two Presidencies' Thesis," *Journal of Politics*, 51 (November 1979), 1195–1205. Sigelman's use of key votes was criticized in Steven A. Shull and Lance T. LeLoup, "Reassessing the Reassessment: Comment on Sigelman's Note on the 'Two Presidencies' Thesis," *Journal of Politics*, 43 (May 1981): 563–564.

[79] Edwards, *At the Margins*, p. 23.

State of the Union message.[80] The OMB designation denotes bills of greatest importance to the President, while Light notes in the case of the State of the Union address that a bill not mentioned there is probably not in the President's top priority. Applying this dual standard, Light formulated the data in Table 3.6 (greater restrictions imposed by the Reagan administration have prevented researchers from accessing OMB data for the years after 1980).

Two important facts emerge from this table. First, the absolute number of bills on the President's high-priority list is very small, keeping in mind that Congress deals with thousands of bills every year; the largest number submitted in a single year by a president (thirty-four) came, not surprisingly, in 1965, at the height of Lyndon Johnson's Great Society. Presidents whose high-priority list is too large are likely to find Congress responding in the way a parent might when a child submits a Christmas list that is too long and expensive—with suspicion that nothing on the list is really important to the child and with a determination to set priorities for the child.

The second fact emerging from the table is that relative presidential success follows the pattern of the other measures. President Johnson's overall success rate is highest (59 percent), followed by Kennedy (53 percent), Carter (49 percent), Nixon (35 percent), and Ford (31 percent). As the reader is no doubt aware, the first three presidents dealt with Congresses controlled by the President's political party.

A final measure sometimes taken as an indicator of presidential success is the President's number of vetoes and record in sustaining vetoes (see our earlier discussion of vetoes). Although veto scores are readily available, these scores by themselves say little about presidential rates of success. The veto is an indisputably important power, but as an aggregate measure it reveals little because of the circumstances under which it is applied and its relatively rare use by most Presidents. The best rule of thumb about the veto is that Presidents who find themselves compelled to rely on the veto as a legislation-shaping

[80] Light notes that the OMB classifies all bills to which it gives clearance according to one of three designations: "in accord," denoting a bill that is part of the President's program; "consistent with," indicating bills that are philosophically consistent with but not a part of the President's program; and "no objection," characterizing bills about which OMB is indifferent. Any bill that comes along which is clearly not consistent with the President's preferences is simply eliminated. See Paul C. Light, "The Focusing Skill and Presidential Influence in Congress," in *Congressional Politics*, ed. by Christopher J. Deering (Chicago: Dorsey, 1989), p. 245.

Table 3.6   Light's Presidential Box Scores, 1961–1980

Year		Agenda Box Score		
		Requested	Passed	Percent
1961		25	15	60
1962	Kennedy	16	7	44
1963		6	3	50
1964	Johnson (1st term)	6	3	50
1965		34	28	82
1966	Johnson	24	14	58
1967	(2d term)	19	8	42
1968		14	4	29
1969		17	7	41
1970	Nixon	12	3	25
1971	(1st term)	8	2	25
1972		3	1	33
1973	Nixon	20	8	40
1974	(2d term)	5	2	40
1975		10	3	30
1976	Ford	6	2	33
1977		21	14	67
1978		8	3	38
1979	Carter	8	2	25
1980		4	1	25

SOURCE: Paul C. Light, "The Focusing Skill and Presidential
Influence in Congress," in *Congressional Politics*, ed. by
Christopher J. Deering (Chicago: Dorsey Press, 1989), p. 247.
Reprinted by permission.

tool are probably relatively ineffective as legislative leaders; ergo, high veto use indicates relatively low positive legislative leadership.[81]

All these quantified measures of presidential success have two notable drawbacks. First, they are all aggregate measures that cannot provide a basis for conclusions about the causes of presidential and congressional behavior. In a penetrating critique of these measures, political scientist George Edwards concluded that they provide at

[81] Franklin Roosevelt is of course an exception to this rule. In modern times, President Ford is a President who fits this equation.

best "tenuous . . . inferences about the causes of behavior of individual members of Congress toward the president."[82]

Second, these measures are only one symptom of a more complex phenomenon and may seduce the reader into believing that high numbers in these various measures both reflect and explain presidential success. High scores may indeed reflect presidential achievement, but the numbers by themselves are not necessarily all that important. Far more important for Presidents is a positive, assertive image built upon a reputation as a tough, positive leader and an ability to succeed when it counts. Comparing President Reagan's support scores with those of Carter would lead one to conclude that Carter's legislative success was greater than that of Reagan, yet most legislators, political pundits, and others would take issue with such an assertion, noting key Reagan victories that represented a marked ideological change from the past despite Reagan's having to deal with a House of Representatives firmly in the hands of the opposition party. In sum, these measures are of some use, but the user should not confuse numerical precision with explanation.

CONCLUSION

The label chief legislator as applied to the President has become a hackneyed truism.[83] In the 1970s and 1980s Congress reasserted itself

---

[82] Edwards, *At the Margins,* p. 17, and generally chap. 2. Edwards used the data compiled by *Congressional Quarterly* to reconstruct four measures: overall support (all the measures on which the President has taken a stand), nonunanimous support (omitting those votes for which the winning side was more than 80 percent), single-vote support (which controls for important bills for which numerous votes were taken), and key votes. Edwards then calculated these indexes for each member of Congress from 1953 to 1986. For more on methodological problems pertaining to measures of presidential success, see Thomas H. Hammond and Jane M. Fraser, "Studying Presidential Performance in Congress," *Political Methodology,* 10 (1984): 211–244.

[83] For example, Bond and Fleisher, *The President in the Legislative Realm.* George C. Edwards III concluded his study of presidential influence in Congress by saying that "the president is in a weak position with regards to Congress." This conclusion represents an appropriate reaction to inflated claims of presidential influence in the popular press and in much of the presidency literature based on inordinate attention to anecdotes and reputation and focusing on a few recent Presidents. See *Presidential Influence in Congress* (San Francisco: Freeman, 1980), p. 205. See also Edwards, *At the Margins.* As the title suggests, the theme of this book is that presidential leadership and influence constitute a relatively marginal explanatory factor in understanding congressional outcomes. Edwards refers to the President's role as that of a "facilitator," yet he also concludes that the President is "a vital centralizing force, providing direction and energy for the nation's policymaking" (p. 224). These arguments are addressed in Chapters 4 and 7.

in national political and policy-making processes. As congressional expert Charles O. Jones noted, "Congress experienced more reform during the 1970s than at any other time in its history."[84] Several examples of this reassertion will be explored in the next three chapters (although some changes did nothing to help Congress in its dealings with the President).[85] These examples will demonstrate Congress's ability to reinject itself into important national processes such as budgeting and war making as well as the limits of those efforts. They will also demonstrate that the presidency is no less a part of the process than it was before the congressional resurgence of the previous two decades.

As for this chapter, the sheer quantity, not to mention quality, of presidential impact on the legislative process discussed up to now— agenda setting, central clearance, liaison and lobbying, party leadership, patronage, public support, and the veto—points to an extensive *institutionalized* presidential presence that underscores the continued pertinence of the chief legislator label. This presence is institutionalized in two respects. First, patterns of presidential intervention are well established and accepted at both ends of Pennsylvania Avenue; second, the institutionalized presidency, composed of the White House Office and the Executive Office of the President, includes personnel and departments that maintain as a primary focus the influencing or "facilitating" of Congress to realize presidential objectives.[86] This does not mean that Presidents always or even usually get what they want from Congress or that every modern President pursues agendas as vigorously as every other. The several measures of presidential success reveal wide fluctuations both within and between presidential terms. Also, no one would dispute that from formulation to enactment, members of Congress inspire and sculpt im-

---

[84] Jones, "Keeping Faith and Losing Congress," p. 442. See also Jones, *The Trusteeship Presidency* (Baton Rouge: Louisiana State University Press, 1988), chap. 3.

[85] Congress's efforts to reassert itself during the 1970s are summarized in Harvey G. Zeidenstein, "The Reassertion of Congressional Power: New Curbs on the President," *Political Science Quarterly,* 93 (Fall 1978): 393–409.

[86] For more on the institutionalized presidency, see John Hart, *The Presidential Branch* (New York: Pergamon, 1987). The presidential branch is understood to be an entity separate from the rest of the executive branch, composed of the cabinet departments and independent agencies. See Alfred Dick Sander, *A Staff for the President* (Westport, Conn.: Greenwood, 1989).

portant bills to suit their political imperatives.[87] Political scientist Richard Pious aptly summarizes this relationship: "Presidents must lead Congress. . . . But presidents rarely succeed as legislative leaders."[88]

However, Congress is a porous and decentralized institution with numerous access points for outside actors seeking to influence its processes. Congressional organization, norms, and procedures almost invite outside influence by virtue of their openness and decentralized nature. As one expert on Congress notes, "Congress is an institution vulnerable to invasion by others."[89] And as the presidential invasion analogy implies, the presidential-congressional struggle usually plays itself out on Congress's home territory. Congress may not be the weaker partner in national policy-making, but it can never reasonably expect—nor would most in Congress seek—to return to the kind of legislative supremacy that typified most of the nineteenth century any more than it can act as though the President were irrelevant to the modern legislative process.

[87] This view parallels what Mark Peterson characterizes as the "tandem-institutions perspective" of executive-legislative relations. See *Legislating Together*, pp. 7–8, 79, 96–97.

[88] Pious, *The American Presidency*, p. 176.

[89] William J. Keefe, *Congress and the American People* (Englewood Cliffs, N.J.: Prentice-Hall, 1988), p. 139.

Chapter 4

The Domestic Realm II: Explaining Presidential-Congressional Interactions

As there are in this state two visible powers—the legislative and the executive—and as every citizen has a will of his own, and may at pleasure assert his independence, most men have a greater fondness for one of these powers than for the other, and the multitude have commonly neither equity nor sense enough to show equal affection to both.
CHARLES MONTESQUIEU, *THE SPIRIT OF THE LAWS* , BOOK 19, CHAP. 27

Most legislative-executive interactions play themselves out in the legislative realm. In the words of journalist Hedrick Smith, "Congress is the principal policy arena of battle. . . ."[1] We have therefore discussed how and why Presidents have come to play such a central role in legislative affairs, focusing on such familiar factors as agenda setting, lobbying, political party, patronage, and public support. Chapter 3 concluded with several useful if imperfect measures of presidential success.

Without question, factors such as party balance in Congress, the size of the President's election victory, the President's public standing, and the impact of interest groups are central to understanding the daily give-and-take between the executive and legislative

[1] Hedrick Smith, *The Power Game* (New York: Ballantine, 1988), p. xviii.

branches. However, we run the risk of losing sight of the forest for the trees if we focus exclusively on these particulars.

The purpose of this chapter is to take a step back and focus on four broader perspectives or "explanations" for presidential-congressional relations. The four—political leadership, history, law, and policy—provide a broader view that can help identify long-term patterns that span particular congresses, administrations, and even decades. These four explanations also return us to the analytic perspective advanced in the introduction to this book, where I argued that modern analysis has often been too narrow and ahistorical by neglecting such bedrock factors as history and law. Attention to these four explanations will help us understand why some Presidents are considered successful in dominating the congressional agenda whereas under other circumstances Congress is more likely to be a dominant player.

In considering the four explanations to follow, it is also important to note that all have a useful perspective, and there is no attempt to rank them by relative explanatory power. Extra attention is given to presidential leadership, however, because of the extent to which this perspective still dominates and even monopolizes analysis of national politics. In addition, these explanations overlap. Historical perspective may be applied to legal analysis, policy analysis may account for political considerations, and so on. This overlap is also evident in the particular cases discussed. Thus, it may be most useful to think of these perspectives as different lenses through which the student or analyst may think about presidential-congressional relations.

POLITICAL EXPLANATION: PRESIDENTIAL LEADERSHIP

Shortly before leaving the presidency Harry Truman observed that his successor, former General Dwight D. Eisenhower, would be in for a rude awakening when he assumed the presidency. Truman predicted: "He'll sit here . . . and he'll say, 'Do this! Do that!' *And nothing will happen.* Poor Ike—it won't be a bit like the Army. He'll find it very frustrating."[2]

---

[2] Richard E. Neustadt, *Presidential Power and the Modern Presidents* (New York: Free Press, 1990), p. 10.

Political scientist Richard Neustadt made a vital point about the modern American presidency when he quoted his former boss, Truman. In observing that presidential power to command is both overrated and overstated, he was arguing that presidential power is primarily the power to persuade. The reliance on persuasion and bargaining has become a hallmark of the presidency, Neustadt observed, because the responsibilities, demands, and expectations now inherent in the presidency have outstripped the powers of the office. As a consequence, Presidents must rely on informal bargaining skills to accomplish their goals. In other words, Presidents must rely on leadership.

No explanation for presidential success has received more attention than that of leadership.[3] The numerous biographies and historical studies of Presidents invariably focus on their leadership abilities pertaining to Congress, the rest of the government, and the people.[4] One way in which the concern over leadership can be seen is by looking at the attention given to the ratings of Presidents (Table 4.1). In 1948 historian Arthur Schlesinger, Sr., polled fifty-five historians, asking them to rank the Presidents from "great" to "failure." Since then, numerous studies have played the ratings game. While the criteria vary, they usually include such traits as the ability of the President to bargain, the desire to seek power and exploit opportunity, and knowing when to seek conciliation versus when and how to rally popular support. As one historian observed, "The best presidents

[3] The leadership theme permeates the literature on the presidency. Note, for example, that Neustadt's book *Presidential Power*, previously cited, is subtitled *The Politics of Leadership from Roosevelt to Reagan.* Most standard works on the presidency focus on the leadership question. See for example, Thomas Cronin, *The State of the Presidency* (Boston: Little, Brown, 1980), chap. 11; Frank Kessler, *The Dilemmas of Presidential Leadership* (Englewood Cliffs, N.J.: Prentice-Hall, 1982), chap. 11 and passim; Erwin C. Hargrove and Michael Nelson, *Presidents, Politics, and Policy* (New York: Knopf, 1984), chap. 4; Larry Berman, *The New American Presidency* (Boston: Little, Brown, 1987), chaps. 6–8; Fred I. Greenstein, ed., *Leadership and the Modern Presidency* (Cambridge, Mass.: Harvard University Press, 1988); David McKay, *Domestic Policy and Ideology: Presidents and the American State, 1964–1987* (New York: Cambridge University Press, 1989); George C. Edwards III and Stephen J. Wayne, *Presidential Leadership* (New York: St. Martin's, 1990). See also the many books of James MacGregor Burns and Barbara Kellerman. An excellent critique of the conventional leadership perspective can be found in William F. Grover, *The President as Prisoner* (Albany: State University of New York Press, 1989).

[4] See Fenton S. Martin and Robert U. Goehlert, *American Presidents: A Bibliography* (Washington, D.C.: Congressional Quarterly, 1987), for a compilation of biographical and historical studies about the presidents.

Table 4.1 Ratings of U.S. Presidents

Schlesinger Poll (1948)	Schlesinger Poll (1962)	Dodder Poll (1970)	DiClerico Poll (1977)	Tribune Poll (1982)	Murray Poll (1982)
Great	Great	Accomplishments of administration	Ten greatest Presidents	Ten best Presidents	Presidential rank
1. Lincoln	1. Lincoln	1. Lincoln	1. Lincoln	1. Lincoln (best)	1. Lincoln
2. Washington	2. Washington	2. F. Roosevelt	2. Washington	2. Washington	2. F. Roosevelt
3. F. Roosevelt	3. F. Roosevelt	3. Washington	3. F. Roosevelt	3. F. Roosevelt	3. Washington
4. Wilson	4. Wilson	4. Jefferson	4. Jefferson	4. T. Roosevelt	4. Jefferson
5. Jefferson	5. Jefferson	5. T. Roosevelt	5. T. Roosevelt	5. Jefferson	5. T. Roosevelt
6. Jackson	Near great	6. Truman	6. Wilson	6. Wilson	6. Wilson
Near great	6. Jackson	7. Wilson	7. Jackson	7. Jackson	7. Jackson
7. T. Roosevelt	7. T. Roosevelt	8. Jackson	8. Truman	8. Truman	8. Truman
8. Cleveland	8. Polk	9. L. Johnson	9. Polk	9. Eisenhower	9. J. Adams
9. J. Adams	Truman (tie)	10. Polk	10. J. Adams	10. Polk (10th best)	10. L. Johnson
10. Polk	9. J. Adams	11. J. Adams			11. Eisenhower
Average	10. Cleveland	12. Kennedy		Ten worst Presidents	12. Polk
11. J. Q. Adams	Average	13. Monroe		1. Harding (worst)	13. Kennedy
12. Monroe	11. Madison	14. Cleveland		2. Nixon	14. Madison
13. Hayes	12. J. Q. Adams	15. Madison		3. Buchanan	15. Monroe
14. Madison	13. Hayes	16. Taft		4. Pierce	16. J. Q. Adams
15. Van Buren	14. McKinley	17. McKinley		5. Grant	17. Cleveland
16. Taft	15. Taft	18. J. Q. Adams		6. Fillmore	18. McKinley
17. Arthur	16. Van Buren	19. Hoover		7. A. Johnson	19. Taft
	17. Monroe	20. Eisenhower		8. Coolidge	20. Van Buren
		21. A. Johnson		9. Tyler	21. Hoover
		22. Van Buren			22. Hayes
					23. Arthur

18. McKinley	18. Hoover	23. Arthur	10. Carter (10th worst)	24. Ford
19. A. Johnson	19. B. Harrison	24. Hayes		25. Carter
20. Hoover	20. Arthur	25. Tyler		26. B. Harrison
21. B. Harrison	Eisenhower (tie)	26. B. Harrison		27. Taylor
	21. A. Johnson	27. Taylor		28. Tyler
		28. Buchanan		29. Fillmore
Below average	Below average	29. Fillmore		30. Coolidge
22. Tyler	22. Taylor	30. Coolidge		31. Pierce
23. Coolidge	23. Tyler	31. Pierce		32. A. Johnson
24. Fillmore	24. Fillmore	32. Grant		33. Buchanan
25. Taylor	25. Coolidge	33. Harding		34. Nixon
26. Buchanan	26. Pierce			35. Grant
27. Pierce	27. Buchanan			36. Harding
Failure	Failure			
28. Grant	28. Grant			
29. Harding	29. Harding			

Note: These ratings result from surveys of scholars ranging in number from 55 to 950.

SOURCES: Henry J. Abraham, *Justices and Presidents: Appointments to the Supreme Court,* 2d ed. (New York: Oxford University Press, 1985), pp. 380–383 (copyright © Henry J. Abraham, 1974, 1985, reprinted by permission of Oxford University Press, Inc.); Arthur Murphy, "Evaluating the Presidents of the United States," *Presidential Studies Quarterly* 14 (1984): 117–126 (permission granted by Center for the Study of the Presidency, publisher). Adapted from Harold W. Stanley and Richard G. Niemi, *Vital Statistics on American Politics* (Washington, D.C.: CQ Press, 1990). Reprinted by permission.

have been strong political leaders with a vision, if not a complete program, of where they think the country should go."[5] All these rankings include such presidents as Lincoln, Franklin Roosevelt, Washington, and Jefferson at the top of their lists—all known for their singular leadership abilities.

Despite the popularity of the ratings game, such rankings of Presidents have been criticized for oversimplifying complex historical and political circumstances, being biased in favor of liberal Democratic presidents, and failing to account for the impact of the political climate of the time.[6] Yet a more particular problem or, rather, bias emerges when the greatness game is applied to presidential leadership of Congress. James MacGregor Burns defines leadership as occurring when

> persons with certain motives and purposes mobilize, in competition or conflict with others, institutional, political, psychological, and other resources so as to arouse, engage, and satisfy the motives of followers. . . . Leadership is exercised in a condition of conflict or competition in which leaders contend in appealing to the motive bases of potential followers.[7]

This definition of leadership does not involve the exercise of naked power but rather efforts on the part of the leader to induce followers to realize certain goals of interest to both—an approach that nicely summarizes what most people conceive to be the appropriate role of the contemporary President in relation to Congress. But what is normally overlooked in the "President-as-leader-of-Congress" perspective is the inherent bias of a model which presupposes that it is the job of the President to lead and that of the Congress to follow. In this view, the president is the Lone Ranger and Congress is Tonto. The leadership model therefore precludes the idea of an equal partnership between the two branches, and it certainly precludes the Whig-

---

[5] Quoted in Michael Nelson, ed., *CQ Guide to the Presidency* (Washington, D.C.: Congressional Quarterly, 1989), p. 146. For more on the presidential ratings game, see pp. 143–148; see also Robert K. Murray and Tim H. Blessing, *Greatness in the White House* (University Park: Pennsylvania State University Press, 1988); Michael Nelson, "Evaluating the Presidency," in *The Presidency and the Political System*, ed. by Nelson (Washington, D.C.: CQ Press, 1990), pp. 3–28.

[6] See Thomas A. Bailey, *Presidential Greatness* (New York: Appleton-Century-Crofts, 1966); Nelson Polsby, "Against Presidential Greatness," *Commentary*, January 1977, pp. 61–64.

[7] James MacGregor Burns, *Leadership* (New York: Harper & Row, 1978), p. 18.

gish view of the presidency that dominated much thinking about presidential power in the nineteenth century. Contemporary efforts by Congress to seek policy initiative—to be an actor rather than a reactor in its dealings with the President—would by definition be circumstances where presidential leadership had "failed."

One problem with the leadership model, then, is that it limits our thinking. Leadership is undeniably important, and Congress willingly seeks presidential leadership on many issues, but this model hampers our thinking in other circumstances. A second, related problem is that the leadership explanation has crowded out other important explanations that, evidence suggests, may be more important in explaining presidential-congressional interactions.

Leadership and Presidential Power

Concern for the appropriate level of presidential leadership skills was articulated by two early twentieth-century presidents. Theodore Roosevelt advocated an aggressive, stewardship role for the President. He argued that Presidents were entitled, even obliged, to act as they saw fit to promote the needs, goals, and interests of the people unless such action was explicitly unconstitutional. Roosevelt's successor, William Howard Taft, articulated a restrained or Whiggish view of the presidency, proposing instead that the President "can exercise no power which cannot be fairly and reasonably traced to some specific grant of power or justly implied and included within such express grant as proper and necessary to its exercise."[8] Both approaches imply some level of presidential leadership skills, but they vary widely as to the scope and limitation of those skills.

While the philosophical debate over the relative merits of the stewardship and Whiggish views of presidential leadership persists, no modern President can ignore the fundamentals of effective executive leadership. To win enactment of important and therefore usually controversial legislation, the President cannot simply submit legislation and sit back to wait for the finished product. The President must often build specialized coalitions in Congress, even across party lines.

[8] See Theodore Roosevelt, *The Autobiography of Theodore Roosevelt* (New York: Scribner's, 1958), pp. 197–200; William Howard Taft, *The President and His Powers* (New York: Columbia University Press, 1916), pp. 139–140. Taft's full perspective on presidential power was actually somewhat more complex in that it did in fact make allowance for other than expressed powers.

Lyndon Johnson, for example, admitted that he could not have gained passage of key civil rights legislation without the support of moderate Republicans despite the fact that his party held substantial majorities in both houses.

Often considered one of the most adept legislative strategists ever to sit in the White House, Johnson knew better than most about the key leadership role of the President. Johnson summarized his philosophy when he said: "There is but one way for a President to deal with the Congress, and that is continuously, incessantly, and without interruption. . . . the relationship between the President and the Congress has got to be almost incestuous. . . . he's got to build a system that stretches from the cradle to the grave, from the moment a bill is introduced to the moment it is officially enrolled as the law of the land."[9] Johnson's extravagant view of how best to lead Congress was based on his own extensive experience in Congress; he was elected to the House in 1936 and to the Senate in 1948 and served as leader of the Democrats for seven years until his ascension to the vice presidency in 1961.

Presidents are the personifications of their administrations. They take personal credit for successes and personal blame for failures, although seldom willingly in the case of the latter. More to the point, Presidents are personal, readily available reservoirs of influence. They are an administration's handiest political balm.

Leadership Qualities and Congress

Several specific leadership qualities bear directly on presidential-congressional interactions.[10] For example, the *timing* of legislative maneuvers can often contribute to a successful outcome. In the aftermath of the rise in Reagan's popularity following the 1981 attempt on his life, members of his administration knew that an unforeseen event had provided them with an opportunity to promote a key proposal. The subsequent successful passage of Reagan's economic program owed much to timing. Lyndon Johnson similarly believed that

[9] Doris Kearns, *Lyndon Johnson and the American Dream* (New York: New American Library, 1976), pp. 236–237.

[10] The discussion in this section is based in part on George C. Edwards III, *Presidential Influence in Congress* (San Francisco: Freeman, 1980), chaps. 5 and 6. See also Paul C. Light, *The President's Agenda* (Baltimore: Johns Hopkins University Press, 1982), esp. the introduction and chap. 1.

sending bills to Congress at the right time was important in securing a favorable outcome.

Consultation plays a vital role in executive-legislative relations. Presidents who do not bother to consult with key members of Congress often find that they have made opponents of potential allies. President Nixon probably lost the support of Senator Margaret Chase Smith (R-Maine) during the consideration of Harrold Carswell for the Supreme Court when his administration informed members of the Senate that she was going to support Carswell when in fact she had not made up her mind. Eventually she voted against Carswell. President Johnson was careful to consult with influential members of Congress at all stages of the legislative process, from bill drafting to final conferences before passage. Johnson was also careful to provide advance notice to Congress to defuse opposition or strengthen support and to anticipate problems when possible.

Presidents have sometimes found their *cabinets* to be an important legislative resource. Cabinet secretaries and their departments can be an important source of expertise and political pressure. Johnson devoted much cabinet meeting time to pending legislation and also directed his cabinet secretaries to apply their departments to legislative ends. Cabinet secretaries and lower department officials also often testify before congressional committees, and Presidents can shape that testimony to their advantage.

A *personal appeal* from the President, whether over the phone or face to face, has always been considered an effective although by no means foolproof means of winning support. Some Presidents, such as Johnson, Ford, Reagan, and Bush, were frequent and effective users of personal appeals. Others, such as Eisenhower and Carter, were less comfortable with the personal approach. Richard Nixon actively avoided substantive personal contact with members of Congress. Phone calls from members of Congress to the President were carefully screened, with most not even getting through to Nixon. Moreover, Nixon rarely used the personal approach, seeing himself more as an administrator than a power broker. Nixon's apparent aloofness and detachment did little to endear him to members of Congress.

As with any resource, the impact of direct involvement by the President may decline when it is employed too frequently. Presidents usually apply personal pressure parsimoniously, especially in the case of close votes on important bills and in instances when the President's prestige is on the line. A good example of both cases is seen when Presidents attempt to beat back a veto override vote. In 1986, for example, Reagan personally contacted twelve senators to win their support to uphold his veto of a congressional effort to block an arms sale to Saudi Arabia. One senator who changed his vote to support Reagan's veto was John P. East (R-N.C.). In doing so, he was persuaded that "the president should be allowed to make foreign policy without being managed at every turn by Congress."[11] In this instance, Reagan's veto was upheld by the precise minimum of thirty-four votes.

In January 1990 George Bush won a battle with Congress over his veto of a Chinese immigration bill. Passed at the end of the first session of the 101st Congress, the measure would have protected Chinese students in the United States from deportation to China after the expiration of their visas in the aftermath of the Chinese government's repression of the democracy movement led largely by Chinese students. In his November 30, 1989, veto message, Bush announced that he would implement protections administratively, arguing that a legislative remedy was an unnecessary infringement on presidential power. Congressional leaders were outraged by the veto, and the prospects for an override seemed great, as the bill had passed unanimously in the House and without a recorded vote in the Senate (usually an indication of unanimous sentiment). On January 24 the House overrode the veto by a vote of 390 to 25; the next day, however, Bush's veto was sustained in the Senate by a vote of 62 to 37, five votes short of the two-thirds needed to override. Observers credited the surprising result largely to Bush's forceful personal intervention, including phone calls and personal notes, and that of former President Richard Nixon. Bush won over supporters by assuring a handful of Republican senators that the students would not be forced out of the country, that an override would be a blow to the President's prestige, and that the President should have final say in such foreign policy matters.[12]

If there is a political coin of the realm in Washington, it is certainly *bargaining*. Although there is no consensus on the extent and

[11] Steven V. Roberts, "Senate Upholds Arms for Saudis, Backing Reagan," *New York Times,* June 6, 1986.

[12] Thomas L. Friedman, "Senate, by 4 Votes, Fails to Override Bush's China Veto," and R. W. Apple, Jr., "Getting Mad, Getting Even," *New York Times,* January 26, 1990; Thomas L. Friedman, "White House Asks Congress Support on China Policies," *New York Times,* January 24, 1990.

effectiveness of bargaining, it is indisputably an integral presidential resource. President Kennedy, for example, struck a bargain with Senator Robert Kerr (D-Okla.) over an Arkansas River project (the Arkansas River ran through Kerr's home state). When Kennedy asked Kerr for help in getting an investment tax credit bill out of the Senate Finance Committee, Kerr responded by raising the Arkansas River bill, insisting on a trade. Kennedy's reply was, "You know, Bob, I never really understood that Arkansas River bill before today."[13] Kerr's project was supported and enacted; in exchange, Kerr backed the Kennedy bill.

Although every President engages in some degree of bargaining, the technique has limitations. First, bargaining resources are limited. The President cannot afford to use bargaining or favor trading as a principal means to obtain action. If bargains appear to be frequent and explicit, it is likely that everyone in Congress will want to make such deals. Like personal contact, bargains are most effective when used prudently and implicitly. Also, members of Congress may not be swayed by the bargaining option, especially if they are motivated by factors such as constituent pressure, ideology, and party ties.

Sometimes presidential influence extends beyond offering incentives, to the application of *coercion*. In a strict sense, the President can do little to twist arms. Some Presidents, such as Eisenhower, found strong-arm tactics to be distasteful. Johnson, by contrast, was not reluctant to employ embarrassment, bullying, and threats to promote his ends. The Nixon administration also employed arm-twisting tactics, although Nixon himself avoided personal involvement. These tactics came into play during the Nixon years over such controversial issues as the antiballistic missile system in 1969 and the unsuccessful Haynsworth and Carswell nominations to the Supreme Court.

In addition, the Nixon administration threatened rebellious representatives with reelection trouble. A well-known example was the administration's support of James Buckley for Senator from New York. The Republican incumbent, Charles Goodell, had become a strong critic of the administration. In response, the administration threw its support all but officially behind Buckley, the nominee of the small New York Conservative party. The weight of the Nixon administration helped Buckley defeat Goodell and the Democratic nominee, Richard Ottinger. Despite this and other periodic suc-

---

[13] Quoted in Edwards, *Presidential Influence in Congress*, p. 129.

cesses for the arm-twisting technique, it frequently does not work and often serves to fan and fortify opposition.[14]

Presidents can provide a variety of *services* to members of Congress. Such services can include presidential visits to home districts, assistance with favored pork barrel and other projects, patronage appointments, constituent service assistance (such as giving out presidential memorabilia and signed photographs, arranging special White House tours, and interceding with federal agencies), access to privileged or other inside information, campaign assistance, and personal favors and amenities for members of Congress (from cuff links to choice theater tickets at Washington's Kennedy Center). The use of amenities and social courtesies lies in the potential to build positive personal relations. President Johnson was careful to apportion credit for important legislation among key legislators early in his term. But as Vietnam-related criticism mounted, he became less generous in giving credit to members of Congress and claimed more credit for himself, further eroding his relations with Congress. As with other tactical devices, services and amenities are of limited effectiveness.[15]

Aside from these direct means of influence, Presidents also marshal *outside pressure.* One way to influence members of Congress is through constituent pressure. Presidents may make direct appeals to geographic or other constituencies to urge that pressure be placed on representatives. Kennedy's legislative chief, Lawrence O'Brien, would often contact governors to urge them to pressure state representatives. Federal agencies may also be called on to mobilize support for presidential policies. Farmers, unions, business groups, and regional or other interests may be persuaded to side with the administration in attempting to swing congressional support. President Johnson forged a coalition that included the major religious denominations and education groups in support of the Elementary and Secondary Education Act of 1965 even before the bill was introduced. In fact, Johnson deliberately held back the bill until both the National

---

[14] See Neustadt, *Presidential Power,* chaps. 2 and 3.

[15] See, for example, Cary R. Covington, "'Guess Who's Coming to Dinner': The Distribution of White House Social Invitations and Their Effects on Congressional Support," *American Politics Quarterly* 16 (July 1988): 243–265.

Education Association and the National Catholic Welfare Conference agreed on its basics.[16]

Presidents often employ *rhetorical skills* and a *public presidency* approach to go over the heads of Congress in an effort to sway public opinion. It is not surprising, then, that Presidents often seek public favor to build support for major legislation or to head off possible opposition.

One of the most dramatic examples of a President seeking public support to sway Congress occurred before the era of television. In 1919 Woodrow Wilson stumped the country by train to rally support for his cherished but besieged League of Nations treaty then before the Senate, giving forty speeches in twenty-two days. Wilson's efforts fell short. After his fortieth speech, he collapsed from exhaustion and then suffered a stroke, and the Senate defeated the treaty by a fifteen-vote margin.

To cite a more recent example, Ronald Reagan met increasing opposition in both Congress and the country to his efforts to cut back on aid to education. (Polls indicated a two-to-one ratio of popular disapproval of the cutbacks.) In response, the White House launched a communications offensive emphasizing the themes of promoting excellence in education, merit pay for teachers, and greater classroom discipline. Reagan made over twenty-five appearances on education, repeating these themes. Several months after the start of the campaign, poll results indicated that the public had come to support Reagan's education program by a two-to-one ratio even though no actual policy changes had occurred. By altering public perceptions, Reagan helped alleviate pressure from Congress.[17]

President Johnson also found a public appeal desirable and even necessary as a way to impel congressional action. When Johnson's tax surcharge bill stalled in the House Ways and Means Committee, he appealed to the people through several public forums, including his 1968 State of the Union address. The impasse was eventually overcome despite some congressional resentment over the public approach.

[16] See Edwards, *Presidential Influence in Congress*, chaps. 5 and 6. See also Light, *The President's Agenda*, esp. the introduction and chap. 1.

[17] Mark Hertsgaard, *On Bended Knee* (New York: Farrar, Straus & Giroux, 1988), pp. 48–49.

President Carter used a public appeal early in his administration when he proposed an energy package to Congress in 1977. He worked to rally public support through a series of television addresses. To symbolize his own commitment to energy conservation, Carter wore a cardigan sweater instead of the traditional suit jacket. Despite Carter's appeal to the public, his energy program faced difficult sailing in Congress.

In addition to working to rally national opinion, Presidents seek to take advantage of changing public sentiments. Immediately after the 1968 assassination of Martin Luther King, Jr., President Johnson pressed congressional leaders to act on his Fair Housing Act, which had been stalled in committee for over two years. Within seven days of King's death the bill was signed into law. A day after Robert Kennedy's assassination Congress enacted the Omnibus Crime Control and Safe Streets Act in 1968, even though the bill had been tied up in Congress for more than a year. In both instances dramatic swings in public sentiment resulting from unforeseen events provided a key impetus to push a presidentially favored proposal through. The presidential public appeal is nothing new,[18] but many analysts have noted that modern communications technology, along with other changes in the political landscape, has had the effect of encouraging Presidents to use the public forum to pressure Congress.[19] Presidents can command network television time almost at will. No modern President would think of launching a major political effort involving Congress without incorporating the means of public communications. Indeed, as Figure 4.1 shows, presidents have progressively expanded their prime-time exposure.

Political scientist Samuel Kernell has argued that modern Presidents "go public" more than their predecessors in an attempt to place themselves and their proposals directly before the people in order to improve their political fortunes in Washington. These efforts may target particular groups or segments of the population, but since virtually any presidential action is news, national coverage usually results. The consequence of this trend is that Presidents, their allies, and their foes have all become much more concerned with public relations as a political tactic. Both allies and critics agree that among

[18] See Jeffrey K. Tulis's excellent study, *The Rhetorical Presidency* (Princeton, N.J.: Princeton University Press, 1987).

[19] See, for example, Jeffrey B. Abramson, F. Christopher Arterton, and Gary R. Orren, *The Electronic Commonwealth* (New York: Basic Books, 1988).

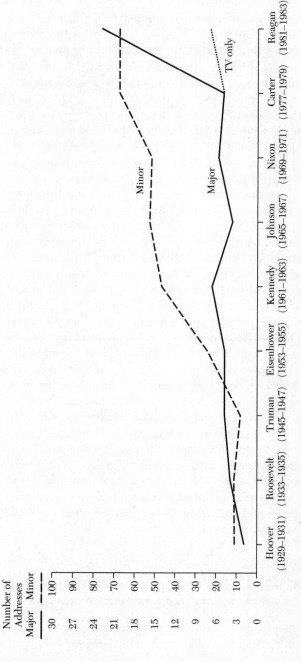

Figure 4.1 Presidential Addresses, 1929–1983 (Yearly Averages for First Three Years of First Term)

NOTE: To eliminate public activities inspired by concerns of reelection rather than governing, only the first three years have been tabulated. For this reason, Gerald Ford's record of public activities during his two and one-half years of office have been ignored.

SOURCES: Data for Hoover, Roosevelt, Truman, Eisenhower, Nixon, and Carter are from William W. Lammers, "Presidential Attention-Focusing Activities," in *The President and the American Public,* ed. Doris A. Graber (Philadelphia: Institute for the Study of Human Issues, 1982), Table 6–1, p. 152. Data for Kennedy, Johnson, and Reagan are from *Public Papers of the Presidents* series. See also Kernell, "Presidency and the People," p. 242. Reprinted by permission from Samuel Kernell, *Going Public* (Washington, D.C.: Congressional Quarterly, 1986), p. 4.

modern Presidents, "no president has enlisted public strategies to better advantage than has Ronald Reagan."[20] Reagan's acting background dovetailed with a growing appreciation for the impact of presidential images to produce a presidency that worked to cultivate Reagan's national image as a means to promote the President's agenda in Congress.

The idea that modern Presidents can obtain powerful political capital from public support is taken further by Theodore J. Lowi. Lowi argues that the country has entered an era of presidentially centered government in which presidential appeals have taken on a plebiscitary nature; that is, Presidents seek popular support or even adoration, as did the autocrats of the ancient Roman and the more recent French empires. The forceful ascendancy of the personal presidency has come at the expense of the separation of powers (especially in a denigration of the role of Congress) and the two-party system, Lowi asserts. The cult of presidential personality has been accompanied by a rise in the formal and informal powers of the presidency, although these heightened powers cannot match public expectations. Under these conditions, the President may operate outside of traditional presidential-congressional relations to impel Congress to act in accordance with the President's wishes.[21]

The emphasis on what powers and skills are most important to Presidents seeking an effective presidency has changed since the 1950s. Communications skills have always been important, but past Presidents known for their communications skills, such as Theodore Roosevelt, Woodrow Wilson, and Franklin Roosevelt, did not rely solely or even primarily on speech making and public oration to gain political results in Congress. Modern Presidents have found that public appeals are an increasingly important supplement to traditional bargaining with Congress. With the erosion of strong party ties and the rise of television as an instrument of political expression, traditional institutional and partisan links between the President and Congress have been further weakened.

Assessment

The sheer length of this list of leadership tools available to the President might lull the reader into the conclusion that presidential per-

---

[20] Samuel Kernell, *Going Public* (Washington, D.C.: CQ Press, 1986), p. 4.

[21] Theodore J. Lowi, *The Personal President* (Ithaca, N.Y.: Cornell University Press, 1985).

suasion is pretty much irresistible when applied with concerted and consistent effort and is all-encompassing as an explanation of presidential-congressional relations. However, the actual presidential record suggests nearly the opposite.

First, the measures of presidential success described in Chapter 3 make it clear that even the most skilled Presidents are often frustrated in their efforts to realize their objectives in Congress. Second, if presidential leadership skills were as powerful an explanation of presidential success as many assume, the actual records of Presidents would be very different. Any reasonably skilled President will treat the term of office as a learning experience. According to political scientist Paul Light, presidential information and expertise develop in a "cycle of increasing effectiveness."[22] By the end of a term a good presidential leader will have learned from experience and mistakes. But what is most revealing about this observation is that, as Light notes, the development of leadership skills varies *inversely* with success, as presidential success is greatest at the *start* of a term and lowest at or near the *end* of a term—an observation that flatly contradicts the centrality of the leadership explanation.

Third, three important studies of presidential influence in Congress concluded that the impact of presidential skills has been overstated, partly because of the natural tendency for such activities to attract press headlines. Two of these studies were produced by George Edwards. According to Edwards's first study, "Presidential legislative skills do not seem to affect support for presidential policies, despite what conventional wisdom leads us to expect."[23] The link between presidential leadership and Congress received even closer scrutiny in a later study in which Edwards examined the three key sources of presidential influence in Congress—party, public support, and legislative skills—to determine executive impact on congressional voting. Relying on four different measures of support for the President applied to the period 1953–1986, Edwards concluded that the impact of presidential leadership on congressional action (or inaction) was indeed marginal.[24]

A parallel quantitative study by political scientists Jon R. Bond and Richard Fleisher also examined the explanatory power of public

---

[22] Light, *The President's Agenda*, p. 37. Light refers to the tendency for presidential influence to decline during the course of a term as the "cycle of decreasing influence."

[23] Edwards, *Presidential Influence in Congress*, p. 202.

[24] George C. Edwards III, *At the Margins* (New Haven, Conn.: Yale University Press, 1989).

approval, party, and presidential leadership, plus ideology. They concluded that none of these factors was especially powerful in explaining roll call votes but that leadership was the least important. In short, Bond and Fleisher found "little support for the theory that the president's perceived leadership skills are associated with success on roll call votes in Congress."[25]

In the conclusion to his later study, Edwards was also careful to note, however, that the study of presidential designs and actions would continue to be important if for no other reason than because "our political system virtually compels the president to attempt to lead Congress."[26] As Edwards concluded,

> it is important to depersonalize somewhat the study of presidential leadership and examine it from a broader perspective. In this way there are fewer risks of attributing to various aspects of presidential leadership consequences of factors largely beyond the president's control. Similarly, one is less likely to attribute incorrectly the failure of a president to achieve his goals to his failure to lead properly. Things are rarely so simple.[27]

It is this caution which informs much of the rest of the analysis in this chapter. The study of presidential leadership is always important if for no other reason than because the practice of good leadership will always be important to Presidents. But we must not confuse prescription with description and explanation. Those who seek a fuller understanding of the presidential-congressional link must look well beyond the quality of leadership.

HISTORICAL EXPLANATION: BUDGETING

Many important answers to questions concerning presidential-congressional relations can be found in an exploration of political history.

[25] Jon R. Bond and Richard Fleisher, *The President in the Legislative Arena* (Chicago: University of Chicago Press, 1990), p. 218. See also pp. x, 221–223.

[26] Edwards, *At the Margins*, p. 1. Mark A. Peterson also warns against concentrating on presidential leadership. See *Legislating Together: The White House and Capitol Hill from Eisenhower to Reagan* (Cambridge, Mass.: Harvard University Press, 1990), pp. 10–11. An interesting study of presidential leadership in domestic affairs makes the case that leadership is indeed more important than Edwards and others would suggest when viewed in the broader context of regime stability and change. See McKay, *Domestic Policy and Ideology*.

[27] Edwards, *At the Margins*, p. 216. Bond and Fleisher make a similar point. See *The President in the Legislative Arena*, p. 231.

The truth of this observation can be seen in Chapters 1 and 2, which provide a historical framework central to the subject of this book. To illustrate with greater specificity the importance of historical perspective, we examine here the case of the evolution of budgetary authority.

From Legislative to Executive Budget

Before 1921 Congress was vested with sole budget-making authority. Although many Presidents and treasury secretaries played important roles in formulating national spending priorities, Congress bore the principal responsibility for the level and disbursement of federal money and had relatively little difficulty formulating annual spending priorities up to the time of the Civil War. The magnitude of wartime spending placed a great strain on the legislative committee structure, however, and Congress responded by dispersing budgetary authority among several committees, including the newly created Appropriations Committee, and separating authority over the appropriation and revenue components of budget making.

In the latter part of the nineteenth century increasing fragmentation of budgeting authority to more congressional committees encouraged railroad interests, land speculators, other business interests, and many individuals seeking government pensions to obtain lucrative concessions in the budget. The fiscal consequence was greater extravagance in the use of public funds. The only public figure to consistently stand up against this abuse was the President. President Grover Cleveland in particular gained a reputation as a "protector of the purse" by his prolific use of the veto. In his first term alone he vetoed 304 bills, almost three times as many as all his predecessors combined. Of those, 241 were aimed at private and general pension bills.

From the early 1900s on, the swell of reformers' cries, including many in Congress, called for giving greater budgetary authority to the President. The motivation was twofold: to rely on executive leadership as a means of providing budgetary unity and to place budgetary authority in the hands of "experts" in the executive branch who would compose budgets based on what was then labeled "the science of budgetmaking,"[28] In doing so, reformers hoped to mini-

---

[28] Quoted in Aaron Wildavsky, *The New Politics of the Budgetary Process* (Glenview, Ill.: Scott, Foresman, 1988), p. 55.

mize the political influence of congressional leaders and committee chairs.

In 1921, Congress enacted the Budget and Accounting Act, which provided for an executive Bureau of the Budget (BOB) and allowed the President to appoint his own budget director. For the first time the BOB would formulate and submit to Congress a comprehensive budget document. Government agencies that formerly dickered directly with congressional committees would now be required to submit their annual proposals to the BOB. At about the same time, however, Congress strengthened its appropriations committees to counterbalance the greater executive role. Moreover, as if to underscore the principle that Congress was still in command of the budget process, it noted in a congressional report accompanying the measure that "the plan outlined does provide for an Executive initiation of the budget, but the President's responsibility ends when he has prepared the budget and transmitted it to Congress."[29] Despite this declaration, budgetary powers continued to shift toward the executive.

In 1933 Congress passed the Economy Act, which centralized and reorganized various budgetary authorities within the executive. Based on the authority granted to the President in this act, President Roosevelt directed that certain authority pertaining to appropriations formerly in the hands of department heads be transferred to the BOB director. In this way, BOB could exert direct pressure on agencies to review and revise their budget estimates in accordance with the President's, as opposed to the agency's, preferences.[30]

In 1939 President Franklin Roosevelt used reorganization authority granted by Congress to bring the BOB into the newly created Executive Office of the President (EOP). This important action, stemming from recommendations of the Brownlow Committee, was designed to strengthen the President's hand in budgeting and executive branch management through a strengthened BOB situated politically and organizationally closer to the President. By executive order, Roosevelt strengthened the powers of the BOB to include assisting the President in formulating an overall fiscal plan for the government, control and supervision of budget administration, enhanced re-

[29] Quoted in Louis Fisher and Neal Devins, "How Successfully Can the States' Item Veto Be Transferred to the President?" *Georgetown Law Journal*, 75 (October 1986): 188.

[30] See Louis Fisher, *Presidential Spending Power* (Princeton, N.J.: Princeton University Press, 1975), p. 40.

search capabilities, enhanced involvement in legislative clearance pertinent to both proposed legislation and executive orders, and informing the President about agency spending patterns. Political scientist Larry Berman referred to the post-1939 BOB as the "born-again Budget Bureau."[31]

In 1970 President Nixon issued an executive order based on reorganization authority granted by Congress to broaden the focus of the BOB from simply preparing the budget to assessing and evaluating existing programs. The office's staff capabilities were enhanced, and the office of the director was moved to the White House. The name of the agency was changed to the Office of Management and Budget (OMB) to reflect its added authority. Nixon's stated intention was to vest the new OMB with a panoply of administrative-technical responsibilities while leaving broad matters of policy to the newly created Domestic Council. Yet OMB soon became heavily involved not only in its "management" function but in policy, a pattern that has accelerated in subsequent decades.[32]

Congress Awakens

Many in Congress had come to recognize even before the late 1960s that Congress had lost serious political ground to the executive on fiscal and budgetary matters.[33] Its disaggregated approach to budgeting and increasing reliance on the executive for information, leadership, and perspective meant that Congress was seriously handicapped if it chose to challenge the President's priorities and assumptions. Conservatives feared congressional inability to stem the federal deficit and deal effectively with economic downturns. Liberals feared continued loss of power to the executive. This sense of congressional impotence combined with dismay over the excesses of the Nixon ad-

[31] Larry Berman, *The Office of Management and Budget and the Presidency, 1921–1979* (Princeton, N.J.: Princeton University Press, 1979), p. 14.

[32] Fisher, *Presidential Spending Power*, p. 48; Berman, *The Office of Management and Budget*, pp. 112–130.

[33] In the Legislative Reorganization Act of 1946 Congress made an effort to establish a legislative budget, setting out procedures similar to those of the 1974 budget act. As in the 1970s and 1980s, Congress was reacting to increased presidential power, a growing deficit, and the fragmentation of congressional power. This effort ceased within three years of enactment. See Lance T. LeLoup, "Fiscal Policy and Congressional Politics," in *Congressional Politics*, ed. by Christopher J. Deering (Chicago: Dorsey, 1989), pp. 275–276.

ministration, including Nixon's expanded use of impoundment power (refusing to spend funds duly appropriated by Congress), resulting in the passage of the Budget and Impoundment Control Act of 1974.[34] The act's purpose was to reassert congressional control over the budget by centralizing and buttressing Congress's budget-related mechanisms—a difficult task for an organization where power has become ever more decentralized and fragmented—and thus to end the practice of presidential impoundment of funds.

Specifically, the act created new House and Senate budget committees to provide a means by which Congress could set overall taxing and spending levels; it created its own budget analysis office—the Congressional Budget Office—which could provide Congress with its own source of budget information to rival OMB; it established a complex series of budgetary timetables, schedules, and procedures; and it reined in impoundment by defining two procedures: deferrals, by which Presidents may delay spending unilaterally, and rescissions, by which Presidents may request that Congress approve the cancellation of spending. Unlike pre-1974 impoundment, Presidents must now obtain congressional approval for any rescission or impoundment action.[35]

Most important, this act sought to provide the means by which Congress could challenge and, if it chose, rearrange the President's budget priorities. Congress's inability to compose its own look at the big budgetary picture had made it that much more dependent on the President at a time when congressional suspicion of the President was at an all-time high.[36]

---

[34] For more on the reasons for the enactment of this act, see John W. Ellwood and James A. Thurber, "The New Congressional Budget Process," in *Congress Reconsidered,* ed. by Lawrence C. Dodd and Bruce I. Oppenheimer (New York: Praeger, 1977), pp. 163–192.

[35] For more on the 1974 act and its consequences, see John W. Ellwood and James A. Thurber, "The Politics of the Congressional Budget Process Re-examined," in *Congress Reconsidered,* ed. by Lawrence C. Dodd and Bruce I. Oppenheimer (Washington, D.C.: Congressional Quarterly, 1981), pp. 246–274; and Allen Schick, *Congress and Money* (Washington, D.C.: Urban Institute Press, 1980), pp. 17–81. For more on impoundment, see James P. Pfiffner, *The President, the Budget, and Congress* (Boulder, Colo.: Westview, 1979).

[36] James A. Thurber, "The Consequences of Budget Reform for Congressional-Presidential Relations," *Annals of the American Academy of Political and Social Science,* 499 (September 1988): 102–105.

Executive Counterpunch

Since the 1974 reform Congress has indeed become a more important player in the budget process, and Presidents have been forced to work more closely with congressional leaders.[37] Yet Presidents have also succeeded in working budgetary reforms to their advantage. For example, the 1974 act created and the Gramm-Rudman-Hollings reforms enhanced a "reconciliation" process that gives the congressional budget committees the power to "reconcile" budget resolutions with congressional authorizations and appropriations by directing that pertinent committees meet pre-set spending targets. In other words, through reconciliation Congress can force itself to limit spending within broad categories in order to abide by preset spending ceilings. The purpose of the change was to provide a means by which Congress could impose some budgetary discipline to keep within overall guidelines.

However, in early 1981 President Reagan's budget director, David Stockman, proposed a radical way to use the then poorly understood reconciliation process to achieve administration objectives. The administration pushed for a reconciliation vote early in the budget process (instead of during September, toward the end of the process, when the reconciliation vote had usually been taken) that set strict ceilings which forced major cuts in domestic programs and major increases in defense spending. Despite strenuous opposition, Reagan won key votes in the Republican-controlled Senate and in the Democratic-controlled House through a coalition of disciplined Republicans and conservative Democrats. Thus, a device designed by congressional reformers to allow Congress to exert greater budget control and responsibility was used successfully by a President to radically alter national budget priorities. One congressional leader called Reagan's actions "the most brutal and blunt instrument used by a President in an attempt to control the congressional process since Nixon used impoundment."[38]

Despite the ambitious design of the 1974 reform, it spawned its own set of problems. According to one assessment, "although the

---

[37] Thurber, "The Consequences of Budget Reform," pp. 105, 112.

[38] Quoted in Howard E. Shuman, *Politics and the Budget* (Englewood Cliffs, N.J.: Prentice-Hall, 1988), p. 262. See also pp. 252–270 and David Stockman, *The Triumph of Politics* (New York: Avon, 1987), chap. 6.

1974 Budget Act appeared to advance the cause of rationality in budgeting by encouraging comprehensiveness and explicitness, it also had the potential of encouraging avoidance and fakery."[39] In the 1980s legislative tinkering with the budget process continued.

Ronald Reagan won the presidency in 1980 in part because of his pledge to slash big government and reduce the federal deficit. In the first year of his presidency Reagan won important budgetary victories in Congress (thanks in part to exploitation of the reconciliation process), including a three-year cut in domestic programs of $135 billion and a massive $1.8 trillion increase in defense spending over five years. At the same time, he also won a three-year 25 percent cut in income taxes. The fear that such a tax cut combined with increased defense spending would result in massive deficits was dismissed by the administration because of an economic theory, supply-side economics, which posited that lower taxes would ultimately result in more profits in the private sector and therefore more tax money for the government. The theory proved false, and the country's total federal deficit doubled during the first four years of the Reagan presidency. As Table 4.2 reveals, annual deficits hovered around $200 billion per year for most of the Reagan era. However, other economic indicators, including inflation and unemployment, remained favorable, helping to buttress Reagan's personal popularity.[40]

Gramm-Rudman-Hollings.   Congress and the President were nevertheless saddled with the specter of serious budget deficits that diverted attention from the President's spending priorities. Congress responded with the Balanced Budget and Emergency Deficit Control Act of 1985, better known as Gramm-Rudman-Hollings (GRH).

Enacted hurriedly by Congress in an atmosphere of deficit-induced crisis, GRH sought to unblock continuing executive-legislative stalemate over the budget by setting into law mandatory deficit reduction figures so that by fiscal year 1991 the federal budget would be balanced. If the projected deficit targets were not met, the OMB was charged with making automatic cuts in accordance with a for-

---

[39] Rudolph G. Penner and Alan J. Abramson, *Broken Purse Strings* (Washington, D.C.: Urban Institute Press, 1988), p. 20.

[40] Lance T. LeLoup, *Budgetary Politics* (Brunswick, Ohio: King's Court Communications, 1988), pp. 27–29.

mula set by Congress. In addition, GRH required the President to submit his budget a month earlier, and it specified other timing requirements.

Doubts about the constitutionality of some aspects of GRH led to an immediate court challenge. In *Bowsher v. Synar*[41] the Supreme Court ruled that the provision in GRH giving the head of the General Accounting Office (GAO) the power to order executive branch cuts in the budget was a violation of separation of powers because the GAO head was removable by Congress. This and other difficulties in the GRH mechanisms impelled Congress to enact the Balanced Budget and Emergency Deficit Control Reaffirmation Act of 1987 (GRH II). This measure repaired the constitutional problem by giving debt-cutting powers to OMB, extending the deficit reduction timetable, strengthening the deficit-cutting mechanism, and placing added limits on what could count toward deficit reduction.

The effects of these remedies were mixed. In an environment where neither Reagan nor Bush (until mid-1990) was willing to propose tax increases, the temptation to meet budget targets through gimmickry was great. For example, the fiscal year 1987 budget target was met by such gimmicks as holding a one-time sale of some federal assets and bumping a $3 billion pay raise for federal employees from the last day of the 1987 fiscal year to the first day of the next year. According to several respected budget analysts, the two GRH reforms "moved budgetary gimmickry from the sidelines to center stage. Where once policy makers resorted to questionable practices to shave a few billion dollars from total spending, now they used such gimmicks as an integral part of fiscal policy."[42]

In December 1989, Senator Daniel P. Moynihan (D-N.Y.) sought to strip away one budget gimmick by proposing a two-year cut in social security taxes. Social security reform enacted in 1983 that was designed to make the system more fiscally sound resulted in a trust fund surplus that amounted to $65 billion in 1990 and was projected to reach $113 billion by 1994. While GRH specifically exempted social security from mandated budget cuts, it also allowed the trust

[41] 478 U.S. 714 (1986).

[42] Lawrence J. Haas, "Endless Tinkering," *National Journal*, November 18, 1989, p. 2831. For more on the GRH sequence, see James A. Thurber, "The Impact of Budget Reform on Presidential and Congressional Governance," in *Divided Democracy*, ed. by James A. Thurber (Washington, D.C.: CQ Press, 1991), pp. 145–170.

Table 4.2 Budget Receipts and Outlays, 1789–1995ᵃ

Fiscal Year	Budget Receipts	Budget Outlays	Budget Surplus or Deficit	Fiscal Year	Budget Receipts	Budget Outlays	Budget Surplus or Deficit
1789–1849	1,160	1,090	+70	1958	79,636	82,405	-2,769
1850–1900	14,462	15,453	-991	1959	79,249	92,098	-12,849
1901–1905	2,797	2,678	+119	1960	92,492	92,245	+247
1906–1910	3,143	3,196	-52	1961	94,388	97,723	-3,335
1911–1915	3,517	3,568	-49	1962	99,676	106,821	-7,146
1916–1920	17,286	40,195	-22,909	1963	106,560	111,316	-4,756
1921–1925	20,962	17,323	+3,639	1964	112,613	118,528	-5,915
1926	3,795	2,930	+865	1965	116,817	118,228	-1,411
1927	4,013	2,857	+1,155	1966	130,835	134,532	-3,698
1928	3,900	2,961	+939	1967	148,822	157,464	-8,643
1929	3,862	3,127	+734	1968	152,973	178,134	-25,161
1930	4,058	3,320	+738	1969	186,882	183,640	+3,242
1931	3,116	3,577	-462	1970	192,812	195,649	-2,837
1932	1,924	4,659	-2,735	1971	187,139	210,172	-23,033
1933	1,997	4,598	-2,602	1972	207,309	230,681	-23,373
1934	3,015	6,645	-3,630	1973	230,799	245,707	-14,908
1935	3,706	6,497	-2,791	1974	263,224	269,359	-6,135
1936	3,997	8,422	-4,425	1975	279,090	332,332	-53,242
1937	4,956	7,733	-2,777	1976	298,060	371,779	-73,719
1938	5,588	6,765	-1,177	TQᵇ	81,232	95,973	-14,741

1939	4,979	8,841	-3,862	1977	355,559	409,203	-53,644
1940	6,548	9,468	-2,920	1978	399,740	458,729	-58,989
1941	8,712	13,653	-4,941	1979	463,302	503,464	-40,161
1942	14,634	35,137	-20,503	1980	517,112	590,920	-73,808
1943	24,001	78,555	-54,554	1981	599,272	678,209	-78,936
1944	43,747	91,304	-47,557	1982	617,766	745,706	-127,940
1945	45,159	92,712	-47,553	1983	600,562	808,327	-207,764
1946	39,296	55,232	-15,936	1984	666,457	851,781	-185,324
1947	38,514	34,496	+4,018	1985	734,057	946,316	-212,260
1948	41,560	29,764	+11,796	1986	769,091	989,815	-220,725
1949	39,415	38,835	+580	1987‡	854,000	1,003,000	-150,000
1950	39,443	42,562	-3,119	1988	909,000	1,064,000	-155,000
1951	51,616	45,514	+6,102	1989	991,000	1,144,000	-152,000
1952	66,167	67,686	-1,519	1990	1,031,000	1,251,000	-220,000
1953	69,608	76,101	-6,493	1991 est.	1,110,000		-279,000
1954	69,701	70,855	-1,154	1992 est.	1,185,000		-362,000
1955	65,451	68,444	-2,993	1993 est.	1,258,000		-239,000
1956	74,587	70,640	+3,947	1994 est.	1,344,000		-211,000
1957	79,990	76,578	+3,412	1995 est.	1,429,000		-128,000

Data for 1789–1939 are for the administrative budget: data for 1940 and all following years are for the unified budget.

° Includes outlays (and deficits) that are off budget under current law and proposed to be included on budget. These transactions began in 1973.

† In calendar year 1976, the federal fiscal year was converted from a July 1–June 30 basis to an October 1–September 30 basis. TQ refers to the transition quarter from July 1 to September 30, 1976.

‡ Figures from 1987 on are rounded to nearest million.

SOURCE: Office of Management and Budget. Adapted from Lance T. LeLoup, *Budgetary Politics* (Brunswick, Ohio: King's Court Communications, 1988). Reprinted Courtesy of King's Court Communications, Brunswick, Ohio.

fund to be used in federal deficit calculations, even though the money was earmarked for social security, lowering the magnitude of the debt by the amount of the social security surplus. Despite general agreement that Moynihan's plan stood no chance of enactment, there was also general agreement that he had succeeded in focusing national attention on the nation's tax and deficit problems. *The New York Times* noted that Moynihan's proposal "struck a nerve in the body politic"[43] and "burst like a firebomb onto the Congressional agenda."[44] Moynihan's efforts did prove fruitful, however, insofar as the social security surplus was eliminated from deficit calculations in 1990.

After Gramm-Rudman-Hollings.   Worsening economic conditions in the latter part of 1990 combined with continuing budget problems to force a new round of budget-related changes. Most people agreed that new, deeper cuts would be necessary for the 1991 budget and future budgets, but most people agreed also that cuts alone would be insufficient and that some kind of tax increase would be necessary. Standing in the way of such an increase was the often repeated promise that became the cornerstone of President Bush's successful 1988 campaign: "Read my lips, no new taxes." Yet in June Bush backtracked on this keystone pledge by announcing that he would in fact consider a tax increase. Weathering the initial political storm, White House and congressional leaders began negotiations on a budget reduction package. Negotiations continued through September, with a plan finally emerging on September 30, the last day of the fiscal year. The fragile compromise called for a $500 billion deficit reduction over the next five years. Bush and congressional negotiators pushed hard for speedy congressional approval, but in what was viewed as a stunning loss for Bush, the plan was defeated in a vote taken a few days later because of the defection of conservative Republicans led by the House minority whip, Newt

[43] David E. Rosenbaum, "Congressional Leaders Take Issue with Moynihan Plan to Cut Taxes," *New York Times,* January 22, 1990. See also David E. Rosenbaum, "Prof. Moynihan Wakes the Class with Truth about Taxes," *New York Times,* January 21, 1990.

[44] Susan F. Rasky, "Democrats Seek Advantage on Tax Cut Plan," *New York Times,* January 24, 1990. My thanks to John Diaz for gathering information on this case.

Gingrich (R-Ga.), who were unhappy with Bush's abandonment of his no new taxes pledge.[45]

The defeat of the compromise package left the administration unprepared, and Bush came under increasing fire during October for his public equivocation over whether he would in fact support a tax increase, a cut in the capital gains tax, and other suggested measures.[46] A new compromise package that included a five-year $490 billion deficit reduction package was finally assembled and passed by Congress at the end of October.

But aside from resolving the 1991 budget, White House negotiators and a small group of congressional leaders also won enactment of some significant changes in budgeting procedures that were considered likely to shift more budget authority to the OMB. First, the new budget regulations called for separate budget caps for the three primary spending areas: domestic, defense, and international aid. By imposing separate caps instead of one overall cap, Congress could not shift funds from one category to another if a category exceeded its cap; instead, cuts would come automatically from within the affected category. Those who anticipated deeper defense cuts in the coming years—the so-called peace dividend—were especially dismayed at this loss of flexibility.

Second, Congress was now required to operate on a pay-as-you-go basis. That is, any new entitlement spending programs or tax reduction that was not "revenue-neutral" (offset by a comparable tax increase or spending cut) would have to be accompanied by a deficit-cutting reconciliation bill to find the needed savings. If such a reconciliation measure did not accompany the bill, a sequester calculated by OMB would automatically cut the necessary funds from other entitlement programs.

---

[45] Congressional liberals were also dissatisfied with the plan because of the brief time for debate, the inclusion of regressive taxes, and proposed cuts in programs such as Medicare. Even so, the measure could have passed even without the support of conservative Republicans; however, a group of about forty Democrats refused to support the package unless Republicans did as well. Susan F. Rasky, "Accord to Reduce Spending and Raise Taxes Is Reached; Many in Congress Critical," *New York Times*, October 1, 1990; Richard L. Berke, "Shouts of Revolt Rise Up in Congressional Ranks," *New York Times*, October 1, 1990; David E. Rosenbaum, "House Votes Stopgap Funds after Budget Pact Defeat," *New York Times*, October 6, 1990.

[46] Maureen Dowd, "George Bush's Communication Breakdown on the Budget," *New York Times*, October 21, 1990.

Third, OMB was given a major additional budget tool. Instead of calculating at the end of the budget year whether the government had exceeded its spending targets (and then triggering appropriate across-the-board spending cuts), OMB was given the power to conduct such assessments and enact sequesters several times throughout the budget year. Finally, the 1990 law again changed deficit reduction targets, calling for deficit limits of $327 billion for 1991, $317 billion for 1992, $236 billion for 1993, $102 billion for 1994, and $83 billion for 1995.[47]

The impact of these changes was expected to be profound. These gains in power for the executive and OMB meant less influence for Congress's CBO, the Joint Committee on Taxation, and the budget committees. According to one assessment, OMB's ability to enact sequesters throughout the budget year meant that "the White House would be able to block any legislation it opposes."[48] Congress's ability to alter the budget's overall fiscal framework would continue only with executive acquiescence, as the numbers behind congressional budget resolutions would be driven by OMB's numbers. Ironically, this OMB-centered system resembles the pre-1974 budget process.[49] The fact that such a potentially sweeping change incorporating the loss of congressional budget power was enacted by Congress was attributable to the plan's complexity, the timing of the proposal (it was offered at a time when Congress was eager to enact the full budget package and then adjourn to conduct fall congressional campaigns), the small number of congressional leaders involved in the bargaining process, the ability of administration negotiators to play off Democratic leaders against each other (in particular by granting concessions to negotiator and powerful Appropriations Committee chair Robert Byrd (D-W.V.)), and the absence of extended public debate over the plan's merits and consequences.[50]

These continuing reform efforts intermixed short-term concerns

---

[47] Lawrence J. Haas, "New Rules of the Game," *National Journal,* November 17, 1990, p. 2796.

[48] Haas, "New Rules," p. 2794.

[49] Haas, "New Rules," p. 2797. See also Lawrence J. Haas, "Off Center," *National Journal,* December 8, 1990, pp. 2971–2973. According to one senior congressional aide, "I don't think people realize just how much power has been shifted from one end of Pennsylvania Avenue to the other." Susan F. Rasky, "Substantial Power on Spending Is Shifted from Congress to Bush," *New York Times,* October 30, 1990.

[50] Haas, "New Rules," p. 2794.

over budgetary stalemate and priorities with long-term concern over interbranch relations. Congress began the 1990s by seemingly placing itself in the very situation in which it had found itself before 1974—able to manipulate specific budget lines but unable to shape the overall budgetary picture. Yet the enhanced sequester power given to the OMB in 1990 posed the potential for even greater executive intrusion into the budget process.

Successive rounds of budget tinkering will undoubtedly ensue. Regardless of the outcome, however, it is clear that (1) the President was, is, and will be an important player in the budget game, (2) the budget system was, is, and will be heavily criticized, and (3) aside from proposals to tinker further with the mechanics of the budget process,[51] the cries of many reformers have focused and will continue to focus on one remedy: more executive control over the budget process.[52]

Assessment

The case of the historical evolution of budgeting clearly illustrates how congressional authority over the budget has been successively delegated to the President, resulting in a significant increase in executive budget-related authority. Several specific lessons emerge from this case.

First, many of those who argue for greater executive control over the budget process accept as a given that an active executive role has been the norm throughout most of our history. The merits of the case aside, it is important to realize that this is a relatively recent phenomenon.

Second, the progressively greater scope of presidential budget authority was challenged only when Congress and the Presidency came into sharp political dispute over claims that the executive had abused its authority during the Nixon and, to a lesser extent, the Rea-

[51] See Wildavsky, *The New Politics of the Budgetary Process,* chap. 10. A comprehensive analysis of budgeting and the deficit problem in the 1980s can be found in Joseph White and Aaron Wildavsky, *The Deficit and the Public Interest* (Berkeley: University of California Press, 1990).

[52] See Penner and Abramson, *Broken Purse Strings,* chap. 7; Loren A. Smith, "Administration," in *The Fettered Presidency,* ed. by L. Gordon Crovitz and Jeremy Rabkin (Washington, D.C.: American Enterprise Institute, 1989), pp. 159–168. National Legal Center for the Public Interest, *Pork Barrels and Principles* (Washington, D.C.: NLCPI, 1988).

gan years. Third, the increase in presidential budget power could not have occurred without congressional willingness to delegate authority to the executive and give the President powers which allowed the executive to unify and consolidate executive branch budgetary dealings through the OMB. Congress was thus an active partner in altering the balance of power. Yet even when Congress has attempted to impose some limits, as in 1921 and 1974, Presidents have found ways to circumvent or exploit existing powers.

Fourth, the power balance between the branches is a dynamic process, subject to shifts dictated by political necessity or initiative. Fifth, the dominant historical trend, as in most areas, has been away from Congress and toward the presidency. This does not mean that Congress is no longer an important player or that Presidents can expect to get whatever they propose, but it does mean that the President's budget has become "The Country's Number One Political and Priorities Document."[53]

LEGAL EXPLANATION: THE LEGISLATIVE VETO

The study of legal relationships was the first important means for studying executive-legislative relations. Both branches are defined by the words of the Constitution, a legally binding document. The study of constitutional law, statutory law (law passed by Congress), and administrative law (legally binding regulations emanating from administrative agencies), while often viewed as the province of lawyers and legal scholars, is no less important to an understanding of interbranch relations than are other perspectives. In recent decades legal perspectives have been neglected in favor of other methods of analysis, but such events as Watergate, Iran-contra, and the bicentennial of the U.S. Constitution have helped redirect attention to the rules and structures that govern interbranch relations. These events serve to remind us that law and politics are not separate; rather, law is the codification of politics.[54]

This section examines a lively and enduring interbranch contro-

---

[53] Shuman, *Politics and the Budget,* p. 1.

[54] For more on the return to legal analysis, see Louis Fisher, "Making Use of Legal Sources," in *Studying the Presidency,* ed. by George C. Edwards III and Stephen J. Wayne (Knoxville: University of Tennessee Press, 1983), pp. 182–198.

versy founded in law and constitutional interpretation. Despite a 1983 Supreme Court ruling that seemingly concluded the legislative veto controversy, both the power and the controversy surrounding it continue.

Congress Gets a Veto

The legislative veto power came into being in the 1930s during the Hoover administration as a means for Congress to maintain some control over administrative actions yet allow administrative agencies and the President more discretion after Congress enacted legislation. A legislative veto, sometimes referred to as a congressional veto, "is an effort by Congress, by one house of Congress, or even by a single committee or chairman to retain control over the execution or interpretation of laws *after* enactment."[55] A legislative veto typically stipulates that Congress must be notified of an action to be taken by the executive branch with the proviso that the action will occur after a specified period of time unless Congress votes (by means short of a public law) within that period to block the action.

A legislative veto differs from regular legislative action in that it does not cross the President's desk for signature or veto, although the authority creating a legislative veto must be enacted in prior legislation that does cross the President's desk. In this way Congress can reserve to itself the right to review and disapprove present and future actions. For example, a law passed by Congress and signed by the President in 1980 required the Federal Trade Commission to present to Congress any proposed FTC regulations. These rules would become effective ninety days after receipt by Congress unless Congress voted by concurrent resolution (a majority vote in both houses) to disallow any of the rules. By definition, a concurrent resolution does not cross the President's desk.

Up to the end of the 1960s most legislative veto provisions pertained to executive branch reorganization. The 1970s, however, wit-

[55] Barbara Hinkson Craig, *The Legislative Veto* (Boulder, Colo.: Westview, 1983), p. 8. See also Louis Fisher and Ronald C. Moe, "Delegating with Ambivalence," *Studies on the Legislative Veto,* Rules Committee, House of Representatives, 96th Congress, 2d sess. (Washington, D.C.: U.S. Government Printing Office, February 1980); James L. Sundquist, *The Decline and Resurgence of Congress* (Washington, D.C.: Brookings Institution, 1981), pp. 344–346; and Louis Fisher, *Constitutional Conflicts between Congress and the President* (Princeton, N.J.: Princeton University Press, 1985), pp. 166–168.

nessed a profound increase in both the number and variety of legislative vetoes. From 1970 to 1980, for example, Congress enacted 248 laws that included 423 legislative veto provisions.[56]

Some of the best known and most controversial legislative veto provisions were enacted in the early 1970s. In 1973, the War Powers Resolution included a provision giving Congress the power to direct the President by concurrent resolution to withdraw American troops from foreign intervention sixty days after the outbreak of hostilities (see Chapter 6). The 1974 Budget Act discussed earlier in this chapter included a legislative veto provision for rescissions (by simple or single-house resolution). The International Security Assistance and Arms Export Control Act of 1976 required the President to inform Congress of any plan to sell weapons to other countries. Congress then had thirty days to disapprove of the sale by concurrent resolution (this was changed to a joint resolution after the *Chadha* case).[57]

Legislative vetoes have been used in such legislation as NASA and Department of Defense reorganization, executive decisions pertaining to the Tariff Commission, disbursement of highway funding to the states, international applications of atomic energy, and federal grant termination for failure to comply with federal civil rights standards. While legislative vetoes have appeared in most varieties of legislation, they seem to be used most often for "distributive" policies, that is, policies pertaining to federal contracts, grants, construction, and other subsidy or pork barrel activities.[58]

Arguments Pro and Con

The legislative veto has engendered a prolonged and heated legal and constitutional debate. President Hoover's attorney general,

---

[56] Craig, *The Legislative Veto,* p. 27.

[57] For more on these cases, see Murray Dry, "The Congressional Veto and the Constitutional Separation of Powers," in *The Presidency in the Constitutional Order,* ed. by Joseph M. Bessette and Jeffrey Tulis (Baton Rouge: Louisiana State University Press, 1981), pp. 195–233.

[58] Joseph Cooper, "The Legislative Veto in the 1980s," in *Congress Reconsidered,* ed. by Lawrence C. Dodd and Bruce I. Oppenheimer (Washington, D.C.: CQ Press, 1985), pp. 368–369; Lawrence C. Dodd and Richard L. Schott, *Congress and the Administrative State* (New York: Wiley, 1979), pp. 235–236; Susan L. Roberts, "The Legislative Veto and the New Politics," a paper delivered at the Annual Meeting of the American Political Science Association, Washington, D.C., August 29–September 4, 1984.

William Mitchell, thought the device was an improper congressional invasion of executive power, and Presidents since Hoover have been similarly skeptical. President Carter said, "Such intrusive devices infringe on the Executive's constitutional duty to faithfully execute the laws. They also authorize congressional action that has the effect of legislation while denying the President the opportunity to exercise his veto."[59] The only recent President to indicate any support for this power was Ronald Reagan, during a 1980 campaign speech. After assuming office, however, Reagan reversed his stand.[60] Despite their doubts, neither President ever vetoed legislation because it contained such a provision.

Members of Congress have also had doubts about the power, in part because of the recognition that legislative vetoes historically were usually advantageous to the executive because they granted Presidents new or broad powers and because the congressional veto check would not often come into play. As Representative Jack Brooks (D-Tex.) wryly noted about one legislative veto in 1977, it was the "best unconstitutional bill you could draw up."[61] Yet doubts in both branches of government have not deterred hundreds of these provisions from being passed and signed into law.

Arguments against the legislative veto rest primarily on three constitutional principles: presentment, bicameralism, and execution. Critics have asserted that this power violates the presentment clause of Article I, Section 7, of the Constitution, which says that "every bill" emanating from the legislature must be presented to the President for signature or veto. While prior enabling authority does pass the President's desk for signature or veto, the legislative veto itself does not. Related to this is the assertion that the legislative veto seems to reverse the normal relationship between the two branches, since the President or an agency takes an action unless Congress "vetoes" the action.

Second, in the case of one-house or committee-instigated legislative vetoes, the principle of bicameralism (Article I, Section 1) is said to be violated in that action may take place without approval from both houses. Third, the power is said to infringe on the executive's constitutional duty to "take care that the laws be faithfully executed"

---

[59] Quoted in Sundquist, *The Decline and Resurgence of Congress*, p. 355.

[60] Sundquist, *The Decline and Resurgence of Congress*, p. 354.

[61] Quoted in Fisher, *Constitutional Conflicts*, p. 167.

(Article II, Section 3) because of the way Congress uses the veto to direct administrative action.

In arguing for the legislative veto, proponents point out that Congress legally delegates rule-making authority to executive branch agencies and the President with regularity, and given that this occurs, it follows that Congress may circumscribe or limit that delegated power by making it subject to subsequent review by Congress. As one member of Congress observed, "If Congress has the power to delegate rulemaking authority, it is axiomatic that it can delegate all that power, or it can condition or limit that delegated power by making it subject to a Congressional veto."[62]

Second, although the legislative veto is not subject to presidential assent, it is based on prior statutory authority, which must cross the President's desk, consistent with presentment. Third, the legislative veto has proved to be an important means by which Congress can conduct administrative oversight. More to the point, despite impressions to the contrary, legislative vetoes have not been foisted on agencies or the President; for the most part, they exist because of mutual consent that this is a reasonable means for interbranch interaction.

Fourth, the argument that the legislative veto violates the finely wrought constitutional principles of bicameralism, presentment, and execution ignores the blending of powers that is a keystone of the national governmental system (see the discussion in Chapter 1). Congress legislates, yet the executive plays an essential role in that process. The President executes the law, yet the administrative apparatus that composes the executive branch was created and is funded by Congress. The mechanics of the legislative process are often subject to shortcuts, such as conducting business by unanimous consent and bypassing committees in certain instances. As political scientist Murray Dry noted, the legislative veto "satisfies the objectives of efficiency and political balance implicit in the separation of powers."[63] As Justice Byron White noted, the legislative veto "no more invades the President's powers than does a regulation not required to be laid before Congress."[64]

---

[62] Quoted in Sundquist, *The Decline and Resurgence of Congress,* p. 355.

[63] Dry, "The Congressional Veto," p. 228.

[64] *Buckley v. Valeo,* 424 U.S. 1 (1976), at 285. Arguments over the legislative veto are summarized in Rules Committee, House of Representatives, "Recommendations on Establishment of Procedures for Congressional Review of Agency Rules," 96th Cong., 2d Sess. (Washington, D.C.: U.S. Government Printing Office, March 1980).

The Court Rules . . .

The arguments for and against the legislative veto came to a head in the court case *Immigration and Naturalization Service v. Chadha.*[65] Speaking for a seven-member majority, Chief Justice Burger stated in June 1983 that the legislative veto violated the presentment clause and the principle of bicameralism, as the *Chadha* case involved a one-house veto. The majority recognized the convenience of the device but rejected this as a justification for the power. Justice White dissented on the merits of the case, saying that the power was entirely consistent with the Constitution and that the legislative veto was "an important if not indispensable political invention that allows the President and Congress to resolve major constitutional and policy differences, assures the accountability of independent regulatory agencies, and preserves Congress' control over lawmaking."[66] Justice Rehnquist dissented on more narrow, technical grounds. The following month the Court upheld two lower court rulings striking down one- and two-house legislative vetoes.[67]

The *Chadha* case was hailed by some but criticized by others. Constitutional specialist Louis Fisher, for example, argued that the Court majority "played fast and free with history" when it rejected the importance of efficiency and convenience in interbranch relations. Indeed, according to Fisher, "efficiency was highly valued by the framers." In the case of legislative vetoes pertaining to presidential action, Fisher pointed out that the President is not in fact deprived of influence, as Presidents are responsible for sending measures to Congress for possible legislative veto. Congress has no power to amend these submissions; it can only vote them up or down. If Congress disapproves, the status quo remains.[68]

. . . But the Veto Remains

After *Chadha*, Congress moved to repeal some legislative veto provisions, but despite the sweeping nature of the *Chadha* case, the legislative veto is still being employed. In fact, from the time of the *Chadha* ruling in 1983 to 1986, Congress enacted 102 legislative veto

[65] 462 U.S. 919 (1983).

[66] Quoted in Craig, *The Legislative Veto,* p. 192.

[67] For more on the *Chadha* case, see Barbara Hinkson Craig, *Chadha* (New York: Oxford University Press, 1988).

[68] Fisher, *Constitutional Conflicts,* pp. 179–180.

provisions involving 24 laws through "ingenious and novel methods"[69] developed jointly between Congress and federal agencies. From 1986 to 1990 an additional 100 provisions were enacted.[70] Most take the form of committee vetoes. To cite some obvious post-*Chadha* examples explicitly stated in statutes, Environmental Protection Agency construction grants approved during the ninety-seventh Congress required approval from the appropriations committees, as did expenditures beyond set dollar amounts for the National Flood Insurance Fund.

Other provisions are more subtle, as they are not written into law. For example, certain appropriations for the District of Columbia were to be spent only with prior approval from certain congressional committees according to procedures described in committee reports. In 1984 an agreement was reached between NASA and the appropriations committees which stipulated that the legislative veto provisions formerly employed to govern NASA spending would no longer be enacted but that NASA would agree to voluntarily comply with committee recommendations concerning spending. In other words, NASA agreed to comply with the wishes of the committees even though they were not legally binding.[71]

An important consequence of the *Chadha* case was that regulations formerly enacted as legislative vetoes continue to be promulgated as not legally binding agreements. The terms of these agreements, as in the cases mentioned above, often appear in committee reports rather than in laws. This means that agencies are not legally bound to such agreements, but both Congress and the agencies understand that it is in the interest of both to continue to make such agreements and abide by them. If an agency agrees to such an arrangement but violates it later, Congress has no immediate legal recourse, but it can penalize the agency through the annual appropria-

[69] Louis Fisher, "Judicial Misjudgments about the Lawmaking Process," *Public Administration Review*, 45 (November 1985): 705. See also Louis Fisher and James Saturno, "Legislative Vetoes Enacted after *Chadha*," Report No. 87–389 GOV, Congressional Research Service, Library of Congress, April 28, 1987.

[70] From communication with Louis Fisher. For an excellent analysis of the political and legal consequences of the *Chadha* case, see Jessica Korn, "The Political Effects of Separation of Powers Jurisprudence: The Case of *Chadha* and the Legislative Veto," a paper delivered at the 1991 Annual Meeting of the American Political Science Association, Washington, D.C., August 29–September 1.

[71] Fisher, "Judicial Misjudgments," pp. 706–707.

tions process or through other oversight means. These agreements "are not legal in effect. They are, however, in effect legal."[72]

Assessment

What prohibition was to liquor, *Chadha* is to the legislative veto. Many legislative-veto-type agreements have been driven underground, although they are in plain view to anyone who reads committee reports, correspondence, and other documents. Some provisions are enforced by relying on House and Senate rules governing internal procedures, as such rules require only the approval of the affected chamber to take effect. Other legislative veto provisions continue to exist and operate in seeming violation of *Chadha*. According to Fisher, *Chadha* has resulted in "a record of non-compliance, subtle evasion, and a system of lawmaking that is now more convoluted, cumbersome, and covert than before."[73]

The legislative veto persists because of the continuing need to accommodate the goals of both Congress and the federal administrative apparatus.[74] If Congress were to rely on the regular lawmaking process to enact into law the sorts of provisions formerly enacted by legislative veto, it would find itself overwhelmed by a flood of legislation concerned with minute administrative matters that would further slow an already time-consuming legislative process. It would also mean that administrative agencies seeking congressional permission to change a procedure set in law would have to devote considerable time and resources to expedite the change.

However, if Congress simply abandoned these efforts to retain control over agency activities, it would result in a bureaucracy even less accountable to elected representatives, a result that most Americans, and most people in government, would find unacceptable. In short, the legislative veto persists because it continues to allow both administrative discretion and congressional influence. Regardless of whether the *Chadha* case was good or bad law, this case provides a clear example of a vital political accommodation between the branches that was not impeded by a sweeping court ruling.

---

[72] Fisher, "Judicial Misjudgments," p. 708.

[73] Fisher, "Judicial Misjudgments," p. 711.

[74] See Daniel P. Franklin, "Why the Legislative Veto Isn't Dead," *Presidential Studies Quarterly*, 16 (Summer 1986): 491–502.

One might be tempted to conclude from this case that law is irrelevant, especially in the post-*Chadha* world. On the contrary, this admittedly unusual case underscores two vital facts about the legal explanation. First, law provides the framework and structure within which political processes operate. Even when those processes operate outside of legal structures, as in this case, an understanding of the legal structure is vital to an understanding of the nature and direction of that process. Second, law is the codified expression of politics. Legislative veto provisions express in law a political arrangement suitable to congressional-executive relations. The *Chadha* case was an expression, if a contrary one, of the Court's perspective on interbranch relations. A legal approach is both powerful and political, therefore making it highly useful for understanding presidential-congressional relations. If the *Chadha* case is good law, the actions of Congress, federal agencies, and even the President suggest that the case is bad politics—a reminder that law and politics are inseparable.

POLICY EXPLANATION: POLICY TYPES

The study of public policy as it affects presidential-congressional relations has long and deep roots. After all, most of the struggles that bring the two branches together concern the nature and direction of national policy. The organization of congressional committees is based on policy subjects, from agriculture to veterans' affairs. White House staff organization also has a strong policy orientation.

One can therefore hardly study presidential-congressional relations without including some attention to policy. Yet most of the attention to policy takes one of two forms: a case study of a particular policy issue or set of issues[75] or a focus on the policy process.[76] Re-

---

[75] For example, see Stephen K. Bailey, *Congress Makes a Law* (New York: Vintage, 1964); Eugene Eidenberg and Roy D. Morey, *An Act of Congress* (New York: Norton, 1969); Ruth Morgan, *The President and Civil Rights* (New York: St. Martin's, 1970); John A. Ferejohn, *Pork Barrel Politics* (Stanford, Calif.: Stanford University Press, 1974); Eric Redman, *The Dance of Legislation* (New York: Simon & Schuster, 1973).

[76] See for example, James L. Sundquist, *Politics and Policy* (Washington, D.C.: Brookings Institution, 1968); William Lammers, *Presidential Politics* (New York: Harper & Row, 1976); Steven A. Shull, *Presidential Policy Making* (Brunswick, Ohio: King's Court Communications, 1979); George C. Edwards III, Steven A. Shull, and Norman C. Thomas, eds., *The Presidency and Public Policy Making* (Pittsburgh: University of Pittsburgh Press, 1985); David C. Kozak and John D. Macartney, eds., *Congress and Public Policy* (Chicago: Dorsey, 1987). The books mentioned in the previous footnote are also concerned with process but focus on a single policy or policy area.

gardless of the particular approach taken, however, policy is typically viewed as something to be explained (otherwise known as the dependent variable); in other words, policy is best understood as the product or outcome of various political forces.

In contrast, a few studies have sought to demonstrate that policy can be an important explanatory force in presidential-congressional relations, and it is with this perspective in mind that we look to policy as an explanatory or independent variable. The best known policy-based explanation posits that Presidents are more likely to be successful in their dealings with Congress in the realm of foreign policy compared with domestic policy, an assertion that will be examined in Chapter 5.

The Arenas of Power

Within the realm of domestic policy, several studies have concluded that different policies, such as those dealing with social benefits, civil rights, crime control, public works, government management, and agriculture, have different political patterns that help explain presidential and congressional actions.[77] As political scientist Steven Shull noted, "variations in the content of policies . . . produce variations in the roles and behavior of actors."[78]

This logic has been taken further by one of the nation's leading policy theorists, Theodore J. Lowi, who argues that different types of policies engender their own unique politics or sets of political relationships.[79] Stated simply, policy causes politics. According to Lowi's scheme, called the arenas of power, particular policies are subsumed under one of four policy categories: distributive, regulatory, redistributive, or constituent. According to the logic of the scheme, each policy type produces its own unique political patterns. For example, the President has far more influence over a redistributive policy,

[77] See Aage R. Clausen, *How Congressmen Decide* (New York: St. Martin's, 1973); John W. Kingdon, *Congressmen's Voting Decisions* (New York: Harper & Row, 1973); and Steven A. Shull, *Domestic Policy Formation: Presidential-Congressional Partnership?* (Westport, Conn.: Greenwood, 1983).

[78] Shull, *Domestic Policy Formation*, p. 10.

[79] Lowi proposed this scheme in "American Business, Public Policy, Case Studies, and Political Theory," *World Politics*, 16 (July 1964): 677–715. See also "Four Systems of Policy, Politics, and Choice," *Public Administration Review*, 32 (July–August 1972): 298–310. Critical discussion of the scheme is summarized in Robert J. Spitzer, "Promoting Policy Theory: Revising the Arenas of Power," *Policy Studies Journal*, 15 (June 1987): 675–689.

such as welfare reform or a tax package, than over a distributive policy, such as river and harbor legislation, where Congress is more influential.[80]

The Four Presidencies

In my own study of presidential-congressional policy-making, I applied the arenas of power scheme to the President's annual legislative programs from 1954 to 1974 (a total of about 5,500 legislative proposals) to observe if policy type had an effect on presidential-congressional interactions. Specifically, I sought to observe the impact of policy type on (1) the degree of presidential influence, (2) the degree of presidential involvement and success, and (3) the degree of political conflict. All three components pertain to the fate of the President's legislative proposals in Congress.[81]

Table 4.3 summarizes these findings. It can be seen from the table that the President's influence is greatest in the area of constituent policies—policies dealing with the running of the government—but that Presidents are less heavily involved in this area than in redistributive policies. The degree of political conflict surrounding constituent policies is lowest of the four policy areas. That is, Congress, the President, and other political figures find themselves fighting and disagreeing less over constituent policies than over any other type. By contrast, presidential influence over regulatory policies is less than for any other policy type. The President's success in this area is lowest, and the degree of political conflict is, not surprisingly, highest.

Political scientist Mark Peterson applied these categories to presidential proposals, examining legislative offerings from Eisenhower to Reagan. He, too, noted that Presidents favor redistributive and constituent policies, that Congress tends to favor distributive policies but that presidential distribution often does not fare well in Congress, and that regulatory policies are the most conflictual.[82]

---

[80] These general patterns are verified in Shull, *Domestic Policy Formation,* p. 147; and Randall B. Ripley and Grace A. Franklin, *Congress, the Bureaucracy, and Public Policy* (Pacific Grove, Calif.: Brooks/Cole, 1991), chap. 8.

[81] Robert J. Spitzer, *The Presidency and Public Policy: The Four Arenas of Presidential Power* (University: University of Alabama Press, 1983). The analysis incorporated three levels: the full universe of about 5,500 presidential legislative proposals, 165 selected cases subjected to more detailed analysis, and 8 case studies.

[82] Peterson, *Legislating Together,* pp. 175–181.

Table 4.3 Rank Orderings for Types of Bills According to Presidential Influence, Presidential Involvement, and Political Conflict

	Degree of Presidential Influence	Presidential Involvement and Success	Degree of Political Conflict
Constituent ("administrative")	1	2–3	4
Redistributive ("public interest")	2	1	2
Distributive ("special interest")	3	2–3	3
Regulatory ("broker")	4	4	1

Note: 1 = highest; 4 = lowest.

SOURCE: Robert J. Spitzer, *The Presidency and Public Policy* (University of Alabama Press, 1983). Reprinted with permission.

These patterns yielded "four presidencies" pertaining to the President's interaction with Congress. The "administrative President" arises when the President proposes constituent policies, or those related to the running of the government, including such areas as government reorganization, election laws, and budgeting. As chief executive, the President is seen as having great authority over such administrative, overhead matters. Thus, Presidents have the greatest success in dealing with Congress when they advance constituent policy legislation. Involvement in this area is less politically rewarding for Presidents than is involvement in other policy areas, however, because constituent policies usually attract little attention or interest in the country.

The "public interest President" results from presidential concern with redistributive policies. These are policies that are broad in scope, affecting broad classes of people. Examples include social security, welfare, and taxation. The nationwide scope of redistributive policies means that Congress looks for presidential leadership in this area, and Presidents in turn are expected to take the lead in addressing these problems. The politics that results may be contentious, but Presidents usually log important successes in this area. Because of the larger scope of and greater interest in redistributive policies in

Congress and the country, presidential success is not as easily realized for these policies as it is for constituent policies. Despite this, Presidents take a strong interest in redistributive policies insofar as decisive presidential involvement in this area is often a litmus test of presidential leadership.

The "special-interest President" emerges when the President proposes distributive policies. These are policies that are narrow in scope and purpose and are also often labeled patronage or pork barrel policies. Presidents can be politically influential when proposing these policies to Congress, but they must pay careful attention to congressional preferences. Distributive policies, such as construction projects, river and harbor legislation, and national park and other land use policies, have direct effects on the economies of the localities where they are targeted, and individual members of Congress take keen interest in such "bread and butter" projects when they involve their districts. Thus, when Presidents challenge congressional preferences in this area, they are likely to face a fierce struggle.

Presidents assume a "presidential broker" role when dealing with regulatory policies. These policies involve the formation and enforcement of laws that manipulate economic and social conduct, usually through the use of sanctions and penalties. Common examples include regulations affecting unfair competition, elimination of substandard goods, gun control, and antitrust activity. Presidents often attempt to take the lead in this area but also are often frustrated, having the least legislative success. Regulatory policies by their nature arouse deep conflicts between those doing the regulating and those being regulated; thus, even Presidents at the peak of power, such as Lyndon Johnson after his election in 1964, often find the enactment of such proposals in Congress to be extremely difficult.[83]

Figure 4.2 summarizes these relationships. The two arrows in the center of the diagram illustrate the tendency of presidents to cast distributive issues in broader, redistributive terms as a means of establishing broad national appeal and the contrary tendency of Congress to cast redistributive issues in distributive terms in order to "disaggregate" such policies. That is, Congress has a tendency to redefine redistributive issues so that they can be broken into discrete parts to

---

[83] The patterns described for regulatory policies are confirmed in Raymond Tatalovich and Byron W. Daynes, eds., *Social Regulatory Policy* (Boulder, Colo.: Westview, 1988).

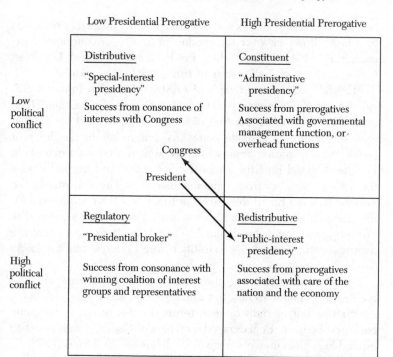

Figure 4.2   The Arenas of Power Applied to Presidential Policy Making

SOURCE: Reprinted by permission from Robert J. Spitzer, *The Presidency and Public Policy* (University, Ala.: University of Alabama Press, 1983), p. 152. Reprinted by permission.

provide specific, concrete benefits for members of Congress in their home districts.[84] Two brief cases illustrate these tendencies.

The Lockheed Case.   An example of Presidents seeking to redefine a distributive issue in redistributive terms is the case of President Nixon's handling of a 1971 bill that provided a $250 million loan guarantee to the Lockheed Aircraft Corporation. Lockheed was the nation's largest defense contractor, with 95 percent of its work tied to government, mostly defense, contracts. In the early 1970s, however, it encountered considerable financial problems as a result of ques-

[84] See Peterson, *Legislating Together*, p. 180.

tionable business practices and cost overruns. Its finanical woes came to a head, however, over the production of a new commercial aircraft, the L-1011 Tristar airbus. Private lenders refused Lockheed further credit, and so the company turned to the government.

This bill was a clear example of a distributive policy in that it provided a specific, concrete benefit to a particular organization. However, the Nixon administration did not defend the bill for what it was—a bailout for a single company—but rather in far different terms. Administration representatives argued that failure to help Lockheed would hurt the national employment picture and hinder the nation's recovery from economic recession. The chairman of the Federal Reserve Board went so far as to say that the board "is not interested in preserving big business as such. . . . We are interested in protecting the national economy."[85] The administration even sent the deputy secretary of defense to testify before Congress that the Lockheed bill was not a defense matter but an economic issue.

By attempting to frame the issue in terms of national employment and economic trends, the administration was trying to define a distributive bill in redistributive terms. In this instance the tactic backfired because it encouraged members of Congress to attempt to expand loan guarantee coverage to small businesses, farmers, and educational and health institutions. If these measures had been added, the bill's potential cost would have ballooned. Eventually, after fierce partisan wrangling, Congress returned to and passed the original Lockheed-only bill.

The Area Redevelopment Act.   A top priority of the newly elected Democratic Kennedy administration was passage of a bill to aid those parts of the country hardest hit by adverse economic times. The purpose of such a measure was to assist areas of the country beset by chronic unemployment and economic hardship. In this respect, area redevelopment was a redistributive policy in that it was designed to manipulate national economic patterns by improving economic conditions for those who were less well off. Several efforts to enact such an area redevelopment bill in the late 1950s were frustrated by the Republican President, Dwight Eisenhower.

On taking office in 1961, Kennedy joined with congressional leaders to propose a $394 million package of loans and grants to pro-

---

[85] Quoted in Spitzer, *The Presidency and Public Policy*, p. 50.

vide aid over a four-year period to urban and rural areas suffering high unemployment and economic hardship. The administration feared that a coalition of Republicans and conservative southern Democrats would sink the bill, but support was won because of two key aspects of the bill.

First, most of the aid provided by the bill would not go directly to needy individuals, as with such redistributive policies as social security or welfare. Rather, most of the money was to go to local governments and private industry in the designated areas, and the program's administrators were to have considerable discretion over these disbursement decisions. Second, areas slated to receive the aid were spread around the country but were concentrated in border and southern states. To drive the point home, a large map was set up in the lobby of the House Speaker's office showing the location of the areas projected to receive aid. One southern representative commented on the "vote-getting proclivities" of the bill.[86] Needless to say, the votes of many conservative southern representatives were won by this provision.

While the design of this bill was redistributive, members of Congress sought and obtained a bill that possessed distributive qualities, as seen especially in the way the bill would be administered. That is, the bill would award discrete, particularized, concrete benefits for which members of Congress could claim credit when it was time to deliver federal checks to local government officials and business leaders. This credit claiming was facilitated because the aid went to intermediaries in geographically depressed regions rather than directly to needy people. In this way, Congress often seeks to disaggregate redistributive policies in a distributive direction.

Assessment

One student of Congress, David Vogler, commented that the policy-as-explanation-for-politics approach is a way to "uncover new ground for understanding the politics of Congress."[87] Among the several explanations of presidential-congressional relations discussed in this chapter, the policy approach is relatively new and underexplored. Even so, the policy explanation holds true despite such factors as dif-

[86] Quoted in Spitzer, *The Presidency and Public Policy*, p. 79.
[87] David J. Vogler, *The Politics of Congress* (Boston: Allyn & Bacon, 1988), p. 271.

ferences in the President's party affiliation, reputed leadership skills, and party support in Congress.[88]

The policy approach also can be used to subsume other explanations. For example, it posits that the politics of regulatory policies is relatively wide open and pluralistic, whereas the politics of distributive policies is lower in visibility and conflict in that it is focused on "subgovernments": close-knit networks of congressional committees, federal agencies, and interest groups that tend to be like-minded and mutually supportive in their approach to policy issues. The scheme asserts that presidential leadership of the sort described at the start of this chapter is more likely to occur and more likely to succeed in the realm of redistributive policies than in other policy areas. In short, the potency of the policy explanation has yet to be fully tested; its promise, however, is considerable.[89]

CONCLUSION

Politics, history, law, and policy are the cornerstones of the presidential-congressional relationship. Any reader or analyst who maintains a grasp of these dimensions can claim considerable insight into the workings of these two institutions. From these perspectives we can also observe the roots and impact of executive hegemony. The normative bias toward executives inherent in the leadership explanation is the most obvious instance of the hegemonic drive. The historical accumulation of budgetary powers by Presidents in the twentieth century was, it now seems, interrupted only briefly and temporarily by the budget reforms of the 1970s and 1980s. The lessons of the legislative veto are less clear, yet the Supreme Court, in siding with the President, continued the pattern of court rulings leaning toward the executive. And the accommodations that members of Congress and federal agencies continue to seek through informal legislative veto

[88] For example, Ripley and Franklin, *Congress, the Bureaucracy, and Public Policy.* Lowi's book on the presidency applies a policy analysis to the evolution of the modern presidency. See *The Personal President* (Ithaca, N.Y.: Cornell University Press, 1985). A similar policy analysis is applied comparatively in T. Alexander Smith, *The Comparative Policy Process* (Santa Barbara, Calif.: Clio, 1975).

[89] Gary King and Lyn Ragsdale emphasize this point in *The Elusive Executive* (Washington, D.C.: CQ Press, 1988), p. 60. Peterson's analysis confirms these policy trends, but he places them in a broader policy-analytic context. See *Legislating Together,* chap. 5.

agreements in the aftermath of the *Chadha* case mock statements by Presidents that such arrangements are illegal or inappropriate. Finally, the policy explanation suggests that the executive-legislative balance may vary in predictable ways according to policy type. This notion does not contradict this book's arguments but does suggest a possible avenue for reconciling apparently conflicting views of presidential-congressional behavior. It is an approach that invites further exploration.

To return to the leadership approach, this chapter began by paying special attention to the leadership explanation as a means of understanding the presidential-congressional dynamic. Leadership is a theme that pervades both scholarly and popular analysis. Yet George Edwards's systematic study of presidential leadership skills in Congress, as well as that of Bond and Fleisher, concluded that legislative skills play at best a small role in explaining administration successes. Edwards focused in particular on the modern President who seemed to possess the greatest such leadership skills, Lyndon Johnson. Taking the Johnson administration as a "best-case" analysis, Edwards found the leadership variable to be at best a marginal explanatory factor, leading to the general conclusion that "while legislative skills may at times gain support for presidential policies, this is not typical. Thus, what seems to be the most manipulatable source of presidential influence is probably the least powerful."[90]

The leadership perspective will continue to be seductive not only because it is seen as "the most manipulatable source of presidential influence" but because of the plain desire for presidential leadership of Congress and the nation. It will also continue to be good advice for Presidents and consonant with the pervasive symbolism that surrounds the office—facts that have been and will continue to be reflected in writings on the presidency.[91]

However, the main conclusion of this chapter is that the explanation for presidential-congressional interactions does not and should not rest solely or even primarily with the President's leadership skills. On an empirical or factual level, the leadership explanation is limited. In a normative respect, it is inherently biased in favor of strong, activist Presidents. The propriety of this bias is not the issue here; what

[90] Edwards, *Presidential Influence in Congress*, p. 10.

[91] For more on these themes, see Cronin, *The State of the Presidency*, chap. 3; Lowi, *The Personal President*; George E. Reedy, *The Twilight of the Presidency* (New York: New American Library, 1987).

is at issue is the fact that this bias undergirds leadership analysis, a fact which is often unrecognized. It may therefore color analytic judgment when applied to the study of presidential-congressional relations.

Second, an appreciation of history, law, and policy is no less important for the manner in which they frame interbranch relations. The four explanations discussed in this chapter provide a more macroscopic, overarching perspective on interbranch relations that allows one to see beyond the particulars of any single case, Congress, or presidential administration. The interweaving of these four factors will be very evident in Chapters 5 and 6.

Chapter 5

Foreign Affairs I: Who Steers the Ship of State?

The President is to be commander-in-chief of the army and navy of the United States. In this respect his authority would be nominally the same with that of the king of Great Britain, but in substance much inferior to it. It would amount to nothing more than the supreme command and direction of the military and naval forces, as first general and admiral of the Confederacy; while that of the British king extends to the *declaring* of war and to the *raising* and *regulating* of fleets and armies—all which, by the Constitution under consideration, would appertain to the legislature.

ALEXANDER HAMILTON, *FEDERALIST* NO. 69

Our external affairs, in short, are all but entirely in the hands of the Chief Executive.

BERNARD SCHWARTZ, *A COMMENTARY ON THE CONSTITUTION OF THE UNITED STATES*, 1963, P. 101.

The first major foreign policy initiative of the Bush administration caught supporters and critics by surprise. On March 24, 1989, President Bush announced that he had reached a bipartisan agreement with opposition Democratic leaders in Congress on an issue that had nearly destroyed the Reagan administration: aid to the Nicaraguan rebels, who were also known as contras. Congress agreed to provide $4.5 million in nonlethal supplies per month to the contras—food, clothing, medical supplies, and shelter—through February 1990, when Nicaragua would hold free elections. But in addition, Bush would not be allowed to send any aid to the contras after November 1989 without specific approval from four congressional committees

137

and congressional party leaders. Failure to receive letters of approval from all these committees and leaders would mean the interruption of aid.

Many of President Bush's critics hailed the agreement, engineered by Secretary of State James Baker, as a positive step toward consensus-based foreign policy. Senator Edward Kennedy (D-Mass.) called the agreement "an excellent compromise."[1] Some conservatives, however, expressed dismay, feeling that the agreement represented an improper encroachment on the President's constitutional powers in foreign affairs. The President's counsel, C. Boyden Gray, expressed public irritation at the agreement and at Baker's failure to consult with him before the agreement was announced. Gray's criticism resulted in a public rebuke by the White House chief of staff, John Sununu.[2]

The agreement was politically significant for several reasons. First, it represented a major departure from the Nicaragua policy of the Reagan administration. Secretary Baker acknowledged as much when he commented that Reagan's policy "basically failed. . . . We had an executive branch going in one direction and a legislative branch going in another."[3] Reagan's unswerving commitment to contra funding and the overthrow of the Sandinista regime led to an open breach with Congress, the infusion of $350 million in American aid, and illegal efforts by the Reagan administration to continue aiding the contras by diverting profits from secret arms deals with Iran, resulting in the Iran-contra investigation.

Second, the bipartisan agreement was spurred by the acknowledgment on all sides that without such an agreement, Congress would have stopped all contra funding after a few months. While this was viewed by some as a sign of weakness on the part of the Bush administration, Bush and others argued that the agreement in fact strengthened the President's hand because it produced more contra aid than could have been obtained by any other means. Also, the abrasive confrontation between Reagan and Congress in the 1980s over this issue helped motivate congressional critics to challenge the

[1] Robert Pear, "Contra Plan: A New Deal," *New York Times,* March 25, 1990.

[2] Robert Pear, "Pact Challenged by Bush Counsel," *New York Times,* March 3, 1989; Bernard Weinraub, "White House Rebukes Counsel on Pact," *New York Times,* March 28, 1989. Gray also said that he thought the agreement was an illegal legislative veto. It was not, however, because the agreement was not written into law.

[3] Bernard Weinraub, "Bush and Congress Sign Policy Accord on Aid to Contras," *New York Times,* March 25, 1990.

President on other policies. As Congressman Lee Hamilton (D-Ind.) noted, "You enhance presidential power when you follow the process."[4]

Third, the provision of the agreement giving four congressional committees veto power over future contra aid was not written into law, setting no legal precedent. Despite this, some remained skeptical. Former President Gerald Ford commented, "In some respects, I think he [Bush] gave up some of his presidential prerogatives."[5]

American policy toward Nicaragua was a major source of presidential-congressional friction in the 1980s.[6] It fired long-standing interbranch disputes over such areas as diplomacy, foreign aid, and war making. It illustrated the consequences of protracted political conflict between the branches as well as the ambiguity of constitutional powers and responsibilities. Above all, it affirmed constitutional scholar Edward Corwin's assessment that the Constitution "is an invitation to struggle for the privilege of directing American foreign policy."[7]

In this chapter, the first of two dealing with foreign affairs, we consider two broad topics: a general consideration of the presidential-congressional balance in foreign affairs and the momentous matter of war-making powers. Chapter 6 deals with other powers in foreign affairs, including treaty making, arms sales, foreign aid, "intermestic" issues, and intelligence activities. Appropriately, we begin the examination of foreign policy with the Constitution.

THE EXECUTIVE-LEGISLATIVE BALANCE AND THE CONSTITUTION

As with other constitutionally mandated powers, responsibility for foreign affairs is both divided and shared between the two

[4] Gerald F. Seib, "Bush Vows to Protect Authority, Yet Brings Congress into Decisions," *Wall Street Journal*, September 12, 1989.

[5] Seib, "Bush Vows to Protect Authority."

[6] Ironically, those disputes were resolved not only by the Bush compromise but by free and open elections held in Nicaragua in early 1990, in which Sandinista leader Daniel Ortega was defeated by a rival coalition led by Violeta Barrios de Chamorro. True to his word, Ortega surrendered the presidency to his opponent a few weeks later. For more on U.S. policy toward Central America in the 1980s, see Nora Hamilton, Jeffry A. Frieden, Linda Fuller, and Manuel Pastor, Jr., eds., *Crisis in Central America* (Boulder, Colo.: Westview, 1988).

[7] Edward S. Corwin, *The President: Office and Powers* (New York: New York University Press, 1957), p. 171.

branches.[8] In Article II, Section 2, the President is empowered to serve as "Commander in Chief of the Army and Navy of the United States, and of the Militia of the several States, when called into the actual service of the United States. . . ." The President also has the power to "make treaties" with two-thirds concurrence of the Senate and to nominate "ambassadors, other public ministers and consuls" subject to Senate approval. The President receives ambassadors and must see that the laws are "faithfully executed." In addition, some infer foreign affairs prerogative from Article II, Section 1, which vests "executive power" in the President. Finally, the presidential oath of office requires that the executive "preserve, protect and defend the Constitution of the United States."[9]

Congress is charged with responsibilities pertaining to foreign affairs in Article I, Section 8. It is to "provide for the common defense and general welfare of the United States" and regulate commerce with other nations. It punishes crimes on the high seas and settles "offenses against the law of nations." Congress also has the power to "declare war, grant letters of marque and reprisal, and make rules concerning captures on land and water."[10] It raises and supports the army and provides for a navy, makes rules governing both, calls up and regulates the militia, and makes all laws considered "necessary and proper" to carry out its other responsibilities.

By number and specificity, congressional powers in foreign affairs

[8] For an insightful examination of the tides of American foreign policy in the twentieth century and the key role played by presidents, see Norman A. Graebner, *America as a World Power: A Realist Appraisal from Wilson to Reagan* (Wilmington, Del.: Scholarly Resources, 1984).

[9] For an excellent synthesis of the executive role in foreign affairs, see Barbara Kellerman and Ryan J. Barilleaux, *The President as World Leader* (New York: St. Martin's, 1991).

[10] "Letters of Marque and Reprisal" refers in its strict sense to a now-outdated power that allowed Congress to authorize private individuals to prey on an enemy nation's shipping and property without being labeled pirates. This practice was outlawed by the Declaration of Paris in 1856. The act of reprisal has a broader meaning, however, in that it also refers to governmentally sanctioned retaliation against another nation for an act of belligerency. Such reprisal may be designed to seize property or to be punitive. That this power is also given to Congress makes it clear that "every act of reprisal is an act of war and therefore requires congressional authorization." Francis D. Wormuth and Edwin B. Firmage, *To Chain the Dog of War* (Urbana: University of Illinois Press, 1989), p. 37. In 1793, Secretary of State Thomas Jefferson noted about reprisal that "Congress must be called upon to take it; the right of reprisal being expressly lodged with them by the Constitution, and not with the executive." Quoted in David Gray Adler, "The Constitution and Presidential Warmaking: The Enduring Debate," *Political Science Quarterly*, 103 (Spring 1988): 8.

are undoubtedly greater,[11] yet the course of the management of foreign affairs bears little connection with any such simple counting of
powers. The immediate and foremost fact of the balance of power in
foreign affairs is that it has been hotly debated for over two centuries.
The second most important fact is that the President has gained by
far the most ground in two centuries. As one constitutional scholar
noted about the text of the Constitution, it is a "marvel at how much
Presidents have spun out of so little."[12]

In 1793, for example, President George Washington issued a
proclamation of neutrality in the war between France and Great
Britain. The political consequence of the proclamation was actually
favorable to Britain, as it barred France from raising troops and
money in the United States. Washington's proclamation came at the
urging of Alexander Hamilton, who sympathized with the British.
But pro-French Americans, led by Thomas Jefferson, criticized the
proclamation, arguing that Washington was usurping congressional
authority. To proclaim neutrality was to proclaim the absence of war;
therefore, the power to do so rested with Congress. Alexander
Hamilton defended Washington's action, saying that conducting foreign relations was an executive function, especially in the absence of
a declaration of war from Congress. To satisfy Jefferson, Washington
omitted any reference to the word *neutrality.*[13]

Even though Washington acted unilaterally, he went before
Congress when it reconvened later in the year to explain his actions
and yield to final congressional action. In Washington's words, "It
rests with the wisdom of Congress to correct, improve, or enforce
this plan of procedure. . . ."[14] Congress responded with "hearty ap-
probation."[15]

While the particulars of the neutrality proclamation were amica-
bly settled, they fired a public dispute that was aired in a series of articles in a Philadelphia newspaper written by Hamilton and James

[11] As W. Taylor Reveley III notes, "The text [of the Constitution] tilts decisively toward
Congress." *War Powers of the President and Congress* (Charlottesville: University of
Virginia Press, 1981), p. 29.

[12] Reveley, *War Powers of the President.*

[13] Sidney M. Milkis and Michael Nelson, *The American Presidency* (Washington, D.C.:
CQ Press, 1990), pp. 81–82.

[14] James D. Richardson, ed., *Messages and Papers of the Presidents* (Washington, D.C.:
Bureau of National Literature, 1913), I, p. 131.

[15] Richardson, *Messages and Papers*, I, p. 135.

Madison, who defended the Jeffersonian position (Madison responded because of the urging of Jefferson). Hamilton wrote under the name Pacificus, and Madison under the name Helvidius. In his essays, Hamilton proposed a sweeping view of the presidential prerogative in foreign affairs, arguing that the foreign realm was the natural and inherent domain of the President. Madison flatly contradicted Hamilton's claim, noting congressional sovereignty in such matters as war and peace and the antirepublican nature of Hamilton's argument.[16]

That two of the Constitution's founders would disagree so categorically about fundamental responsibilities so soon after ratification of the Constitution underscores the intensity and persistence of both the constitutional and political debate, yet the actions of other Presidents have been more instructive than the Hamilton-Madison debate. Jefferson, Lincoln, and Franklin Roosevelt, for example, also made similar unilateral foreign policy decisions in times of crisis. Like Washington, however, they were quick to seek subsequent congressional approval and acknowledge that the actions were temporary and had been prompted by emergency situations that would not otherwise justify them.[17]

ARE THERE "TWO PRESIDENCIES"?

Whatever the balance between the two branches, most people agree that presidential-congressional relations are importantly different in the realm of foreign affairs compared with domestic matters. One aspect of this distinction has been extensively debated in recent years. In a brief article that has received more attention than its author could have guessed, political scientist Aaron Wildavsky argued that since the end of World War II Presidents have had far greater success in realizing their foreign policy goals than their domestic policies

[16] The full Pacificus and Helvidius letters can be found in the collective published works of Hamilton and Madison. Excerpts appear in Christopher H. Pyle and Richard M. Pious, *The President, Congress, and the Constitution* (New York: Free Press, 1984), pp. 55–60. Interestingly, Hamilton's position on presidential war powers found little sympathy or support among his contemporaries, including other Federalists. See Charles A. Lofgren, "War-Making under the Constitution: The Original Understanding," *Yale Law Journal*, 81 (March 1972): 700.

[17] Thomas E. Mann, "Making Foreign Policy," in *A Question of Balance*, ed. by Thomas E. Mann (Washington, D.C.: Brookings Institution, 1990), pp. 6–7.

in Congress. This observation led Wildavsky to conclude that there are actually "two presidencies," one for domestic policy and the other for foreign policy. "In the realm of foreign policy," Wildavsky asserted, "there has not been a single major issue on which Presidents, when they were serious and determined, have failed."[18]

Wildavsky's thesis found widespread favor at first, but his arguments came to be challenged on several grounds. First, it was noted that his observation was timebound in that the period of his study—the 1950s and early 1960s—was a time of low congressional assertiveness and relatively high consensus, especially in foreign policy. With the rise of discontent over the Vietnam war and other foreign policy misadventures, such as the presidentially authorized covert CIA meddling in Chile's 1973 presidential election that resulted in the assassination of Salvadore Allende, Congress became more informed and assertive in foreign affairs.[19]

Second, several studies concluded that the higher approval rates in Congress for presidential foreign policy proposals reported by Wildavsky had dropped to almost the same level as approval rates for domestic policy by the late 1960s and 1970s.[20] The only exceptions (by no means unimportant) seemed to be in the Senate and for Republican presidents.[21]

Third, political scientist George Edwards concluded in a careful

---

[18] Aaron Wildavsky, "The Two Presidencies," in *Perspectives on the Presidency,* ed. by Aaron Wildavsky (Boston: Little, Brown, 1975), p. 449.

[19] Donald A. Peppers, "The Two Presidencies: Eight Years Later," in Wildavsky, *Perspectives on the Presidency,* pp. 462–471.

[20] Lance T. LeLoup and Steven A. Shull, "Congress versus the Executive: The 'Two Presidencies' Reconsidered," *Social Science Quarterly,* 59 (March 1979): 704–719; Lee Sigelman, "A Reassessment of the 'Two Presidencies' Thesis," *Journal of Politics,* 41 (November 1979): 1195–1205; exchange between Shull/LeLoup and Sigelman in *Journal of Politics,* 43 (May 1981); Jeffrey E. Cohen, "A Historical Reassessment of Wildavsky's 'Two Presidencies' Thesis," *Social Science Quarterly,* 63 (September 1982): 549–555. See also Steven A. Shull, ed., *The Two Presidencies: A Quarter Century Assessment* (Chicago: Nelson-Hall, 1991).

[21] Harvey G. Zeidenstein, "The 'Two Presidencies' Thesis Is Alive and Well and Has Been Living in the U.S. Senate since 1973," *Presidential Studies Quarterly,* 11 (Fall 1981): 511–525; Richard Fleisher and Jon R. Bond, "Are There Two Presidencies? Yes, but Only for Republicans," *Journal of Politics,* 50 (August 1988): 747–767. Karen M. Kedrowski and James Warner find support for the two presidencies thesis by concluding that Congress is able to exert more influence over foreign policy vis-à-vis the President to the extent that Congress is able to emphasize the policy's domestic consequences. "Modeling Executive-Legislative Relations: More on the Two Presidencies," a paper presented at the 1990 Annual Meeting of the American Political Science Association, San Francisco, August 30–September 2.

analysis that the two presidencies phenomenon was confined mostly to the Eisenhower presidency. More to the point, his explanation for greater presidential success in foreign affairs, to the extent that it existed, ruled out bipartisanship (opposing political parties submerging their differences for the sake of unity abroad) and deference (the fact that congressional leaders are more likely to defer to the President's wishes in foreign affairs because they cannot match the President's expertise and preeminence in this realm). Instead, Edwards concluded that Eisenhower succeeded because his foreign policy was relatively liberal; therefore, he was able to win over key Democratic votes yet still hold on to his Republican congressional core. Subsequent Republican presidents, said Edwards, offered more conservative foreign policies that found less favor with Democrats.[22]

Finally, Wildavsky bowed to his critics in a 1989 reassessment when he wrote, " 'The Two Presidencies' is time and culture bound."[23] He also noted, however, that the two presidencies debate had been defined in relatively narrow terms.

Indeed, the two presidencies debate has suffered from narrow vision. I argue that Wildavsky's concept received such wide, quick, and persistent acceptance precisely because its applicability extended far beyond the narrow measures of presidential success and roll call votes of the sort discussed here and at the end of Chapter 3. These studies offer important analysis, but they largely ignore the multiplicity of foreign policy streams within which the executive and legislative interact, as well as the broader legal and historic context. (As one study that relied on this sort of analysis conceded, "much foreign policy does not require legislation and does not show up on roll calls."[24]) *As a matter of law, there are indeed two presidencies.*

Nowhere is this more clear than in the context of Supreme Court decisions. The courts have ruled on relatively few cases dealing directly with the balance of powers between the executive and legislative branches, but in a few important cases the Supreme Court justices made it abundantly clear where they thought the law stood on the existence of two presidencies. For example, in *U.S. v. Curtiss-*

---

[22] George C. Edwards III, *At the Margins* (New Haven, Conn.: Yale University Press, 1989), pp. 65–69.

[23] Duane M. Oldfield and Aaron Wildavsky, "Reconsidering the Two Presidencies," *Society*, 26 (July/August 1989): 55.

[24] Jon R. Bond and Richard Fleisher, *The President in the Legislative Arena* (Chicago: University of Chicago Press, 1990), p. 171, fn. 6.

Wright Export Corp., Justice Sutherland identified what he termed "the very delicate, plenary and exclusive power of the President as the sole organ of the federal government in the field of international relations. . . ."[25] In *Chicago and Southern Airlines v. Waterman Steamship Corp.*, the Court referred to "the President . . . as the Nation's organ for foreign affairs. . . ."[26] The *Chicago* ruling also noted that Congress possesses far greater discretion to grant its authority in foreign affairs to the President, should it choose to do so, than is the case with domestic authority.[27] This same point was made in *Zemel v. Rusk.*[28] Even in the well-known case of *U.S. v. Nixon*, when the Court ruled against President Nixon's claim that the doctrine of executive privilege prevented the courts or Congress from forcing him to turn over transcripts of conversations taped in the White House, the Court noted several times in its decision that its ruling might have been more sympathetic to the President if the tapes and conversations in question had involved foreign affairs, such as military or diplomatic matters.[29]

While many of these statements by the Court are what lawyers call dicta—comments made in passing in a court decision that do not bear directly on the particular legal issues of the case—they reflect an understanding that (1) the presidential-congressional balance in foreign affairs is substantially different from what it is in domestic affairs, (2) executive authority in foreign affairs is indeed greater than in domestic affairs (leaving aside for the moment the question of exactly where the boundary lies), and (3) Congress may delegate to the President, if it chooses, greater powers and a greater degree of discretion than would be permissible for domestic affairs.[30] None of this

---

[25] 299 U.S. 304, at 320 (1936).

[26] 333 U.S. 103, at 111 (1948). See also 109–110, 115.

[27] 333 U.S. 103, at 109.

[28] 381 U.S. 1, at 17 (1965). "It is important to bear in mind . . . that because of the changeable and explosive nature of contemporary international relations, and the fact that the Executive is immediately privy to information which cannot be swiftly presented to, evaluated by, and acted upon by legislature, Congress—in giving the Executive authority over matters of foreign affairs—must of necessity paint with a brush broader than it customarily wields in domestic areas."

[29] 418 U.S. 683, at 706, 710.

[30] As the Court said in *Curtiss-Wright*, "Congressional legislation . . . within the international field must often accord to the President a degree of discretion and freedom from statutory restriction which would not be admissible were domestic affairs alone involved." 299 U.S. 304, at 320 (1936).

means that foreign policy is necessarily bipartisan, that Congress invariably defers to the President in foreign policy, or that Presidents score higher batting averages in Congress for foreign than for domestic proposals. It does mean, however, that the fundamental legal, historical, and political context of presidential-congressional relations is different for foreign affairs. And if this fact is not clearly evident in an analysis of roll call votes, then we must look well beyond roll calls.[31]

WHY PRESIDENTIAL ASCENDANCY?

Alexander Hamilton was among the first but certainly not the last to attempt to justify presidential preeminence in foreign policy by looking to the Constitution. The explanation for executive ascendancy begins with the ambiguities of the Constitution but by no means ends there.

First, Congress by its nature is more likely to be drawn to substantively and geographically particularistic concerns, that is, the concerns of the constituents of the states and districts represented by those in Congress. Thus, service by members of Congress on the agriculture and public works committees, for example, is likely to be of greater interest to constituents because of the immediate impact those committees have on representatives' home districts than is service on the foreign affairs and foreign relations committees. Similarly, as the only nationally elected political leader, the President often is viewed as a more purely national leader, who is more likely to receive political credit for and thus benefit from foreign policy initiatives.

Second, the President benefits from the unitary nature of the position. Although the modern presidency incorporates a large administrative apparatus, the President can act authoritatively as a single individual. Especially in times of emergency and crisis, the President can act with decisiveness, secrecy, and dispatch.[32] Even presidential

[31] The fundamental distinction between foreign policy and domestic policy as it affects presidential-congressional relations is amply confirmed by most constitutional scholars. See, for example, Corwin, *The President*, pp. 171–181; Bernard Schwartz, *A Commentary on the Constitution of the United States*, 2 vols. (New York: Macmillan, 1963), pp. 96–102; Louis Fisher, *President and Congress* (New York: Free Press, 1972), p. 33; Louis Henkin, *Foreign Affairs and the Constitution* (New York: Norton, 1972), pp. 37–65; Cecil V. Crabb, Jr., and Pat M. Holt, *Invitation to Struggle* (Washington, D.C.: CQ Press, 1989), pp. 10–11.

[32] These concerns were expressed early in the country's history. See, for example, John Jay's comments in *Federalist* No. 64, *Federalist Papers* (New York: New American Library, 1961), p. 392.

critics acknowledge the necessity that a country speak with a single voice to the rest of the world. The President is the obvious person to fulfill such a role.

Third, Presidents are always on hand. Until about the middle of this century Congress would hold session for only part of the year. Many responsibilities therefore fell on presidential shoulders out of simple necessity, including many pertaining to foreign affairs.

Fourth, strong Presidents set precedent. Although the history of presidential-congressional relations is marked by periods in which each has held some degree of ascendancy, the cumulative impact of unilateral presidential actions in areas including war making, diplomacy, and intelligence has been to buttress arguments that presidential assertiveness in those areas is appropriate, if not constitutional. Indeed, "Powers [in foreign affairs] which Congress has continued to dispute without resolution have been exercised by the President as though the disputes had been resolved in his favor."[33]

Finally, court decisions, including those just cited, have generally supported an expansive interpretation of the presidential prerogative in foreign affairs.[34] The courts have largely avoided constitutional challenges to presidential initiatives abroad (often arguing that such questions are "political" and thus not justiciable by the courts) but in a few cases have spoken to presidential power. Perhaps the strongest statement favoring presidential authority in foreign affairs came in *U.S. v. Curtiss-Wright Export Corp.*[35]

Three reasons can be offered for the courts' apparent deference and the infrequency of rulings in such cases. First, the wording of Ar-

---

[33] Henkin, *Foreign Affairs and the Constitution,* p. 38.

[34] For more on factors contributing to executive dominance in foreign affairs, see Kellerman and Barilleaux, *The President as World Leader,* chap. 3.

[35] The *Curtiss-Wright* case has been heavily criticized. In particular, Congress had specifically authorized the action taken by President Roosevelt that led to the court case; thus, the President was not even acting as a "sole organ." More generally, Justice Sutherland's view of the President's constitutional powers in foreign affairs was unprecedented for its scope, the reach of the decision extended well beyond the facts of the case, and Sutherland's view of presidential history was "shockingly inaccurate." See Charles A. Lofgren, *"United States v. Curtiss-Wright Export Corporation:* An Historical Reassessment," *Yale Law Journal,* 83 (November 1973); 32. See also David M. Levitan, "The Foreign Relations Power: An Analysis of Mr. Justice Sutherland's Theory," *Yale Law Journal,* 55 (April 1946): 467–497; Gerhard Casper, "Constitutional Constraints on the Conduct of Foreign and Defense Policy: A Nonjudicial Model," *University of Chicago Law Review,* 43 (Spring 1976): 463, 475; Adler, "The Constitution and Presidential Warmaking," pp. 30–33. While the views of *Curtiss-Wright* may be legal dicta, and erroneous dicta at that, they nevertheless reflect and feed contemporary political and legal thinking about the President's role in foreign affairs.

ticle II of the Constitution is more vague and less clear than that of Article I. Thus, Presidents possess more leeway to interpret the wording to fit their political goals; the courts in turn have less firm interpretive ground upon which to stand.

Second, and related to the first reason, an aura of nearly monarchical dimensions has surrounded the presidential office for most of the country's history. Phrases such as "the Sun King complex," "the textbook presidency," "the cult of the presidency," and "the American monarchy" refer to enduring popular images of the President as moral leader, problem solver, and benevolent omniscient father figure. In no realm is this image more vital than in foreign affairs.[36] Historian Arthur Schlesinger's well-known study of the presidency, appropriately titled *The Imperial Presidency,* argues precisely that the development of the modern strong presidency occurred through presidential adventurism in foreign affairs.[37] This image has affected the courts in that they often seem to believe that they lack the "competence, expertise, equipment, and guidelines for resolution of foreign affairs cases."[38] Add to this the "embarrassment, chaos, and confusion that may attend the exercise of judicial review against a presidential [foreign policy] act"[39]—imagine a court ordering the President to withdraw American troops from some faraway battlefield!—and it is not too difficult to understand why the courts typically tread lightly in foreign affairs.

Third, the courts have generally been reluctant to enter into interbranch disputes between the President and Congress on the grounds that such disputes should be settled through the usual processes of legislation and political negotiation. The justification for this

---

[36] See Louis Koenig, *The Chief Executive* (New York: Harcourt Brace Jovanovich, 1975), pp. 5–6; Thomas E. Cronin, *The State of the Presidency* (Boston: Little, Brown, 1980), chap. 3; George Reedy, *The Twilight of the Presidency* (New York: New American Library, 1987), chap. 2. For a more general treatment of this theme during the Reagan era, see John Kenneth White, *The New Politics of Old Values* (Hanover, N.H.: University Press of New England, 1990).

[37] Arthur M. Schlesinger, Jr., *The Imperial Presidency* (Boston: Houghton Mifflin, 1973).

[38] David Gray Adler, "The Supreme Court and Presidential Power in Foreign Affairs: Curtiss-Wright and Judicial Deference," paper presented at the 1990 Annual Meeting of the Western Political Science Association, Newport Beach, Calif., March 22–24, 1990, p. 23.

[39] Adler, "The Supreme Court," p. 23.

reluctance is usually the doctrine of "political questions," referring to disputes that are considered inappropriate for resolution in the judicial realm.

Given the trend toward executive ascendancy in general matters of foreign affairs, has this been the pattern in war making as well? If so, has this resulted in a tendency toward executive-made war, as many of the Constitution's founders predicted?

WAR POWERS AND MILITARY FORCE

Most would agree that the power over war and peace is the most momentous governmental power. Few governmental powers therefore require more care, caution, and deliberation in their exercise. Yet it is also the nature of war that it often occurs with speed and surprise, on the one hand, or gradually, incrementally, and inexorably, on the other. American entry into World War II, for example, occurred because of Japan's devastating surprise attack on the American naval base at Pearl Harbor. American involvement in Vietnam, by contrast, was a gradual process that started with a handful of American advisers in the late 1950s and culminated with the commitment of over 500,000 American troops by 1968. Despite changes in the nature of warfare over two centuries, the Constitution's founders were keenly aware of the momentous, serendipitous nature of war.

The Founders and War

Although ambiguity surrounds many of the founders' deliberations, little uncertainty exists concerning the construction of war powers. The power to initiate and oversee the conduct of war was vested in Congress. "In contrast to the English system, the Framers did not want the wealth and blood of the Nation committed by the decision of a single individual."[40] In a draft of the Constitution circulated to the convention members on August 6, 1787, the legislature was to have the power "to make war." In subsequent debate, this phrase was changed to "declare war." As Madison's notes revealed, he and El-

[40] Johnny H. Killian, ed., *The Constitution of the United States of America* (Washington, D.C.: U.S. Government Printing Office, 1987), p. 335.

bridge Gerry "moved to insert *'declare,'* striking out *'make'* war; leaving to the Executive the power to repel sudden attacks."[41]

Thus, the purpose of the change was not to enhance the President's power but to permit the executive to take actions to repel sudden attacks.[42] Only one delegate to the convention, Pierce Butler, proposed giving the President war-making powers, but his proposal found no support. Indeed, Gerry noted with dismay that he "never expected to hear in a republic a motion to empower the Executive alone to declare war."[43] Both Madison and James Wilson assured the convention that the power of war and peace was a legislative, not an executive, function, a view that was also echoed in state ratifying conventions.[44]

In addition to repelling sudden attacks on the nation, it also was understood that the President would direct and lead the armed forces and put them to any use specified by Congress, as the President was dependent on and responsible to final legislative authority. Jefferson summarized the thinking of many when he wrote to Madison in 1789, "We have already given in example one effectual check to the Dog of war by transferring the power of letting him loose from the Executive to the Legislative body, from those who are to spend to those who are to pay."[45]

---

[41] Max Farrand, *The Records of the Federal Convention of 1787,* 4 vols. (New Haven, Conn.: Yale University Press, 1966), II, p. 318. As early as 1552, the verb *declare* has been synonymous with the verb *commence,* as in "to begin or initiate." See Wormuth and Firmage, *To Chain the Dog of War,* pp. 19–20. This interpretation appears in James Kent, *Commentaries on American Law,* 4 vols. (Boston, Mass.: Little, Brown, 1896), I, p. 55.

[42] See Lofgren, "War-Making under the Constitution," pp. 672–702. Some have attempted to argue that the wording change from *make* to *declare* in fact left Presidents with war-making powers. See Barry Goldwater, "The War Power Act Controversy," *Congressional Digest,* 62 (November 1983): 267–275.

[43] Farrand, *Records of the Federal Convention,* II, p. 318.

[44] Farrand, *Records of the Federal Convention,* I, pp. 64–65, 70. See also David Gray Adler, "The President's War-Making Power," in *Inventing the American Presidency,* ed. by Thomas Cronin (Lawrence: University Press of Kansas, 1989), pp. 121–122.

[45] Quoted in Gerald Gunther, *Constitutional Law* (Mineola, N.Y.: Foundation Press, 1975), p. 436. See Gunther's discussion on war powers. Alexander Hamilton summarized the President's responsibility to Congress in regard to war making in *Federalist* No. 69. A useful historical accounting of the evolution of war powers is found in Demetrios Caraley, ed., *The President's War Powers: From the Federalists to Reagan* (New York: Academy of Political Science, 1984).

Imperfect Wars

American courts have identified two types of war—"perfect," or general, war (sometimes also called "solemn" war) and "imperfect," or limited, war. A perfect war is one that "destroys the national peace and tranquillity, and lays the foundation of every possible act of hostility." An imperfect war "does not entirely destroy the public tranquillity, but interrupts it only in some particulars, as in the case of reprisals."[46] In simpler terms, a perfect war is usually understood to be of a larger scale and preceded by a formal declaration, as in the world wars. An imperfect war refers to a more limited military engagement not accompanied by any formal, general declaration. Without doubt, most American military engagements have been of the latter type.

The question raised by an imperfect war is whether the executive possesses greater authority to act in smaller or more localized military conflicts. By experience and history, the answer would seem to be yes. Yet by the Constitution and legal interpretation, authority over imperfect wars lies with Congress no less than does authority over perfect wars.

Remember that the Constitution grants Congress the power to declare war, but also to "grant letters of marque and reprisal." This obscure and seemingly arcane reference refers precisely to "a broad spectrum of armed hostilities short of declared war."[47] As Jefferson noted in 1793 in regard to military reprisals, "Congress must be called upon to take it; the right of reprisal being expressly lodged with them by the Constitution, and not with the executive."[48] Madison and Hamilton also noted that military reprisal was a warlike act and therefore fell under the authority of Congress.[49] (Such a conclusion would not, of course, preclude Congress from authorizing the President to stage a military reprisal.) Similarly, Justice Joseph Story noted in 1833 that "this power of reprisal . . . is nearly related to,

[46] Quoted in Wormuth and Firmage, *To Chain the Dog of War*, p. 55.
[47] Adler, "The Constitution and Presidential Warmaking," p. 8.
[48] Quoted in Adler, "The Constitution and Presidential Warmaking," p. 8.
[49] See Jules Lobel, "Covert War and Congressional Authority: Hidden War and Forgotten Power," *Pennsylvania Law Review*, 134 (June 1986): 1035, 1045–1047.

and plainly derived from that of making war. It is but an incomplete state of hostilities. . . ."[50]

This interpretation was validated in three early Supreme Court cases that dealt with limited military engagements—imperfect wars—in the first decade of the nineteenth century. In *Bas v. Tingy*,[51] *Talbot v. Seeman*,[52] and *Little v. Barreme*,[53] the Supreme Court ruled that when presidential decisions contradicted an act of Congress, the latter prevailed, and that Congress was vested with war powers. As Chief Justice John Marshall noted in the *Talbot* case, "The whole powers of war being, by the Constitution of the United States, vested in congress, the acts of that body alone be resorted to as our guides in the enquiry."[54] In other words, "Congress may initiate action short of general war, . . . the initiation both of general war and of action short of general war belongs to Congress, and . . . it is for Congress to prescribe the dimensions of the war."[55]

The Evolution of the War Power

As with many shared powers, the practice of war making and the deployment of troops was shaped by necessity, ambition, and enterprise. During the nineteenth century American armed forces were used by Presidents on their own authority to suppress piracy and the slave trade, in "hot pursuit" of criminals across frontiers, and in protecting American lives and property in primitive or backward areas. This limited use of military forces by the President came to be accepted because it did not involve the initiation of hostilities against foreign governments.

Some presidents, such as James K. Polk, Ulysses S. Grant, and William McKinley, interpreted the powers of the commander in

---

[50] Joseph Story, *Commentaries on the Constitution of the United States* (Durham, N.C.: Carolina Academic Press, 1987), p. 412. An extended study of imperfect and undeclared wars similarly concludes that "the Framers recognized congressional power to determine the use of limited force against other nations to redress grievances . . . the Framers intended to vest limited as well as general war-making power in Congress rather than the President." Edward Keynes, *Undeclared War: Twilight Zone of Constitutional Power* (University Park: Pennsylvania State University Press, 1982), p. 37.

[51] 4 U.S. (4 Dall.) 36 (1800).

[52] 5 U.S. (1 Cranch) 1 (1801).

[53] 6 U.S. (2 Cranch) 170 (1804).

[54] *Talbot v. Seeman*, 5 U.S. (1 Cranch) 1 (1801), at 28.

[55] Wormuth and Firmage, *To Chain the Dog of War*, p. 63.

chief more broadly, while others, such as the early presidents, as well as James Buchanan, and Grover Cleveland, were more deferential to the war powers of Congress. Regardless of these differences, however, the dominant view of the time was that the President could deploy the military outside of U.S. borders as long as the military was not used to commit an "act of war" (using military force against a sovereign nation without that nation having declared war on or used force against the United States).[56]

This pattern changed in the twentieth century. Presidents from Theodore Roosevelt on began to use the military against sovereign nations without congressional authorization, as Roosevelt did with the Navy against Colombia to prevent it from suppressing the U.S.-instigated Panamanian insurrection in 1903. Presidents William Howard Taft and Woodrow Wilson both used American troops freely in Central America and the Caribbean without congressional authorization. President Franklin Roosevelt exercised even greater discretion over use of American troops abroad prior to the start of World War II.[57]

The accompanying box summarizes significant American military engagements from 1789 up to the Vietnam war. It is important to note first that Congress has declared war on only five occasions.[58] The other fourteen major military engagements listed reflect the vital interplay between the President and Congress.

In all three of the "other actions" in the nineteenth century, Congress provided legal authorization for presidential action. Of the eleven nondeclared wars in the twentieth century, only three were accompanied by congressional authorization (Mexico, 1914; pre–World War II, 1939; and Lebanon, 1958). In the eight instances when Presidents acted without congressional authorization, political consensus generally supported the President's actions, as was the case with the Boxer Rebellion, for example. Similarly, when opinions shifted against these presidential actions, for example, during the Soviet incursion in 1919 and the Nicaraguan incursion in 1926, the

---

[56] See Gunther, *Constitutional Law*, pp. 437–439.

[57] For more on this, see Louis Fisher, *Constitutional Conflicts between Congress and the President* (Princeton, N.J.: Princeton University Press, 1985), chap. 9. For more on Roosevelt, see Richard M. Pious, *The American Presidency* (New York: Basic Books, 1979), pp. 53–55.

[58] The Civil War was not accompanied by a declaration of war because it was not considered a conflict with another sovereign nation; rather, it was a domestic insurrection.

Major U.S. Armed Actions[1] Overseas, with Relevant Congressional Action, 1789–1965

A. DECLARED WARS

1. War of 1812.   Congress declared war on Great Britain, June 17, 1812. Madison's review of grievances did not actually call for war, but Congress resolved the matter with a joint resolution declaring war.

2. Mexican War, 1848.   U.S. troops under General Zachary Taylor were ordered by President Polk to occupy the land between the Nueces and Rio Grande Rivers, territory also claimed by Mexico. This was done without any authorization from Congress. Mexican troops surprised and mauled an American unit, and Polk sent a message to Congress asking that it recognize the existence of hostilities. Congress responded by a resolution declaring that a state of war existed between the U.S. and Mexico.

There was opposition to the war from the beginning, which grew stronger with time. The House added a rider to a resolution honoring General Taylor on January 3, 1848, stating that the war was begun "unnecessarily and unconstitutionally" by the President.

3. Spanish-American War, 1898.   President McKinley at first merely requested Congress' permission to use military and naval forces to effect a cessation of hostilities between Spain and its rebellious possession, Cuba, and to establish a stable government in the latter. The Senate added a provision to this request recognizing the independence of Cuba. This provision was opposed by the President and deleted in the conference with the House. A resolution was passed giving the President discretionary authority to use military force to satisfy U.S. aims with respect to Spain and Cuba. Spain responded by declaring war on the U.S. In response, McKinley ordered Dewey to attack the Philippines. He then asked for a declaration of war, which Congress gave, stating that war had existed from the day Spain declared it against the U.S.

4. World War I, 1917–1918.   President Wilson asked Congress to recognize that the course of the German government amounted to

---

[1] Armed action means the confrontation of U.S. forces with those of a foreign government or revolutionary faction, usually, but not always resulting in an actual clash.

SOURCE: "War Powers Legislation," Hearings, Committee on Foreign Relations, U.S. Senate, 92d Congress, 1st sess. (Washington, D.C.: U.S. Government Printing Office, 1972), pp. 298–302.

war against the United States. Congress responded by a joint resolution declaring that a state of war existed between the Imperial German Government and the U.S. War was not declared against Austria-Hungary until December, 1917, eight months after the declaration against Germany.

5. World War II.   After the Japanese attack on Pearl Harbor on December 7, 1941, President Roosevelt went before Congress the next day, and asked for a declaration of war, dating from the time of the Pearl Harbor attack. Germany and Italy, who were allies of Japan, then declared war on the United States. On December 11, 1941, President Roosevelt asked that Congress recognize a state of war between the U.S. and Germany and the U.S. and Italy, a request to which Congress acceded the same day.[2]

B. OTHER ACTIONS

Armed Action	*Congressional Action*

Undeclared naval war with France, 1798–1800. This was a limited war, fought essentially for the protection of American merchant ships which were being harassed by French naval vessels. This contest included some land actions, i.e., the capture by U.S. marines of a French privateer under the guns of the forts in the Dominican city of Puerto Plata.	Congress:
	
	    1. Created a Navy Department.
	    2. Voted appropriations for new warships.
	    3. Abrogated treaties and consular conventions with France.
	    4. Authorized the enlistment of a "provisional army" for the duration of the emergency.
	    5. Authorized seizure and bringing into port of armed French vessels which had been preying on American shipping. Did not authorize seizure of unarmed French vessels.[3]

[2] For an account of the moves short of war by which the U.S. sought to aid Britain in its fight against Germany, see part B of this Appendix.

[3] Two days before Congress authorized the seizure of French ships, a lone U.S. naval vessel had been sent out on patrol to protect U.S. coastal waters between Long Island and the Virginia Capes.

Armed Action	Congressional Action
War with Tripoli, 1801–1805. The so-called Barbary pirates exacted tribute from countries whose ships plied the Mediterranean. The European nations paid, finding this the easiest way. When Jefferson became President the Pasha of Tripoli, feeling tribute paid by U.S. was insufficient, declared war. Jefferson sent warships to the Mediterranean which, after several naval actions, succeeded in winning a treaty from Tripoli more favorable than any other nation had yet secured from her. During this conflict a few U.S. marines were landed with U.S. Agent William Eaton, with a view to raising a force to free the crew of the Philadelphia. This expedition penetrated as far as Derna, on Tripoli's eastern frontier, and probably influenced the Pasha to make peace.	In 1802 Congress passed a law entitled "An Act for the Protection of the Commerce and Seamen of the United States against the Tripolitan Cruisers." It authorized the President to protect commerce and seamen, to seize and make prizes of vessels belonging to Tripoli, and all other acts of precaution and hostility as in a state of war. This amounted to subsequent approval of Jefferson's actions, plus the authority which only Congress could grant: to take prizes and to give commissions to privateers. An act levying revenue duties to pay the cost of the naval operations was likewise approved.
Second Barbary War, 1815. The Dey of Algiers declared war against the U.S. Two U.S. naval squadrons were sent to the Mediterranean. Stephen Decatur, commander of one of the squadrons, dictated peace to Algiers, and then to Tunis and Tripoli, ending the Barbary blackmail as far as the U.S. was concerned. Within a year, European warships took action against the Barbary corsairs, and the payment of tribute ended entirely.	Congress authorized the expedition against Algiers. Specifically, it authorized the use of armed vessels, "as may be judged requisite by the President." The same legislation made it lawful to take prizes.

Armed Action	*Congressional Action*
Boxer Rebellion, 1900. In 1900 a series of anti-foreign disorders erupted in China, fomented by a secret society known to Westerners as Boxers. This uprising was encouraged by elements within the Imperial Government, but it was not, strictly speaking, a war waged by that government. The high point of the rebellion came when the Boxers rampaged through Peking, and laid siege to the foreign legations there. An international force was organized to lift the siege, and a U.S. contingent of 2,500 men was sent by President McKinley to join this international force. These U.S. troops came from forces already mobilized for the Spanish-American War and the Philippine Insurrection. For many years thereafter the U.S. maintained a guard at Peking and other military forces at certain places on Chinese territory, pursuant to authority acquired from the Chinese.	None—Congress was not in session at the time. There was little protest when Congress did reconvene, however.
Nicaragua, 1926–1933. The U.S. employed military occupation to end civil war and establish elections and regular government. President Coolidge undertook the occupation on his own responsibility. Henry L. Stimson was sent as the President's personal representative, and managed to work out an agreement accepted by contending Nicaraguan factions, ex*cept* for Gen-	Resolutions were introduced in Congress requesting immediate withdrawal of armed forces from Nicaragua. Hearings were held by the Foreign Relations Committee and the ensuing report, Senate Report 498, 70th Congress, defended retention of troops in Nicaragua until settlement worked out by Stimson could be carried out. This report expressed no opinion on the con-

Armed Action

eral Sandino, one of the Liberal generals, and his followers. Sandino carried on guerrilla warfare against the Nicaraguan government and U.S. forces for the remainder of the occupation. At its height, over 5,000 sailors and marines were either in Nicaragua or in transit there.

Congressional Action

stitutionality of dispatching troops to Nicaragua in the first place. Mexico and the U.S. backed rival factions in the Nicaraguan dispute. This added to existing tensions between the U.S. and Mexico. This tension evoked a "sense of the Senate" resolution, introduced by Sen. Frazier of North Dakota, that the President not exercise his powers as Commander in Chief to send any of our armed forces into Mexico, or to mobilize troops on the Mexican border, or assemble fighting units of the navy in waters adjacent to Mexico, while Congress was not in session. If the President contemplated such action, the resolution directed him to call Congress into special session and explain his reasons for proposed military moves.

This resolution did not contest the President's powers as Commander in Chief, but it did represent an attempt to curb his initiative in bringing about situations that might become dangerous, or lead to armed clashes. It was not adopted, but public opinion grew increasingly opposed to intervention by U.S. troops in any foreign country. The policy of intervention in Latin America was ended during the 1930's, and the country attempted to insulate itself against involvement in foreign wars through the Neutrality Acts.

Armed Action	*Congressional Action*
China, 1927. In 1927, anti-foreign disorders, which had taken place repeatedly since 1911, reached a climax. There was fighting at Shanghai between Nationalist and anti-Nationalist forces, which led to the landing of 1,250 Marines, who joined an international force that reached 13,000 men. A naval guard had to be stationed at the American consulate in Nanking. A small contingent of sailors was landed at Hankow at the beginning of the year, and a tiny contingent of Marines in April. A U.S. and a British warship fired on Chinese soldiers to protect the escape of Americans and other foreigners from Nanking. By the end of 1927, the U.S. had 44 naval vessels in Chinese waters, and 5,670 men ashore. Other countries also sent considerable forces to the area. After U.S. signed an agreement with Nationalist China in 1928 which constituted recognition, U.S. troops were gradually withdrawn.	No specific action was taken by Congress with respect to the landing of troops. However a resolution calling for the end of America's special privileges in China won overwhelming approval in the House.
Pre-War Moves, 1939–1941. After the outbreak of World War II in Europe, the U.S. took a number of actions designed to safeguard its security and that of the Western Hemisphere and to aid the allied powers against Nazi Germany. Among these actions were the following: 1. Troops were sent to garrison air and naval bases obtained from Great	President Roosevelt did not seek specific congressional authorization for many of the actions he took to aid Britain and other nations fighting the Axis. However, despite fierce opposition, Congress passed the Lend-Lease Act. It also passed the first peacetime conscription law in U.S. history (which it renewed by a margin of one vote) and passed

Armed Action	*Congressional Action*

Britain in exchange for overage destroyers. These bases were located in Newfoundland, Bermuda, St. Lucia, Jamaica, Antigua, Trinidad, British Guiana, and the Bahamas. 2. Greenland was placed under American control, and the U.S. was given permission to build bases there by agreement with the Danish Minister in Washington, an agreement disavowed by the captive Danish government. 3. The President ordered troops to occupy Dutch Guiana, under agreement with the Dutch government in exile. 4. Iceland was taken under U.S. protection for strategic reasons, after the British had indicated they could no longer garrison their base there, and after agreement had been secured from the Icelandic government. 5. The President ordered the navy to patrol the ship lanes to Europe. These patrols began to convoy lend-lease shipments as far as Iceland, where the British navy picked them up. Clashes with German U-boats resulted from this activity.

Korean Police Action, 1950–1953. North Korean troops crossed the borders of South Korea June 25, 1950. The UN Security Council, called into special session, denounced the invasion as an act of aggression, called for an immediate cease-

the bill permitting the arming of merchant ships. In addition, Congress repealed those sections of the Neutrality Act of 1939 which forbade trade with belligerents, established combat zones into which U.S. ships were not to sail, and prevented the arming of merchantmen. In short, President Roosevelt did not seek the authorization of Congress for certain moves he made as Commander in Chief, but he did obtain what was in effect the endorsement of Congress for his policy of assisting one side in an international conflict.

A few members of both houses voiced criticism that the President had usurped Congress' power to declare war. Resolutions were introduced in 1951 to declare war against North Korea and Communist China, and also for an orderly withdrawal of U.S.

Armed Action	*Congressional Action*
fire, and requested member nations to render every assistance to see that its resolution was enforced. On June 27, President Truman announced that he had ordered U.S. air and sea forces to give the Korean government troops cover and support; that he had ordered the 7th Fleet to prevent any attack on Formosa as well as to prevent any Chinese Nationalist sea or air operations against the Chinese mainland. Later that day the Security Council adopted a resolution calling upon the members of the UN to furnish such assistance to the Republic of Korea as might be necessary to restore international peace and security in the area. In response to this resolution, President Truman ordered ground forces to Korea to repel the North Korean attack. Since the Korean action was undertaken under UN sponsorship, other countries also sent contingents, but that of the U.S. was by far the largest.	forces. None of these resolutions came to a vote.
	If Congress did not formally accept, neither did it as a whole contest the contention of the Executive that it acted in response to the call of the UN Security Council. The State Department, in its memorandum defending the authority of the President to repel the attack in Korea, pointed to the debates on the UN Charter in which it was asserted that by becoming a party thereto, the U.S. would be obligated by commitments the organization would undertake, including commitments to international policing, and that it would be within the power of the Executive to see that these agreements were carried out. The Senate had approved the UN Charter, and there was some feeling, particularly at the outbreak of the Korean conflict, that it had therefore authorized, at least implicitly and in a general way, actions that might be taken under it. Furthermore the entire Congress had passed the UN Participation Act.
Landing of Troops in Lebanon, 1958. Lebanon has always preserved a delicate internal balance between Christians and Moslems. This was threatened by certain Moslems, reportedly encouraged by President Nasser of	The "Eisenhower Doctrine," a joint resolution, had been passed by Congress in 1957 authorizing the President to use U.S. armed forces to assist any nation in the Middle East requesting help against Communist aggression.

Armed Action	Congressional Action
the UAR. When a pro-Nasser coup took place in Iraq in July of 1958, the President of Lebanon sent an urgent plea for assistance to President Eisenhower, saying that his country was threatened both by internal rebellion and "indirect aggression." President Eisenhower responded by sending 5,000 marines to Beirut to protect American lives and help the Lebanese maintain their independence. This force was gradually increased to 14,000 soldiers and marines, who occupied strategic positions throughout the country.	President Eisenhower stressed the provocative nature of Soviet and Cairo broadcasts in justifying the landing of troops.
After the matter had been taken to the UN, and the General Assembly had passed a resolution calling on member states to respect one another's integrity and refrain from interfering in one another's internal affairs, and also requesting that arrangements be made for the withdrawal of troops, the situation stabilized somewhat. U.S. troops were then gradually withdrawn on a schedule worked out with Lebanese authorities.	
Deployment of Troops, Thailand, 1961–1970. In 1961 a detachment of 259 Marines was sent to Thailand to set up a helicopter maintenance facility for ferrying supplies to anti-Communist forces in Laos, when the military situation in that country began to	In 1969 Congress voted to prohibit a commitment of U.S. ground troops to Laos or Thailand, as an amendment to the defense appropriations bill.

Armed Action

deteriorate. In 1962, when anti-Communists fled across the Mekong into Thai territory, and it appeared that Pathet Lao might move into Thailand, U.S. forces numbering 5,000 men were sent into Northeast Thailand to guard against that possibility. The UK, Australia, and New Zealand also sent in small units, in a show of SEATO solidarity. As the threat receded, the U.S. and other troops were gradually withdrawn. The building of U.S. air bases in Thailand began around 1964, and by 1965 U.S. air strikes against the Vietcong and North Vietnam were being flown from Thailand. These air bases in Thailand are still maintained.

Intervention in the Dominican Republic, 1965. On April 24, 1965, a revolt broke out in Santo Domingo, capital of the Dominican Republic. On April 28 President Johnson ordered a contingent of several hundred marines to land there, stating that Dominican "military authorities" had requested assistance, as they could no longer guarantee the safety of American citizens living in the Dominican Republic. The President stated that assistance would also be available to protect nationals of other countries as well.

The first U.S. contingent num-

Congressional Action

Congressional leadership was informed before the move was made into the Dominican Republic. Several resolutions were offered supporting the President's action in the Dominican Republic. The most prominent was H. Res. 560, endorsing the use of force individually or collectively by any country in the Western hemisphere to prevent a Communist takeover. It passed the House by a vote of 312–52.

Many members of Congress felt that the President had overestimated the extent of Communist penetration of the revolutionary movement. Others have charged

Armed Action

bered only 400 men, but on May 2 the President announced he was sending in 200 more, with an additional 4,500 to follow at the earliest possible moment. Eventually U.S. forces in the Dominican Republic were to number 21,500. Total personnel involved numbered over 30,000.

In announcing the dispatch of additional troops to the Dominican Republic, President Johnson cited increasing Communist control of the revolution, plus increasing needs for food and medical supplies, etc.

A peace commission from the Organization of American States succeeded in achieving a cease-fire among the contending Dominican groups, and on May 6, 1965, the OAS voted to create an Inter-American Peace force, to assist in restoring peace and order. As various elements of this Inter-American Peace Force began to arrive in the Dominican Republic, the U.S. withdrew a proportionate number of its forces. By the end of 1965 this Inter-American force numbered 9,400, with U.S. troops serving as part of that force. An Ad Hoc Commission of the OAS worked out a formula to restore constitutional government, and finally on September 3, 1965 a civilian, Hector Garcia Godoy, was inaugurated as provisional president. All U.S. troops were gradually withdrawn.

Congressional Action

that the intervention was motivated not so much by a desire to save lives and property as by a desire to prevent a Communist takeover in the country, a desire which, in their view, arose from an inaccurate assessment of the danger of such a takeover. Some argued that the U.S. should have consulted the OAS before it intervened in the Dominican Republic, something which it did not do.

Presidents eventually reversed their intervention decisions—a pattern that has repeated itself in recent decades.[59] Including the major engagements listed in the box, the United States by one count engaged in 153 military actions abroad from 1789 to 1970 (aside from the five declared wars).[60]

After World War II, this nation emerged for the first time from its predominantly isolationist posture in world affairs, assuming instead an assertive internationalist and interventionist role. This trend opened the door to a more active military role, with military initiatives occurring because of presidential initiative and congressional acquiescence.

President Harry Truman committed American troops to Korea in 1950 without congressional authorization. Truman offered no explanation for declining to seek congressional assent. He did inform congressional leaders of his order to send American troops moments before informing the press, but in the words of Senator Robert A. Taft (R-Ohio), there was "no pretense of consulting the Congress."[61] In a State Department bulletin, the administration asserted that "the President, as Commander in Chief of the Armed Forces of the United States, has full control over the use thereof."[62] The following year Secretary of State Dean Acheson defended Truman's actions before a congressional hearing, asserting that the President had acted properly by carrying out American foreign policy and that Congress could not interfere.

One may dispute the extent to which Truman's actions broke new ground, but the Truman administration's claims to a constitutional basis for executive war making and failure to seek legislative authorization did represent a major departure from his predecessors, including Franklin Roosevelt. For the first time a President claimed unqualified war-making powers founded in the Constitution. The invocation of the President's authority as commander in chief of the

[59] For more on the relationship between public opinion and war, see John E. Mueller, *War, Presidents, and Public Opinion* (New York: Wiley, 1973). An excellent historical treatment of this relationship is found in Richard J. Barnet, *The Rockets' Red Glare* (New York: Simon & Schuster, 1990).

[60] "War Powers Legislation," Hearings before the Committee on Foreign Relations, U.S. Senate, 92nd Cong., 1st sess. (Washington, D.C.: U.S. Government Printing Office, 1972), pp. 359–375.

[61] Quoted in James L. Sundquist, *The Decline and Resurgence of Congress* (Washington, D.C.: Brookings Institution, 1981), p. 107. Sundquist provides an excellent account of the Korean case; see pp. 107–110.

[62] Quoted in Gunther, *Constitutional Law*, p. 439.

military ignores the fact that the commander in chief is responsible to Congress and that this power bestows no independent authority to make war without congressional authorization.[63] Yet this fact has been swept aside by Truman and most of his successors.

President Dwight Eisenhower, by contrast, took care to seek congressional authorization in the two major military confrontations of his administration: Formosa and the mideast. In the Formosa Resolution of 1954, Congress empowered the President to employ American forces to defend the island of Formosa, off the coast of China. In the Middle East Resolution of 1957, the Cuba Resolution of 1962 (under President Kennedy), and the 1964 Gulf of Tonkin Resolution (under President Johnson), the concept of seeking congressional authorization was dropped. Instead, the terminology of the resolutions implied acceptance of the idea that the President already had the power to use the armed forces in the ways mentioned in the resolutions.

Among these resolutions, the Gulf of Tonkin Resolution (see the accompanying box) represents the extreme point of Congress's surrender of its power over war to the President. Enacted in 1964 at Johnson's behest after an alleged attack on an American vessel off the coast of North Vietnam, the resolution provided the President with a blank check to make war in southeast Asia when, where, and by whatever means the executive saw fit. As the accompanying box states, Section 2 of the resolution gives the President the authority to act militarily "as the President determines" without reference to any limits as to area or scope of conflict within southeast Asia. In Section 3 the President is given the power to determine when the resolution will expire. Such was congressional compliance that the resolution was passed unanimously by the House and with only two dissenting votes in the Senate.[64]

In the period from Truman to Johnson Congress literally removed itself from the war-making process. In the words of political analyst James Sundquist, "The power of decision over war and peace—held in such tight and rigid control by the Congress in its pe-

---

[63] See Henkin, *Foreign Affairs and the Constitution*, pp. 50–54; Adler, "The President's War-Making Power," pp. 126–130; Wormuth and Firmage, chap. 7. See also Hamilton's *Federalist* No. 69. The executive power clause in Article II is an even weaker reed upon which to prop presidential war making. See Adler, "The President's War-Making Power," pp. 130–132.

[64] The two dissenters were Wayne Morse (D-Oreg.) and Ernest Gruening (D-Alaska).

The Gulf of Tonkin Resolution

The text of the Resolution. H.J.Res. 1145, 73 Stat. 384 (1964):

Whereas naval units of the Communist regime in Vietnam, in violation of the principles of the Charter of the United Nations and of international law, have deliberately and repeatedly attacked United States naval vessels lawfully present in international waters, and have thereby created a serious threat to international peace; and

Whereas these attacks are part of a deliberate and systematic campaign of aggression that the Communist regime in North Vietnam has been waging against its neighbors and the nations joined with them in the collective defense of their freedom; and

Whereas the United States is assisting the peoples of southeast Asia to protect their freedom and has no territorial, military or political ambitions in that area, but desires only that these peoples should be left in peace to work out their own destinies in their own way: Now, therefore, be it

Resolved by the Senate and House of Representatives of the United States of America in Congress assembled,

Sec. 1. The Congress approves and supports the determination of the President, as Commander in Chief, to take all necessary measures to repel any armed attack against the forces of the United States and to prevent further aggression.

Sec. 2. The United States regards as vital to its national interest and to world peace the maintenance of international peace and security in southeast Asia. Consonant with the Constitution of the United States and the Charter of the United Nations and in accordance with its obligations under the Southeast Asia Collective Defense Treaty, the United States is, therefore, prepared, as the President determines, to take all necessary steps, including the use of armed force, to assist any member or protocol state of the Southeast Asia Collective Defense Treaty requesting assistance in defense of its freedom.

Sec. 3. This resolution shall expire when the President shall determine that the peace and security of the area is reasonably assured by international conditions created by action of the United Nations or otherwise, except that it may be terminated earlier by concurrent resolution of the Congress.

[The Gulf of Tonkin Resolution was repealed in January 1971. See 84 Stat. 2053.]

riod of self-assertion in the decade before World War II—slipped virtually wholly from its grasp."[65] Similarly, presidents from Eisenhower through Nixon all asserted unrestricted executive authority to commit American forces without prior congressional consent. Congress generally acquiesced in this arrangement until 1973.

THE WAR POWERS RESOLUTION

The 1960s and 1970s saw American engagement in the longest war in the nation's history.[66] Although the scale of American involvement was less than that in World War II, for example, the length of the war combined with growing doubts about its justification and its progressively greater human and material costs to fan the flames of discontent in this country. Congressional leaders pressed for means to curtail the President's relatively free hand, and this in turn sparked renewed interest in reinvigorating congressional influence over war making. During the early 1970s Congress succeeded in passing legislation to cut off funding for the bombing of Cambodia. Yet President Nixon vetoed the legislation, leaving the government in the ironic position of continuing the Vietnam war as long as Nixon could sustain a veto with the support of one-third plus one member of one house of Congress. Congressional pressure and frustration culminated in the passage of the War Powers Resolution in 1973. Although vetoed by Nixon, the bill was enacted over the veto.

The resolution incorporates three key provisions (see the accompanying box). First, it provides that the President must consult with Congress "in every possible instance" before introducing U.S. forces into hostilities (Section 3). Second, the President must submit a written report to Congress within forty-eight hours of the introduction of American forces into hostilities [Section 4(a)(3)]. Third, the President must withdraw forces within sixty to ninety days unless Congress provides appropriate authorization [Section 5(b)]. Congress may also direct the President to withdraw forces at any time by pas-

---

[65] Sundquist, *The Decline and Resurgence of Congress*, p. 110.

[66] For more on the unique nature of Vietnam's impact on American foreign policy, see Graebner, *America as a World Power*, chap. 9.

The War Powers Resolution of 1973*

SHORT TITLE
Section 1. This joint resolution may be cited as the "War Powers Resolution."

PURPOSE AND POLICY
Section 2. (a) It is the purpose of this joint resolution to fulfill the intent of the framers of the Constitution of the United States and insure that the collective judgment of both the Congress and the president will apply to the introduction of United States armed forces into hostilities, or into situations where imminent involvement in hostilities is clearly indicated by the circumstances, and to the continued use of such forces in hostilities or in such situations.

(b) Under article 1, section 8, of the Constitution, it is specifically provided that the Congress shall have the power to make all laws necessary and proper for carrying into execution, not only its own powers but also all other powers vested by the Constitution in the government of the United States, or in any department or officer thereof.

(c) The constitutional powers of the president as commander-in-chief to introduce United States armed forces into hostilities, or into situations where imminent involvement in hostilities is clearly indicated by the circumstances, are exercised only pursuant to (1) a declaration of war, (2) specific statutory authorization, or (3) a national emergency created by attack upon the United States, its territories or possessions, or its armed forces.

CONSULTATION
Section 3. The president in every possible instance shall consult with Congress before introducing United States armed forces into hostilities or into situations where imminent involvement in hostilities is clearly indicated by the circumstances, and after every such introduction shall consult regularly with the Congress until United States armed forces are no longer engaged in hostilities or have been removed from such situations.

REPORTING
Section 4. (a) In the absence of a declaration of war, in any case in which the United States armed forces are introduced—

*SOURCE: Public Law 93–148, 87 Stat. 555 (November 7, 1973).

1) into hostilities or into situations where imminent involvement in hostilities is clearly indicated by the circumstances;

(2) into the territory, airspace or waters of a foreign nation, while equipped for combat, except for deployments which relate solely to supply, replacement, repair, or training of such forces; or

(3) in numbers which substantially enlarge United States armed forces equipped for combat already located in a foreign nation;

the President shall submit within 48 hours to the Speaker of the House of Representatives and to the president pro tempore of the Senate a report, in writing, setting forth—

(A) the circumstances necessitating the introduction of United States armed forces;

(B) the constitutional and legislative authority under which such introduction took place; and

(C) the estimated scope and duration of the hostilities or involvement.

(b) The president shall provide such other information as the Congress may request in the fulfillment of its constitutional responsibilities with respect to committing the nation to war and to the use of United States armed forces abroad.

(c) Whenever United States armed forces are introduced into hostilities or into any situation described in subsection (a) of this section, the president shall, so long as such armed forces continue to be engaged in such hostilities or situation, report to the Congress periodically on the status of such hostilities or situation as well as on the scope and duration of such hostilities or situation, but in no event shall he report to the Congress less often than once every six months.

CONGRESSIONAL ACTION
Section 5.   (a) Each report submitted pursuant to section 4(a) (1) shall be transmitted to the Speaker of the House of Representatives and to the president pro tempore of the Senate on the same calendar day. Each report so transmitted shall be referred to the Committee on Foreign Affairs of the House of Representatives and to the Committee on Foreign Relations of the Senate for appropriate action. If, when the report is transmitted, the Congress has adjourned sine die or has adjourned for any period in excess of three calendar days, the Speaker of the House of Representatives and the president pro tempore of the Senate, if they seem it advisable (or if petitioned by at least 30 per-

cent of the membership of their respective houses) shall jointly request the president to convene Congress in order that it may consider the report and take appropriate action pursuant to this section.

(b) Within sixty calendar days after a report is submitted or is required to be submitted pursuant to section 4(a) (1), whichever is earlier, the president shall terminate any use of United States armed forces with respect to which such report was submitted (or required to be submitted), unless the Congress (1) has declared war or has enacted a specific authorization for such use of United States armed forces, (2) has extended by law such sixty-day period, or (3) is physically unable to meet as a result of an armed attack upon the United States. Such sixty-day period shall be extended for not more than an additional thirty days if the president determines and certifies to the Congress in writing that unavoidable military necessity respecting the safety of the United States armed forces requires the continued use of such armed forces in the course of bringing about a prompt removal of such forces.

(c) Notwithstanding subsection (b), at any time that United States armed forces are engaged in hostilities outside the territory of the United States, its possessions and territories without a declaration of war or specific statutory authorization, such forces shall be removed by the president if the Congress so directs by concurrent resolution.

CONGRESSIONAL PRIORITY PROCEDURES FOR JOINT RESOLUTION OR BILL

Section 6.   (a) Any joint resolution or bill introduced pursuant to section 5(b) at least thirty calendar days before the expiration of the sixty-day period specified in such section shall be referred to the Committee on Foreign Affairs of the House of Representatives or the Committee on Foreign Relations of the Senate, as the case may be, and such committee shall report one such joint resolution or bill, together with its recommendations, not later than twenty-four calendar days before the expiration of the sixty-day period specified in such section, unless such house shall otherwise determine by the yeas and nays.

(b) Any joint resolution or bill so reported shall become the pending business of the house in question (in the case of the Senate the time for debate shall be equally divided between the proponents and the opponents), and shall be voted on within three calendar days thereafter, unless such house shall otherwise determine by yeas and nays.

(c) Such a joint resolution or bill passed by one house shall be referred to the committee of the other house named in subsection (a) and shall be reported out not later than fourteen calendar days before the expiration of the sixty-day period specified in section 5(b). The joint resolution or bill so reported shall become the pending business of the house in question and shall be voted on within three calendar days after it has been reported, unless such house shall otherwise determine by yeas and nays.

(d) In the case of any disagreement between the two houses of Congress with respect to a joint resolution or bill passed by both houses, conferees shall be promptly appointed and the committee of conference shall make and file a report with respect to such resolution or bill not later than four calendar days before the expiration of the sixty-day period specified in section 5(b). In the event the conferees are unable to agree within forty-eight hours, they shall report back to their respective houses in disagreement. Notwithstanding any rule in either house concerning the printing of conference reports in the Record or concerning any delay in the consideration of such reports, such report shall be acted on by both houses not later than the expiration of such sixty-day period.

CONGRESSIONAL PRIORITY PROCEDURES FOR CONCURRENT RESOLUTION
Section 7.   (a) Any concurrent resolution introduced pursuant to section 5(c) shall be referred to the Committee on Foreign Affairs of the House of Representatives or the Committee on Foreign Relations of the Senate, as the case may be, and one such concurrent resolution shall be reported out by such committee together with its recommendations within fifteen calendar days, unless such house shall otherwise determine by the yeas and nays.

(b) Any concurrent resolution so reported shall become the pending business of the house in question (in the case of the Senate the time for debate shall be equally divided between the proponents and the opponents) and shall be voted on within three calendar days thereafter, unless such house shall otherwise determine by yeas and nays.

(c) Such a concurrent resolution passed by one house shall be referred to the committee of the other house named in subsection (a) and shall be reported out by such committee together with its recommendations within fifteen calendar days and shall thereupon become the pending business of such house and shall be voted upon within three calendar days, unless such house shall otherwise determine by yeas and nays.

(d) In the case of any disagreement between the two houses of Congress with respect to a concurrent resolution passed by both houses, conferees shall be promptly appointed and the committee of conference shall make and file a report with respect to such concurrent resolution within six calendar days after the legislation is referred to the committee of conference. Notwithstanding any rule in either house concerning the printing of conference reports in the Record or concerning any delay in the consideration of such reports, such report shall be acted on by both houses not later than six calendar days after the conference report is filed. In the event the conferees are unable to agree within forty-eight hours, they shall report back to their respective houses in disagreement.

INTERPRETATION OF JOINT RESOLUTION
Section 8. (a) Authority to introduce United States armed forces into hostilities or into situations wherein involvement in hostilities is clearly indicated by the circumstances shall not be inferred—

(1) from any provision of law (whether or not in effect before the date of the enactment of this joint resolution), including any provision contained in any appropriation act, unless such provision specifically authorizes the introduction of United States armed forces into hostilities or into such situations and states that it is intended to constitute specific statutory authorization within the meaning of this joint resolution; or

(2) from any treaty heretofore or hereafter ratified unless such treaty is implemented by legislation specifically authorizing the introduction of United States armed forces into hostilities or into such situations and stating that it is intended to constitute specific statutory authorization within the meaning of this joint resolution.

(b) Nothing in this joint resolution shall be construed to require any further specific statutory authorization to permit members of the United States armed forces to participate jointly with members of the armed forces of one or more foreign countries in the headquarters operations of high-level military commands which were established prior to the date of enactment of this joint resolution and pursuant to the United Nations Charter or any treaty ratified by the United States prior to such date.

(c) For purposes of this joint resolution, the term "introduction of

United States armed forces" includes the assignment of members of such armed forces to command, coordinate, participate in the movement of, or accompany the regular or irregular military forces of any foreign country or government when such military forces are engaged, or there exists an imminent threat that such forces will become engaged, in hostilities.

(d) Nothing in this joint resolution—

(1) is intended to alter the constitutional authority of the Congress or of the president, or the provisions of existing treaties; or

(2) shall be construed as granting any authority to the president with respect to the introduction of United States armed forces into hostilities or into situations wherein involvement in hostilities is clearly indicated by the circumstances which authority he would not have had in the absence of this joint resolution.

SEPARABILITY CLAUSE
Section 9.   If any provision of this joint resolution or the application thereof to any person or circumstance is held invalid, the remainder of the joint resolution and the application of such provision to any other person or circumstance shall not be affected thereby.

EFFECTIVE DATE
Section 10.   This joint resolution shall take effect on the date of its enactment.

Passed over presidential veto Nov. 7, 1973.

---

sage of a concurrent resolution [Section 5(c)].[67] The sixty-to ninety-day period does not begin, however, until the President submits a written report under the terms of Section 4(a)(1) or unless Congress decides on a date when such a report should have been submitted but was not and acts accordingly to start the sixty-day clock in motion [Section 5(b)].[68]

[67] This provision has been a source of controversy because it allows Congress to direct the President to withdraw troops at any time by concurrent resolution, which is a legislative enactment that does not cross the President's desk (see the discussion of the legislative veto in Chapter 4.) The provision has not been excised from the law, but in the one instance where Congress invoked its power to define the length of presidentially initiated U.S. military involvement—the Lebanon case in 1983–1984—Congress acted through the regular legislative process.

[68] Presidents have almost always submitted reports but have deliberately avoided doing so under Section 4(a)(1), thereby not starting the clock.

Despite what initially was considered a successful attempt to involve Congress more meaningfully in war making, the War Powers Resolution has been the focus of much criticism and debate. Some critics have argued that it attempts improperly to tie the President's hands. Others view it as a weak and inadequate act that has had no important impact on presidential war making or state that it has served as an invitation for the President to conduct war freely for sixty days.[69] In any case, no President from Ford to Bush has fully complied with its terms, and all have questioned the act's constitutionality, mostly on the grounds that the act improperly infringes on the President's constitutional prerogatives. This raises the added objection that the act lacks any mechanism to force the President to comply (aside from the concurrent resolution provision), as it provides no means to impel the President to submit an initial report or even to consult with Congress.

The War Powers Resolution in Operation; or, "Oh, What a Lovely War"

In 1975 the War Powers Resolution was invoked on four occasions. The first three occurred in April and involved the evacuation of refugees and American citizens from Vietnam and Cambodia in the waning days of the Vietnam war. In these instances consultation and reporting occurred, but the rescue attempts were concluded within forty-eight hours.

The fourth instance occurred in May, when an American cargo

---

[69] For more on this debate, see Stephen Carter, "The Constitutionality of the War Powers Resolution," *Virginia Law Review*, 70 (February 1984): 101–134; Richard E. Cohen, "Marching through the War Powers Act," *National Journal*, December 30, 1989, p. 3120; Daniel P. Franklin, "Why the Legislative Veto Isn't Dead," *Presidential Studies Quarterly*, 16 (Summer 1986): 491–502; Kenneth M. Holland, "The War Powers Resolution: An Infringement on the President's Constitutional and Prerogative Powers," in *The Presidency and National Security Policy*, ed. by R. Gordon Hoxie (New York: Center for the Study of the Presidency, 1984); Robert A. Katzmann, "War Powers: Toward a New Accommodation," in *A Question of Balance*, ed. by Thomas E. Mann; Michael Rubner, "The Reagan Administration, the 1973 War Powers Resolution, and the Invasion of Grenada," *Political Science Quarterly*, 100 (Winter, 1985/86); Robert Scigliano, "The War Powers Resolution and the War Powers," in *The Presidency in the Constitutional Order*, ed. by Joseph M. Bessette and Jeffrey Tulis (Baton Rouge: Louisiana State University Press, 1981), pp. 115–153; Marc E. Smyrl, *Conflict or Codetermination? Congress, the President, and the Power to Make War* (Cambridge, Mass.: Ballinger, 1988); William Spong, Jr., "The War Powers Resolution Revisited: Historical Accomplishment or Surrender?" *William and Mary Law Review*, 16 (Summer 1975): 823–882.

vessel, the *Mayaguez*, was captured by a Cambodian gunboat. President Ford ordered retaliatory air strikes against Cambodia and called up the Marines, who launched a costly invasion of Koh Tang Island in the erroneous belief that the *Mayaguez's* crew was being held there. Despite problems with the military operation, the crew was returned two days later, although apparently not as a result of the military assaults. Ford's actions prompted euphoria at a time when the country was still feeling the sting of Vietnam. In this instance Ford did not consult with Congress, but he did inform some members of Congress of the operation as it was being carried out and provided a report.

In April 1980 President Jimmy Carter launched an unsuccessful military effort to rescue American hostages being held in Iran. He did not consult with Congress, citing the need for secrecy. He did submit a brief report to Congress, but he also argued that the War Powers Resolution did not apply, asserting that the mission was a humanitarian effort and therefore outside the provisions of the resolution.

Lebanon.   The presidency of Ronald Reagan saw several clashes between the executive and legislative branches over the deployment of American troops abroad. In August 1982 Reagan sent Marines to Lebanon to serve as part of an international force including French and Italian (and later British) troops to help bring peace to that wartorn nation. Despite agreement that a state of hostilities existed, Reagan submitted a report to Congress "consistent with" the War Powers Resolution rather than "under" or "pursuant to" its terms. Thus, he did not set in motion the sixty- to ninety-day limit the resolution imposes.

The continued presence of American troops in Lebanon in what was considered an untenable military situation raised doubts about the mission.[70] Such doubts were aggravated when Marines were killed in several bombing incidents. In one instance 241 Marines were killed when a Moslem fundamentalist drove a truck full of explosives into Marine headquarters on October 23, 1983.

In the absence of the automatic triggering of the war powers

---

[70] The Joint Chiefs of Staff, it was later revealed, had unanimously opposed sending the Marines to Lebanon. See Cecil V. Crabb, Jr., and Pat M. Holt, *Invitation to Struggle: Congress, the President and Foreign Policy* (Washington, D.C.: CQ Press, 1989), p. 148. In all, 264 Marines were killed and 134 were wounded.

clock, Congress stepped up debate and criticism of Reagan's decision. After protracted negotiations between the administration and
congressional leaders, Congress passed and the President signed a
bill giving Reagan the authority to keep the troops in Lebanon for
eighteen months. Despite uneasiness over the length of this period,
many in Congress felt it politically prudent to see that this period extended past the 1984 elections. The legislation represented mutual
concession, as this marked the first time the act had been formally invoked, yet the length of time granted to the President to maintain the
troops in Lebanon was so long that it had no immediate impact.

Congressional leaders also believed that Reagan would acknowledge the legitimacy of the war powers framework. Instead, the President made it clear that he did not consider himself bound by the act
(even though he signed it into law rather than veto it) and that he
would consider keeping troops in Lebanon past the eighteen-month
deadline.[71]

By early 1984 the military situation was deteriorating steadily. On
February 7, 1984, Reagan ordered the remaining Marines withdrawn
to American ships.

Grenada.   On October 25, 1983, President Reagan launched an invasion of the tiny Caribbean island of Grenada (population 110,000).
The operation involved almost 10,000 soldiers from all service
branches. In 1979 the ruling government of Prime Minister Eric
Gairy was overthrown in a coup led by Maurice Bishop. In October
1983 Bishop was overthrown. The Reagan administration had viewed
the reformist Bishop regime with suspicion, and it feared a new
regime more sympathetic to Cuba. Also, about 1,000 Americans were
living on the island at the time, 600 of whom were medical students.

Reagan briefed congressional leaders the night before the invasion and submitted a report on the day of the invasion. Despite overwhelming military superiority, American forces took about a week to
win control of the island. Nineteen American soldiers were killed,
and 116 were wounded; 24 Cubans were killed, as were 45 Grenadi-
ans (27 were killed accidentally when American forces bombed a
mental hospital). By the end of October both houses of Congress had
taken steps to begin the sixty-day war powers clock, but by December only about 300 American personnel were still on the island.

---

[71] Fisher, *Constitutional Conflicts between Congress and the President*, p. 317.

Critics of the invasion questioned whether the American civilians on Grenada had in fact been in danger and, if so, whether an armed invasion was the appropriate response. They also criticized the fact that news reporters were not allowed to accompany the invading American troops, as had been the practice in previous wars. The Defense Department claimed that reporters were excluded for their own safety, but after the invasion the Defense Department announced new rules for press coverage of similar military actions that would allow a few reporters to accompany troops.[72]

The Gulf of Sidra.   On April 14, 1986, President Reagan ordered air strikes against port and military installations in Libya in response to Libya's reputed support of terrorism. The air strike was prompted by two incidents: the terrorist bombing of a nightclub in West Germany frequented by American soldiers and American naval maneuvers in the Gulf of Sidra. Libya claimed all of the gulf as its territorial waters, but the Reagan administration ordered maneuvers to be conducted there nevertheless.

President Reagan summoned congressional leaders to the White House for a late afternoon briefing after American F-111 bombers had already left their bases in Britain (they were joined in the raid by carrier-based aircraft). After the mission, the Reagan administration admitted that the naval maneuvers held inside the gulf had been designed to provoke Libya's leader, Muammar Qaddafi, into military action to provide a basis for an American response. The air strikes also were an attempt to assassinate Qaddafi, who narrowly escaped death when planes bombed his residence.[73]

The Persian Gulf.   The Iran-Iraq war of the 1980s spilled over into the Persian Gulf, a central shipping lane for oil, and oil tankers became targets of raids by both countries. Although American ships had been patrolling the gulf and the Indian Ocean, patrols were stepped up in 1986 in response to requests by Kuwait that its oil tankers be

---

[72] See Rubner, "The Reagan Administration, the 1973 War Powers Resolution, and the Invasion of Grenada," pp. 627–647.

[73] See Seymour M. Hersh, "Target Qaddafi," *New York Times Magazine,* February 22, 1987, p. 17. Hersh quoted an Air Force intelligence officer involved with the raid: "There's no question that they [the Reagan administration] were going for Qaddafi. It was briefed that way. They were going to kill him" (p. 20). Qaddafi's home and workplace were primary targets. See Edward Schumacher, "Wide Damage Seen; Daughter of Qaddafi Is Said to Have Died," *New York Times,* April 16, 1986.

"reflagged" under U.S. registry to provide a basis for armed American protection. American ships and personnel were involved in several skirmishes. In one instance an Iraqi Exocet missile hit the frigate *U.S.S. Stark* on May 17, 1987, killing thirty-seven crew members and injuring twenty-one. The attack was apparently a mistake and Iraq immediately apologized, but it underscored the vulnerability of American vessels to harm from missiles, mines, and small attack speedboats. On July 3, 1988, the *U.S.S. Vincennes* mistook an Iranian passenger jet for a hostile craft and shot it down, killing all 290 passengers and crew members.

As with the Lebanon case, many in Congress were concerned that the American purpose and mission were ill defined. Despite the fact that the Persian Gulf was considered "the most dangerous body of water in the world for shipping" and that American service personnel were given "imminent danger" pay, the Reagan administration argued that the War Powers Resolution did not apply.[74] In response, 112 members of Congress filed suit in federal court to force the President to comply.[75] In early 1988 the Reagan administration announced that it was cutting back on the American presence in the gulf. The direct military threat to shipping subsided with the declaration of an Iran-Iraq truce shortly thereafter.

The Invasion of Panama. General Manuel Noriega ruled Panama, a nation of 2.4 million people, with an iron hand and U.S. support in the 1980s. Noriega's connections with drug trafficking were common knowledge, and he became loudly anti-American as criticism of his regime escalated. In October 1989 a failed coup attempt brought criticism to the Bush administration for its failure to intervene militarily on the side of the insurgents. Bush had called repeatedly for an armed uprising against Noriega, and many saw his failure to intervene as a sign of administration weakness.

On December 17 an unarmed American soldier stationed at the large U.S. base in Panama was killed by Panamanian soldiers. Citing an escalating threat to American lives and property, Bush authorized a massive assault on Panama on December 20. Labeled Operation

---

[74] See John T. McQuiston, "The Persian Gulf: A Deadly Corridor," *New York Times*, May 18, 1987; John H. Cushman, Jr., "U.S. Fleet in Gulf: Mission Inscrutable," *New York Times*, May 19, 1987.

[75] *Lowry et al. v. Reagan*, 676 F. Supp. 333 (D.D.C. 1987). The suit was dismissed on October 17, 1988 [*Lowry v. Reagan*, No. 87–5426 (D.C. Cir. 1988)].

Just Cause, the invasion involved a total of 27,000 American soldiers, including the 13,000 already stationed there before the assault. A primary goal of the attack was the capture of Noriega, who took refuge at the Vatican Embassy on December 24. After two weeks of negotiation, Noriega surrendered to American forces. A civilian government was installed within hours of the start of the assault.

In military terms the operation was considered a success. Most Panamanian defense forces put up little resistance, but Noriega's "dignity battalions" proved to be unexpectedly tough. The American effort was criticized for underestimating the opposition, failing to protect Americans vulnerable to capture, failing to secure the television and radio stations in the early going, and poor operational security. According to one Pentagon official, "As a model for future operations, it leaves something to be desired."[76] According to Defense Department (DOD) figures, 23 U.S. soldiers and 3 U.S. civilians were killed and 324 American soldiers were wounded. Panamanian military losses were 314 troops killed and 124 wounded. The official DOD count of Panamanian civilian deaths was 202. However, this figure was hotly disputed and is more reasonably estimated to be between 300 and 700, although one estimate placed the number at 4,000.[77] About 1,500 civilians were wounded, and at least 13,000 were displaced because of the fighting and destruction.[78]

The Bush administration had kept congressional leaders informed of developments before the invasion and told them by phone of the attack plans a few hours before it began. The administration sent a formal notice to Congress shortly after the invasion but added, "We continue to maintain that the War Powers Act is unconstitutional."[79] Similar to Reagan, Bush notified Congress "consistent with" the War Powers Resolution rather than formally pursuant to its terms; thus, the sixty-day clock was not begun, as Congress took no action to do so.[80]

[76] Bernard E. Trainor, "Flaws in Panama Attack," *New York Times,* December 31, 1989.

[77] The 4,000 number was aired in a segment of the CBS News program *60 Minutes* broadcast on September 23, 1990. See Mark A. Uhlig, "In Panama, Counting the Invasion Dead Is a Matter of Dispute," *New York Times,* October 28, 1990.

[78] Uhlig, "In Panama." See also David E. Pitt, "The Invasion's Civilian Toll: Still No Official Count," *The New York Times,* January 10, 1990.

[79] Martin Tolchin, "Legislators Express Concern on the Operation's Future," *New York Times,* December 22, 1989.

[80] Cohen, "Marching through the War Powers Act."

Most in Congress supported the invasion; ironically, congressional criticism of Bush's failure to act in October might have encouraged Bush to launch the December invasion in order to neutralize his reputed "difficulties in projecting himself as a tough, decisive leader."[81] One headline appearing on the front page of *The New York Times* blared, "War: Bush's Presidential Rite of Passage."[82] One congressional critic, Representative Patricia Schroeder (D-Colo.), said that "Noriega himself is the toxic waste of a polluted Reagan-Bush foreign policy. Noriega was A-O.K. as long as he did our bidding."[83] Despite the large scale of the operation, most U.S. forces were withdrawn by mid-February.

The Iraqi War. The warlike proclivities of Iraq's ruler, Saddam Hussein, were fully revealed to the world during Iraq's decadelong war with Iran. But American hostility toward Iran prompted the United States to provide military and other support to Iraq during the war Iraq had started. In 1990 this tenuous alliance turned sour when Saddam turned his attention to Iraq's vulnerable, oil-rich neighbor, Kuwait. After protracted negotiations between the two nations over oil production and debt repayment, Iraq invaded Kuwait on August 2, quickly overrunning that nation's small army. Despite nearly unanimous international outcry, Saddam fortified his forces. Fearing an assault on Saudi Arabia and an interruption of oil supplies, President Bush began a massive American troop buildup on August 7, dubbed Operation Desert Shield. Bush's decision emerged from a small circle of administration advisers. The only member of Congress informed of the decision before the beginning of troop deployment was Senator Sam Nunn (D-Ga.), chairman of the Armed Services Committee (Congress was not in session during this time, although Bush could have easily contacted other congressional leaders if he had chosen to do so). Within two weeks of the invasion nearly 100,000 troops had been deployed in and around Saudi Arabia.[84]

In a message to Congress on August 10 Bush said, "I do not be-

---

[81] R. W. Apple, Jr., "Bush's Obsession," *New York Times,* December 26, 1989.

[82] R. W. Apple, Jr., December 21, 1989.

[83] Tolchin, "Legislators Express Concern."

[84] Michael Wines, "Largest Force since Vietnam Committed in 15-Day Flurry," *New York Times,* August 19, 1990.

lieve involvement in hostilities is imminent; to the contrary, it is my belief that this deployment will facilitate a peaceful resolution of the crisis."[85] Bush's statement was designed at least in part to head off an early invocation of the War Powers Resolution by virtue of the assertion that hostilities were not imminent. Throughout the crisis Bush worked with considerable success to seek bipartisan support at home and obtain international approval for action against Iraq. In particular, Bush won a vote of confidence from the Arab League, Soviet support, and a series of United Nations Security Council votes calling for economic sanctions as well as military action if Iraq did not withdraw from Kuwait by January 15, 1991. *The New York Times* called Bush "a superb crisis manager."[86]

As Bush continued to accelerate the military buildup and escalate his rhetoric, a chorus of dissent and criticism arose from liberals and conservatives. Such influential conservative voices as former U.S. Ambassador Jeane Kirkpatrick; columnists Robert Novak, Patrick Buchanan, and George Will; and the *Washington Times* all urged caution or questioned the logic of the U.S. buildup.[87] On Capitol Hill several congressional committees subjected administration representatives to unexpectedly tough questioning about proposed accelerated arms sales to Saudi Arabia. Many in Congress also began to insist that any move to war had to include close consultation with Congress as well as a formal congressional declaration or other authorization. Such sentiments came not only from Democratic leaders but from such prominent Republicans as the Senate minority leader, Robert Dole (R-Kan.), and Senator Richard Lugar (R-Ind.). "Lawmakers who were prepared to wink at the Constitution when American forces were called to action in Libya, Grenada and Panama without prior Congressional approval [saw] the gulf as a very different matter."[88] In response, the White House repeatedly rejected the assertion that a congressional authorization was necessary, saying that

[85] R. W. Apple, Jr., "U.S. Says Its Troops in the Gulf Could Reach 100,000 in Months," *New York Times,* August 11, 1990; Carroll J. Doherty, "Members Back Sending Troops to Gulf, but Worry about a Drawn-Out Crisis," *CQ Weekly Report,* August 11, 1990, pp. 2598–2599.

[86] "Chief Trumpet," *New York Times,* August 12, 1990.

[87] Randall Rothenberg, "Thunder on the Right," *New York Times,* September 6, 1990. Columnist Pat Buchanan ridiculed the "quest for global democracy" used as justification for the incursion as "messianic globaloney."

[88] Susan F. Rasky, "Congress and the Gulf," *New York Times,* December 17, 1990.

the President's power as commander-in-chief was a sufficient basis upon which to initiate hostilities.[89]

Congressional dismay was fanned when on November 8 (two days after the midterm congressional elections) Bush announced that he was more than doubling U.S. troop strength in the Persian Gulf by sending an additional 150,000 troops (who by then were joined with troops from over twenty other nations) and canceling plans to rotate the troops already there. These actions presaged a shift in policy from defense to offense. American troop strength reached about 400,000 by the end of 1990.

On November 20, fifty-three House members and one senator (Tom Harkin, D-Iowa) filed suit in U.S. District Court to obtain an injunction barring Bush from using force to push Iraq from Kuwait without first seeking congressional authorization. The suit, *Ronald V. Dellums et al. v. George Bush*, was turned aside in a ruling handed down on December 12 by Judge Harold H. Green. In his opinion Green said that the issue was not yet "ripe," meaning that it would have been premature for the court to rule since Congress as a whole had not yet taken a stand on the issue. At the same time, however, Green added that Congress alone possessed the power to declare war.[90]

Despite these congressional warnings and actions, the Bush administration continued war preparations. In the first three months of the crisis, according to columnist George Will, planning, preparations, and decisions were "the President's business."[91]

After the November elections, many within as well as outside of Congress began to urge that Congress formally debate and come to a decision on the future of American involvement. On January 10 both houses of Congress began lengthy debates on two proposals. One, sponsored by the Democratic leadership, directed the President to

---

[89] Rasky, "Congress and the Gulf." See also Thomas L. Friedman, "Senators Demand Bush Ask Congress before Iraq Move," *New York Times*, October 18, 1990.

[90] 752 F. Supp. 1141 (D.D.C. 1990). Judge Green rejected the administration's contention that it needed only consult with Congress before going to war and that a war declaration need not come before the initiation of hostilities. Neil A. Lewis, "Lawmakers Lose a Suit on War Powers," *New York Times*, December 14, 1990. In a nonbinding party caucus vote on December 4, House Democrats agreed that Bush should not initiate any military action without formal congressional approval. Susan F. Rasky, "House Democrats Caution Bush on War," *New York Times*, December 5, 1990.

[91] George Will, "Congressional Involvement Needed," *Cortland Standard*, November 21, 1990.

continue the use of sanctions against Iraq but left open the option of use of force if the President renewed the request. That resolution failed in votes taken in both houses on January 12.[92] That same day both houses approved President Bush's request of January 8, sponsored by Republican leaders and some Democrats, that it enact a measure authorizing him to use military force consistent with United Nations Security Council Resolution 678, subject to notification to the Speaker of the House and the president pro tempore of the Senate that other means to force Iraqi compliance had failed. The measure also included a specific invocation of the War Powers Resolution (the second after Lebanon), declaring that Congress was granting the necessary statutory authorization under Sections 5(b) and 8(a). That resolution passed by a vote of 52 to 47 in the Senate and 250 to 183 in the House (see the accompanying box).[93] The relatively close vote reflected similar divisions in the country. A *New York Times*/CBS News poll taken January 11–13 reported that 47 percent of those polled favored military action, with 46 percent supporting continued reliance on sanctions.[94]

Observers were virtually unanimous in praising Congress for the high quality of the debate, the absence of grandstanding and undue delay, and the high participation rate—at least 93 senators and 268 House members participated in the debate. According to *Washington Post* columnist David Broder: "Never in 35 years have I seen more lawmakers talking seriously with each other about the choice they were about to make. Never have I seen more of them retire to their offices to write their own speeches explaining how and why they reached their decision. . . . This time, they were legislators."[95]

About eighteen hours after the January 15 deadline for Iraqi

[92] The vote defeating the sanctions measure was 53 to 46 in the Senate and 250 to 183 in the House. Adam Clymer, "Congress Acts to Authorize War in Gulf," *New York Times*, January 13, 1991.

[93] Clymer, "Congress Acts." In the House, the measure was supported by 86 Democrats and 164 Republicans; it was opposed by 179 Democrats, 3 Republicans, and 1 independent. In the Senate, the measure was supported by nine Democrats and forty-three Republicans; opposing the measure were forty-five Democrats and two Republicans. Adam Clymer, "Congress in Step," *New York Times*, January 14, 1991.

[94] Andrew Rosenthal, "Americans Don't Expect Short War," *New York Times*, January 15, 1991.

[95] David S. Broder, "Congress Fulfills Its Responsibility," *Syracuse Post-Standard*, January 15, 1991.

Congressional Resolution on the Gulf Crisis of 1991

PL 102–1

To authorize the use of United States Armed Forces pursuant to United Nations Security Council Resolution 678.

WHEREAS the Government of Iraq without provocation invaded and occupied the territory of Kuwait on August 2, 1990; and

WHEREAS both the House of Representatives (in H.J. Res. 658 of the 101st Congress) and the Senate (in S. Con. Res. 147 of the 101st Congress) have condemned Iraq's invasion of Kuwait and declared their support for international action to reverse Iraq's aggression; and

WHEREAS, Iraq's conventional, chemical, biological, and nuclear weapons and ballistic missile programs and its demonstrated willingness to use weapons of mass destruction pose a grave threat to world peace; and

WHEREAS the international community has demanded that Iraq withdraw unconditionally and immediately from Kuwait and that Kuwait's independence and legitimate government be restored; and

WHEREAS the U.N. Security Council repeatedly affirmed the inherent right of individual or collective self-defense in response to the armed attack by Iraq against Kuwait in accordance with Article 51 of the U.N. Charter; and

WHEREAS, in the absence of full compliance by Iraq with its resolutions, the U.N. Security in Resolution 678 has authorized member states of the United Nations to use all necessary means, after January 15, 1991, to uphold and implement all relevant Security Council resolutions and to restore international peace and security in the area; and

WHEREAS Iraq has persisted in its illegal occupation of, and brutal aggression against Kuwait; Now, therefore, be it

Resolved by the Senate and House of Representatives of the United States of America in Congress assembled,

Section 1.
SHORT TITLE

This joint resolution may be cited as the "Authorization for Use of Military Force Against Iraq Resolution."

Section 2.
AUTHORIZATION FOR USE OF U.S. ARMED FORCES

(a) AUTHORIZATION.—The President is authorized, subject to subsection (b), to use United States Armed Forces pursuant to United Nations Security council Resolution 678 (1990) in order to achieve implementation of Security Council Resolutions 660, 661, 662, 664, 665, 666, 667, 669, 670, 674, and 677.

(b) REQUIREMENT FOR DETERMINATION THAT USE OF MILITARY FORCE IS NECESSARY.—Before exercising the authority granted in subsection (a), the President shall make available to the Speaker of the House of Representatives and the President pro tempore of the Senate his determination that—

(1) the United States has used all appropriate diplomatic and other peaceful means to obtain compliance by Iraq with the United Nations Security Council resolutions cited in subsection (a); and (2) that those efforts have not been and would not be successful in obtaining such compliance.

(c) WAR POWERS RESOLUTION REQUIREMENTS.—

(1) SPECIFIC STATUTORY AUTHORIZATION.—Consistent with section 8(a) of the War Powers Resolution, the Congress declares that this section is intended to constitute specific statutory authorization within the meaning of section 5(b) of the War Powers Resolution.

(2) APPLICABILITY OF OTHER REQUIREMENTS.—Nothing in this resolution supersedes any requirement of the War Powers Resolution.

Section 3.
REPORTS TO CONGRESS

At least once every 60 days, the President shall submit to the Congress a summary on the status of efforts to obtain compliance by Iraq with the resolutions adopted by the United Nations Security Council in response to Iraq's aggression.

---

withdrawal the allies initiated a massive air assault in an operation now dubbed Desert Storm. From then to February 23 the United States and its allies flew almost 100,000 air missions against targets in Kuwait and Iraq. As the air missions were combined with naval and land artillery bombardment, extremely heavy damage was inflicted on Iraqi troops, communications and transportation means, and supplies.

Iraq's primary military response was the firing of Scud missiles against targets in Saudi Arabia and Israel. The damage from these missiles was minor, as most were destroyed by U.S. Patriot antimissile missiles. Allied leaders hoped to destroy Iraq's nuclear, biological, and chemical capabilities and inflict as much damage as possible on its forces before launching a ground war.

After a brief pause, during which the Iraqis were again warned to leave Kuwait, the allies launched a massive ground assault on February 23. In a war lasting 100 hours, demoralized and battered Iraqi troops were routed by well-equipped forces that moved rapidly to encircle Iraq's static trench defenses. Remarkably, allied casualties were far lighter than anticipated. During the air war only twenty-three Americans were killed, thirty-four wounded, and thirty-nine listed as missing.[96] During the four-day ground war, 72 Americans were killed and about 200 were wounded (these figures include 28 killed and 90 wounded when a Scud missile hit an American military barracks in Saudi Arabia on February 25). About forty-five allied planes were lost, including thirty-six in combat. Over 100,000 Iraqi soldiers surrendered outright, and tens of thousands were killed in the allied bombardment and ground attack. Hundreds of Kuwaiti oil wells were set on fire by retreating Iraqi forces, and Iraq itself was bombed into a virtually preindustrial state. Yet despite the stunning defeat Saddam Hussein retained control of his country, and the United States did not intervene directly to overthrow him.

Once the air and ground war began, Congress closed ranks behind Bush and the war. Nationwide support for Bush reached an unprecedentedly high 90 percent in public opinion polls. However, the national euphoria over the brief and successful military campaign did not satisfy nagging questions. Despite praise for Congress's role, the institution was criticized for delaying action until January, especially since Bush's decisions in August and November to commit troops were unilateral and had the effect of presenting Congress with a fait accompli. After the initiation of the war, by contrast, Congress had virtually no say in the war's conduct, and its members were given little more information than was the general public. Also, the careful planning that contributed to the military victory did not seem to find any parallel in postwar planning, as the administration seemingly

---

[96] "U.S. Casualties," *New York Times*, February 28, 1991.

gave little thought to a postwar mideast policy that might seek to avoid future regional instability.[97]

Despite continued administration claims before the outbreak of hostilities that the President possessed adequate authority on his own to begin military action, the President nevertheless chose to go to Congress for the necessary authorization, and Congress reaffirmed its war power in its January vote. Many in Congress, such as the majority leader, Richard Gephardt (D-Mo.), were unambiguous in saying that any unilateral presidential action would be grounds for impeachment. Yet even with expressions of dissatisfaction on both sides, most in the executive and legislative branches seemed satisfied that a reasonable constitutional balance had been struck.[98]

Presidential War Making

Despite Congress's attempts to reinject itself into the war-making process, it is evident that Presidents who wish to project American military strength still have considerable ability to do so. Several reasons help explain this persisting trend.

First, even when taken at face value, the War Powers Resolution includes a number of loopholes which provide many openings for Presidents with a predilection to military action. For example, the resolution says, "Nothing in this joint resolution . . . is intended to alter the constitutional authority of the . . . president. . . ." [Section 8(a)(2)(d)]. Other loopholes and ambiguities, such as the concern that the sixty- to ninety-day period in fact provides the President with an open invitation to make war for that period of time, are highlighted by the cases summarized above. Presidents have also argued that parts of the act are simply impractical. In discussing the *Mayaguez* incident, President Ford noted later that many key legislators were out of town, thus making consultation difficult. He also noted that legislators have other concerns which minimize the attention they can focus on a single problem, that the need to gain a con-

---

[97] Christopher Madison, "Holding Their Fire," *National Journal,* February 16, 1991, pp. 390–393.

[98] For more on the war with Iraq, see Marcia Lynn Whicker, Raymond A. Moore, and James P. Pfiffner, eds., *The Presidency and the Persian Gulf War* (Lexington, Ky.: University Press of Kentucky, 1992).

gressional consensus may inhibit speed of action, and that information may leak from Congress.[99]

Second, the historical record indicates that Presidents usually
benefit politically when they engage in foreign military operations.
Most foreign policy crises and operations, especially when brief, usually boost the President's popularity ratings. The close association between foreign policy initiatives and upturns in the President's standing has been carefully documented.[100] More to the point, Congress is
less likely to challenge the President if it perceives that the public
supports the President's actions. And court challenges of presidentially inspired military actions by members of Congress or others typically result in dismissal or approval of the status quo, consistent with
the courts' reluctance to interfere with ongoing military actions.[101]

Third, a military action perceived as successful invariably out-
weighs seemingly mundane constitutional and legal questions. The
military necessity of both the *Mayaguez* and Grenada incidents was
questioned, for example, yet such questions were overshadowed by
national feelings of euphoria. Moreover, although members of
Congress recognized in the *Mayaguez* incident that President Ford
had not followed the law, they muted their criticism because of the
positive public reaction to his actions.[102]

Fourth, Congress has by no means been unified in opposing presidential military initiatives, as the Panamanian and Iraqi operations illustrated. Many in Congress support presidential actions for ideological or partisan reasons. Many believe that the President indeed has
the constitutional prerogative to make war. Some would just as soon
let the President take the lead regardless of the Constitution, given
the political risks of military adventures that fail. And once a military
operation has begun, members of Congress invariably are reluctant
to interfere in a way that might be interpreted later as having con-

[99] John Spanier and Eric M. Uslander, *American Foreign Policy Making and the Democratic Dilemmas* (New York: Holt, Rinehart & Winston, 1985), pp. 73–74.

[100] See, for example, Theodore J. Lowi, *Incomplete Conquest: Governing America* (New
York: Holt, Rinehart & Winston, 1981), pp. 313–315; Theodore Lowi, *The Personal
President* (Ithaca, N.Y.: Cornell University Press, 1985), chap. 1. This trend has broken
down in a few instances, such as during Vietnam and the Iranian hostage crisis, when
the involvement stretched on without the prospect of a "winning" outcome.

[101] See Christopher N. May, *In the Name of War: Judicial Review and the War Powers
since 1918* (Cambridge, Mass.: Harvard University Press, 1989).

[102] James W. Davis, *The American Presidency* (New York: Harper & Row, 1987), p. 196.

tributed to the defeat of or harm to American soldiers. This was a key consideration in the reluctance of Congress to force Reagan's hand in Lebanon.

Fifth, with very few exceptions, the courts have been loath to hear or rule substantively on legal challenges to presidential use of the military brought by members of Congress or others. Challenges to unilateral presidential actions brought by members of Congress in the cases of Vietnam (with a few exceptions), the Persian Gulf, and Iraq, for example, have all come to naught.[103]

Admittedly, congressional attempts to limit unilateral presidential action or involve members of Congress more meaningfully have met with at best limited success. Still, the War Powers Resolution has served as a focal point for debate over war making. More important, it has probably helped routinize the flow of information between the President and Congress when military situations arise. And the fact that no President to date has challenged the War Powers Resolution in court suggests that Presidents are more wary of congressional prerogative than their public rhetoric suggests.

CONCLUSION: PACIFICUS PREVAILS

The Constitution's "invitation to struggle" over foreign policy has not resulted in stalemate. Despite the fact that the document leans toward Congress, especially in the area of war powers, the President has indeed become the nation's primary organ of foreign affairs. One may be tempted to conclude that the Constitution is therefore simply irrelevant to the definition of foreign policy powers, yet this conclusion would be incorrect. If the Constitution were irrelevant, Presidents would not have labored to justify their war-related and other adventures in constitutional terms.

The first lesson to derive from this discussion of foreign policy is that the Constitution as symbol is often more important than the Constitution as fact. If the country accepts the President's claim that the powers of the commander in chief are adequate to justify a military invasion, for example, then that assertion is more important politically than a purely constitutional-historical reading of Article II.

[103] For more on the Vietnam cases, see Keynes, *Undeclared War,* chap. 6. See also Clinton Rossiter, *The Supreme Court and the Commander in Chief* (Ithaca, N.Y.: Cornell University Press, 1976).

The second lesson is that there is enough room for doubt as to the document's meaning and intent that Presidents have been able to make a plausible case for their actions. The third lesson is that political consensus can outweigh constitutional structures. That is, when the other two branches acquiesce to presidential actions, constitutional forms may matter little. This holds true especially when presidential actions curry popular favor.

In a letter to Thomas Jefferson written in 1798, James Madison observed, "The constitution supposes, what the History of all govts demonstrates, that the Ex. is the branch of power most interested in war, & most prone to it. It has accordingly with studied care, vested the question of war in the Legisl."[104] The twentieth-century presidential assumption of war powers may indeed have been a necessary or desirable development, but presidential actions have only endorsed the truth of Madison's judgment. Until Vietnam, most liberals and conservatives did not question presidential preeminence, especially in relation to the war power, agreeing with political scientist Clinton Rossiter that the President "alone will be the judge of what is 'best' for the survival of the republic."[105]

Yet Vietnam made clear to political observers of all stripes that a foreign policy scheme closer to the framers' original design, incorporating a more active congressional role, is essential to a consensus-based foreign policy. The political and human costs of presidential war are simply too great. Despite this realization, however, the assumptions of presidential preeminence remain largely intact. Hamilton might have lost the Pacificus-Helvidius debate in his own time, but he certainly captured the debate in the modern era, Vietnam notwithstanding, especially after the Iraq war.

The enactment of the War Powers Resolution was prodded by Vietnam, but its roots are traceable back to 1951, when a growing number in Congress began to sense that the normal ebb and flow between the two branches had become a one-way channel to the execu-

---

[104] Quoted in "War Powers Legislation," p. 154.

[105] Clinton Rossiter, *The American Presidency* (New York: New American Library, 1960), p. 23. See also Henry Steele Commager, "Does the President Have Too Much Power?" *Congressional Record*, April 2, 1951; J. William Fulbright, "American Foreign Policy in the 20th Century under an 18th-Century Constitution," *Cornell Law Quarterly*, 47 (Fall 1961), reprinted in "War Powers Legislation," Hearings before the Committee on Foreign Relations, U.S. Senate, 92nd Congress, 1st Session (Washington, D.C.: U.S. Government Printing Office, 1972), pp. 46–53, 63–66. Both Commager and Fulbright, among many others, altered their views during the Vietnam War.

tive since the advent of the New Deal.[106] Whatever criticisms may be leveled against the act, one fact is clear: This move by Congress was not an assertion but a *re*assertion of congressional power. Despite its alleged flaws, the act has demonstrated that presidential-congressional cooperation in modern war making, whether involving perfect or imperfect wars, is eminently feasible, if not desirable. In Chapter 6 we will see a similar pattern of congressional reassertion efforts in other areas of foreign policy.

[106] Louis Fisher demonstrated that the genesis of the War Powers Resolution predated Vietnam. See "War Powers: The Need for Collective Judgment," in *Divided Democracy*, ed. by James A. Thurber (Washington, D.C.: CQ Press, 1991), pp. 199–218.

Chapter 6

Foreign Affairs II: Ah, Diplomacy!

> If the observation be well founded that wise kings will always be served by able ministers it is fair to argue that as an assembly of select electors possess, in a greater degree than kings, the means of extensive and accurate information relative to men and characters, so will their appointments bear at least equal marks of discretion and discernment. The inference which naturally results from these considerations is this, that the President and senators so chosen will always be of the number of those who best understand our national interests. . . .
>
> JOHN JAY, *FEDERALIST* NO. 64

Senate minority leader Robert Dole (R-Kan.) set off a flurry of debate in 1990 when he proposed that the United States consider reducing foreign aid by 5 percent to the five top aid-receiving nations—Israel, Egypt, the Philippines, Turkey, and Pakistan—and funnel the money saved to eastern Europe and Panama.[1] The proposal met with fierce criticism from several quarters, especially from Israel, which receives more foreign aid than any other nation.

The importance of Dole's proposal lay primarily in the considerations behind it. First, it was a signal that many congressional leaders, and perhaps the Bush administration as well, were beginning to lose patience over Israel's apparent unwillingness to engage in serious peace negotiations in the middle east.

Second, it reflected the severe limitations imposed by continuing

---

[1] For fiscal year 1990 the combined economic and military aid proposed in President Bush's budget for the five nations was $3.0 billion for Israel, $2.1 billion for Egypt, $618 million for the Philippines, $614 million for Turkey, and $541 million for Pakistan. The proposed total for all foreign aid was $11.8 billion. See Thomas L. Friedman, "Senator Dole's Jackpot Question on Foreign Aid Stirs Up Congress," *New York Times*, January 21, 1990.

high federal deficits. Money could not be responsibly allocated for a new purpose without taking it from somewhere else in the budget.

Third, it reflected congressional desire to redirect foreign aid priorities toward nations that merited consideration for American dollars because of recent political changes. In the process, Dole's remarks underscored the fact that Congress, no less than the President, was in a position to reshape the nature of foreign aid if it so chose (although some suggested that Dole's comments might have come at the private urging of the Bush administration).[2]

In Chapter 5 we discussed the general balance between the President and Congress in foreign affairs and that balance as it pertains to war powers. Our attention turns now to other important tools of foreign policy used by the President and Congress, notably, those short of war. They include agreements with other nations, arms sales, foreign aid, "intermestic" issues, and intelligence activities. In each instance the presidential-congressional debate outlined in Chapter 5 repeats itself. That is, modern Presidents claim and often exert ascendancy, yet Congress in fact shares these responsibilities and has in some instances moved to reassert its involvement.

TREATIES AND EXECUTIVE AGREEMENTS

Treaty making is treated succinctly in Article II, Section 2, of the Constitution, which gives the President the power "by and with the advice and consent of the Senate, to make treaties, provided two thirds of the Senators present concur. . . ." The House of Representatives is excluded from the treaty process, yet it becomes involved out of necessity when the enactment of appropriations or enabling legislation is required. The requirement for a two-thirds vote reflected the founders' desire to avoid a treaty approval process that was too easy. Many sought to avoid foreign entanglements or agreements entered into frivolously. As Gouverneur Morris noted, "The more difficulty in making treaties, the more value will be set upon them."[3]

Treaty-making power was discussed frequently at the Constitu-

---

[2] Susan F. Rasky, "Dole, the G.O.P. and Israel: How Much Criticism Is Too Much?" *New York Times,* April 30, 1990.

[3] Max Farrand, *The Records of the Federal Convention of 1787* (New Haven, Conn.: Yale University Press, 1966), II, p. 393. See also pp. 547–548.

tional Convention. Initially, the founders proposed that power over treaties remain solely in the hands of the legislature, as had been the case under the Articles of Confederation. But late in the convention the founders yielded to the argument that the President should "make treaties" with the Senate. The exclusion of the House was defended by Alexander Hamilton and John Jay in the *Federalist Papers* when they argued that the Senate's smaller size and institutional continuity, attributable to senators' longer terms of office and staggered election cycle, would facilitate secrecy and dispatch in the treaty process.[4]

The founders envisioned that the President actually would consult with the Senate while treaty formulation was under way and not simply present the Senate with a fait accompli. In fact, "the Senate was to be a kind of Presidential council affording him advice throughout the treaty-making process and on all aspects of it. . . ."[5] Writing in *Federalist* No. 75, Hamilton went further by saying that power over treaties was more legislative than executive in that "the particular nature of the power of making treaties. . . . will be found to partake more of the legislative than of the executive character. . . ."[6]

President Washington pursued joint presidential-Senate responsibility with an Indian treaty in 1789, seeking Senate advice by going to the chamber in person. In addition to informing the Senate about the most recent developments, he sought the opinions of senators about how to proceed in future negotiations. However, Washington expected the Senate to provide its consent then and there, whereas the senators felt that they were being rushed and needed time to analyze, discuss, and deliberate. When the senators objected and proposed a delay, Washington became visibly angry, declaring, *"This defeats every purpose of my coming here."*[7] Resolution of the issue was postponed until the following week; so ended the brief experiment with

[4] See *Federalist* Nos. 64, 69, and 75.

[5] Louis Henkin, *Foreign Affairs and the Constitution* (New York: Norton, 1972), p. 131.

[6] The Federalist Papers (New York: New American Library, 1961), p. 450. For an excellent discussion of the joint nature of the treaty power, see Louis Fisher, "Congressional Participation in the Treaty Process," *University of Pennsylvania Law Review*, 137 (May 1989): 1511–1522.

[7] Quoted in Charlene Bangs Bickford and Kenneth R. Bowling, *Birth of the Nation: The First Federal Congress 1789–1791* (New York: First Federal Congress Project, 1989), p. 88.

in-person consultation. Washington and his successors relied instead on consultation in written form. Yet some Presidents have chosen to avoid Senate consultation, leading to a Senate role that has tended to emphasize the consent role more than the advice role.[8]

Despite this fact, the Senate (and Congress as a whole) has been more active in peace-related matters than war-related matters. According to one study, an inverse relationship exists between the active involvement of Congress and the presence of military hostilities in a situation. Stated another way, the greater the possibility of armed conflict, the less likely Congress is to play a key role.[9]

Although the Senate as an institution typically enters the treaty-making process when treaties are presented to the Senate by the President, individual senators often have participated in negotiations with other countries. As early as 1814 President Madison appointed two members of Congress to negotiate a peace treaty with Great Britain. More recently the United Nations Charter received key input from Senators Arthur Vandenberg (R-Mich.) and Thomas Connally (D-Tex.) in 1945. President Kennedy's negotiations with the Soviet Union over the nuclear test ban treaty of 1963 occurred with Senate members present. Many observers argue that the absence of senators during the Wilson administration's negotiations over the League of Nations agreement at the end of World War I contributed to the treaty's defeat by the Senate in 1919. After that experience, senators were often appointed to important international conferences, especially by Presidents Warren Harding, Herbert Hoover, Franklin Roosevelt, Harry Truman, and Jimmy Carter.[10]

The relationship between the Senate and the President in the treaty process often is viewed as one of conflict, characterized by presidential defeat, especially in light of the requirement for two-thirds approval. Examples such as the defeat of the League of Nations Treaty by the Senate, the withdrawal of the SALT II Treaty by President Carter in 1980 in the face of vocal Senate opposition, and

---

[8] See Larry Berman, *The New American Presidency* (Boston: Little, Brown, 1986), pp. 36–37.

[9] See James A. Robinson, *Congress and Foreign Policy-Making* (Homewood, Ill.: Dorsey, 1967), pp. 67–69.

[10] Louis W. Koenig, *The Chief Executive* (New York: Harcourt Brace Jovanovich, 1986), pp. 205–206; Congressional Quarterly, *Guide to the Congress* (Washington, D.C.: Congressional Quarterly, 1971), p. 202; Fisher, "Congressional Participation in the Treaty Process," p. 1517.

Carter's protracted battle to win ratification of the Panama Canal Treaty in 1978 all seem to support the proposition that the Senate is a graveyard for treaties. Yet from 1789 to 1988, only twenty treaties—about 1 percent—have been voted down on the floor of the Senate (Table 6.1). About 15 percent have been accepted by the Senate after alteration. The very nature of treaty making has provided the President with an immediate advantage in dealing with the Senate. Since the process of negotiating treaties falls clearly, although not necessarily exclusively, on the President, the executive and his or her staff members are most closely associated with the construction of the treaty document. (The President not only may invite members of Congress to participate but may allow key legislators to have a say in the selection of the negotiating team.) Thus, the administration is likely to have control over, if not a monopoly on, information about the content and political process leading up to an agreement. The proposed treaty is presented to the Senate as the President's document, carrying the weight and prestige of the chief executive. Since the President also is recognized as the nation's chief spokesperson to the rest of the world, the political initiative rests with the President in a way it does not with routine legislation.

The treaty-making process actually incorporates three stages. First, the President's representatives, usually including the secretary of state, engage in negotiations that culminate in a treaty with one or more other nations. Such negotiations sometimes span decades and several administrations, as was the case with the Panama Canal Treaty. Congress may offer advice and opinions about negotiations, but such opinions have no special legal weight. Second, the document is transmitted to the Senate, which has several options. It can approve the treaty, reject it, amend it (in which case it may have to go back to the foreign country for reapproval), or attach reservations and understandings designed to clarify its provisions and language. Third, at the conclusion of Senate deliberations, the treaty must be "proclaimed by"—that is, accepted by—the President.[11] As this sequence reveals, the President retains the political initiative throughout. At the same time, Senate involvement at every stage is by no means precluded. But if the Senate is to be involved at any stage other than ratification, it must be at the President's request.

---

[11] Cecil V. Crabb and Pat M. Holt, *Invitation to Struggle* (Washington, D.C.: 1989), pp. 13–14.

Table 6.1 Treaties Killed by the Senate as of June 1988

Date of Vote	Country	Vote Yea	Vote Nay	Subject
March 9, 1825	Colombia	0	40	Suppression of African slave trade
June 11, 1836	Switzerland	14	23	Personal and property rights
June 8, 1844	Texas	16	35	Annexation
June 15, 1844	German Zollverein	26	18	Reciprocity
May 31, 1860	Mexico	18	27	Transit and commercial rights
June 27, 1860	Spain	26	17	Cuban Claims Commission
April 13, 1869	Great Britain	1	54	Arbitration of claims
June 1, 1870	Hawaii	20	19	Reciprocity
June 30, 1870	Dominican Republic	28	28	Annexation
January 29, 1885	Nicaragua	32	23	Interoceanic canal
April 20, 1886	Mexico	32	26	Mining claims
August 21, 1888	Great Britain	27	30	Fishing rights
February 1, 1889	Great Britain	15	38	Extradition
May 5, 1897	Great Britain	43	26	Arbitration
March 19, 1920	Multilateral	49	35	Treaty of Versailles
January 18, 1927	Turkey	50	34	Commercial rights
March 14, 1934	Canada	46	42	St. Lawrence Seaway
January 29, 1935	Multilateral	52	36	World Court
May 26, 1960	Multilateral	49	30	Law of the Sea Convention
March 8, 1983	Multilateral	50	42	Montreal Aviation Protocol

SOURCE: *Congress A to Z* (Washington, D.C.: Congressional Quarterly, 1988), p. 501. Reprinted with permission.

Note: Two-thirds majority vote is required for Senate consent to the ratification of treaties. In many cases treaties were blocked in committee or withdrawn before coming to a vote in the Senate.

Although the treaty process favors the President's political predilections, the chief executive cannot take Senate support for granted. A President must lay careful political groundwork to improve the likelihood of ratification even when substantial support for a proposed treaty already exists.

Ending Treaties

One question about which the Constitution is silent is that of treaty termination. Constitutional scholar Louis Fisher notes that Article V vests federal statutes and treaties with the same status, yielding the conclusion that Congress possesses the power to end a treaty by means of the normal legislative process.[12] Others have argued that since the Senate must ratify treaties, it follows that Senate consent is necessary to terminate a treaty. In legal parlance, this is referred to as the principle of "symmetrical construction."[13] At the same time, several Presidents have claimed for themselves the power to end treaties. For example, President Franklin Roosevelt ended a commerce and friendship treaty with Japan two years before U.S. entry into World War II.

More recently, a political and legal challenge was raised against President Carter's termination of treaties with the Republic of China (Taiwan) as a prelude to full recognition of the People's Republic of China (mainland China). The key bone of contention was the Mutual Defense Treaty of 1954, which allowed either party to end the treaty on a year's notice. Carter announced the termination of the treaty in December 1978, while Congress was out of session. Senator Barry Goldwater (R-Ariz.) filed suit in federal court to block Carter's action. A federal district court sided with Goldwater, but the U.S. Court of Appeals ruled that the President possessed the power to terminate the treaty. In the case of *Goldwater v. Carter*,[14] a divided Supreme Court sided with Carter and upheld the lower court's ruling.

The ruling in the *Goldwater* case also clarified an important point

[12] Louis Fisher, *Constitutional Conflicts between Congress and the President* (Princeton, N.J.: Princeton University Press, 1985), p. 269.

[13] This argument is made by David Gray Adler, *The Constitution and the Termination of Treaties* (New York: Garland, 1986), pp. 342–343.

[14] 444 U.S. 996 (1979).

about recognition of foreign governments. The termination of the treaty with Taiwan was a necessary step toward the full recognition of the Beijing government, which was the goal of Carter's actions. Justice Brennan noted in his opinion, "Our cases firmly establish that the Constitution commits to the President alone the power to recognize, and withdraw recognition from, foreign regimes."[15] Brennan was not, however, speaking for a voting majority in the case.

If past actions are any judge, the power to end a treaty may indeed be shared. According to political scientist David Adler's important study, treaty termination actually occurs rarely. But when it occurred from the period of 1789 to 1985, ten treaties were terminated by the President alone; seven by Congress, and two by the Senate.[16]

In order to better appreciate the politics of the treaty process, I present two examples of recent treaty disputes. One ended in ratification, and the other in withdrawal from the Senate. Both examples illustrate the fine presidential-Senate balance when each holds a vested interest in the outcome.

Treaty-Making Success: The Panama Canal Treaties

Since the American-inspired Panamanian revolution in 1903, a ten-mile-wide strip of land running through the middle of Panama has been controlled by the United States. Control of the strip allowed the United States to construct the Panama Canal and maintain complete control over its operation. The terms of the agreement granting American control "in perpetuity" were so favorable to the United States that despite treaty renegotiations in 1936 and 1955, Panamanians grew increasingly resentful over continued American domination. In contrast, most American leaders felt little necessity to alter significantly the terms of the relationship, as it was very advantageous to this country.

---

[15] 444 U.S. 996 (1979), at 1007.

[16] According to Adler, the ten cases of presidential termination occurred in 1911, 1927, 1933, 1939, 1939, 1941, 1944, 1954, 1962, and 1985. The congressional cases occurred in 1865, 1874, 1883, 1915, 1936, 1951, and 1976. The two instances involving the Senate alone occurred in 1856 and 1921. See *The Constitution and the Termination of Treaties*, pp. iv, 190, 238. For more on treaty termination, see "Termination of Treaties: The Constitutional Allocation of Power," Committee on Foreign Relations, U.S. Senate, 95th Cong., 2d sess., December 1978 (Washington, D.C.: U.S. Government Printing Office, 1979).

In the early 1960s riots broke out in Panama and the American-controlled Canal Zone. Although the immediate cause of the riots had to do with whether the Panamanian flag would be flown along with the American flag in the zone, the riots were symptomatic of growing resentment in Panama over continued American domination.

In the spring of 1964 treaty renegotiations began, and they did not conclude until 1977. During the long negotiating process, some in Congress kept a watchful eye on negotiations development, especially the House Merchant Marine and Fisheries Committee and its subcommittee on the Panama Canal. Both committees were sources of opposition to changes that might arise from a new treaty, and in 1975 the House passed an amendment barring the use of funds to support relinquishing U.S. rights to the Canal Zone. This measure failed in the Senate but was reintroduced in the House in 1976 and 1977.

Treaty negotiations ended during the summer of 1977, and two treaties were transmitted to the Senate on September 16. One, the Panama Canal Treaty, superseded the 1903 treaty and abolished the Canal Zone. The United States maintained the right to manage, maintain, and operate the canal through a new administrative apparatus that would include Panamanians until the end of 1999, when complete control of the canal would pass to Panama. At that time the United States would relinquish its control over administration of the canal and increase payments to Panama in order to continue to obtain favored treatment. The other treaty, the Neutrality Treaty, asserted that the canal would operate under a permanent state of neutrality and that Panama alone would operate the canal after 1999. The only special concession said that U.S. warships would be allowed expeditious canal transit.

From the start, treaty ratification was an open question. Polls showed a large number of undecided senators, and many in the government and in the country simply assumed that the canal belonged to the United States. Indeed, public opinion surveys revealed overwhelming opposition to treaty ratification, although citizens who were better informed about the treaties were more likely to support them.[17] Part of the suspicion surrounding the treaty sprang from the

---

[17] Bernard Roshco, "The Polls: Polling on Panama—Si, Don't Know; Hell no!" *Public Opinion Quarterly*, 42 (Winter 1978): 551–562.

concern that relinquishing legal control would mean that American security needs might be compromised.[18]

Thus, when President Carter tackled the task of winning treaty ratification in the Senate, he faced several political obstacles, and he began to lay the political groundwork in the spring of 1977 by meeting with key members of the Senate to apprise them of developments and solicit their views. In addition to rallying public opinion, Carter needed to satisfy members of his own administration and a Congress that had maintained a long-term interest in the affairs of the Panama Canal. "Few foreign policy issues in the history of the United States have involved the Congress more than negotiations and relations regarding the Panama Canal."[19] Although this degree of congressional involvement is not typical in foreign affairs, the Panama case reveals much about the interaction between the President and Congress in regard to treaties.

Despite the fact that House ratification is not needed for treaties, the House had made its political weight felt in previous attempts to influence funding affecting the canal. During the ratification process the House served as an important forum for generating both support for and opposition to the treaties. In particular, three House committees held hearings on the canal and the treaties: Merchant Marine and Fisheries, International Relations, and Armed Services. In the Senate, hearings were conducted by the Judiciary, Armed Services, and Foreign Relations committees. The hearings of the Senate Foreign Relations Committee were the most lengthy and extensive. In addition, no fewer than 42 of the Senate's 100 members traveled to Panama, as did many members of the House. Extensive activity was seen on the floor of the Senate as well as in committees. Floor debate continued for thirty-eight days, the second longest treaty debate in the Senate's history (only the Treaty of Versailles debate was longer). No fewer than eighty-eight changes were proposed and voted on. Of these, over twenty reservations, understandings, and conditions were added.

Most of the senators who visited Panama did so to gather information, but some engaged in direct negotiations with the Panama-

[18] These and other basic facts are drawn from Cecil V. Crabb, Jr., and Pat M. Holt, *Invitation to Struggle* (Washington, D.C.: CQ Press, 1984), chap. 3.

[19] William L. Furlong, "Negotiations and Ratification of the Panama Canal Treaties," in *Congress, the Presidency and American Foreign Policy,* ed. by John Spanier and Joseph Nogee (New York: Pergamon, 1981), p. 78.

nian leadership. The act of senators engaging in such negotiations after the conclusion of treaty terms between the executive heads of government was highly unusual and represented a degree of Senate involvement not seen since consideration of the Treaty of Versailles. President Carter found it necessary to respond to the specific concerns of undecided senators. In one key incident, a freshman senator—Dennis DeConcini (D-Ariz.)—succeeded in attaching an amendment to the treaty (with Carter's consent) which allowed the United States to use military force to keep the canal open after the year 2000. This addition infuriated the Panamanians, and some emergency bargaining occurred to find compromise wording satisfactory to both the Senate, including DeConcini, and Panama. Carter's concession on the DeConcini amendment was obviously a move to win his support, yet it nearly destroyed the treaty process.

DeConcini's pivotal influence illustrated a larger point about ratification. Senators who remained undecided found themselves in the best political position to influence the terms of the treaty and also to extract concessions (often unrelated to the treaty issue) from the President in exchange for their support. Indeed, some senators who initially had committed themselves to the treaty backed off in an attempt to gain leverage with the White House.[20]

After months of intense investigation, bargaining, and debate the Senate approved the Neutrality Treaty on March 16, 1978, and the Canal Treaty the following April 18. Both passed by the same 68–32 margin—one vote more than the necessary two-thirds.

The unpopularity of the treaty, plus the keen interest of many members of Congress, made the ratification process exceptionally difficult for Carter. Yet Carter almost certainly made the ratification process more difficult by underestimating Senate sensibilities. According to political scientist Richard Pious, Carter "bungled his dealings with the Senate. . . . some of the problems could have been avoided had the Senate been brought in at an early stage. . . ."[21]

---

[20] Crabb and Holt, *Invitation to Struggle,* p. 91.

[21] Richard M. Pious, *The American Presidency* (New York: Basic Books, 1979), p. 338. A similar conclusion was reached by George D. Moffett III, who noted that despite the fact that Carter dealt "from a position of unusual strength," the victory "came at a debilitatingly high political price." *The Limits of Victory: The Ratification of the Panama Canal Treaties* (Ithaca, N.Y.: Cornell University Press, 1985), pp. 9, 11. See also William L. Furlong and Margaret E. Scranton, *The Dynamics of Foreign Policymaking: The President, the Congress, and the Panama Canal Treaties* (Boulder, Colo.: Westview, 1984).

Treaty-Making Failure: The SALT II Treaty

Since 1968, the United States has engaged in systematic talks with the Soviet Union designed to control aspects of the nuclear arms race. For the Nixon, Ford, and Carter administrations, these talks were known by the acronym SALT (Strategic Arms Limitation Talks). The two most important treaties emerging from this process were SALT I, completed and ratified in 1972, and SALT II, completed in 1979 but withdrawn from the Senate shortly after completion. Although SALT II was not brought to a vote before the full Senate, it was withdrawn because of the clear sense that it could not achieve the necessary two-thirds vote.[22]

SALT II negotiations began in November 1972 and stretched on for seven years, spanning three presidential administrations. The treaty dealt with a variety of complex issues, but in general it set limits on the numbers of "strategic delivery vehicles"—that is, the vehicles (including missiles and bombers) used to deliver nuclear warheads—each side could have. It also included a three-year "protocol" addressing controversial issues dividing the two nations and a statement addressing President Carter's "deep cuts" proposal, which called for significant reductions in weapons numbers set out in prior agreements. The negotiating process stretched on during Carter's first two years in office because of disagreements over how to deal with particular weapons systems, such as the cruise missile and the Soviet Backfire bomber.

As with the Panama Canal treaties, the President had to deal domestically not only with the Senate but with the House, his own administration, and public opinion. In Congress, key members had been vocal about the negotiations process since the early 1970s. Certain House members had been influential in shaping the SALT debate in this country, and various attempts were made to influence the nature and direction of the treaty through control of funding (members of Congress had been excluded from actual negotiations up to that time).

In fact, Carter made good on his campaign promise of involving

---

[22] This account is drawn from Stephen J. Flanagan, "The Domestic Politics of SALT II: Implications for the Foreign Policy Process," in *Congress, the Presidency and American Foreign Policy*, ed. by John Spanier and Joseph Nogee, chap. 3. See also John Spanier and Eric M. Uslander, *American Foreign Policy Making and the Democratic Dilemmas* (New York: Holt, Rinehart & Winston, 1985), pp. 204–217.

key legislators by including them within his inner circle of advisers, and some were actually involved in negotiations. Some Senate hard-liners were also consulted by the Carter administration in an attempt to include their views in order to ultimately win their support. In all, a group of thirty senators and fourteen House members were appointed as advisers to and participants in the SALT negotiations. These efforts prompted the Senate minority leader, Howard Baker (R-Tenn.) to praise Carter for his bipartisan approach. In addition, prevailing congressional sentiment often was used as a bargaining chip with the Soviets, as the U.S. negotiators would sometimes argue for or against a certain proposed provision based on predictions about what the Senate would or would not accept.

Despite these careful steps, SALT II encountered a series of roadblocks. For example, many in Congress sought to impose "linkage," that is, to link the SALT agreement to other issues not related to the nuclear balance in an attempt to alter Soviet policy in other areas. Others were concerned that some of Carter's negotiators, such as Arms Control and Disarmament Agency head Paul Warnke, would not be sufficiently tough. Others believed that the treaty gave away too much or that some provisions would be difficult to verify. These and related criticisms were presented forcefully at a time when Congress was moving to assert itself generally in policy-making and the presidency was still laboring under the consequences of Vietnam and Watergate.

The final provisions of the treaty were worked out in May 1979, and the agreement was signed on June 14. By the time the treaty was sent to the Senate, the public SALT debate had been going on for several years. Thus, the major issues were well known to the principals. The Senate Foreign Relations Committee held four months of both open and closed hearings on the treaty. Consideration of the military consequences of the treaty were undertaken by the Senate Armed Services Committee.

After narrowly averting several attempts to kill the treaty, the Foreign Relations Committee reported the treaty favorably by a lukewarm vote of 9–6. In addition, it attached twenty-three conditions to the ratification resolution. It thus became clear that the treaty would not be approved without changes, yet Carter had made it clear that the treaty would not be renegotiated. The force of "linkage" also entered in as congressional critics noted with alarm the presence of Cuban troops in Africa and the taking of American hostages in Iran in November. Shortly thereafter, a group of nineteen senators urged Carter to put off a vote on the treaty. Finally, Carter asked the Senate to postpone consideration of the treaty in the aftermath of the Soviet invasion of Afghanistan in December. The treaty was never brought back to the Senate, although its terms were followed generally by both sides throughout the 1980s.

The withdrawal of SALT II was facilitated by external events but also by persistent divisions within the government over the goals and purposes of the SALT process. Some observers have suggested that the substantial involvement of Congress was instrumental to SALT's demise. Yet it was the exclusion of key representatives from SALT I negotiations that did much to energize congressional opposition to the SALT process that followed.

Assessment: Treaties, the President, and Congress

The Panama Canal treaties and the SALT II Treaty were both high-visibility treaty efforts involving a single presidency—that of Jimmy Carter. Nevertheless, they reveal much about the politics of treaty making. First, the rise of congressional assertiveness in the 1970s has reinvigorated the role of Congress such that Presidents must now take greater care when laying the political groundwork for the approval of major or controversial treaties. In any era, however, a President who ignores the Senate imperils any impending treaty.

Second, the President cannot ignore the House. Through the appropriations process, committee investigations, and the ability to gain public attention, the House (especially through key committees) can have a profound impact on the treaty process.

Third, the door to greater direct involvement by members of Congress in the actual process of formulating treaties, despite the possible pitfall of involving too many hands in the negotiating process, is open. Such involvement is consistent with the intent of the Constitution's framers. Moreover, political circumstances make such efforts desirable, and nothing in the Constitution bars such greater involvement.

Fourth, political bargaining occurs over treaty support just as it does over more mundane domestic political issues. While one might question the trading of a vote for an important treaty in exchange for funding for an unrelated pet project in a senator's home state, such processes are part of the currency of presidential-congressional relations.

Fifth, one of the central facts of the modern Congress is that it is organizationally more decentralized than in its past history. Party and chamber leaders possess less control over the behavior of members, and committees and committee chairs are extremely influential. Thus, a President who needs to win two-thirds support in the Senate must be sensitive to the concerns of a variety of influential senators, including party, committee, ideological, and regional leaders.

Sixth, the two-thirds requirement means that thirty-four senators can veto any treaty. The extraordinary majority requirement gives a relatively small number of legislators disproportionately great influence. Most treaties are relatively uncontroversial and deal with minor matters, but treaties that are likely to raise questions also invite senators to use the two-thirds threshold as a lever to extract concessions from the President, whether related or unrelated to the treaty issue at hand.

Seventh, treaties belong in a political sense primarily to the President. It is the job of the chief executive to build coalition support by any available means. The initiative is the chief executive's, but so too is the burden. Given the historical record, it is clear that Presidents have carried this burden with considerable success. Yet in recent years Presidents increasingly have avoided the treaty route altogether in favor of a means of reaching international agreements that sidesteps the Senate.

Executive Agreements

Agreements with other countries may be achieved not only by treaties but also by executive agreements. An executive agreement is an understanding reached between heads of state or their designees. It can be oral or written and may require either prior congressional authorization or later congressional approval. The key fact about an executive agreement is that it does not go to the Senate for approval. It does, however, have the force of law and also possesses "a similar dignity" to treaties.[23] Although executive agreement power is not stipulated in the Constitution, it is generally recognized as coming from

---

[23] This was stated in *United States v. Pink*, 315 U.S. 203, at 230 (1942).

Table 6.2 Treaties and Executive Agreements, 1789–1988

Years	Treaties	Executive Agreements
1789–1839	60	27
1839–1889	215	238
1889–1929	382	763
1930–1939	142	144
1940–1949	116	919
1950–1959	138	2,229
1960–1969	114	2,324
1970–1979	173	3,040
1980–1988	136	3,094
Total	1,476	12,778

SOURCE: *Guide to Congress,* 3d ed. (Washington, D.C.: Congressional Quarterly Inc., 1982), 291; Department of State, Treaty Affairs Staff, Office of the Legal Adviser. Reprinted with permission.

four sources: presidential responsibility to represent the country in foreign affairs, presidential authority to receive ambassadors, the President's role as commander in chief of the military, and the President's obligation to "take care that the laws be faithfully executed."[24]

Many executive agreements involve routine matters from fishing rights to postal agreements. Yet some important international agreements were concluded through the executive agreement route, including the exchange of fifty American destroyers for some British military bases in 1940 by President Franklin Roosevelt and British Prime Minister Winston Churchill and a series of agreements between the President and South Vietnamese leaders promising military and other assistance in the 1950s and 1960s.

Executive agreements date back to the founding of the country. In 1792 the postmaster general reached an agreement involving international postal arrangements. Executive agreements have been used frequently since then, but dating from World War II, the number of executive agreements has skyrocketed (Table 6.2). In fact, about 95 percent of all international understandings since the war have taken the form of executive agreements.

[24] See Fisher, *Constitutional Conflicts,* pp. 272–283.

A Treaty or an Agreement?   The rise in executive agreements is attributable partly to this nation's greater role in international military, political, and economic affairs since World War II, but it also represents presidential efforts to make foreign policy commitments without having to go through the laborious treaty process. This trend is founded partly on the President's relatively greater political influence, congressional willingness to allow the President wide latitude in this area, and the fundamental legal ambiguity in deciding when an understanding ought to be treated as a treaty and when it can be handled as an executive agreement. This ambiguity has been exploited for many years by Presidents. Theodore Roosevelt, for example, found Congress unwilling to approve a proposed treaty with the Dominican Republic in 1905. In response, Roosevelt proceeded to implement the treaty as an executive agreement.[25]

Constitutional scholar Bernard Schwartz relates this anecdote from 1954 about the distinction between a treaty and an executive agreement in regard to

> a request addressed to the State Department by a Senator asking them how to distinguish a treaty, which must be approved by the Senate, from an executive agreement, which need not. The State Department unhelpfully defined a treaty as "something they had to send to the Senate in order to get approval by a two-thirds vote. An executive agreement was something they did not have to send to the Senate." This reply, said the Senator who had sent the request, "reminded me of the time when I was a boy on the farm, and asked the hired man how to tell the difference between a male and a female pigeon. He said, 'You put corn in front of the pigeon. If he picks it up, it is a he; if she picks it up, it is a she.' "[26]

In practical terms, this ambiguity has come to mean that an international understanding is likely to be handled as an executive agreement unless it deals with a politically important subject and Congress expresses sufficient objections to avoidance of the treaty route. Presidents often test the political waters by suggesting that an understanding might be treated as an executive agreement. President Carter did

---

[25] Bernard Schwartz, *A Commentary on the Constitution of the United States*, 2 vols. (New York: Macmillan, 1963), II, p. 150.

[26] Quoted in Schwartz, *A Commentary*, II, pp. 150–151. A useful scheme for understanding the distinctions between treaties and agreements can be found in Loch K. Johnson, *The Making of International Agreements* (New York: New York University Press, 1984), p. 7.

exactly this with both the Panama Canal treaties and the SALT II agreement. In both cases, however, congressional objections were sufficiently strenuous that he decided to deal with them as treaties.

The increased presidential reliance on executive agreements as a means to circumvent treaties has raised some objections because it robs the Senate of advice and consent.[27] But without a clear legal definition, political forces will probably continue to operate by forcing the President into the treaty route only when Congress complains loudly.

The Case Act.   Congressional dissatisfaction with the President's greater use of executive agreements (including some agreements arrived at secretly without the knowledge of Congress) culminated in the passage of the Case Act (also called the Case-Zablocki Act) of 1972. For example, Congress was not informed of important executive agreements reached between the President and Ethiopia in 1960, Laos in 1963, Thailand in 1964 and 1967, and Korea in 1966.[28] The Case Act says that the secretary of state must transmit to Congress the text of all executive agreements within sixty days of their completion, including secret agreements (although access to information about secret agreements is restricted to key members of Congress).

Some have criticized the Case Act as being too weak. The act did not define executive agreements, and thus Presidents have applied their own definitions, which have excluded understandings that many in Congress believed were agreements. For example, President Nixon promised South Vietnamese President Thieu that the United States would "respond with full force" if North Vietnam violated the Paris Peace agreement, but he did not inform Congress. The pledge proved to be an embarrassment, as Congress declined to provide assistance when South Vietnam was overrun in 1975. One representative estimated in 1975 that from the time of the passage of the Case Act to that year, Presidents had entered into from 400 to 600 understandings with other governments that had not been reported to

[27] See Lawrence Margolis, *Executive Agreements and Presidential Power in Foreign Policy* (New York: Praeger, 1986).

[28] See Benjamin I. Page and Mark P. Petracca, *The American Presidency* (New York: McGraw-Hill, 1983), pp. 269–270. The greater presidential reliance on executive agreements is discussed in Loch Johnson and James M. McCormick, "Foreign Policy by Executive Fiat," *Foreign Policy*, 28 (Fall 1977); pp. 117–138.

Congress.[29] The trend of noncompliance declined somewhat throughout the 1970s but has persisted to the present. Some agreements have been reported to Congress more than a year after completion. Some are never reported.[30]

Despite these problems, Congress is probably in a better position with the act in place. Aside from refusing funding for agreements with which it disagrees, Congress can threaten public disclosure of controversial secret agreements. It can also act to amend or counter them through legislation.[31] And while an executive agreement is by definition a solely presidential action, Congress can make a strong argument for at least being informed of agreements that bind the nation to obligations involving other nations.

ARMS SALES AND THE CHANGING ROLE OF THE UNITED STATES IN THE WORLD

For about the first twenty years after the end of World War II American foreign policy was characterized by a relatively strong degree of bipartisanship. Republicans and Democrats in Congress and the White House shared a deep antipathy for communism and the Soviet Union. During this cold war era, arms sales, foreign aid programs, and direct military efforts usually focused on some aspect of anticommunism. The President provided the principal leadership, and Congress generally followed.

During the mid-1960s, however, dissent began to rise in Congress and throughout the country over the conduct of the Vietnam war. Although the conduct of the war was in many respects consistent with past policies, many Americans began to question the monolithic view of communism that had been the basis of U.S. policy up to that time. This questioning evidenced itself in growing divisions between the executive and legislative branches of government. American involvement in the Vietnam war began with the approval and

---

[29] Robert E. DiClerico, *The American President* (Englewood Cliffs, N.J.: Prentice-Hall, 1990), p. 47. See also James W. Davis, *The American Presidency* (New York: Harper & Row, 1987), p. 216.

[30] Johnson, *The Making of International Agreements,* pp. 123–131.

[31] See Harvey G. Zeidenstein, "The Reassertion of Congressional Power: New Curbs on the President," *Political Science Quarterly,* 93 (Fall 1978): 397.

support of Congress, but it soon became identified with the two presidents most heavily committed to waging the war: Johnson and Nixon. As the institutional rift between the branches widened, so too did presidential-congressional differences over other aspects of foreign policy.

The immediate evidence of this rift was seen in repeated congressional efforts to end or otherwise limit American involvement in Vietnam. However, this rift also was seen in other areas, such as in the handling of arms sales.

In 1974, for example, an amendment passed by Congress required the President to report arms sales of over $5,000 to Congress (although multiple sales under that amount did not have to be reported), and it provided a mechanism by which Congress could move to block some arms sales. This act helped prod Congress to challenge proposed presidential arms sales. In 1978 members of Congress fought unsuccessfully to block the sale of fighter jets to Egypt and Saudi Arabia. Congress succeeded, however, in stalling or forcing the withdrawal of proposed arms sales in the late 1970s to Turkey, Chile, Argentina, Libya, Iraq, and other nations.[32]

Congress continues to take a keen interest in arms sales not only because of their impact on the international balance of power but also because of their domestic consequences. With the decline of the cold war in the early 1990s, many people predicted a severe shrinkage in domestic arms production, yet in 1990 the United States eclipsed the Soviet Union as the largest supplier of weapons to the third world. The demand for American-made weapons resulted from their successful performance during the 1990–1991 war with Iraq and pressure from U.S. companies seeking to compensate for declining sales to their own government.[33]

The Saudi Arms Deal

The Reagan administration revived efforts to exert greater presidential prerogative, but Reagan too encountered opposition to major

---

[32] Spanier and Uslander, *American Foreign Policy Making and the Democratic Dilemmas*, pp. 12, 47, 88.

[33] According to the Congressional Research Service, the United States sold $18.5 billion in arms to third world nations in 1990, up from $7.8 billion in 1989. The largest single client was Saudi Arabia. Robert Pear, "U.S. Ranked No. 1 in Weapons Sales," *New York Times*, August 11, 1991.

arms sales proposals. For example, in 1985 Reagan planned to propose to sell a billion-dollar arms package to Saudi Arabia, including F-15 jet fighters, M-1 tanks, helicopter gunships, and other equipment. This plan was scratched before it was formally proposed, however, because of informal but overwhelming Senate opposition that would have ensured defeat of the package. This sentiment grew partly from the American experience with Iran in 1979, when billions of dollars of American military and other hardware that had been sold to the Shah of Iran fell into the hands of the unfriendly Khomeini regime during that country's revolution.[34]

In the spring of 1986 the Reagan administration proposed a scaled down $354 million missile package for Saudi Arabia that included air-to-sea Harpoon missiles, air-to-air Sidewinder missiles, and ground-to-air shoulder-held Stinger missiles. Congressional resistance to even this modified package was stiff because of Saudi support for Syria and the Palestine Liberation Organization (PLO), Saudi refusal to support Egypt and Jordan in the peace process, and the continued belligerence of Saudi Arabia toward Israel.

The arms sale would proceed unless Congress voted to block the sale within fifty days. Both the Republican-controlled Senate and the Democratic-controlled House voted to disapprove the sale, and President Reagan vetoed the disapproval on May 21. The relatively rapid and lopsided vote against the arms sale was partly a function of the administration's decision to cancel the negative vote by presidential veto rather than working earlier to block the initial vote.

Congressional critics voiced concern over using arms sales as a primary means of diplomacy and in particular about the inclusion of Stinger missiles in the package. Persistent concerns were voiced that given the volatility of the middle east, such weapons might find their way into the hands of terrorists (the Stinger was referred to as a "terrorist's delight" because of its small size, portability, and destructive capability).

The White House argued that Saudi Arabia had remained a friend of the United States, was a key source of oil, and was a moderate voice in the Arab world. It also argued that the package was needed to counter Soviet and Iranian influence in the region. Then, in a significant concession, the President eliminated the Stingers

---

[34]This account is taken from Robert J. Spitzer, *The Presidential Veto* (Albany: State University of New York Press, 1988), pp. 94–96.

from the package. White House pressure to uphold the Reagan veto was facilitated by a recurring argument, namely, that the President's ability to conduct foreign policy could be impaired if his wishes were openly denied by Congress. At least one senator changed his vote in favor of the President in response to this argument. As a result of the last-minute pressure from the White House, the veto was upheld in the Senate by the minimum margin required.[35]

FOREIGN AID

The pattern of presidential-congressional relations with respect to foreign aid has followed a similar path in recent years. Beginning in the 1970s, Congress pressed the President to tie foreign aid to progress on human rights. In 1973 Congress enacted the Foreign Assistance Act, in which it inserted two provisions expressing the opinion or "sense" of Congress that the President should deny foreign aid to any country that practiced incarceration of its citizens for political purposes. One provision stated this as a general principle; the other specifically referred to the government of Chile, which had recently undergone a coup (with the covert assistance of the American Central Intelligence Agency) that deposed its elected president, Salvador Allende, and replaced him with a harsh military regime. The human rights abuses of Chile's new Pinochet regime provoked Congress into tying American aid to human rights practices. Similar human rights–related restrictions were tied to aid packages for Argentina, Cambodia, El Salvador, Guatemala, Haiti, Mexico, Nicaragua, South Africa, South Korea, and Uganda.

Two members of Congress, Representative Charles Vanik (D-Ohio) and Senator Henry Jackson (D-Wash.), spearheaded an effort to link American trade relations with the Soviet Union to Soviet human rights practices and especially to more liberal emigration policies for Soviet dissidents, Jews, and others. Despite resistance by the White House, which felt that quiet diplomacy could accomplish more, the policy was enacted in 1974. Some have argued that this policy, often referred to as the Jackson-Vanik law, actually resulted in a restriction of emigration from the Soviet Union.[36]

[35] For more on this and other arms sales, see Bruce W. Jentleson, "American Diplomacy: Around the World and along Pennsylvania Avenue," in *A Question of Balance*, ed. by Thomas E. Mann (Washington, D.C.: Brookings Institution, 1990), pp. 161–166.

[36] See Dan Caldwell, "The Jackson-Vanik Amendment," in *Congress, the Presidency and American Foreign Policy*, chap. 1.

Nevertheless, Congress strengthened language tying aid to human rights practices in 1976, 1978, 1979, and 1980. This effort was facilitated during the Carter administration, as Carter elevated the concern for human rights as a coordinate policy goal, applying it not just to foreign aid but to the overall conduct of foreign policy, including policy toward the Soviet Union. Congress worked progressively to apply rigorous standards concerning human rights to security assistance and multilateral aid programs but was less rigorous in programs involving development assistance and food aid, since these programs were targeted at more fundamental human needs.

Interbranch struggle intensified during the Reagan administration, which sought a more conciliatory policy toward nations with a record of human rights abuses such as South Africa, El Salvador, Chile, and the Philippines under Ferdinand Marcos. The thinking of the Reagan administration was articulated by members of the administration such as the representative to the United Nations, Jeane Kirkpatrick. She argued that the United States should continue to aid its allies even if human rights problems exist because such nations support the United States, do not violate human rights to the same degree as other nations, and would probably improve their human rights practices.[37] Others in Congress and elsewhere argued that the United States was in the best position to influence the human rights practices of these nations.[38]

In the late 1980s Congress urged the President to support a lifting of some Jackson-Vanik restrictions. At the end of 1989, for example, thirty-three members of Congress signed a letter urging President Bush to temporarily waive Jackson-Vanik measures as a reward for the loosening of Soviet emigration restrictions before Bush met with Soviet President Mikhail Gorbachev. Such an action was seen as paving the way for improved Soviet-U.S. trade and Soviet achievement of most-favored-nation (MFN) trading status.[39] Yet President Bush resisted such efforts because of the Soviet Union's failure to meet the goal of writing an open emigration policy into law.

Similar issues were raised with China. In this instance Bush resisted pressure from Congress to eliminate China's MFN status in

[37] Jeane Kirkpatrick, "Human Rights and American Foreign Policy: A Symposium," *Commentary*, November 1981, pp. 42–45.

[38] For example, Alan Tonelson, "Human Rights: The Bias We Need," *Foreign Policy*, 49 (Winter 1982–1983): 52–74.

[39] Ronald D. Elving, "Hill Is Pressing Jackson-Vanik," *CQ Weekly Report*, December 2, 1989, p. 3311. Among other things, MFN status would reduce duties on Soviet goods.

the aftermath of its ruthless suppression of the democracy movement during the summer of 1989.

In general, the political pattern of presidential-congressional relations follows closely that noted for war making and other foreign policy areas. The President continues to be the dominant actor even when Congress attempts to reassert its role in various foreign policy areas. Political initiative typically belongs to the President, but Congress can meaningfully affect the course of policy when it possesses the will.

"INTERMESTIC" ISSUES

Cheap and plentiful gas and oil supplies were taken for granted in the United States until 1973, when Arab nations imposed an oil embargo on nations that supported Israel during the Arab-Israeli war of that year. For the first time Americans recognized their interdependence, as seen in the relationship between gasoline prices in the United States and events across the globe. This is an example of an "intermestic" issue, and it is an area in which political patterns between the President and Congress resemble those of conventional domestic politics.

One long-standing intermestic policy has been the use of food. Since 1954 the Food for Peace program (also known as PL 480) has served the twofold purpose of providing food for humanitarian, diplomatic, and political purposes abroad and providing a means for disposing of domestic agricultural surpluses. The program expanded in high-surplus years and contracted when surpluses were small. In high-surplus years, the program has provided American farmers with a major subsidy.

The Food for Peace program has grown steadily over the years, largely because of domestic political pressure and support from the Foreign Agricultural Service of the Department of Agriculture, relevant agriculture commodity subcommittees, farmers' groups, and shipping interests. Although the program has served an important foreign policy objective, its political impetus lies in conventional interest group politics.

In the 1970s an executive-legislative dispute arose over the increasing tendency to use the Food for Peace program abroad to reward political allies and coax other nations toward greater cooperation with the United States. Many in Congress opposed this use of the program, arguing that its purpose should be fundamentally humanitarian. Even though this debate persists because strategic considerations continue to influence the distribution of food abroad, the program continued to thrive throughout the 1980s (despite budget cutbacks in other foreign aid programs) in large part because of solid domestic support.[40]

Domestic political forces also play an important role in trade and tariff policies. American steel and auto manufacturers and the unions representing workers in those areas take a keen interest in policies that affect the importation of foreign-made steel and autos. With American jobs apparently at stake, these groups lobby Congress and the President to see that they are not driven out of business by foreign competition. In this way, vital domestic concerns expressed through conventional domestic political means can shape foreign policy.

Not all intermestic issues involve jobs and the economy. Jewish organizations take a strong interest in U.S. policy toward Israel. Greek-Americans and Turkish-Americans are represented by groups that work to influence American policy toward those traditionally antagonistic nations. Opponents of abortion have pressed Congress and the President to cut family planning aid to third world nations that use abortion as a means of limiting population. Civil rights and other African-American groups pressed the U.S. government persistently and with considerable success to toughen its stand toward the white supremacist apartheid regime in South Africa.[41] In all these intermestic issues domestic political forces substantially influence the political configuration of foreign policy as it is shaped by the President and Congress.

THE PRESIDENT, CONGRESS, AND INTELLIGENCE

Control over sensitive information pertaining to national security and intelligence matters represents a key source of presidential ascen-

---

[40] Randall B. Ripley and Grace A. Franklin, *Congress, the Bureaucracy, and Public Policy* (Pacific Grove, Calif.: Brooks/Cole, 1991), pp. 164–165.

[41] See Jentleson, "American Diplomacy," pp. 156–161.

dancy. Intelligence gathering occurs through executive agencies. Executive Order 12333, issued by President Reagan in 1981, listed twelve agencies composing the intelligence community. Five of them are affiliated with the Department of Defense, and the rest with the Executive Office of the President or a cabinet agency. They are

Central Intelligence Agency (CIA)
National Security Agency (NSA)
Bureau of Intelligence and Research, Department of State
Defense Intelligence Agency (DIA)
Army Intelligence
Navy Intelligence
Marine Intelligence
Air Force Intelligence
Federal Bureau of Investigation (FBI)
Department of Energy Intelligence Office
Department of Treasury Intelligence Office
Staff elements of the Director of Central Intelligence[42]

In principle, the role of Congress in relation to intelligence is no different from its role in other areas. It provides the legal basis for such agencies, approves their budgets, and oversees their actions. In reality, however, Congress had little impact on governmental intelligence until the 1970s.[43]

The need for intelligence has always existed, but the executive appetite for information and secrecy accelerated with this nation's expanded role in international affairs after World War II.[44] In 1947 Congress passed the National Security Act, which created the CIA (its forerunner was the Office of Strategic Services, which had been formed to gather intelligence during the war). Yet Congress paid lit-

---

[42] See *Weekly Compilation of Presidential Documents*, 17 (December 7, 1981): 1336–1348. For more on these organizations, see David Wise and Thomas B. Ross, *The Invisible Government* (New York: Random House, 1974); Jeffrey T. Richelson, *The U.S. Intelligence Community* (Cambridge, Mass.: Ballinger, 1985).

[43] For more on this relationship, see Ripley and Franklin, *Congress, the Bureaucracy, and Public Policy*, chap. 7; and Christopher J. Deering, "National Security Policy and Congress," in *Congressional Politics*, ed. by Christopher J. Deering (Chicago: Dorsey, 1989), pp. 284–305.

[44] For more on the executive branch's obsession with secrecy and deception, see John M. Orman, *Presidential Secrecy and Deception* (Westport, Conn.: Greenwood, 1980). See also Gregory F. Treverton, *Covert Action: The Limits of Intervention in the Postwar World* (New York: Basic Books, 1987); Loch K. Johnson, *America's Secret Power* (New York: Oxford University Press, 1989).

tle attention to the agency or its activities, and other intelligence agencies, such as the DIA and the NSA, were created by executive order. Because funds for these agencies were included in lump sum appropriations, members of Congress were unaware of not only the purposes but the actual amounts budgeted. Congressional interest in intelligence was aroused only when embarrassing problems arose, as when the Soviet Union shot down an American U-2 spy plane caught flying over Soviet territory in 1960, and in the aftermath of the disastrous Bay of Pigs invasion, when a CIA-sponsored invasion of Cuba by anti-Castro Cuban exiles failed. A handful of representatives were informed of intelligence activities, but they rarely questioned executive priorities. As the chair of one "watchdog" committee, Senator John Stennis (D-Miss.) said, "You have to make up your mind that you are going to have an intelligence agency and protect it as such and shut your eyes and take what is coming."[45]

Congress was finally emboldened to involve itself more actively in intelligence-related matters when it was revealed that both the CIA and the FBI had been involved in illegal surveillance and investigation of Americans (mostly Vietnam war protestors) in the late 1960s and early 1970s at the behest of the Nixon administration and that the CIA had played an active role in the violent overthrow of the popularly elected Allende government in Chile in 1973. Several important congressional investigations helped bring these activities to light, especially that headed by Senator Frank Church (D-Idaho) in 1975 and 1976. Executive branch authorization of such activities at home and abroad raised fundamental questions about control over and misuse of the American intelligence establishment.[46]

In 1974, Congress passed the Hughes-Ryan Amendment, which required that covert actions of the CIA—that is, operations designed to do more than gather information—be reported to the appropriate congressional committees. The act did not have dramatic consequences, as the executive was to report "in a timely fashion," and the CIA and the President interpreted this to mean after the conclusion of an operation.

---

[45] Quoted in Frank Kessler, *The Dilemmas of Presidential Leadership* (Englewood Cliffs, N.J.: Prentice-Hall, 1982), p. 110.

[46] See "Alleged Assassination Plots Involving Foreign Leaders," an interim report of the Senate Select Committee to Study Governmental Operations with Respect to Intelligence Activities, #94–465, 94th Cong., 1st sess. (Washington, D.C.: U.S. Government Printing Office, 1975).

In 1975 President Ford created a special commission to examine CIA activities. Based on the commission's findings, Ford directed the CIA to refrain from engaging in further assassination plots. This action followed revelations that the CIA had plotted to assassinate Fidel Castro and other heads of government deemed unfriendly.

As a result of these revelations, each house of Congress created a permanent select committee on intelligence. Although the jurisdiction of each committee is slightly different, both are designed to provide meaningful oversight. Each committee has a substantial staff and the power to compel testimony, demand information, and review reports. In addition, the committees exercise control over budgetary authorization (that is, granting legal permission to spend appropriated money) for intelligence agencies. The concern for secrecy has meant that the committees cannot operate with the same openness as other congressional committees. Despite fears that Congress cannot keep secrets, both committees have favorable records of not disclosing national security information.[47]

To help ensure that the committees would engage in meaningful oversight and would not be co-opted by the intelligence agencies, as had happened in the past, a limit was put on the number of terms a member could serve on the committees, and the committee chair is rotated. In 1980, Congress passed the Accountability for Intelligence Activities Act, which stipulated that the two intelligence committees would be the sole funnels for information about covert activities. It required that the committees be fully informed of all intelligence activities, and it terminated the Hughes-Ryan Amendment. Despite wording designed to strengthen and clarify the role of Congress, the act also granted the President wide discretion and freedom of action in covert operations.[48]

Iran-Contra

Although Congress assumed a more active role in intelligence activities, controversial covert operations continued. Beginning in 1981, the Reagan administration engaged in a large-scale covert program to aid the contra rebels fighting against the Sandinista regime in

---

[47] See Crabb and Holt, *Invitation to Struggle*, chap. 6; and Gregory F. Treverton, "Intelligence: Welcome to the American Government," in *A Question of Balance*, pp. 78–80.

[48] DiClerico, *The American President*, pp. 48–52.

Attempts by Congress to Restrict Aid to the Nicaraguan Contras, 1982–1986

In December 1981 Reagan administration officials told members of the House and Senate intelligence committees about the President's secret decision to channel funds and weapons to the contras through the CIA. Some members expressed concern over this policy.

Public Law/Statute	Date Signed	Law to Which Provision Was Attached
PL 97–269 96 STAT 1142, sec.102	9/27/82	Intelligence authorization bill for FY 1983 (exact wording was classified, known only to members of the congressional intelligence committees and members of the administration). This was Congress's first legislative attempt to restrict the nature and quantity of aid to the contras, who were fighting to overthrow the Nicaraguan regime. In the early 1980s aid to the contras was still "covert," though Nicaragua and other nations were already aware of the support given by the CIA and the DOD.
PL 97–377 96 STAT 1865, sec.793	12/21/82	Continuing appropriations bill for FY 1983. For the first time, a law passed by Congress included a specific prohibition attempting to curtail President Reagan's efforts to support the contras. It said: "None of the funds provided in this Act may be used by the Central Intelligence Agency or the Department of Defense to furnish military equipment, military training or advice, or other support for military activities, to any group or individual, not part of a country's armed forces, for the purpose of overthrowing the Government of Nicaragua or provoking a military exchange between Nicaragua and Honduras." This wording was essentially that which appeared in PL 97–269. At this point Congress was re-

Attempts by Congress to Restrict Aid to the Nicaraguan Contras, 1982–1986 (cont.)

Public Law/Statute	Date Signed	Law to Which Provision Was Attached
		sponding to Reagan's refusal to alter his contra policy. Note that the act refers only to the CIA and the DOD. At this point Congress was unaware of the financing being conducted out of the White House. This effort was spearheaded by Representative Edward Boland (D-Mass.). Boland did not seek to renew this wording the following year, because the Senate (then controlled by Republicans) would not accept it. The provision quoted above was aimed at imposing two basic restrictions: (1) that military aid be used solely to interdict arms shipments from Nicaragua to leftist rebels in El Salvador, and (2) that the aid not be used to overthrow the existing Nicaraguan government or provoke conflict between Nicaragua and Honduras.
PL 98–212 97 STAT 1452, sec.775	12/8/83	DOD appropriations bill for FY 1984. This provision placed a $24 million cap on U.S. aid for military and paramilitary operations in Nicaragua. The chair of the House Intelligence Committee, Edward Boland, led the opposition to covert aid. He attempted to eliminate all such aid. Reagan had hoped to obtain $35 million to $50 million in aid, so the $24 million figure represented a compromise.

PL 98–215 97 STAT 1475, sec.108	12/9/83	Authorization for intelligence activities for FY 1984. Same as PL 98–212. During 1983 Reagan launched a major public campaign to buoy his efforts to aid the contras. By removing the cloak of secrecy, Reagan hoped to rally public support. It had the opposite effect, however.
PL 98–473 98 STAT 1935–37, sec.8066	10/11/84	Continuing appropriations bill for FY 1985. In this provision Congress agreed to allow the President to spend $14 million on contra guerrilla military operations after February 28, 1985, provided that both houses of Congress agreed. For the first time in eight years Congress had called a halt to a "covert" CIA activity. The key section said: "During fiscal year 1985, no funds available to the Central Intelligence Agency, the Department of Defense, or any other agency or entity of the United States involved in intelligence activities may be obligated or expended for the purpose or which would have the effect of supporting, directly or indirectly, military or paramilitary operations in Nicaragua by any nation, group, organization, movement, or individual." During 1984 Reagan continued to attempt to rally public support.
PL 98–618 STAT 3304, sec.801	11/8/84	Authorization bill for intelligence-related activities for FY 1985. The wording in this bill was essentially the same as that of PL 98–473. It also applied to any unexpended funds allocated in PL 98–115.

Attempts by Congress to Restrict Aid to the Nicaraguan Contras, 1982–1986 (cont.)

Public Law/Statute	Date Signed	Law to Which Provision Was Attached
PL 99–83 99 STAT 254–55, sec.722	8/8/85	International Security and Development Cooperation Act of 1985. The relevant provision barred the expenditure of any money for military support of the contras, although it did provide a mechanism by which the President could request such money from Congress at a later date. The provision did provide for $27 million in "humanitarian assistance" (through March 31, 1986), but neither the CIA nor the DOD could be involved in administering the humanitarian assistance.
PL 99–88 99 STAT 324–25	8/15/85	Supplemental appropriations for FY 1985. Replicated the provisions of PL 99–83. Questions concerning the disposition and use of this humanitarian aid were and continue to be raised. Questions were also raised, starting in 1985, about the possible unlawful division of U.S. foreign aid designated for other countries. For example, in fiscal years 1984 and 1985 U.S. arms aid to Honduras was $77 million and $61 million, respectively, yet the total Honduran military budget for each year was only about $50 million.
PL 99–169 99 STAT 1003, sec.105	12/4/85	Intelligence authorization act for FY 1986. The relevant provision barred the CIA from using its contingency funds to resume covert military aid to the contras. It also broadened the definition of *humanitarian* to include items such as radios and trucks.

PL 99–190 99 STAT 1211, sec. 8050	12/19/85	Continuing appropriation resolution for FY 1986. Appropriations had to conform to the stipulations laid out in PL 99–169.
PL 99–569 100 STAT 3191, sec. 106	10/27/86	Intelligence authorization act for FY 1987. Approved Reagan's request for $100 million in aid to the contras, including $70 million for military aid and $30 million for nonmilitary assistance. The CIA and DOD could resume their involvement, but they and other government intelligence agencies were barred from using contingency funds to give the contras aid above the $100 million total.
PL 99–591 STAT 3341–109, sec. 9045	10/30/86	Appropriations act for FY 1987. Followed the terms of PL 99–569. The passage of the $100 million aid package represented a significant political victory for Reagan and was the culmination of a protracted political struggle lasting most of the summer.

Nicaragua. In December of that year the administration informed the intelligence committees of its support for the contras.

In 1982 Congress enacted for the first time an amendment aimed at curtailing Reagan's support for the contras. Successively stronger amendments were enacted in 1983, 1984, and 1985 and were attached to authorization and appropriation bills. These amendments were known collectively as the Boland Amendments, named after Representative Edward Boland (D-Mass.), their prime sponsor. The strongest wording was enacted in 1984, barring all military and covert assistance to the contras during fiscal year 1985.

The accompanying box lists the public law numbers, dates of enactment, and pertinent text of these amendments. In all, twelve of these amendments appeared in six pairs of authorization and appropriations bills. The most wide-ranging of these amendments was that attached to PL 98–473. The wording barred all contra funding during fiscal year 1985 originating from the CIA, the Defense Department, "or any other agency or entity of the United States involved in intelligence activities . . . for the purpose or which would have the effect of supporting, directly or indirectly, military or paramilitary operations in Nicaragua by any nation, group, organization, movement, or individual." Despite the inclusive nature of this wording, the Reagan administration argued during the Iran-contra congressional hearings that this wording did not apply to the covert activities of the National Security Council then under investigation.[49]

In 1985 and 1986 the administration succeeded in gaining from Congress permission to extend some support to the contras. Yet in 1986 information also began to surface indicating that several of Reagan's national security advisers and other members of the administration had been involved with an off-the-books operation to fund the contras covertly by selling arms to Iran and using the profits to purchase weapons for the contras. This operation was designed to maintain funding for the contras despite the congressional ban. These revelations prompted President Reagan to appoint a three-member board in November 1986 to investigate NSC operations. The three members—former senator and secretary of state Edmund Muskie, retired lieutenant general Brent Scowcroft, and former senator John Tower (the group's head)—were hamstrung by time and staff limita-

---

[49] Joel Brinkley and Stephen Engelberg, eds., *Report of the Congressional Committees Investigating the Iran-Contra Affair* (New York: Random House, 1988), p. 414.

tions and by a limited mandate. The "Tower Commission Report" was completed three months later.[50]

Throughout the summer of 1987 a joint House-Senate committee cochaired by Senator Daniel Inouye (D-Hawaii) and Representative Lee Hamilton (D-Ind.), both former Intelligence Committee chairs, conducted its own hearings as part of a larger and more thorough investigation of the Iran-contra affair. The committee's majority report concluded that members of the NSC and others (including private business people) had consciously attempted to circumvent the law through misuse of the NSC and by private means. The political damage accompanying these revelations was enhanced by the fact that the scheme had included selling arms to Iran, an avowed enemy of the United States that was in the market for weapons to use in its protracted war with Iraq. In addition, the activities represented an abuse of covert operations.

In short, the findings against the Reagan administration included the following:

- Violating the law—the Boland Amendments—and stated U.S. foreign policy by funneling funds and other assistance to the contras through other nations or private individuals.[51]
- Disobeying legal requirements to report to Congress about these covert activities. In particular, President Reagan issued a secret executive order in January 1986, authorizing the sale of American arms to Iran by the CIA. The purpose of the sale was to obtain the release of American hostages in Lebanon.[52] Reagan told CIA Director William Casey to not inform Congress of the order; Congress learned about the deal ten months later, when a Lebanese newspaper broke the story.[53] According to the Intelligence Oversight Act of 1980, the Presi-

[50] *Arms for Hostages: The Official Report of the President's Special Review Board* (New York: Bantam, 1987).

[51] Some in the Reagan administration argued that Congress could not control foreign affairs by withholding appropriations and that if Congress did so, the President could continue to pursue his goals by soliciting private funding. These arguments are demolished in Louis Fisher, "How Tightly Can Congress Draw the Purse Strings?" *American Journal of International Law*, 83 (1989): 758–766.

[52] The background paper accompanying Reagan's directive, written by Oliver North, said, "This approach . . . may well be our *only* way to achieve the release of the Americans held in Beirut. . . . If all of the hostages are not released after the first shipment of 1,000 weapons, further transfers would cease." Quoted in Treverton, "Intelligence," p. 86.

[53] The story appeared in a Lebanese weekly newspaper called *Al-Shiraa* on November 3, 1986.

dent was required to report all such executive orders to Congress in a "timely fashion."[54] Reporting procedures within the executive branch were also circumvented.

- Violation of antiterrorist laws and the administration's stated policy of refusing to deal with terrorists to gain the release of hostages. An administration report on terrorism released in 1986 had asserted that the United States "will make no concessions to terrorists. It will not pay ransoms, release prisoners, change its policies or agree to other acts that might encourage additional terrorism."[55]
- Attempting to cover up the illegal activities by lying to Congress, shredding documents, and erasing computer memories.[56]

Congress's lengthy investigation did not, however, resolve all the pertinent questions. Subsequent charges leveled in the press claimed that the congressional investigation consciously avoided paths of inquiry that might have led to President Reagan's impeachment. According to one participant in the committee inquiry, "We don't want to go after the President" because of Reagan's continued popularity, his advanced age, the impending end of his term of office, and a desire to avoid any inquiry that might disrupt negotiations with the Soviets.[57] The congressional investigators were criticized for rushing to complete the inquiry; failing to obtain Reagan's telephone logs, calendars, and computer-stored memos; and failing to follow up on information suggesting that Reagan knew about the connection between the Iran arms deal and aid for the contras.[58]

The accompanying box summarizes the major events in the Iran-contra story. One important observation to be drawn from this chronology is that it spanned the entire eight years of the Reagan presidency. Without doubt, aiding the contras was a priority of the Reagan administration. Second, the endeavor was sweeping in its scope. It involved a panoply of administration people and several for-

---

[54] Quoted in DiClerico, *The American President*, p. 51. See also Johnson, *America's Secret Power*, pp. 224–225.

[55] "Vice President's Task Force on Combatting Terrorism," *Public Report* (Washington, D.C.: U.S. Government Printing Office, 1986), p. 7.

[56] Administration lies are summarized in David Hoffman, "The Political Sleights of the Contra Scandal," *Washington Post National Weekly Edition*, April 24–30, 1989.

[57] Seymour M. Hersh, "The Iran-Contra Committees: Did They Protect Reagan?" *New York Times Magazine*, April 29, 1990, p. 64.

[58] Hersh, "The Iran-Contra Committees," p. 47. See also Steven Waldman, "The Committee That Couldn't Shoot Straight," *Washington Monthly*, September 1988, pp. 43–50.

Long Trail of the Iran-Contra Case

Aug. 4, 1981. Maj. Oliver L. North of the Marine Corps is assigned to the White House with the National Security Council.

December 1981. President Reagan signs a "finding" authorizing a covert Central Intelligence Agency operation to support the Nicaraguan rebels.

December 1982. Congress passes the first of several Boland Amendments barring use of Federal money to overthrow the Government of Nicaragua.

1984. North is assigned by security council superiors as the White House link to the rebels, or contras.

October 1984. Congress passes a stricter version of the Boland Amendment, cutting off all military aid to the contras. The ban held until October 1986.

February 1985. Using dummy corporations abroad, Lieutenant Colonel North and two associates, Richard V. Secord, a former Air Force major general, and Albert Hakim, an Iranian-born arms dealer and businessman who is now an American, make the first of six arms purchases for the contras. Money comes from private contributors and a secret $32 million contribution by King Fahd of Saudi Arabia. Colonel North and his associates eventually spend $16.5 million for military aid for the contras. Mr. Hakim, Mr. Secord and a third associate, Thomas C. Clines, retain $4.4 million in commissions.

1985. Press accounts link Colonel North to a private network supplying military aid to the contras, prompting Congressional letters of inquiry. Colonel North helps prepare answers denying any involvement but later admits the denials were false.

July 1985. Israeli Government officials tell Robert C. McFarlane, the national security adviser, that Iran wants to open a "political discourse" with the United States, an overture that leads to the first shipment of American arms to Iran and to the release of one of the seven American hostages held by terrorists.

July 1985. Mr. Secord agrees to begin an airlift to supply the contras.

Nov. 19, 1985. Mr. McFarlane assigns Colonel North to handle logistics for a second shipment of Hawk missiles to Iran. He turns to Mr. Secord for assistance. The North-Secord-Hakim network ferrying arms to the contras also acts as the agent for future secret shipments of American arms to Iran.

April 4, 1986. Colonel North outlines a plan to divert $12 million in profits from the Iran arms sales to the contras. The memorandum is prepared for Rear Adm. John M. Poindexter, who succeeded Mr. McFarlane as the National Security Council adviser, to relay to the President. Admiral Poindexter later testifies that he never showed President Reagan the memo.

May 25, 1986. Mr. McFarlane, Colonel North and other American officials fly to Teheran with spare parts for Iran's Hawk antiaircraft missiles. They meet for four days with Iranian officials, but fail to win the release of all the American hostages.

Aug. 6, 1986. Colonel North meets with 11 members of the House Intelligence Committee and denies raising money for the contras or offering them military advice. Colonel North later testifies that he lied in this session.

Nov. 3–6, 1986. Press accounts say Washington sent arms to Iran.

Nov. 12–19, 1986. Colonel North and other White House officials prepare inaccurate chronologies of events in the Iran affair to deal with any repercussions that might arise.

Nov. 21, 1986. Colonel North is told that Justice Department officials will inspect his files the next day, and he begins shredding documents.

Nov. 22, 1986. Justice Department officials discover in Colonel North's office an April 1986 memo to the President mentioning the diversion of money to the contras.

Nov. 24, 1986. Attorney General Edwin C. Meese 3d goes to the White House and tells the President of the diversion of funds.

Nov. 25, 1986. Mr. Meese announces the diversion. The President announces the resignation of Admiral Poindexter and the dismissal of Colonel North.

Feb. 26, 1987. A Presidential commission, headed by former Senator John G. Tower to study the operations of the National Security Council, concludes that the President's top advisers were responsible for creating the chaos that led to the Iran-contra Affair. The report asserts that Mr. Reagan was largely out of touch with operations by the council staff.

July 7, 1987. Under a grant of limited immunity, Colonel North begins six days of televised testimony before Congressional committees investigating the Iran-contra affair. He says he has no idea whether the President knew of the diversion of funds. He also says that the Director of Central Intelligence, William J. Casey, approved the diversion and that the sales were originally intended as an exchange for the hostages.

Nov. 18, 1987.   The Congressional Iran-contra committees, which heard more than 250 hours of testimony from 28 public witnesses, conclude Mr. Reagan failed to live up to his constitutional mandate to "take care that the laws be faithfully executed." The committees say he bore "the ultimate responsibility" for wrongdoing by his aides. It finds Mr. North to have been the point man in a "cabal of zealots."

March 16, 1988.   Colonel North, Admiral Poindexter, Mr. Secord and Mr. Hakim are indicted on charges of conspiring to defraud the Government by illegally providing the contras with funds from the sale of American weapons to Iran.

March 18, 1988.   Colonel North resigns from the Marine Corps and says he might subpoena the Government's "highest-ranking officials" to defend himself.

Nov. 21, 1988.   Federal District Judge Gerhard A. Gesell says he will grant Mr. North's lawyers "wide latitude" to cross-examine Government witnesses about "involvement in sensitive matters."

Nov. 30, 1988.   The White House announces that it intends to stop the release of secret documents Mr. North wants to use in his defense.

Dec. 12, 1988.   Judge Gesell gives defense lawyers until Jan. 3 to select 300 classified documents for public disclosure in the trial.

Dec. 30, 1988.   President Reagan and Vice President George Bush are subpoenaed to testify as defense witnesses; Judge Gesell later refuses to enforce the subpoenas.

Jan. 5, 1989.   Lawrence M. Walsh, the special counsel, asks the court to dismiss the two main charges against Mr. North because of problems over the use of classified documents, leaving 12 criminal counts against him.

Feb. 21, 1989.   Main stage of Mr. North's trial opens after 11 months of delays and pretrial maneuvering.

April 6–13, 1989.   Mr. North begins six days of testimony.

April 20, 1989.   After reading final instructions for two hours, Judge Gesell sends case to the jury.

May 4, 1989.   Jury convicts Mr. North of three counts, obstructing Congress, destroying documents and accepting an illegal gratuity and acquits him of the other nine charges. On appeal, North's conviction was later overturned on procedural grounds.

eign countries. Third, it raises a central question about the entire venture: How much did President Reagan know about the affair? While there may never be a satisfactory answer to this question, there is no doubt that his desire to aid the contras led to violation of the law and subversion of the separation of powers between the President and Congress.[59]

At the same time, the Iran-contra affair dramatized Congress's continuing difficulty in influencing the conduct of covert operations and exercising meaningful influence over an intelligence process that is structured to serve the President. One potentially important agreement arising from Iran-contra was reached between Congress and President Bush in 1989, when the President agreed to define "timely notice" (notification of Congress of covert operations) as being within "a few days" except under unusual circumstances. The agreement, expressed in a letter, was the culmination of months of negotiations and was finally completed after Congress began moves to enact a definition legislatively.[60]

Despite Congress's renewed efforts in the 1970s and 1980s, it continues to be handicapped because of its lack of involvement with and influence over the NSC, which has acquired principal control over the formulation and coordination of national security matters. Some have suggested that nominees for the national security adviser position be subject to congressional ratification. Despite this and other suggestions, few significant reforms have been enacted.[61]

CONCLUSION

The excerpt from *Federalist* No. 64 at the beginning of this chapter reflected John Jay's belief that the President and the Senate possessed at least equivalent wisdom in directing the country's "national interests." The distribution of powers between the executive and leg-

---

[59] This case was carefully summarized in an episode of *Frontline*, a television news and public affairs series on the Public Broadcasting System. The episode was titled "High Crimes and Misdemeanors;" it was hosted by Bill Moyers, and broadcast November 11, 1990. See also Theodore Draper, *A Very Thin Line: The Iran-Contra Affair* (New York: Hill & Wang, 1991).

[60] Stephen Engelberg, "Bush to Tell Congress of Covert Plans," *New York Times*, October 28, 1989. See also Johnson, *America's Secret Power*.

[61] Harold Hongju Koh, "Why the President (Almost) Always Wins in Foreign Affairs: Lessons of the Iran-Contra Affair," *Yale Law Journal*, 97 (June 1988): 1257–1258. For more on Iran-contra, see *The Iran-Contra Puzzle* (Washington, D.C.: Congressional Quarterly, 1987); Frederick M. Kaiser, "Causes and Conditions of Inter-Branch Conflict: Lessons from the Iran-Contra Affair," paper delivered at the 1989 Annual Meeting of the American Political Science Association, Atlanta, Ga., August 31–September 3.

islative branches in the Constitution in regard to foreign affairs veri-
fies this sentiment. Yet the path of foreign policy from 1789 to the
present is anything but a straight line, as the realm of foreign policy
has come to be accepted, with important exceptions, as being primarily the domain of the President.

No piece of information better summarizes this conclusion than
the dramatic rise in executive agreements. Treaties on important
subjects continue to appear on the Senate agenda, but they are no
longer the primary means for conducting business, important or
otherwise, with other countries. This evolution may be a necessary
adaptation to the modern role of the United States in a complex
world—as may be the case with House involvement in the treaty process—but it also means a shift in the way the President and Congress
do business. Unless Congress is prepared to surrender its foreign affairs responsibilities entirely, the principle of separation of powers
impels it to adapt appropriately, as it has attempted to do through
such acts as the War Powers Resolution and the Case Act. In no
other realm is it more clear that "the president claims the silences of
the Constitution."[62] Congress will continue to hold a vested interest
in policies and action pertaining to arms sales, foreign aid, intermestic issues, and intelligence activities. Its interest may consist merely
of endorsing the President's proposals—an acceptable outcome, but
only if congressional acceptance is based on adequate information
and time—or reordering presidential priorities.

While Congress continues to possess the ability to play a major
role in foreign affairs, recent history demonstrates vividly what happens when one branch of the government abandons separation of
powers and interbranch checks. The Iran-contra affair may be taken
as a classroom case of one-branch government in operation. Quite
simply, those in the executive branch who hatched and carried out
this bizarre scheme—it was bizarre not only because it was illegal but
because it had so little chance of succeeding—formulated, enacted,
and judged this plan entirely within the confines of the National Security Council (including the CIA) in the basement of the White
House.

Impatient with congressional and popular objections to contra
aid, individuals in the Reagan administration simply decided that
their judgment was correct, the Constitution be damned. According

---

[62] Pious, *The American Presidency*, p. 333.

to a former staff director of the Senate Intelligence Committee, the CIA chief and other intelligence chiefs in the government in the 1970s differed from those of the Reagan administration in that the former were " 'so immersed in the constitutional questions that they could recite chapter and verse. Questions of law and balance occurred naturally to them.' By contrast, the Reagan leadership was dominated by 'advocates, people who were always trying to get around the roadblocks, who were looking for a way to get it done.' "[63]

In short, an American foreign policy that is monopolized by the executive branch is liable to be more efficient but entirely at odds with the tenets of the American governing system. This concern for efficiency was, of course, one reason why the office of President was created and vested with authority in foreign affairs. Yet legislative involvement is no less vital a part of the system. The sacrifice of some efficiency was readily accepted by the founders in exchange for the necessary and important judgment of the legislative branch. It is, as has been often said, a cost of democracy. As James Madison presciently observed, "There can be no liberty where the legislative and executive powers are united in the same person. . . ."[64]

Many have pondered this dilemma and ways in which an appropriate balance between the branches might be struck. One thoughtful response was generated by Warren Christopher, a former deputy secretary of state and deputy attorney general who proposed "a new 'compact' between the Executive and Congress on foreign policy decision-making, based on mutually reinforcing commitments and mutually accepted restraints."[65]

Christopher's "compact" is predicated on the distinctive characteristics and capabilities of the two branches. It calls for (1) affirmation of the President's authority to articulate and manage foreign policy, (2) full executive cooperation with Congress in congressional efforts to fulfill its foreign policy obligations, especially through the appropriations process and as a forum for generating and discussing ideas, (3) renewal of bipartisanship in foreign policy, (4) an acknowledgment by both Congress and the President that the government

[63] Quoted in Treverton, "Intelligence," p. 81. This attitude was reflected by President Reagan, who, according to former National Security Adviser Robert C. McFarlane, had "disdain" for Congress. Reported in "High Crimes and Misdemeanors," PBS.

[64] Federalist Papers (New York: New American Library, 1961), No. 47, p. 302.

[65] Warren Christopher, "Ceasefire between the Branches: A Compact in Foreign Affairs," *Foreign Affairs*, 60 (Summer 1982): 998.

must provide sufficient resources for diplomatic and foreign aid efforts, and (5) acknowledgment that American foreign policy cannot operate as efficiently as that of undemocratic nations.[66]

Christopher's compact is important because it accepts, and works to operate within, the constitutional framework while allowing for the more complex, dynamic, and executive-centered nature of contemporary American foreign policy. One cannot help but conclude that American foreign policy will operate best when it strikes a balance between democracy and efficiency. That means working within the constitutional framework of shared powers, that is, striking a balance between the executive and legislative branches.

[66] Christopher, "Ceasefire," pp. 999–1004.

Chapter 7

Conclusion: Is the Separation of Powers Obsolete?

The tyranny of the legislatures is the most formidable dread at present, and will be for many years. That of the executive will come in its turn; but it will be at a remote period.

THOMAS JEFFERSON, FROM A LETTER TO JAMES MADISON, MARCH 15, 1789
JEFFERSON'S LETTERS, 1950, P. 108

The presidential-congressional relationship has changed dramatically since 1789. The twentieth-century presumption that presidents should lead Congress contrasts starkly with the nineteenth-century assessment of this relationship. Justice Joseph Story noted in the early 1800s, "The Executive is compelled to resort to secret and unseen influences, to private interviews, and private arrangements, to accomplish his own appropriate purposes instead of proposing and sustaining his own duties and measures by a bold and manly appeal to the nation in the face of its representatives."[1]

The assessment of distinguished British observer James Bryce, cited in Chapter 3, bears repeating. He wrote in 1891, "The expression of his [the President's] wishes conveyed in a message has not necessarily any more effect on Congress than an article in a prominent party newspaper. . . . in fact, the suggestions which he makes, year after year, are usually neglected. . . ."[2] Even in 1908 political

---

[1] Quoted in George B. Galloway, *History of the House of Representatives* (New York: Crowell, 1961), pp. 236–237.

[2] James Bryce, *The American Commonwealth*, 2 vols. (New York: Macmillan, 1891), I, p. 206.

scientist and soon to be activist President Woodrow Wilson wrote that "the president . . . is not expected to lead Congress, but only to assent to or dissent from the laws it seeks to enact and to put those which receive his signature or are passed over his veto into execution. . . ."[3]

Modern Presidents have not abandoned the subterfuge and private deal making referred to by Story, but neither do they shirk from "a bold and manly appeal to the nation," to Congress, or to the bureaucracy. Presidential activism—or what has been labeled by legal scholar Arthur Miller "executive hegemony"[4]—is a truism of the modern presidency. This does not mean that Presidents will necessarily succeed in realizing their objectives or that Congress will stand quietly by while Presidents issue orders. But Presidents typically possess the primary initiative to recommend, orchestrate, and act. This initiative exists as a result of law, tradition, deference, and desire in the context of constitutional ambiguity sufficient to open the door to these changes. Congress possesses similar capabilities to act, buttressed by a more clear constitutional mandate, but Congress acts less frequently, less systematically, and with less coordination and unity of purpose.

This chapter will return to the arguments that began this book. In the process, we will examine the two primary objections most often heard about the presidential-congressional relationship. One posits that despite the many reforms and changes of the last several decades, Congress is an ineffectual and even inept partner in the presidential-congressional waltz. The other, contrary argument posits that Congress has become "imperial" in its relationship to the President—that it has sapped presidential powers, bound the President hand and foot, and in the process crippled effective national governing.

Neither of these arguments is new, although they took on new life in the 1980s. Both arguments reject, implicitly or explicitly, an accommodation between the branches founded in the separation of powers. Both arguments accept, or at least invite the prospect of, a presidentially centered, congressionally subordinate government. Before addressing these arguments, however, we will summarize the ex-

---

[3]Woodrow Wilson, *Constitutional Government in the United States* (New York: Columbia University Press, 1908), p. 40.

[4]Arthur S. Miller, "Separation of Powers: An Ancient Doctrine under Modern Challenge," *Administrative Law Review*, 28 (Summer 1976): 304.

ecutive hegemony perspective emerging from this book and list one objection to it.

THE PRESIDENTIAL-CONGRESSIONAL RELATIONSHIP: MARGINAL OR HEGEMONIC?

At the outset of this book I proposed two broad arguments about this crucial governmental relationship. The first argument stated that Congress's constitutional designation as the first branch of government has in effect been lost to the presidency. Congress is still a part of the three-branch system, but for the most part the political nation revolves around the executive, not the legislature. In Chapters 1 and 2 we considered the constitutional foundation of a legislative-oriented (although not necessarily dominated) system incorporating clear limits and checks on legislative power. With minor variations, Congress fulfilled its contemplated mission throughout the late eighteenth and nineteenth centuries, yet with the dawn of the twentieth century came the rise of a progressively more vigorous, activist, and assertive executive. The process was gradual but occurred almost without interruption in the decades to follow, such that the typical presidential ambitions and agendas of the nineteenth century would seem utterly archaic and inadequate for a typical twentieth-century presidency. This is not to argue that Congress simply withdrew from its responsibilities during the last two centuries but rather to say that in substantive terms, a greater portion of the expanding universe of national policy concerns came from or responded to executive rather than legislative imperatives. In tactical terms, one might say that Congress switched from primarily offensive to defensive tactics in its dealings with the executive. I admit that this brief summary is broad and sweeping and that many important details do not conform entirely to this pattern. I submit also, however, that the presidential-congressional relationship conforms to this general conclusion more accurately than to any other.[5] In the words of political scientist Jef-

---

[5] For a similar argument and conclusion, see Stephen Skowronek, "Presidential Leadership in Political Time," in *The Presidency and the Political System*, ed. by Michael Nelson (Washington, D.C.: CQ Press, 1990), 117–161. This is not to ignore the cyclical, ebb-and-flow nature of executive-legislative relations that Skowronek and others have observed and that has been chronicled in this book as well. But these cycles, taken together, yield executive accretion over the long term.

frey Cohen, "the development of the modern presidency has fundamentally altered the relationship between the president and the
Congress. . . ."[6]

In Chapter 3 we considered the means by which the modern domestic "legislative presidency" has come to play a central role in virtually every aspect of the modern legislative process. Presidents may
not succeed in realizing important components of their ambitious
agendas through the congressional process, but the only stigma
greater than presidential failure is a presidential failure to *try*. (For
the interested reader, the two appendixes following this chapter consider both the electoral and structural features that tend to propel
the President toward center stage. The electoral features of Congress
tend to emphasize the inherently local nature of its electoral roots
and the tendency to view congressional elections in presidential
terms, as with the coattail effect and the interpretation of midterm
elections. Structurally, Congress is internally decentralized and com-
petitive by virtue of seniority and the committee system, for example,
at a time when potentially unifying factors, such as party and leadership, are less important than at earlier times in its history. Congress is
capable of unity and decisiveness, but its institutional inertia invites
the President to step in.)

Chapter 4 examined the presidential-congressional relationship
from four perspectives—leadership, history, law, and policy—to ex-
plicate more precisely how each of these perspectives frames interbranch relations. We found leadership to be less important as an explanation than the extensive attention it has received would suggest.
The historical case of budgeting illustrated the ebb and flow of initiative and inertia in this annual national governing ritual. The law-re-
lated case of the legislative veto provided an example in which a
statutory solution to a particular problem of interbranch relations
viewed as favorable to Congress was to some extent thwarted by an
important court ruling, and the policy approach demonstrated that
the nature of executive-legislative relations varies with the type of
policy.

The very notion of policy type led to an extended consideration of
foreign policy in Chapters 5 and 6. I argued that there are indeed
two presidencies, one domestic and one foreign, by virtue of law and

[6] Jeffrey E. Cohen, "The Impact of the Modern Presidency on Presidential Success in
the U.S. Congress," *Legislative Studies Quarterly*, 7 (November 1982): 515.

tradition. Congress continues to play a central role in such areas as war making, diplomacy, and foreign aid, but the President stands on higher ground at the outset because of the existence of the two presidencies. The historical patterns in these areas leading toward presidential hegemony largely mimic those described in such domestic areas as budgeting.

How does this conclusion square with assessments which assert that Presidents operate, in the words of political scientist George Edwards, "at the margins" of the presidential-congressional relationship and are not really leaders or directors of Congress but rather facilitators in that Presidents "are essentially limited to exploiting rather than creating opportunities for leadership. . . ."?[7] Edwards finds party and public opinion rather than the President's leadership to be especially salient explanatory factors. In a similar vein, political scientists Jon R. Bond and Richard Fleisher find that the President is "a relatively weak legislative actor. . . ."[8] They conclude that presidential success in Congress is determined more by Congress-centered factors (party and ideology) than by President-centered factors (public support and leadership skills).

First, these studies are extremely important for their careful attention to specific factors that have influenced presidential success in congressional roll call votes in recent years. Second, they are important in their attempt to deemphasize the excessive attention given to presidential leadership in explaining presidential-congressional relations (see Chapter 4). Third, they seek to apply more systematic, quantitative analysis to a subject where these methods are not often applied (although roll call votes often serve as a basis for data analysis).

These studies are, however, limited in their scope and applicability. The focus on the specific concept of presidential success as measured by roll call votes precludes the multiplicity of decision points where the two branches interact before a roll call vote, in other words, most of that with which this book deals. This focus precludes any issue or conflict that does not include roll call votes (especially important in the realm of foreign policy). Of necessity, these studies are timebound as well. As political scientist Mark Peterson notes,

[7] George C. Edwards III, *At the Margins* (New Haven, Conn.: Yale University Press, 1989), p. 212.

[8] Jon R. Bond and Richard Fleisher, *The President in the Legislative Arena* (Chicago: University of Chicago Press, 1990), p. x.

"The plain language of presidential success and failure suggests little about the many legislative roads that lead them, from inertia to concerted action, from acclaim to flat rejection."[9]

In short, to apply the label marginal to the President's relations with Congress is to ignore or reject 200 years of institutional and political development that has been characterized by political scientist Stephen Skowronek as "an evolutionary sequence culminating in the expanded powers and governing responsibilities of the 'modern presidency.' "[10] To reject the marginal label is not, however, to embrace the notion of the President as an unerringly successful leader of Congress, for marginal and leader are not the only two choices in a system of limited, shared powers in a three-branch government. The notion of a hegemonic presidency summarizes the steady accretion of powers, responsibilities, and symbols to the executive, a process that Congress for the most part has not been able to match. That Presidents do not score higher on success indexes is only an indication that Presidents still need the consent of Congress and that Congress can at times modify, redirect, or overrule presidential priorities.

The second argument I advanced at the start of this book is that contemporary governing problems have been in part misdiagnosed by those who would seek to lay at the feet of traditional separation of powers the blame for much of what is perceived to be wrong with modern governing. These problems are usually summarized by such terms as paralysis, deadlock, drift, and decay. It is to these critiques that we now turn.

THE INEFFECTUAL CONGRESS/ASCENDANT PRESIDENT ARGUMENT

Lamentations over Congress's inability to govern effectively pockmark that institution's history. Political scientist Henry Jones Ford offered a not-unsympathetic diagnosis of congressional behavior in 1898 that might easily have come from today's newspapers:

> Congress does the best it can do in the circumstances, for it is really the most diligent legislative body in the world, but the harder it works the

---

[9] Mark A. Peterson, *Legislating Together: The White House and Capitol Hill from Eisenhower to Reagan* (Cambridge, Mass.: Harvard University Press, 1990), p. 77.

[10] Skowronek, "Presidential Leadership in Political Time," p. 117.

more it flounders in the mass of legislation thrust upon it. Only a small proportion of the bills on the calendar can ever be reached. Contending interests struggle for attention and pull this way and that. An interest that gets on top in the scramble plunges violently towards its goal, anxious above all things to attain its object while the opportunity serves. Of course there is a great deal of haphazard work. Imagine the plight of a large board of directors, who, instead of dealing directly with the general officers of the company, have to deal with numerous busy committees of their own, possessed by all sorts of ideas, and abounding with schemes conceived in behalf of all sorts of interests! What opportunity would there be for the establishment of a steady and consistent policy and for the exercise of judgment and deliberation in the dispatch of business?[11]

Ford's assessment mirrors that of many contemporary critics: Congress's size and decentralized structure invite special-interest peddling and corruption, hinder efficient policy-making, encourage an "everyone for themselves" mentality, and promote parochial, shortsighted solutions to pressing national problems. But above all, Congress is fundamentally ineffectual, unable to govern effectively—unless it yields to presidential direction and leadership.[12]

Some have argued that congressional ineffectiveness has not followed a straight line but rather has been cyclical.[13] Most point to the reforms enacted in the era after Vietnam and Watergate as attempts to increase congressional effectiveness vis-à-vis the presidency. Several of these efforts, such as the War Powers Resolution, the Case Act, and the Budget and Impoundment Control Act, have received

[11] Henry Jones Ford, *The Rise and Growth of American Politics* (New York: Da Capo, 1967), pp. 229–230.

[12] Alan L. Clem, *Congress: Powers, Processes, and Politics* (Pacific Grove, Calif.: Brooks/Cole, 1989), p. v. See also James MacGregor Burns, *The Deadlock of Democracy* (Englewood Cliffs, N.J.: Prentice-Hall, 1963). These complaints against Congress often surface in the press. See, for example, Gregg Easterbrook, "What's Wrong with Congress?" *Atlantic Monthly*, December 1984, pp. 57–84; a four-part series of articles by Sara Fritz in the *Los Angeles Times*, January 24–27, 1988; John E. Yang, "Chaotic Congress: Lawmakers' Inability to Clear Up Gridlock Is a Rising Frustration," *Wall Street Journal*, March 21, 1988; and Paula Dwyer and Douglas Harbrecht, "Congress: It Doesn't Work. Let's Fix It," *Business Week*, April 16, 1990, pp. 54–63.

[13] See James L. Sundquist, *The Decline and Resurgence of Congress* (Washington, D.C.: Brookings Institution, 1981); Allen Schick, "Politics through Law: Congressional Limitations on Executive Discretion," in *Both Ends of the Avenue*, ed. by Anthony King (Washington, D.C.: American Enterprise Institute, 1983), pp. 154–184; Burt Solomon, "Pendulum of Power," *National Journal*, November 18, 1989, pp. 2816–2817.

attention in this book.[14] Yet according to the ineffectual Congress view, these efforts have had little impact on congressional malaise because Congress's problems are rooted in the very nature of the institution.[15]

Terms and Parties

A long strain of prescriptive literature has advocated various reforms to facilitate presidential leadership and minimize congressional obstruction and inaction, usually through efforts that would also strengthen the political parties.[16] Many have proposed that the terms for members of the House be extended to four years, coterminous with the president's election, and that senatorial terms be lengthened similarly to eight years. This presumably would lead to a greater likelihood that the same political party would control both branches at the same time, minimizing the often-heard complaint that modern governing is typified by deadlock, paralysis, and gridlock stemming from divided party control.

Evidence of this divided party control is easily seen in the fact that from 1952 to 1992 the presidency and both houses of Congress were controlled by the same political party for only fourteen years. From 1968 to 1992 same-party control existed for only four years. As a 1950 report critical of the current system noted, "If the elections for these offices always coincide, recurrent emphasis upon national issues would promote legislative-executive party solidarity."[17]

The idea of a four-year term for members of the House was not

[14] These and other reforms receive special attention in Harvey G. Zeidenstein, "The Reassertion of Congressional Power," *Political Science Quarterly,* 93 (Fall 1978): 393–409. See also Leroy N. Rieselbach, *Congressional Reform* (Washington, D.C.: CQ Press, 1986), esp. pp. 155–158; and Charles O. Jones, *The Trusteeship Presidency* (Baton Rouge: Louisiana State University Press, 1988), pp. 58–59.

[15] Michael L. Mezey, "The Legislature, the Executive and Public Policy: The Futile Quest for Congressional Power," *Congress and the Presidency,* 13 (Spring 1986): 1–20.

[16] Nelson Polsby provides a general survey of this strain of thought in "Congress-Bashing for Beginners," *The Public Interest,* 100 (Summer 1990): 15–23. An interesting parties-oriented reform proposal is outlined in Theodore J. Lowi, *The Personal President* (Ithaca, N.Y.: Cornell University Press, 1985), chap. 7.

[17] Committee on Responsible Parties, American Political Science Association, *Toward a More Responsible Two-Party System* (New York: Rinehart, 1950), p. 75. See also President's Commission for a National Agenda for the Eighties, *The Electoral and Democratic Process in the Eighties,* Paul G. Rogers, chairperson (Englewood Cliffs, N.J.: Prentice-Hall, 1981), pp. 7, 26, 35–36, 73–74; Charles M. Hardin, *Presidential Power and Accountability* (Chicago: University of Chicago Press, 1974), chap. 10.

considered at the Constitutional Convention of 1787. At that time, representatives in state legislatures served one-year terms, although at one point the convention approved a three-year term for House members.[18] Still, the question of term lengths has been the basis of long-standing controversy. In fact, the proposal to change term lengths to a four- and eight-year cycle was advanced with renewed vigor during the commemoration of the bicentennial of the Constitution. As one critic observed, "The midterm election cannot result in a clearly defined change in governmental direction. . . . All it can do is deadlock the government. . . ."[19] The coterminous term proposal was advanced in other important writings during the bicentennial as well.[20]

The End of Congressional Lawmaking

This despair that Congress as currently constituted can never play an effective role in national affairs has prompted some critics to propose even more drastic structural change. Political scientist Samuel Huntington concluded that the "resumption by Congress of an active, positive role in the legislative process would require a drastic restructuring of power relationships. . . ."[21] Huntington's proposal was to take from Congress and give to the President that which has been the very core of Congress's power and importance: the power to legislate. Since Congress no longer legislates effectively, Huntington argued, "the sensible course is to abandon it for other functions."[22] The other functions to which Huntington refers are constituent service and administrative oversight.

The Huntington critique is echoed in a more recent and more ex-

---

[18] See Max Farrand, *The Records of the Federal Convention of 1787*, 4 vols. (New Haven, Conn.: Yale University Press, 1966), I, pp. 214–215.

[19] James L. Sundquist, *Constitutional Reform and Effective Government* (Washington, D.C.: Brookings Institution, 1986), p. 115. Herman Finer advocated a coterminous election cycle but argued that it would "enhance the political leadership of Congress." *The Presidency* (Chicago: University of Chicago Press, 1960), pp. 344–345.

[20] See Donald L. Robinson, ed., *Reforming American Government* (Boulder, Colo.: Westview, 1985); Sundquist, *Constitutional Reform;* Donald L. Robinson, *To the Best of My Ability* (New York: Norton, 1987), pp. 270–271; and Committee on the Constitutional System, *A Bicentennial Analysis of the American Political Structure*, January 1987, pp. 10–11 and passim.

[21] Samuel Huntington, "Congressional Responses to the Twentieth Century," in *The Congress and America's Future*, ed. by David Truman (Englewood Cliffs, N.J.: Prentice-Hall, 1973), p. 34.

[22] Huntington, "Congressional Responses," p. 37.

tensive study of the President and Congress. According to political scientist Michael Mezey, our national governing system is characterized by an inability to make good policy that results from defects in the constitutional structure. Not only did separation of powers build conflict into the political system, it produced "a constitution against government, a system incapable of [producing sound] policy actions. . . ."[23] Mezey uses as his yardstick of good policy that which is informed, timely, coherent, effective, and responsible. "Congress," he says, "seems structurally incapable of producing public policy" that meets these criteria.[24]

Not only does Congress fail to meet these criteria of efficiency, it also falls short as a representative democratic institution. Mezey's yardstick for democratic policy-making includes four criteria: popular government, majority rule, responsiveness, and accountability. According to Mezey, voters pay little attention to issues when they vote for members of Congress and rarely hold individual representatives accountable for their policy decisions, narrow interest groups exert disproportionate influence over congressional actions, and political structures are designed to limit Congress's responsiveness to the people.[25]

Like Huntington, Mezey proposes to give the President primary responsibility for national policy-making. This not only would eliminate the sticky hands of Congress but also would encourage the executive to focus more on the objective merits of good policy and less on political bargaining and expediency. In this view, Congress should focus its efforts on representing its constituencies rather than on policy-making (despite Mezey's assertion that Congress does a poor job of representation as well). Congress would, however, still be allowed to debate important policy matters.[26]

Is Change Desirable?

Those who seek coterminous presidential-congressional terms and stronger parties are looking for a structure that will encourage consistency, strength, and more efficient policy-making. These goals are admirable, but it is important to note that some recent studies

---

[23] Michael L. Mezey, *Congress, the President, and Public Policy* (Boulder, Colo.: Westview, 1989), p. 18.

[24] Mezey, *Congress, the President, and Public Policy*, p. 142.

[25] Mezey, *Congress, the President, and Public Policy*, pp. 143–146.

[26] Mezey, *Congress, the President, and Public Policy*, pp. 189–202.

have cast considerable doubt on the assumption that divided party control engenders presidential-congressional stalemate; indeed, "party control of both branches is no guarantee of legislative productivity."[27]

I argue that the primary impact of such a reform would be to strengthen the President's hand and control over Congress. Worse, the realization of this greater cohesion (assuming that these changes would have that effect) would occur "at the expense of legislative branch autonomy."[28] Elimination of the midterm election is considered desirable because "all it [the midterm election] can do is deadlock the government, or tighten an existing deadlock. . . ."[29] In other words, midterm elections retard presidential action since the historical trend of such elections is that they cut into the presidential mandate of the previous election.

Any change that would give the President greater influence over Congress would facilitate the executive's ability to realize its goals. But the farther the system moves in this direction, the closer it approaches a one-branch system of government, invoking what political scientist Clinton Rossiter labeled "constitutional dictatorship."[30] And given the rise of the modern strong presidency under the existing constitutional arrangement, what kind of governing could we expect under the regime proposed by reformers? To state this criticism more pointedly, "Unity borne of subservience is a hollow victory for democratic governance."[31]

This question presses even more forcefully with regard to the reforms of Huntington and Mezey, as they actually propose to remove Congress's core power over lawmaking. Mezey's analysis in particular

---

[27] Roger H. Davidson, "The Presidency and Three Eras of the Modern Congress," in *Divided Democracy*, ed. by James A. Thurber (Washington, D.C.: CQ Press, 1991), p. 76. See also David R. Mayhew, *Divided We Govern* (New Haven: Yale University Press, 1991).

[28] Mark P. Petracca, Lonce Bailey, and Pamela Smith, "Proposals for Constitutional Reform: An Evaluation of the Committee on the Constitutional System," *Presidential Studies Quarterly*, 20 (Summer 1990): 517.

[29] Sundquist, *Congressional Reform*, p. 115.

[30] Clinton Rossiter, *Constitutional Dictatorship* (New York: Harcourt, Brace and World, 1948).

[31] Petracca, Bailey, and Smith, "Proposals for Constitutional Reform," p. 517. For a response to the Petracca critique, see James L. Sundquist, "Response to the Petracca-Bailey-Smith Evaluation of the Committee on the Constitutional System," *Presidential Studies Quarterly*, 20 (Summer 1990): 533–543.

paints an unalterably bleak picture, arguing that Congress has never been able to make good policy or fulfill most of its other obligations. Yet the assumptions and standards that underlie Mezey's analysis merit scrutiny.

In particular, the standards he applies for good policy, while admirable in the abstract, are inappropriate as a realistic measure of Congress's abilities. Mezey notes that he derived his criteria from the rational-comprehensive model of decision making described by economist Charles Lindblom.[32] In a famous article, Lindblom compared the rational-comprehensive model with what he labeled the "successive limited comparison" or "muddling through" model of decision making (later known as incrementalism). While the rational-comprehensive model was appealing because it is logical and wide-ranging, Lindblom concluded that it was both descriptively and prescriptively deficient. Incrementalism was less ordered and planned but fit the real world of decision making far better and indeed was a more useful approach for decision makers. The rational-comprehensive approach has not been abandoned, but its analytic and prescriptive limits have long been recognized. In Lindblom's words, the rational-comprehensive approach "is in fact not workable for complex policy questions. . . ."[33] Numerous other studies of decision making have confirmed this assessment.[34]

Therefore, the yardstick Mezey applies to measure Congress's deficiencies is one by which any large, complex decision-making organization will be found wanting. At no time in its history could Congress hope to meet such criteria. Moreover, the rational-comprehensive model and other successive models have been applied mostly

---

[32] Mezey, "The Legislature, the Executive and Public Policy," p. 18, fn. 4.

[33] Charles E. Lindblom, "The Science of 'Muddling Through,'" *Public Administration Review*, 19 (Spring 1959): 81. See also Lindblom's *The Intelligence of Democracy* (New York: Free Press, 1965), esp. chap. 9. As Lindblom and a coauthor noted in another work, what "decision-makers generally do in the face of a complex problem, even when they try to be rational, does not at all approximate rational decision-making as it is conventionally described. . . ." David Braybrooke and Charles E. Lindblom, *A Strategy of Decision* (New York: Free Press, 1970), p. vi. The literature on decision making is abundant and prolific. Theoretical formulations of decision making have moved generally away from the strictly rational and toward such models as the organizational, cybernetic, and even "garbage can."

[34] For example, see Graham Allison, *Essence of Decision* (Boston: Little, Brown, 1971). Allison compared the rational-comprehensive model with organizational and bureaucratic models and found the rational model to be the least applicable.

to bureaucratic organizations characterized by hierarchy, division of labor, supervision, and other organizational traits not applicable to an elective body such as Congress.

In short, the criteria Mezey applies to Congress are inappropriate because (1) their applicability to real-world decision making is limited, (2) they apply poorly if at all to complex problems, and (3) they are derived from analyses of bureaucratic rather than elective organizations. This does not mean that critics should apply a lowest-common-demoninator standard to Congress, but an unfair standard is as inappropriate as no standard.[35]

A similar argument can be made for Congress's alleged inability to make policy that is democratic. The standards for democratic policy as Mezey defines and applies them (popular government, majority rule, responsiveness, and accountability), while laudable in the abstract, reflect problems common to Congress and the electorate: Lack of attention to issues and issue-based voting in the electorate, low levels of voter turnout, disproportionate influence of special interests, and institutional structures that inhibit responsiveness to majorities are traits endemic to American elections. It is neither fair nor reasonable to single out Congress because of its inability to meet these criteria.

THE IMPERIAL CONGRESS/WEAK PRESIDENT ARGUMENT

Another school of thought expresses dissatisfaction with the presidential-congressional balance from the opposite perspective, arguing that the modern Congress has too long dominated and hamstrung the presidency. From the 1940s to the 1960s this complaint emanated primarily from liberals who objected to the efforts of congressional conservatives to resist the advance of progressive presidential agendas.[36] As former Kennedy administration aide Theodore Sorensen noted, "The powers of Congress are enormous. . . .

---

[35] For a critique of Mezey from the perspective of democratic theory, see Joseph Cooper, "Assessing Legislative Performance: A Reply to the Critics of Congress," *Congress and the Presidency*, 13 (Spring 1986): 21–40.

[36] Polsby, "Congress-Bashing for Beginners," p. 15. Sentiments supporting enhanced executive authority at the direct or indirect expense of Congress were suggested by a series of governmental commissions formulated to recommend measures to enhance executive authority over budgeting, administration, and related areas. See, for example,

Congress could cut off the President with one part-time secretary if it does not like the way he is operating his staff, for example."[37]

In the 1980s this theme was picked up with renewed vigor primarily by conservatives who rankled at congressional moves toward reassertion in the 1970s and 1980s and who felt frustrated when Democratic Congresses succeeded in amending or thwarting many of Ronald Reagan's initiatives. Critics applied such descriptions as "the tethered presidency,"[38] "the fettered presidency,"[39] and "the imperial Congress"[40] to their complaints against Congress, arguing that the lessons of the 1960s and 1970s had been misapplied or overapplied. Former President Gerald Ford argued that we have "not an imperial presidency but an imperiled presidency."[41] According to another assessment, "The tethered presidency is no remedy for past sins of *imperium.*"[42]

One outspoken critic of Congress's alleged imperium, former federal judge Robert Bork, stated flatly that "the office of the president of the United States has been significantly weakened in recent years and . . . Congress is largely, but not entirely, responsible."[43] Bork was himself the center of executive-legislative controversy in

---

President's Committee on Administrative Management, *Administrative Management in the Government of the United States,* January 8, 1937 (Washington, D.C.: U.S. Government Printing Office, 1937), better known as the Brownlow Commission, appointed by Franklin Roosevelt.

[37] Theodore C. Sorensen, "The Case for a Strong Presidency," in *Has the President Too Much Power?,* ed. by Charles Roberts (New York: Harper's Magazine Press, 1974), p. 28. Unlike other liberals, such as Arthur Schlesinger, Jr., and Henry Steele Commager, Sorensen has maintained a consistent stand on this issue. See his *Watchman in the Night* (Cambridge, Mass.: MIT Press, 1975).

[38] Thomas M. Franck, ed., *The Tethered Presidency* (New York: New York University Press, 1981).

[39] L. Gordon Crovitz and Jeremy A. Rabkin, eds., *The Fettered Presidency* (Washington, D.C.: American Enterprise Institute, 1989).

[40] Gordon S. Jones and John A. Marini, eds., *The Imperial Congress* (New York: Pharos, 1988).

[41] Gerald R. Ford, "Two Ex-Presidents Assess the Job," *Time,* November 10, 1980, pp. 30–31.

[42] Franck, *The Tethered Presidency,* p. x.

[43] Robert H. Bork, "Foreword," *The Fettered Presidency,* p. ix. See also Bork's "Epilogue" in *Pork Barrels and Principles: The Politics of the Presidential Veto* (Washington, D.C.: National Legal Center for the Public Interest, 1988), and other publications of conservative think tanks, including the American Enterprise Institute and the Heritage Foundation.

1987, when, after lengthy, controversial, and much-publicized hearings, the Senate rejected his nomination by President Reagan to the Supreme Court.

The "Legalism" Critique

One line of criticism begins with Hamilton's famous statement in the *Federalist Papers* (No. 70) that "Energy in the executive is a leading character in the definition of good government."[44] For Congress to shackle that energy is tantamount to an invitation to bad government, according to some. Gordon Crovitz and Jeremy Rabkin criticize Congress for "excessive legalism," that is, "a disturbing trend toward excessive reliance on legal standards in the formulation or control of public policy." These legalisms are used to bind the presidency, they argue. Examples span domestic and foreign affairs and include Congress's establishment of independent counsels to investigate allegations of executive branch wrongdoing, the War Powers Resolution, and the thrust of the Iran-contra investigation, which wrongfully focused on "technical questions of legality instead of on the policy merits of what had been done,"[45] according to Crovitz and Rabkin. Their preference is for greater reliance on "presidential discretion" and a concomitant diminution of "the ever-increasing involvement of Congress in all aspects of executive branch affairs."[46]

The "Imperial" Congress

A second strain of criticism asserts more aggressively that Congress has simply become "imperial." According to Gordon Jones and John Marini, Congress has assaulted the separation of powers by robbing the executive of its rightful constitutional powers. Not only has

---

[44] This sentence from *Federalist* No. 70 is often quoted by those who seek to use it as a touchstone for presidential activism, but it is typically divorced from its context. The "energy" to which Hamilton referred pertained to the ability of the President to act during various emergencies (some of which he specifies) and in "the steady administration of the laws." Executive energy was not defined or described by Hamilton as a blank check for presidents to creatively exercise powers that they did not already possess. See *The Federalist Papers* (New York: New American Library, 1961), pp. 423–424.

[45] Crovitz and Rabkin, *The Fettered Presidency*, p. 3. This criticism of Congress parallels Mezey's argument that Congress relies on "automatic decisionmaking mechanisms" such as the War Powers Resolution to break interbranch stalemates. See Mezey, *Congress, the President, and Public Policy*, pp. 162–163.

[46] Caspar W. Weinberger, "Dangerous Constraints on the President's War Powers," in *The Fettered Presidency*, p. 95.

Congress relied on "legalisms" to confine the President by "criminalizing policy differences," it has engaged in "micromanagement of executive agencies" through enactment of complicated rules regulating administrative agencies and behavior, especially in foreign affairs; has turned the budget into a pork barrel trough that has inflated the budget and widened the federal deficit; and has insulated itself from the people through the rise of incumbency (which therefore means Congress is unaccountable), which in turn encourages government employees to develop greater loyalty to Congress than to the President because of the Congress's greater average longevity in office.[47]

The remedies offered to restore the executive to its allegedly rightful place include urging the President to ignore laws the executive considers unconstitutional, especially in but not limited to the area of foreign affairs; readily fire executive branch officials who disagree with the President and reward those who are loyal; work to impose greater party discipline on members of Congress; assert a greater executive role in all aspects of the legislative process; ignore or challenge congressional micromanagement of federal agencies; fire all heads of independent agencies and then rehire them on a temporary basis to encourage their loyalty to the President; seek repeal of the two-term constitutional limit on presidential terms; ignore American Bar Association (ABA) recommendations for federal court nominees and eliminate the ABA's power to accredit law schools; urge the President to object loudly and vocally to Supreme Court decisions with which the executive disagrees and defend executive privilege even if the Supreme Court rules against that power; and use the President's ability to rally public opinion to support the administration's goals and use the confirmation process to that end as well. Recommendations for changes in Congress include elimination of omnibus appropriation bills, adoption of a balanced budget amendment, reduction of congressional committee and staff power, extension of greater rights to the minority party in Congress, and reduction of congressional perquisites such as the franking privilege.[48]

Executive Absurdism

The imperial Congress/weak President perspective must first be identified as one that springs more from ideology and partisanship

[47] Jones and Marini, *The Imperial Congress*, pp. 4–11.

[48] Jones and Marini, *The Imperial Congress*, pp. 353–362.

than does the ineffectual Congress/ascendant President argument. Liberals advocated a stronger presidency during the Roosevelt-Truman-Kennedy-Johnson era in large measure because these liberal Democratic presidents were attempting to enact a progressive agenda through Congresses that were often resistant. Similarly, conservatives turned on Congress in the 1970s and 1980s because of their fury over its efforts to thwart the programs—or investigate the misdeeds—of the Nixon, Ford, and Reagan administrations (although the brief Ford administration was untouched by scandal). Liberal-conservative clashes over politics and policy are the legitimate stuff of American politics, but when that debate is cast in abstract, institutional terms involving the possibility of structural shifts between the branches of government, partisan motives must be identified and reconciled with the consequences of proposed changes.[49] (After all, only a fool changes the rules of the game because of losing a contest or two.)

Conservative frustration in the 1980s was not limited to anger at the Democratic-controlled Congress. Some even argued that Ronald Reagan had betrayed conservatism and the presidency itself. Gordon Crovitz, for example, argued that Reagan actually weakened the presidency during his terms in office, not because of the Iran-contra scandal, the savings and loan mess, or Reagan's retreat on environmental protections but because Reagan failed to launch sufficiently strong assaults on the Budget and Impoundment Control Act, the War Powers Resolution, and the actions of special prosecutors.[50] Crovitz's opinion, however, is one that finds little support among supporters, critics, or analysts of the Reagan era.[51]

The legalism critique is an especially ironic one in that conservative legal scholars have argued for many years that the national gov-

---

[49] One hint of partisan motives in *The Imperial Congress* is the fact that of the sixteen contributors to the edited volume, four used fictitious names to hide their identity. No explanation is offered for why any protection was needed, and such a practice is virtually unknown in the literature of American politics. See Jones and Marini, pp. 363–366.

[50] L. Gordon Crovitz, "How Ronald Reagan Weakened the Presidency," *Commentary*, September 1988, pp. 25–29.

[51] See, for example, Lester Salamon and Michael S. Lund, eds., *The Reagan Presidency and the Governing of America* (Washington, D.C.: Urban Institute Press, 1984); John L. Palmer and Isabel V. Sawhill, eds., *The Reagan Record* (Cambridge, Mass.: Ballinger, 1984); Sidney Blumenthal and Thomas B. Edsall, eds., *The Reagan Legacy* (New York: Pantheon, 1988); and Charles O. Jones, ed., *The Reagan Legacy* (Chatham, N.J.: Chatham House, 1988).

erning system needs a greater adherence to and reliance on rule of law instead of administrative or presidential discretion.[52] Indeed, an important critique of Congress holds that bad policy has resulted from vaguely drawn congressionally made law or from the absence of law altogether.[53] To complain that Congress has become too legalistic and too precise in lawmaking is to reveal dissatisfaction with the content of the laws, not the process by which they came about. This is evident in the invocation of Iran-contra, where the "technical questions of legality" about which Crovitz and Rabkin complain are what beginning students of American government call "the law of the land." Questions of legality were the primary focus of the Iran-contra inquiry precisely because the Reagan administration was accused of violating the law. To complain about "excessive reliance on legal standards" is to complain that Congress is behaving in the way it was designed to behave and the way by which Congress is most unambiguously accountable for its actions.

The imperial Congress critique receives special attention here because of its unvarnished promotion of structural changes in the presidential-congressional balance stemming from the political frustrations of the 1980s. Indeed, this critique takes its dissatisfaction with the presidential-congressional relationship to the precipice of American democracy. As the evidence marshaled in this book attests, the prevailing trend in presidential-congressional relations has been toward executive hegemony. Buried in Jones and Marini's scorn for Congress are a few familiar complaints against Congress, such as its interest in pork barreling. For the most part, however, they reject constitutional sharing of powers when Congress is participating in the sharing. For example, the complaint about congressional micromanagement of presidential and administrative matters is a reference to Congress's traditional oversight function, which has a long constitutional, statutory, and political basis. One may quibble with the politics of oversight but not with its constitutionality.[54]

---

[52] For example, see F.A. Hayek, *Road to Serfdom* (London: Routledge, 1944), chap. 6. Hayek says, "Though this ideal [rule of law] can never be perfectly achieved, since legislators as well as those to whom the administration of the law is entrusted are fallible men, the essential point, [is] that the discretion left to the executive organs wielding coercive power should be reduced as much as possible. . . ." p. 54.

[53] See Theodore J. Lowi, *The End of Liberalism* (New York: Norton, 1979), esp. chaps. 5 and 11.

[54] See Louis Fisher, *The Politics of Shared Power* (Washington, D.C.: CQ Press, 1987), chaps. 3 and 4.

In sum, Jones and Marini attribute no faults to the President and offer a menu of suggestions that cannot even be labeled a constitutional dictatorship, as they urge Presidents to ignore laws with which Presidents may disagree and rule the executive branch like a petty fiefdom. So much for rule of law.

Even among conservatives sympathetic to the frustrations that give rise to the imperial Congress critique, there is some wariness about translating partisan acrimony into structural change. As one conservative author noted, "to leap from such practical measures to a philosophic defense of a presidential monopoly in foreign policy could lead alarmingly close to compromising traditional conservative commitments to limited government and national independence."[55] Congressman Mickey Edwards (R-Okla.) voiced similar concerns: "Frustrated over repeated defeats in the House and Senate, conservatives have turned to that branch of government they control—the executive—and have proposed to yield important concentrations of power in the hope that something good will happen. It is a dangerous gamble."[56]

WERE THE FOUNDERS WRONG?

Dissatisfaction with the constitutional balance between the President and Congress is the prevailing characteristic of the critiques we have discussed. Leaving aside the mundane question of the likelihood of winning enactment of any of the changes discussed here (a question we can set aside with good conscience because our interest in possible reform lies in what it reveals about underlying opinions about the presidential-congressional relationship), we must consider whether the system of shared powers is fatally flawed for a nation entering its third century of existence. Here I argue that critics mistake lack of political will for structural defects. The ineffectual Congress/ascendant President critique in particular reflects dismay at an alleged inability to govern and make good policy. The assumption is that con-

---

[55] Samuel Francis, "Imperial Conservatives?", *National Review,* August 4, 1989, p. 89.

[56] Mickey Edwards, "Of Conservatives and Kings," *Policy Review,* 48 (Spring 1989): 30. Edwards's concerns are nicely illustrated by the debate over granting the President item veto powers. See Robert J. Spitzer, *The Presidential Veto* (Albany: State University of New York Press, 1988), chap. 5.

stitutional structures prevent decisive action. These critics presume that answers exist or could be found more readily under an altered structure.

Separation of Powers and Alternatives

We again return to the first argument of this book—that the executive-legislative relationship has evolved to a point where we now operate in an executive-centered rather than legislative-centered system. Given an executive-centered system, we face three alternatives. The first, expressed in the previous sections of this chapter, is to accelerate the executive-centered nature of the system and in so doing abandon in fact if not in law the tripartite system of government. Such a change may be an improvement, but I argue simply that as the United States grapples with difficult and perilous problems requiring complex and sometimes rapid decisions, a sharing of powers is *more,* not less useful.

The second alternative is to seek a modified renewal of the separation of powers between the President and Congress—modified, that is, to accept executive hegemony. The third, theoretical option is to return to the congressional-centered system of our first century—an option that is certainly not realistic and probably not desirable.

Retaining an Executive-Hegemonic Separation of Powers

In regard to the complaint that the existing presidential-congressional relationship is incapable of coming to terms with problems, I would note that in our executive-centered system we observe a direct relationship between expeditious government action and the degree of urgency or crisis. Documentation released during the summer of 1974 linking unconstitutional and illegal actions with Richard Nixon and top members of his administration accelerated impeachment efforts and the first resignation of a sitting President in August of that year. The budget crisis of the mid-1980s propelled the passage by Congress of the Gramm-Rudman deficit reduction act in record speed in the fall of 1985. The Iraqi crisis propelled President Bush in August 1990 to send 100,000 American troops to Saudi Arabia in just over two weeks, with congressional acquiescence. The following January Congress deliberated and on January 12 affirmed a presidential proposal to authorize him to initiate hostilities after the January 15 United Nations deadline for Iraqi withdrawal from Kuwait. Despite the compressed time frame and sense of urgency, Congress demonstrated its abilities to act with speed and, by most accounts, with responsibility. The sentiments of most observers regarding congressional handling of the Iraqi crisis were summarized by veteran Washington reporter David Broder: "The debate served superbly well the requirements of representative government, informing the public and reflecting the electorate's divided views. From freshmen casting their first votes to the most senior members, there was—for all the anguish over the consequences—a real sense of pride that their Congress had met the responsibility the Constitution laid at its door."[57]

Barring a crisis directly involving an interbranch dispute, such as Watergate or Iran-contra, the President and Congress have little difficulty making quick and, given the circumstances, reasonable decisions when circumstances warrant. Even the Watergate and Iran-contra cases yield to this logic; action became possible according to the extent to which information was unambiguous.

The rest of the time—which is to say most of the time—good decision making demands the input of varying perspectives. A good President is one who makes not only a timely decision but a good decision. The difficulty in formulating good decisions is that they rarely emerge from small, like-minded groups of people. Good decision making requires the airing of competing views, exposure to criticism, and a willingness to revise or even abandon preferred alternatives. To cite one well-known example, Lyndon Johnson's progressive isolation from critics and critical perspectives encouraged successive misjudgments and miscalculations by his administration about American involvement in Vietnam.[58] As leadership specialist James MacGregor Burns notes, "A more effective way to handle choice . . . is to use conflict deliberately to protect decision-making options and power, and, even more, to use conflict to structure [the] political environ-

[57] David S. Broder, "Congress Fulfills Its Responsibility," *Syracuse Post-Standard,* January 15, 1991.

[58] See, for example, Townsend Hoopes, *The Limits of Intervention* (New York: McKay, 1969); Larry Berman, *Planning a Tragedy* (New York: Norton, 1982); George Reedy, *The Twilight of the Presidency* (New York: New American Library, 1987).

ment so as to maximize 'constructive' dissonance, thus allowing for more informed decision-making. Perhaps the chief means of doing this is to create a system of 'multiple access' and 'multiple advocacy' around the decision-maker."[59]

In his landmark study of governmental decision making, psychologist Irving Janis emphasizes the vital importance of avoiding conformity, seeking competing viewpoints, and resisting insulation from outside forces. Failure to avoid these problems may result in defective decision making obfuscated by the illusion that good policy has resulted from the existence of consensus among the decision makers. That is, the mere fact that the decision makers agree with each other often deludes them into thinking that they have arrived at the best policy.[60]

Through the separation of powers, the Constitution created a system to minimize these decision-making defects. In this area the Constitution's founders were wise, perhaps more than they knew. Congress was expected to provide a popular voice, and the President some measure of efficiency and administrative order. Yet Congress also provides a vital added perspective that conforms to the tenets of good decision making and policy-making. Moreover, the continued involvement of Congress in decision making conforms with the tenets of democratic theory. After all, "democratic regimes are based on a fundamental skepticism about the superior wisdom or virtue of any single individual, group, or institution."[61] To construct a system where the President can "operate in the absence of explicit presidential-congressional agreements"[62] is to invite more Vietnams and Iran-contras.

For Congress to continue as a meaningful participant in this capacity, it must retain its formal independence from the President (bearing in mind the many ways in which Congress is informally de-

---

[59] James MacGregor Burns, *Leadership* (New York: Harper & Row, 1978), p. 410. Burns points out that congressional structure conforms to this model but that the executive branch emphasizes "single-minded judgment and execution"; therefore, it is vital that the executive build such a multiple advocacy system to ensure against defective decision making (pp. 410–411). See also Richard E. Neustadt and Ernest R. May, *Thinking in Time* (New York: Free Press, 1986), chap. 13.

[60] Irving Janis, *Groupthink* (Boston: Houghton Mifflin, 1982).

[61] Cooper, "Assessing Legislative Performance," p. 24.

[62] Mezey, *Congress, the President, and Public Policy*, p. 192.

pendent on the executive—see Chapter 3), especially if we accept presidential hegemony as inevitable or desirable.[63] Remember also that presidential hegemony does not necessarily mean a weak Congress. I argued early in the book against thinking of the presidential-congressional balance as a seesaw: The seesaw analogy precludes the best of times, when the President and Congress work together constructively, and the worst of times, when they become locked in stalemate. The ideal should be "a modern 'constitutional presidency,' a presidency equipped to act effectively but also required to act cooperatively."[64] The President should continue to exercise executive initiative, but Congress should retain its rights and abilities to investigate, question, and above all legislate.

The Rules and Outcomes

The primary fallacy of the imperial Congress/weak President critique is fairly simple: It confuses the rules of the game with the outcome of particular contests. It is an axiom of political science that rules shape outcomes and that rules are not neutral. The separation of powers is certainly not neutral, but its biases are well understood. To those who would change the rules because of political or ideological frustrations, political scientist Nelson Polsby observes, "There is something uncivil . . . about insisting upon constitutional reforms to cure political ailments."[65] As James Q. Wilson commented, "Separated powers are a fine idea, it would seem, except when they prevent me from having my own way."[66] President Reagan, to pick an example, did not need an item veto; he needed a Congress more strongly in the hands of conservative Republicans and a greater willingness to use his existing veto powers to confront Congress.[67]

[63] Let me state for the record that I do not offer the executive-hegemonic model because I necessarily find it the most desirable. It is simply my belief that this model strikes the most judicious balance between what exists and what is possible given the impact of the forces that have brought the nation to this point.

[64] Lester Salamon, "Conclusion: Beyond the Presidential Illusion—Toward a Constitutional Presidency," in *The Illusion of Presidential Government*, ed. by Hugh Heclo and Salamon (Boulder, Colo.: Westview, 1981), p. 292.

[65] Nelson Polsby, "Congress-Bashing for Beginners," p. 17.

[66] James Q. Wilson, "Does the Separation of Powers Still Work?" in *Analyzing the Presidency*, ed. by Robert E. DiClerico (Guilford, Conn.: Dushkin, 1990), p. 100.

[67] See Spitzer, *The Presidential Veto*, pp. 88–104, 141–142.

The contradictions and roadblocks of the separation of powers invite political frustration, even in a system of executive hegemony. But a primary objective of Presidents and members of Congress should be constructive engagement—learning to live with the contradictions, not striving to eliminate them as a category.[68] The presidential Machiavelli, Richard Neustadt, outlined in his classic work a blueprint for this constructive engagement in which he urged Presidents to bargain and persuade rather than bully and order.[69]

The Presidency and Democracy

The defense of separation of powers is not merely a defense of the devil we know. In the context of modern executive hegemony, it is functional, useful, even vital. Separation of powers provides no insurance against policy that is bad, slow, or distasteful because there is no insurance against these outcomes under this or any system. (Nor is it a given that slow policy is necessarily bad policy.) It does help to ensure, however, that competing values—efficiency versus democracy, secrecy versus accountability, speed versus deliberation—will continue to be able to compete.

It is important to remember, too, that the separation of powers is pretty much unique.[70] The United States is virtually alone among modern nations in having an independent and influential legislative branch. Comparisons between the American system and others are useful for scholarly purposes but are inherently suspect among those who criticize the American system for being unlike other democratic systems or who seek to transplant parliamentary features onto the U.S. Constitution. This is not to argue against ever making structural changes but to point out that we have no yardstick for calculating the consequences of such actions and to suggest that we already have a structure that reinforces and is compatible with the underlying values we claim to hold dear.

Finally, we must remind ourselves that the founders favored a

[68] Peterson writes about "treating the president and Congress as a decision-making system." He notes that compromise and consensus are indeed far more typical of this relationship than is normally supposed. *Legislating Together,* pp. 79, 96–97.

[69] Richard E. Neustadt, *Presidential Power and the Modern Presidents* (New York: Free Press, 1990).

[70] For a discussion of American exceptionalism, see Byron E. Shafer, " 'Exceptionalism' in American Politics?" *PS,* 22 (September 1989): 588–594.

separation of and limitations on powers because they feared the tyrannical and narcotic consequences of too much power concentrated in too few hands. Is this fear obsolete? Hardly. The very conditions of modern governing that impel reformers to advocate a more executive-centered system are also the conditions under which the pernicious consequences of concentrated power in a single branch should be feared even more. Far too often in recent decades we have observed a stubborn unwillingness on the part of the President and his minions to accede to public accountability and "an all too common White House disbelief in the assumptions and values of democratic political life."[71]

In his testimony before the special congressional committee investigating Iran-contra in 1987, Oliver North aggressively, even proudly defended the illegal activities in which he and others in the Reagan administration engaged: "And I am admitting to you that I participated in preparation of documents for the Congress that were erroneous, misleading, evasive and wrong, and I did it again here when I appeared before that committee convened in the White House Situation Room, and I make no excuses for what I did."[72]

Many members of Congress expressed outrage at these and other violations of law and at the underlying belief among members of the Reagan administration that illegality was somehow acceptable if it was the wish of the President. Representative Lee Hamilton's (D-Ind.) reaction summarized nicely the case against important policy made solely by the executive branch (and therefore the case against abandonment of the separation of powers): "Foreign policies were created and carried out by a tiny circle of persons, apparently without the involvement of even some of the highest officials in our government. The administration tried to do so secretly what the Congress sought to prevent it from doing. The administration did secretly what it claimed to all the world it was not doing. Covert action should al-

---

[71] Bruce Miroff, "Secrecy and Spectacle: Reflections on the Dangers of the Presidency," in *The Presidency in American Politics,* ed. by Paul Brace, Christine B. Harrington, and Gary King (New York: New York University Press, 1989), p. 161. Mezey notes that this trend has arisen in many nations: "In the twentieth century, the democratic state has been repeatedly challenged by those who have been all too willing to eliminate democratic practices ostensibly to maximize managerial values." *Congress, the President, and Public Policy,* p. 17. According to Allen Schick, "It is the misfortune of Congress to be unappreciated when it guards against abuses in executive power." "Politics through Law," p. 181.

[72] *The Iran-Contra Puzzle* (Washington, D.C.: *Congressional Quarterly*, 1987), p. C-84.

ways be used to supplement, not to contradict, our foreign policy. It should be consistent with our public policies. It should not be used to impose a foreign policy on the American people which they do not support."[73] Since the time of these comments much evidence has emerged which suggests that top Reagan administration officials and Reagan himself knew or approved of the major components of the Iran-contra scheme. Even if we assume this wider level of participation, however, we are still talking about a very narrow circle of participants in the executive branch.

James Madison summarized these sentiments and concerns concisely when he wrote: "There can be no liberty where the legislative and executive powers are united in the same person. . . ."[74]

---

[73] *The Iran-Contra Puzzle*, p. C-96.

[74] *The Federalist Papers*, No. 47, p. 302. Madison was actually summarizing Montesquieu but concurring with his sentiments.

Appendix I

The Politics of the Modern Presidency

Both the President and Congress owe their final loyalty, in theory at least, to those who elect them. Even if our national representatives are merely pawns of wealthy special interests, they still must acquire their positions by electoral means. Both also bear the burden of enacting, implementing, and overseeing national policy. Yet even though the President and Congress seem to face similar conditions, the consequences of these electoral and policy imperatives are markedly different for the two branches, and the differences have widened in recent decades.

We note at the outset that their respective constituencies and organization are very different. The President's constituency is the entire nation; members of Congress are responsible to the states or districts that elected them. The President heads a large, diverse, hierarchical, bureaucratic organization composed of thousands of offices and millions of employees who make countless legally binding decisions daily; Congress, by contrast, is composed of 535 members, all of whom seek a share in power and a majority of whom must give their consent for laws to be enacted.

PRESIDENTIAL ELECTIONS

The Constitution's framers struggled to come up with an acceptable method to select the President. Initial plans called for the President to be elected by the legislature, and some also favored direct election by the people. The first plan was ultimately rejected for the obvious reason that the President would be too dependent on and beholden to Congress. Direct election was rejected largely because of mistrust of the people's judgment.

The Electoral College

The method for presidential election finally included in the Constitution was by any standard unusual and by modern standards arcane, if not bizarre. However, it did satisfy the goals of presidential election separate from the Congress and avoidance of direct popular election.

According to Article II, Section I, each state is designated to cast a set number of electoral votes equal to the total number of senators and representatives that state sends to Congress. The presidential candidate receiving the largest number of popular votes in each state wins all the electoral votes of that state. That candidate's slate of electors (none of the electors may be members of Congress or hold national office) are thus selected to cast their electoral votes, an event which occurs about a month after the general election. To be elected President, a candidate must receive an absolute majority of Electoral College ballots. According to the formula, there are currently 538 Electoral College votes, based on the number of representatives in Congress (435 members of the House and 100 senators, plus three votes allocated to the District of Columbia). A winning margin is 50 percent plus one, or 270 votes.

The initial purpose of the Electoral College was to exercise independent judgment, with the aim of filtering popular choices to emerge with a winning candidate. But with the rise of political parties and competing slates of electors pledged to support their candidate, the Electoral College ceased to operate in this manner, becoming instead a rubber stamp for the political parties.

Many have argued over the years that this system is archaic and unnecessary. In fact, over 500 proposals to reform or abolish the Electoral College have been introduced into Congress, and a vigorous debate persists concerning this institution.[1]

[1] For more on this debate, see Neal R. Peirce, *The People's President: The Electoral College in American History and the Direct Vote Alternative* (New York: Simon & Schuster, 1968); Judith A. Best, *The Case against Direct Election of the President* (Ithaca, N.Y.: Cornell University Press, 1975); Lawrence D. Longley and Alan G. Braun, *The Politics of Electoral College Reform* (New Haven, Conn.: Yale University Press, 1975); Martin Diamond, *The Electoral College and the American Idea of Democracy* (Washington, D.C.: American Enterprise Institute, 1977). Best and Diamond argue in favor of retaining the Electoral College system.

The Nomination Process

Any candidate aspiring to the presidency faces two successive hurdles: the nomination process and the general election. Accomplishing victories in both is a prodigious, time-consuming, expensive process that often leaves the victor and the victor's campaign team politically and personally exhausted at the very time when their energy needs to be greatest—at the start of a presidential term, which follows only two months after the November election.

The Nomination Process Opens Up.   The methods employed by the major parties to select presidential candidates have changed substantially over the last two centuries.[2] Yet the predominant trend in nomination politics has been a progressive opening up or "democratizing" of the process to larger segments within the parties.

The method of nomination that emerged from the period of Jacksonian democracy was the national nominating convention. First employed by the Anti-Masonic party, the method was quickly adopted by the major parties by the 1830s. Simply stated, a national party convention is an assemblage of party delegates selected by various means from localities around the country who come together to nominate the presidential and vice presidential candidates and make party policy, such as rules governing delegate selection and stands on national issues. The convention system of the last century operated similarly to the contemporary convention system for the national parties. What has changed dramatically, however, is the method used to select delegates.

By the late 1800s the convention system came under increasing criticism from progressives and party reformers for being too heavily controlled by a handful of party leaders. This criticism provided the impetus for a new, more open method of nomination: the direct primary. For presidential selection, the introduction of the primary

[2] For more on the evolution of the nomination process and party reform, see Gerald Pomper, *Nominating the President* (New York: Norton, 1966); Austin Ranney, *Curing the Mischiefs of Faction* (Berkeley: University of California Press, 1975); William J. Crotty, *Political Reform and the American Experiment* (New York: Harper & Row, 1977); William J. Crotty, *Party Reform* (New York: Longman, 1983); James W. Ceaser, *Reforming the Reforms* (Cambridge, Mass.: Ballinger, 1982); Nelson W. Polsby, *Consequences of Party Reform* (New York: Oxford University Press, 1983); Stephen J. Wayne, *The Road to the White House* (New York: St. Martin's, 1988); and Nelson W. Polsby and Aaron Wildavsky, *Presidential Elections* (New York: Free Press, 1988).

meant that voters in states that adopted some form of the primary method (as opposed to selecting delegates by state caucuses or conventions) could now support the nominee they preferred by voting for that nominee's convention delegate slate. While the direct primary had sweeping effects on party nominations at the state and local level around the country, its impact on the presidential selection process was delayed, as most states continued to rely on state caucuses and conventions to nominate delegates to the national convention until the 1960s.

The most recent major reform of the nomination process occurred in the 1970s. The 1968 nomination process produced a bitter struggle between party regulars and reformers, primarily within the Democratic party, over a variety of symbolic and substantive issues. Numerous efforts at party reform were implemented which ensured wider and broader representation within the Democratic party and an increase in the number of states using primaries to select delegates. These changes proved to be advantageous to the candidacy of long-shot Democratic Senator George McGovern. More than anything else, McGovern's nomination represented a sharp break with the past in that he was the *least* favored prospect among the contenders in the eyes of traditional party leaders. The ideological zeal that was so crucial to realizing his nomination proved to be his downfall in the general election, and the incumbent Richard Nixon defeated McGovern by sweeping over 60 percent of the popular vote.

Problems with an Open Process. The McGovern campaign revealed an apparent dilemma for the Democratic party in regard to the nomination process of recent decades: The effort required to win the presidential nomination may preclude a successful fall campaign. Moreover, many view the current, more open nomination process as one which tends to produce weak candidates. Whether this impression is true of the nomination process or not, many in the Democratic party continue to view this as a primary reason for the party's inability to win the presidency from 1968 to 1988, except for Jimmy Carter's successful bid in 1976.[3]

[3] See Polsby, *Consequences of Party Reform,* chap. 5; Pope McCorkle and Joel Fleishman, "Political Parties and Presidential Nominations: The Intellectual Ironies of Reform and Change in the Mass Media Age," in *The Future of American Political Parties,* ed. by Joel Fleishman (Englewood Cliffs, N.J.: Prentice-Hall, 1982), pp. 140–168. Even Carter's 1976 election is viewed as symptomatic of the party's problems. Critics allege that almost any Democrat could have beaten Gerald Ford that year.

The opening up of the nomination process has had other effects.[4] It has encouraged more serious contenders to enter the nomination fray (counting parties not running an incumbent). In 1972, eleven Democrats entered the race, the largest field since 1912. In 1976, thirteen Democrats vied for the nomination. In 1980, ten Republicans entered the race; in 1984, nine Democrats ran; and in 1988, eight Democrats and six Republicans sought the nomination. In addition, these reforms have lengthened the nomination season, a trend exacerbated by a related key trait of the nomination process—that it is a "front-loaded" process. Tremendous political and symbolic importance is attached to early victories, which then lead to the early victor being dubbed the "front-runner," a designation which greatly enhances the fund-raising and momentum-building aspects of the early winner's campaign.[5]

Since the 1970s the first two important nomination contests have been the Iowa caucuses, usually held in January of the presidential election year, and the New Hampshire primary, usually held in early February. Preparations for these and subsequent contests must begin early, as a victory or a better than expected showing is crucial to the

---

[4] The characteristics and consequences of the current nomination process are nicely summarized in Robert E. DiClerico and Eric M. Uslander, *Few Are Chosen: Problems in Presidential Selection* (New York: McGraw-Hill, 1984), chap. 1. See also Alexander Heard and Michael Nelson, eds., *Presidential Selection* (Durham, N.C.: Duke University Press, 1987); and William Crotty and John S. Jackson III, *Presidential Primaries and Nominations* (Washington, D.C.: CQ Press, 1985).

[5] Recent research has concluded that the front-loaded, momentum-building nature of the early contests is actually more complex and unpredictable than many assume in that the particular political circumstances at the time may overwhelm the short-term advantages for a dark horse who suddenly does better than expected. Still, early victories are essential, and since the 1950s no candidate has been elected President who did not win the New Hampshire primary. See Larry M. Bartels, *Presidential Primaries and the Dynamics of Public Choice* (Princeton, N.J.: Princeton University Press, 1988), chaps. 10 and 11; and Lee Sigelman, "The 1988 Presidential Nominations: Whatever Happened to Momentum?" *PS*, 22 (March 1989): 35–39.

A key drawback to being dubbed the front-runner is that it heightens the expectations for success imposed on the front-runner's campaign. If the front-runner does not meet these new expectations, the candidate's campaign may precipitously decline. See Gary R. Orren, "The Nomination Process: Vicissitudes of Candidate Selection," in *The Elections of 1984*, ed. by Michael Nelson (Washington, D.C.: CQ Press, 1985), pp. 27–82; and Gary R. Orren and Nelson W. Polsby, eds., *Media and Momentum: The New Hampshire Primary and Nomination Politics* (Chatham, N.J.: Chatham House, 1987).

continued survival of a campaign.[6] Recent successful nominees in both parties were all early entrants into the nomination field.

The Convention as Rubber Stamp.   This greater emphasis on the primaries as a winnowing, trial-by-fire process has also had the effect of deemphasizing the importance of the national convention. The traditional purposes of party conventions include choosing presidential and vice-presidential nominees, setting party rules, establishing the party platform, and providing a forum for unifying the party after the bruising primary process. Yet these functions are now effectively orchestrated before the convention or are determined by the presidential nominee's preferences.

These trends are attributable first to the fact that the front-loaded nature of the nomination process tends to force most entrants out of the race relatively early, freeing delegates and resources for the remaining candidates. Second, since most delegates are now chosen in primaries, party leaders can hope to control the convention only by obtaining victories in the primaries. By the time of the convention, one nominee has typically won the support of a numerical majority of delegates. In fact, no national convention since 1952 has needed to hold more than one round of balloting to determine its nominee.

Third, the intense media coverage that conventions now receive has curtailed the kind of bargaining for which conventions were once famous, as it is difficult to conduct meaningful bargaining under the media's omnipresent eye. Fourth, the dramatic increase in the number of convention delegates also inhibits bargaining as well as control of the convention by party leaders. In 1960, for example, about 1,500 delegates were seated at the Democratic convention, and about 1,300 at the Republican convention. In 1988, 4,160 delegates attended the Democratic convention and 2,277 attended the Republican.[7] As a consequence of these factors, the convention has become little more than a rubber stamp for the survivor of the primary process.

[6] The Iowa contest is examined in Peverill Squire, ed., *The Iowa Caucuses and the Presidential Nominating Process* (Boulder, Colo.: Westview, 1989). The significance of the New Hampshire primary is discussed in Orren and Polsby, *Media and Momentum.*

[7] Wayne, *The Road to the White House*, pp. 131–132.

The General Election

Active campaigning by presidential candidates is a relatively recent practice.[8] The first presidential candidate to aggressively stump the country making speeches to large groups was the Greenback party's 1880 nominee, General James B. Weaver of Iowa, who reportedly traveled 20,000 miles, made 100 speeches, shook 30,000 hands, and was heard by 500,000 people. Despite this effort, Weaver received only about 3 percent of the vote.[9] The first major party nominee to duplicate these personal efforts was Democrat William Jennings Bryan, a fiery orator who reportedly made more than 600 speeches and was heard by nearly 5 million people during the 1896 presidential campaign. Bryan's opponent, Republican William McKinley, literally conducted his campaign from his front porch yet won the election. Since that time few presidential aspirants have felt sufficiently secure about their election chances to forgo an aggressive personal campaign.

Today's presidential campaign has two overriding features. First, planning and preparation start early. As the section on nominations made clear, a presidential aspirant must begin several years before the election to have any hope of succeeding. Similarly, an incumbent President seeking reelection generally devotes increasing time during the final two years of the term to election-related activities. In terms of the President's attitude toward governing, this usually means a decline in new policy initiatives around election time to minimize the likelihood of making new enemies[10] and increased attention to the race itself, that is, more presidential activities aimed at fund-raising, criticizing the opposing party, and rallying public sentiment.

The second primary feature of the presidential campaign is that it

---

[8]To mention a few good books on presidential elections: John Kessel, *Presidential Campaign Politics* (Homewood, Ill.: Dorsey, 1980); James I. Lengle and Byron Shafer, eds., *Presidential Politics* (New York: St. Martin's, 1983); DiClerico and Uslander, *Few Are Chosen;* Watson, *The Presidential Contest;* Herbert B. Asher, *Presidential Elections and American Politics* (Chicago: Dorsey, 1988); Polsby and Wildavsky, *Presidential Elections;* Wayne, *The Road to the White House.*

[9]William B. Hesseltine, *Third Party Movements in the United States* (New York: Van Nostrand, 1962), p. 54.

[10]The connection between presidential policy initiatives and their electoral cycles is chronicled in Edward R. Tufte, *Political Control of the Economy* (Princeton, N.J.: Princeton University Press, 1978); and Robert J. Spitzer, *The Presidency and Public Policy: The Four Arenas of Presidential Power* (University: University of Alabama Press, 1983), pp. 106–108.

is run by a large campaign organization. According to analyst John Kessel, the modern campaign organization deals with four primary activities: campaign operations, public relations, research, and finance.[11]

Campaign operations center on basic questions concerning where and how to campaign, given limited time and resources. For example, the structure of the Electoral College encourages candidates to concentrate their efforts in the more populous states.

Public relations (PR) has always been a concern of political aspirants and leaders, but only in the twentieth century has skill in this area become a full-fledged occupation. No modern presidential campaign is complete without its own in-house PR division and added assistance from an outside campaign management firm hired for its expertise. PR activities focus on generating favorable news for the mass media; producing campaign literature, including everything from issue papers to bumper stickers; and developing television strategies. While television is a part of the mass media, the enormous costs and potential impact of television dictate concerted efforts to manage and shape the "electronic campaign." Symptomatic of television's perceived importance is that fact that since the 1970s over half of all presidential campaign budgets have gone toward television expenditures.[12]

The research component of a campaign involves the application of particularized research skills to immediate, pressing campaign problems. Pollsters, specialists on issues, speechwriters, and others apply their skills during the campaign to enhance the President's standing. Campaign polling was used in the 1950s and 1960s simply to tell candidates how well they were doing, but by the 1980s polling results were being used to shape campaign strategies.

An old truism says that money is the mother's milk of politics.

[11] The following discussion is drawn, unless otherwise indicated, from John H. Kessel, *Presidential Parties* (Homewood, Ill.: Dorsey, 1984), pp. 357–383.

[12] The emphasis here is on television's *perceived* importance. While it is obvious that campaigns devote tremendous resources to television, there is considerable doubt as to whether the actual impact of television is proportional to this level of spending and attention. For more on this, see Thomas E. Patterson and Robert D. McClure, *The Unseeing Eye* (New York: Putnam, 1976); Thomas Patterson, *The Mass Media Election* (New York: Praeger, 1980); Michael J. Robinson and Margaret A. Sheehan, *Over the Wire and on TV* (New York: Russell Sage Foundation, 1983); Montague Kern, *Thirty-Second Politics: Political Advertising in the Eighties* (New York: Praeger, 1989); Sig Mickelson, *From Whistle Stop to Sound Bite* (New York: Praeger, 1989).

The presidential race has become a very expensive activity, even allowing for the federal cap on spending imposed in 1976. Modern campaigns now rely on several fund-raising sources, including reliance on professional fund-raisers, mass appeals (often through direct mail), and funding from the federal government. While governmental restrictions now limit the amount of money a presidential campaign can spend, a loophole in the current law allows groups unaffiliated with the campaigns to spend as much money as they like on behalf of their candidates. In 1984, for example, about $16 million was raised independently of but in support of the Reagan campaign, compared with about $1 million raised for Democratic challenger Walter Mondale. The real impact of this money is less than the dollar figures imply, however, as most of it was spent on fund-raising and operating costs.[13]

Presidents leave the election behind them when they assume office. Yet they are in a real sense prisoners of the endless presidential cycles defined by the election process.

PRESIDENTIAL CYCLES

The actions and imperatives of every presidency are shaped and molded by the President's electoral cycle. The "normal" presidential cycle—one not interrupted by resignation, death, or defeat at the polls—consists of two consecutive four-year terms.[14] We know, however, that the President's opportunities and resources are not distributed equally across this time period. Political scientist Richard Neustadt observed "a certain rhythm in the modern Presidency."[15]

[13] Asher, *Presidential Elections and American Politics*, pp. 220–221.

[14] The two-term limit was an informal practice begun by George Washington. It was followed voluntarily by Presidents until Franklin Roosevelt, who was elected to four terms. After Roosevelt's death, the Twenty-second Amendment to the Constitution was added (in 1951), barring Presidents from being elected more than twice. In actual fact, the average term length for Presidents in the twentieth century has been about five years.

[15] Richard E. Neustadt, *Presidential Power and the Modern Presidents* (New York: Free Press, 1990), p. 169. Neustadt observed that the initial two years of a presidency constitute a learning period for a new chief executive devoted to learning the job, establishing routines, and setting patterns with Congress. In the fourth year, a "period of pause," the incumbent must become preoccupied with reelection. And in the final two years of the eight-year cycle, attention increasingly turns away from the incumbent and toward the incumbent's successor.

A study of presidencies of the 1960s and 1970s by political scientist Paul Light concluded that presidential success in office hinged on two conflicting cycles: a cycle of decreasing influence and a cycle of increasing effectiveness. Presidential resources, and therefore capacity for influence, are greatest immediately after election (this holds true, but to a lesser degree, for the President's influence after reelection). Ironically, Presidents and their staffs possess the least experience and skill at the start of the administration and are thus in a poor position to exploit their influence. The administration acquires experience and skill as it progresses but also loses resources. Thus, the capacity for effectiveness increases while the resources needed to succeed diminish. This paradoxical pattern has been labeled the no-win presidency. White House aides have observed that maximizing the President's success under these conditions hinges on running up a large electoral margin, maintaining high positive public approval, and holding a partisan majority in Congress.[16]

Aside from the cyclical qualities of the presidency driven by its ties to the electoral process, the office of President has its own bureaucratic and symbolic imperatives that are also common to "the presidential experience."[17]

THE CHIEF EXECUTIVE

For our present purposes, we examine three aspects of the presidential job: management, symbolism, and special-interest focus point. These three aspects are not inclusive but emphasize sides of the job not directly related to the legislative activities discussed in the rest of this book.

The first, a managerial function, is narrower and more formal and bureaucratic. Article II of the Constitution vests "the executive power" in the President, along with the power to "take care" that the laws are carried out. The executive is also granted the power of commander in chief of the military and may require written opinions from executive department heads.

[16] Paul C. Light, *The President's Agenda* (Baltimore: Johns Hopkins University Press, 1982), pp. 32, 202–206. See also Kessel, *Presidential Parties*, chap. 3.

[17] See Bruce Buchanan, *The Presidential Experience* (Englewood Cliffs, N.J.: Prentice-Hall, 1978).

President as Manager

Like a corporate chief executive officer (CEO), the President sits astride an enormous governmental apparatus composed of the Executive Office of the President, fourteen cabinet departments headed by presidentially appointed secretaries, and scores of independent agencies. Staffing these agencies are roughly 2.7 million civilian and 2.5 million military personnel.

Unlike a CEO, however, the President cannot expect to exercise the kind of policy authority over the bureaucracy that a CEO might in a corporation. The federal bureaucracy is not a neat hierarchy but an ad hoc assemblage of departments, agencies, and bureaus that respond not only to the President but to Congress, special interests, and their own professional norms. Presidents who seek to exert political and policy control over the bureaucracy cannot simply manage but must take account of these additional political forces. Much of the President's effort is expended in simply attempting to make the administration his administration, although there is a considerable debate about whether the President's influence over the bureaucracy ought to be as great as some would like.[18]

President as Father Figure

The second aspect of the President's role as chief executive is largely symbolic. It embodies the perception of the President as, in the words of political scientist Thomas Cronin, "benevolent, omnipotent, omniscient, and highly moral."[19] This "cult of the presidency" summarizes enduring popular feelings that the President is the source of prosperity as well as of answers and reassurance in times of trouble. In short, the symbolic dimension of being chief executive means being the nation's father figure. Even the scandal-rocked administrations of Richard Nixon and Ronald Reagan have had little long-term impact on the strength and depth of this sentiment.[20] This symbolic

---

[18] See Richard P. Nathan, *The Administrative Presidency* (New York: Wiley, 1983).

[19] See Thomas E. Cronin, *The State of the Presidency* (Boston: Little, Brown, 1980), p. 76.

[20] A study by Harold M. Barger of the coverage of the presidency in precollege texts revealed that these books uniformly ignore scandal and corruption in the White House and emphasize mythical, heroic images of the presidency. See "Suspending Disbelief: The President in Pre-College Textbooks," *Presidential Studies Quarterly*, 20 (Winter

dimension of the presidency means that a shrewd chief executive can use symbols to curry popular support and enhance a political base; it also means that the expectations for and demands placed on the presidency invariably outstrip the office's ability to get things done. Popular disaffection is inevitable when the gap between expectations and performance grows too great.[21]

The President and Special Interests

The attention the President receives as national leader often obscures the fact that the executive office is also the focal point of special-interest pressure.[22] During the campaign process presidential candidates seek to build coalitions and raise money by currying the favor of important groups and organizations representing veterans; minority groups; unions; the elderly; various manufacturing, financial, and occupational sectors; and many other constituencies. After election, Presidents seek political allies from organized interests as a means of realizing enactment of their programs in Congress. In turn, interest groups seek access, recognition, and support.

Presidents have institutionalized a means for channeling interest group access through the White House Office of Public Liaison, which was formally established in 1974. During the Reagan administration this office provided a key conduit between the White House and the business community as well as a link to various evangelical Protestant and Catholic groups that were considered politically important.[23] Yet contacts with special interests often occur directly as

1990): 55–70. Many books discuss the nature and consequences of this symbolic quality of the presidency. See, for example, Harold M. Barger, *The Impossible Presidency* (Glenview, Ill.: Scott, Foresman, 1984); and Theodore J. Lowi, *The Personal President* (Ithaca, N.Y.: Cornell University Press, 1985). The appropriateness of the phrase "scandal-rocked" applied to the Nixon and Reagan administrations is confirmed in Shelley Ross, *Fall from Grace* (New York: Ballantine, 1988).

[21] For more on the President's pursuit of popular support, see George C. Edwards III, *The Public Presidency* (New York: St. Martin's, 1983).

[22] See, for example, Benjamin I. Page and Mark P. Petracca, *The American Presidency* (New York: McGraw-Hill, 1983), chap. 7; Joseph Pika, "The President and Interest Groups," in *Dimensions of the Modern Presidency*, ed. by Edward N. Kearny (St. Louis: Forum, 1981), pp. 59–80.

[23] Kay Lehman Schlozman and John T. Tierney, *Organized Interests and American Democracy* (New York: Harper & Row, 1986), p. 326.

well. Most often, these contacts are made between top administration aides and interest group representatives.[24]

CONCLUSION

Several conclusions about presidential behavior can be drawn from this discussion. First, the modern presidential campaign is highly personalized and therefore divorced from and independent of party and congressional races. Presidential candidates seek the party label no less aggressively than in the past, but they do so because of the two-party monopoly, which all but forecloses a successful third party effort. The political parties no longer control a monopoly of resources, such as jobs and money, and party leaders can no longer dictate the nomination.

Second, the concern of incumbent Presidents for reelection taints policy and their political relations with Congress. Presidents are discouraged from launching new initiatives as an election approaches, and the disjunction between the branches encourages mutual inter-branch scapegoating. For presidential challengers, the more crowded field of contestants rewards early success and any effort that helps voters distinguish one candidate from the others. The nomination process has become a marathon that begins with a sprint. For the victor, the early opportunities at the start of an administration are tempered by lack of experience. This becomes more clear when one considers the size of the executive branch, the chief executive's routine managerial and symbolic qualities, and the President's underestimated susceptibility to special interests. In Appendix 2 we turn to the parallel electoral and institutional forces that shape congressional behavior.

[24] Businesses and trade associations, for example, often hire lobbyists with White House connections to ensure such links. United Technologies, a company that relies heavily on defense contracts, employed former Representative Clark MacGregor (R-Minn.) to lobby on their behalf. MacGregor relied on his Washington contacts in the White House and elsewhere to effectively perform his job. See Jeffrey M. Berry, *The Interest Group Society* (Boston: Little, Brown, 1984), p. 194.

Appendix II

The Politics of the Modern Congress

It is impossible to understand the impact of Congress on national politics and its relations with the presidency without also understanding the basic features of this institution. Many have remarked that the American national legislature is unique among the legislatures of the world in its structure, formal detachment from the executive branch, and ability to shape national policy.[1] These unique electoral, structural, and political characteristics therefore merit scrutiny, particularly as they pertain to executive-legislative relations.

CONGRESSIONAL ELECTIONS

The Constitution's founders finally agreed that the national Congress would consist of two houses. However, as was discussed in Chapter 1, considerable controversy arose concerning the system of representation and the lengths of terms. The famed "Great Compromise" at the Constitutional Convention outlined a plan acceptable to both large and small states in creating one house in which representation would be based on population and a second house with equal representation for each state. The House of Representatives would be the popular branch in that its members would be elected frequently (every two years was the compromise between one- and three-year terms) and by direct vote. The Senate, in contrast, would be elected less frequently (the six-year term was also a compromise among those want-

[1] Gerhard Loewenberg and Samuel C. Patterson, *Comparing Legislatures* (Boston: Little, Brown, 1979), pp. 33–35.

ing terms ranging from three to nine years) and by state legislatures. This indirect method of election was viewed as a means for checking the other house's popular excesses.

The size of the Senate has never been an issue, as each new state was entitled to only two senators. Population-based representation in the House proved more vexing, however, and that body was progressively increased in size from 105 members in the First Congress to 435 after the 1910 Census, when a decision was made to freeze the number of seats for fear that the body would simply become too unwieldy. As the nation's population continued to grow and be redistributed around the country, seats would be juggled from state to state after each decennial census.[2]

In recent years population trends have reflected relative growth in the south and west, resulting in more congressional representation for those states and less for the northeast and midwest. New York State, for example, had forty-one seats in the House of Representatives in the 1960s, thirty-nine in the 1970s, thirty-four in the 1980s, and thirty-one in the 1990s. In contrast, California reaped the biggest gains. In the 1960s it had thirty-eight representatives in the House; that number increased to forty-three in the 1970s, forty-five in the 1980s, and fifty-two in the 1990s.

The Congressional Race

Congressional elections share at least three key traits that are also reflected in the institution. First, they are candidate-centered. That is, factors such as political party affiliation, issue positions, and national political tides have a minimal impact on the outcome of most congressional races.[3]

Second, reelection of incumbents is the overwhelming pattern. In 1988, 98 percent of House incumbents who sought reelection won. Despite the spread of antiincumbentism in the 1990 elections, the return rate that year was 97 percent. Measured another way, from

[2] Gary C. Jacobson, *The Politics of Congressional Elections* (Boston: Little, Brown, 1987), pp. 8–10. The size of the House was temporarily expanded when Alaska and Hawaii were admitted as states in 1959.

[3] See Randall B. Ripley, *Congress: Process and Policy* (New York: Norton, 1983), p. 76; Thomas E. Mann, *Unsafe at Any Margin* (Washington, D.C.: American Enterprise Institute, 1978); and Morris Fiorina, "The Presidency and Congress: An Electoral Connection?" in *The Presidency and the Political System*, ed. by Michael Nelson (Washington, D.C.: CQ Press, 1990), pp. 443–470.

1964 to 1980 the average vote received by House incumbents increased from 60 to 65 percent.[4] Buttressing the candidate-centered nature of congressional elections is the fact that while voters continued to approve of their individual members of Congress, their cynicism about national governing institutions (including Congress as a whole) grew during the same period.[5]

Third, the reelection process for members of the House is essentially continuous, and representatives are keenly sensitive to the connections between their actions and their impending reelection. Much of the behavior of members of Congress is explainable in terms of their perpetual concern for reelection.

CONGRESSIONAL CYCLES

Every presidential election revives discussion about the ability of the successful candidate to encourage voters to support congressional candidates of the same party as the President when they would not otherwise do so. When this occurs, it is said that the President has coattails.

The Coattail Effect

This phenomenon is widely discussed but also often misunderstood. Many assume, for example, that the wider the presidential candidate's margin of victory, the greater the coattail effect or assume that the coattail effect is present in every presidential election, yet neither assumption is necessarily true. In 1972, for example, Richard Nixon was reelected with over 60 percent of the popular vote and won the electoral vote of forty-nine states, yet the Republican party gained only twelve seats in the House and lost two seats in the Senate. Perhaps the Republicans would have done even worse if Nixon had not done so well, but Nixon demonstrated little in the way of coattails

[4] By one assessment, the electoral bonus of incumbency—that is, extra votes received because of incumbency—rose from less than 2 percent in the 1950s to 5 percent in the 1960s and 8 percent in the 1970s. See Fiorina, "The Presidency and Congress," p. 449.

[5] Jacobson, *The Politics of Congressional Elections*, p. 2. This paradox is discussed in Richard F. Fenno, "If, as Ralph Nader Says, Congress Is the 'Broken Branch,' How Come We Love Our Congressmen So Much?" in *Congress in Change*, ed. by Norman J. Ornstein (New York: Praeger, 1975), pp. 227–281. See also Glenn R. Parker, *Characteristics of Congress* (Englewood Cliffs, N.J.: Prentice-Hall, 1989), chap. 3.

when 1972 is compared to other presidential election years. One study of coattail effects concluded that a successful presidential candidate is most likely to possess coattails in congressional districts where no incumbent is running.[6]

Many believe that the coattail effect is on the decline or at least is less important, an allegation supported by declining party loyalties among voters, the decline of political parties as a vital force in national elections, and the increasing tendency for candidates to rely on their own nonparty resources, such as contributions from political action committees. Until the New Deal era, from one-quarter to one-half of the members of the President's party in Congress faced defeat when the President performed poorly; today, that figure would probably be below 10 percent.[7] Another indication of the decline of the coattail effect is the rise in the number of congressional districts with split results, that is, House districts where the President won a majority of the vote but the district elected a representative from the opposition party.

Midterm Elections

The electoral concerns of the President and Congress converge in nonpresidential election years as well. The election of all 435 members of the House and one-third of the Senate during the middle of the presidential term invites presidential attempts to fortify the executive party's strength in Congress, yet the overwhelming trend has been the opposite. With the exception of the midterm election of 1934,[8] the President's party has lost seats in the House (with only a third of the Senate elected every two years, its results are a less accurate gauge of the mood of the country) in every instance in the twentieth century.

This midterm dip has been labeled the surge and decline phenomenon and is predicated on the assumption that the President's party usually does better during presidential election years than the national partisan balance would otherwise predict because of the

---

[6] George C. Edwards, *The Public Presidency* (New York: St. Martin's, 1983), pp. 86–88.

[7] Fiorina, "The Presidency and Congress," p. 453. See also Gary C. Jacobson, *The Electoral Origins of Divided Government* (Boulder, Colo.: Westview, 1990), p. 81.

[8] This midterm election occurred during a time of swelling support for Franklin Roosevelt, first elected in 1932, and a time when the country was undergoing a fundamental shift toward the Democratic Party.

strength of the winning presidential candidate. Thus, when the President's party loses congressional seats during the midterm election, it is considered a normal adjustment to the President's previous victory. The problem with this explanation is that the correlation between presidential and congressional votes has declined in recent years, and two other factors—incumbency and the condition of the economy—are now given greater weight in explaining midterm swings.[9]

The Electoral Link

It is clear that congressional elections are distinct from presidential elections, yet they are linked too, depending on the political conditions of a particular year. Long presidential coattails and a weak midterm swing away from the President's party will yield a stronger partisan tie between the branches than will the reverse situation. But a weak and stratified party system, mass media campaigns, independent fund-raising, weak out-party challenges, and incumbency all lead to a tenuous electoral link between the branches that has been reflected in the norm of divided government since 1968.[10] Thus, the President casts a shadow over congressional elections, but it is only a shadow.

One other important fact links congressional and presidential elections. Congress has been the primary breeding ground for Presidents throughout American history. Of the forty men who have served as president from George Washington to George Bush, twenty-four have served in at least one house of Congress.

CONGRESSIONAL STRUCTURES

Like the presidency, Congress is a unique institution with its own structural and institutional characteristics. Some of these characteristics are written into law, but most are unwritten traditions or "norms"

---

[9] As Gary Jacobson points out, while surge and decline still occurs, the seats that are lost during the midterm decline are less likely to be those won in the last presidential election surge. From 1946 to 1966 an average of 40 percent of the seats that changed hands from one party to the other were recaptured seats lost during the previous election. But from 1968 to 1988 only 15.6 percent of seat switches were recaptures. See Jacobson, *The Electoral Origins of Divided Government*, p. 19.

[10] See Jacobson, *The Electoral Origins of Divided Party Government*.

that are essential to Congress's daily operation. Spanning these characteristics is one central fact about the Congress of the twentieth century: Congress is a relatively decentralized institution. Just as Congress must be attentive to the structural and political features of the executive branch, Presidents seeking congressional support must curry favor not only with party and congressional leaders but also with committee and subcommittee chairs, regional leaders, and others representing particular interests. They must also play to partisan and ideological imperatives.

Chamber Leaders

Since the establishment of the modern two-party system in Congress in the post–Civil War period, leadership in Congress has been based on partisan divisions. Although members of Congress are elected as representatives of small geographic regions, they are also elected as Republicans or Democrats. The party that holds the numerical majority in each house uses that majority to select the chamber leaders. Leadership selection takes place in party caucuses—assemblies of party members in each chamber—at the start of each two-year Congress.

In the House the chief chamber leader is the Speaker, who also serves as the leader of the majority party. Each party then has its majority and minority leaders and majority and minority assistant floor leaders, called whips.

The Senate has no position comparable to that of the Speaker of the House. The chief presiding officer is the president of the Senate, designated by the Constitution to be the U.S. Vice President. This position is ceremonial, however, and the Vice President participates only to cast a tie-breaking vote. The next highest officer is the president pro tempore, also a ceremonial position that is awarded to the most senior member of the majority party in the Senate. The most important Senate leaders are the majority and minority leaders, followed by the majority and minority whips.

Congressional leaders work to provide centralization, coherence, and a measure of party discipline to their chambers. The principal job of the leaders is to rally support for or opposition to partisan programs. This is done by negotiating with committee leaders, resolving jurisdictional disputes between committees, scheduling floor action for bills, using rules and procedures to best advantage, and gathering support for important votes. Unlike some of their predecessors, current leaders have limited resources at their disposal. Still, they can employ persuasion, use their bill-scheduling authority to reward or punish, influence committee assignments, appoint special committees, direct campaign contributions toward or away from members, and use White House contacts to exert pressure.

Congressional leaders are expected to pay their first allegiance to the members of their party in Congress. Yet leadership is also important as the primary means for linking the President with Congress. Ironically, the decline in leadership power has probably increased the tendency of leaders to either rely on or react to the President. In the case of congressional leaders of the same party as the President, leaders' reputations rise and fall according to their success in implementing the President's priorities. Even when the major party in Congress is not that of the President, its actions are keyed to the President's political stance. In other words, congressional leadership strategies typically revolve around presidential actions and preferences.[11]

Seniority

Although it is a custom and not a formal rule, seniority—a system by which length of continuous service is rewarded with enhanced power and perquisites in the institution—has been the principal means for selecting leaders of standing committees and resolving other power-related matters in both houses of Congress. Length of service in Congress is called congressional seniority, whereas length of service on a committee is known as committee seniority.

Prior to the twentieth century, seniority was only one of several criteria used to select committee chairs and other leaders. But in the latter part of the nineteenth century, as legislation became more complex and the average length of congressional careers increased, so too did reliance on seniority (although it came to the House more slowly than to the Senate, where terms were longer and experience was more venerated). In this century the norm of seniority has been

---

[11] Barbara Sinclair, "Congressional Leadership: A Review Essay and a Research Agenda," in *Leading Congress,* ed. by John J. Kornacki (Washington, D.C.: Congressional Quarterly, 1990), pp. 134–35, 138–139. See also Roger H. Davidson, "The Senate: If Everyone Leads, Who Follows?" in *Congress Reconsidered,* ed. by Lawrence C. Dodd and Bruce I. Oppenheimer (Washington, D.C.: CQ Press, 1989), pp. 297–301.

violated only occasionally and only under unusual circumstances.[12] In recent years, however, members of Congress have had less patience with ineffectual committee leadership.

Seniority is the basis for determining formal status on congressional committees. The committee chair is typically the most senior member of the majority party, which holds numerical majorities on all committees. The most senior member of the minority party on each committee is known as the ranking minority member and is also accorded some deference by virtue of continuous years of committee service. Aside from access to and influence on committees, seniority affects the assignment of office space, access to congressional patronage, and the respect of colleagues. Party leaders in both houses are not selected according to seniority, but lengthy service in Congress is generally a prerequisite for serving as a chamber leader. Because the principle of seniority rewards length of continuous service, it has tended to empower representatives elected from "safe" constituencies, that is, districts or states that reelect a representative by consistently high percentages.[13]

The Committee System

Congressional committees constitute the heart of Congress. Much important work is done there. Policy is formulated, reputations are made, and power is wielded. This fact was noted by Woodrow Wilson, who wrote in 1886 that "Congress in its committee-rooms is Congress at work."[14]

The importance of committees is seen partly in their workload. Virtually all bills introduced into Congress are referred to one or more committees. During the 100th Congress (1987–1988), for example, 6,263 measures were introduced in the House, and 3,325 in

[12] The evolution of the seniority system is chronicled in Nelson W. Polsby, Miriam Gallagher, and Barry Rundquist, "The Growth of the Seniority System in the U.S. House of Representatives," *American Political Science Review*, 63 (September 1969): 787–807. Seniority in relation to the selection of committee chairs was violated in three instances in 1975 and twice in 1990.

[13] For more on seniority, see Barbara Hinckley, *The Seniority System in Congress* (Bloomington: Indiana University Press, 1971); and Congressional Quarterly, Inc., *How Congress Works* (Washington, D.C.: Congressional Quarterly, 1983), pp. 109–112.

[14] Woodrow Wilson, *Congressional Government* (Cleveland, Ohio: Meridian, 1956), p. 69.

the Senate. Of these, a total of 713 bills[15] were enacted into law. Most of the rest died in committee. In the same Congress, the House maintained 22 regular standing committees and 132 subcommittees; the Senate had 16 standing committees and 85 subcommittees. In the House, according to Democratic party caucus rules, no member can chair more than one subcommittee. The Senate also imposes restrictions on chairing multiple committees. The effect of this principle is that most members of the Senate, including very junior members, have the opportunity to wield added power as a committee or subcommittee chair, as do many junior House members. In addition, various special, select, and joint committees also engage in important work.

The average senator sits on ten committees or subcommittees, while the average House member serves on seven. In 1987 Senate committees alone employed about 1,000 staff members, while House committees employed almost 2,000 staff people.

Committees are important not only because virtually all legislation is funneled through them but also because they are recognized for their members' expertise, specialization, and experience. This deference to committee recommendations means that committee actions are usually respected by the full House and Senate.

Since the 1970s, however, deference to committees has undergone some change. Committee actions are somewhat more likely to be challenged on the floor, as more members have developed their own expertise on selected issues. In the 1970s an influx of new members of Congress prompted a move to grant junior members more influence. In addition, the autonomy of subcommittees was increased, and this had the effect of limiting the power of the committee chair.[16]

Subcommittees

Many committees have long relied on subcommittees to handle most of their important work. Subcommittees hold initial hearings and

[15] This is the number of public bills enacted into law. See Norman J. Ornstein, Thomas E. Mann, and Michael J. Malbin, *Vital Statistics on Congress 1989–1990* (Washington, D.C.: CQ Press, 1990), p. 160.

[16] See Norman J. Ornstein and David W. Rohde, "Political Parties and Congressional Reform," in *Parties and Elections in an Anti-Party Age,* ed. by Jeff Fishel (Bloomington: Indiana University Press, 1978), pp. 280–294; and Barbara Hinckley, *Stability and Change in Congress* (New York: Harper & Row, 1988), pp. 128–132, 144–146.

provide the first recommendation on bills. The key role of subcommittees represents an extension of the principle that has made committees important, namely, that Congress must rely on specialization and division of labor to deal with the overwhelming amount of work it faces annually.

Subcommittees gained a greater role in the 1970s with the adoption of the so-called subcommittee bill of rights. Approved in 1973, this agreement ensured that subcommittees would have clearly defined jurisdictions, could meet with or without approval of the committee chair, and would have their own budgets and staffs. Committee members could also choose at least one subcommittee assignment.

Seniority is also the principle used for selecting subcommittee chairs, although it is violated more frequently than is the case with committee chairs. From 1959 to 1981 about 5 percent of all subcommittee chairs owed their positions to violations of seniority. This percentage remained constant before and after the changes of the 1970s.[17]

The number of subcommittees has grown, and their workload has increased as well. In the 1950s subcommittees held about 30 percent of all hearings; by the late 1970s subcommittees were holding over 90 percent of all hearings. Their impact was and is felt in committee work but also is felt on the chamber floor, where the extension of specialization and decentralization is shown by the key influence exerted by subcommittee chairs acting as legislative shepherds. The greater role of subcommittees has also meant that they have generated even more business in Congress.[18]

Informal Caucuses

In addition to the fragmenting effects of seniority and the committee system, leaders must contend with a vast array of informal caucuses, groups, alliances, cliques, and coalitions that serve to unify like-

[17] Randall Ripley, *Congress: Process and Policy* (New York: Norton, 1988), p. 60.

[18] Hinckley, *Stability and Change in Congress,* pp. 165–170. For more on the committee and subcommittee system, see Richard F. Fenno, *Congressmen in Committees* (Boston: Little, Brown, 1973); Steven S. Smith and Christopher J. Deering, *Committees in Congress* (Washington, D.C.: CQ Press, 1984); Congressional Quarterly, Inc., *How Congress Works,* pp. 79–108.

minded congressional groups. Each party in each chamber has its own party caucus, which addresses particular policy and issue related concerns. The House Democratic party caucus was the vehicle used to institute many of the reforms of the 1970s. An important party caucus of the 1950s and 1960s, the boll weevils, was composed of conservative southern Democrats. This regional group was revitalized during the 1980s and provided President Reagan with key support for his conservative agenda.

A variety of other unofficial congressional groups have sprung up in recent years. Some are active and influential, while others are paper organizations that exist mostly to attract favorable public attention. In 1988, sixty such organizations existed in the House, twenty-six were in the Senate, and thirty-seven were joint. The number of members has varied from 5 to 200, and their concerns have ranged from the arts to wine. Among the more important have been the state caucuses, composed of the representatives from larger states, which have been influential in promoting state and regional concerns.

Assessments of the impact of these groups are divided. Without question, some caucuses have provided key influence in promoting the passage of important legislation. Some view these groups as a positive basis around which like-minded legislators can organize to promote legitimate interests. Others complain that they simply add to the list of parochial interests that must be satisfied in order to enact important legislation. As Speaker of the House Tip O'Neill observed, the "House has over-caucused itself."[19]

Party and Ideology

Political party affiliation is central to the organization and operation of Congress. At the same time, members of Congress rely heavily on signals or cues from their parties and party leaders to help them decide how to vote on the thousands of bills that come before Congress every year. In fact, despite the generalized decline of political parties as a national political force in recent decades, party affiliation as an explanation for congressional voting actually increased during the

---

[19] Quoted in Roger H. Davidson and Walter J. Oleszek, *Congress and Its Members* (Washington, D.C.: 1990), p. 294; see also pp. 182–184, 294–299.

1980s, although the amount of party-based voting in Congress varies from issue to issue.[20]

For members of Congress whose party is the same as that of the President, the pull to support the President is great. First, even without presidential coattails, both are likely to share the same or similar constituencies. Second, like it or not, members of the President's party will be identified with the President's record and goals. Third, the party label itself is an important binding tie, as it was the banner under which they were elected. Fourth, the President can provide a variety of concrete rewards for party loyalty.[21]

Closely related to partisan considerations is the ideological leaning of members of Congress, which also shapes the behavior of representatives as well as their attitudes toward presidential actions and programs. The fact that ideology plays a role in congressional behavior is attributable to several factors. First, the process by which individuals win office is one that by definition attracts people with fairly well developed, sophisticated, and strongly held views of politics. Second, ideology bears directly on congressional campaigns, as issues and the voting records of incumbents can figure prominently in such contests. Third, ideology is a source of voting cues for members of Congress (second to party cues).[22] For Presidents lacking a partisan majority in Congress, ideology can be an important basis for coalition building for presidential iniatives.

Congress and Special Interests

Special-interest access and influence is often considered Congress's great weakness, as witnessed by periodic investigations and exposés of bribery, influence peddling, and other misdeeds. It is readily apparent in both congressional elections and congressional behavior.

---

[20] David J. Vogler, *The Politics of Congress* (Boston: Allyn & Bacon, 1988), pp. 117–119.

[21] Jon R. Bond and Richard Fleisher, *The President in the Legislative Arena* (Chicago: University of Chicago Press, 1990), pp. 14–16. For more on the role of party, see Julius Turner and Edward Schneier, *Party and Constituency* (Baltimore: Johns Hopkins University Press, 1970); Jeff Fishel, *Party and Opposition* (New York: McKay, 1973).

[22] Bond and Fleisher, *The President in the Legislative Arena*, pp. 18–22. For more on the importance of ideology, see Jerrold Schneider, *Ideological Coalitions in Congress* (Westport, Conn.: Greenwood, 1979); John W. Kingdon, *Congressmen's Voting Decisions* (New York: Harper & Row, 1981).

Elections and Influence.   The high rate of reelection of incumbents has done little to stem the pervasive presence of specialized interests in the congressional campaign process. Chief among these   interests are the ubiquitous political action committees (PACs)—organizations attached to corporations, trade associations, unions, and other entities with political interests that raise money to contribute to campaigns. PACs proliferated in the 1970s primarily as an unintended consequence of campaign finance reforms. Thousands of PACs operate today, and they have accounted for a substantial and growing amount of the funding of congressional races. In 1984, for example, PACs contributed about 42 percent of the total campaign contributions for House incumbents and 23 percent for Senate incumbents.[23]

Many assume that PACs are literally purchasing the loyalties of representatives when they contribute to congressional campaigns, but the truth is more complex. PAC contributions are most important as reinforcement. PAC giving tends to favor incumbents overwhelmingly: In the 1989–1990 period, for example, about 84 percent of all PAC money, or $79 million, went to incumbents.[24] The reasoning behind this pattern is entirely logical: A PAC would rather get a small political "return" from betting on a winner than no return from betting on a loser even if the loser holds positions more friendly to that PAC. Even if they cannot buy votes, PACs can at least hope for access and a more sympathetic ear from members of Congress. Yet there are also instances when special-interest money can swing votes, an outcome that is more likely when the issue involved is more narrow and less visible.[25]

Structures and Influence.   The decentralized, fragmented nature of congressional decision making greatly facilitates access by specialized interests. It also means that lobbyists must expend greater effort, since important decisions arise from many decision points in

[23] Alan L. Clem, *Congress: Powers, Processes, and Politics* (Pacific Grove, Calif.: Brooks/Cole, 1989), p. 84.

[24] *Federal Election Commission Record*, 16 (November 1990):6.

[25] See H. R. Mahood, *Interest Group Politics in America* (Englewood Cliffs, N.J.: Prentice-Hall, 1990), p. 96. See also Jeffrey M. Berry, *The Interest Group Society* (Boston: Little, Brown, 1984), pp. 171–175. For more on PACs, see Michael J. Malbin, ed., *Money and Politics in the United States* (Washington, D.C.: American Enterprise Institute, 1984); and Larry Sabato, *PAC Power* (New York: Norton, 1985).

Congress. Lobbyists rely on a wide array of techniques to influence congressional decision making. These efforts can be focused narrowly to sway key legislators in what are labeled "iron triangles"— close, accommodative relationships between congressional committees, bureaucratic agencies ,and private interests. These "subgovernments" operate in relative anonymity, a fact which enforces the likelihood that the policy which emerges will benefit the members of the triangle. Yet such influence is not necessarily uniform. One study concluded that the impact of subgovernments on policy-making varies with the type of policy.[26] Still, the involvement of specialized interests in the policy process extends from congressional hearings to congressional oversight.

CONCLUSION

The sum total of these organizational characteristics points to an institution where centrifugal forces predominate despite the efforts of chamber leaders. Insulation results from candidate-centered congressional elections, incumbency, and the declining impact of presidential coattails, as well as seniority, the committee system, and patterns of influence and access. This situation invites presidential leadership in the legislative sphere yet also makes success for the President difficult.[27]

Presidents must take care to deal with Congress's multiple power centers. A positive working relationship with Congress begins with its party leaders. This helps strengthen the hand of the President, since it demonstrates respect for the opinions of chamber leaders, and it helps the chamber leaders, as it allows them to represent themselves to the rest of the chamber as a presidential conduit. In addition, Presidents must be sensitive to important subgovernment leaders, including committee chairs, caucus leaders, and influential private in-

---

[26] See Randall B. Ripley and Grace A. Franklin, *Congress, the Bureaucracy, and Public Policy* (Pacific Grove, Calif.: Brooks/Cole, 1991). For more on this relationship, see Morris P. Fiorina, *Congress: Keystone of the Washington Establishment* (New Haven, Conn.: Yale University Press, 1989); and Theodore J. Lowi, *The End of Liberalism* (New York: Norton, 1979).

[27] Ripley, *Congress: Process and Policy,* 1983 edition, p. 160. See 1988 edition, p. 185.

terests. Presidential success turns on the President's recognition that Congress incorporates numerous decision points. A lack of support at any one of those points can mean the end of a presidential initiative.

Institutional Apples and Oranges?

The President and Congress are indeed separate institutions, but they must come together to share important governing powers. As in a marriage, each must be sensitive to the unique traits of the other if they are to have even a chance of establishing a successful working relationship.

Both branches are concerned with their own elections; both apply institutional resources to enhance their chances of reelection. Regardless of whether a congressional election coincides with a presidential election, the participants, as well as journalists and other pundits, focus incessant attention on the connections between the two. As we have noted, the President may have coattails and midterm swings may be affected by the President's political standing. Unfortunately, factors that are more important to explaining these outcomes, such as incumbency and economic conditions, are seldom given their due. As a result, the actual electoral link between the two institutions is usually exaggerated. As historian James MacGregor Burns has argued, we have not two but four national parties: presidential Democrats and Republicans and congressional Democrats and Republicans.[28] Moreover, the impact of each on the other's reelection is not considered reciprocal. That is, the President may have an impact on congressional races, but congressional elections do not seem to have a similar impact on the presidential race—a conclusion symptomatic of the broader pattern of presidential preeminence that emerges in this book.

Even greater divergence between the branches is evidenced in their structural makeup and norms. For all the organizational diversity of the executive branch, it is at least formally bureaucratic and hierarchical in nature. Congress is quite the opposite in that it is an institution composed of numerous semiautonomous power centers. Party and chamber leaders attempt to push the institution toward greater centralization, but the countervailing forces of seniority, the

---

[28] James MacGregor Burns, *The Deadlock of Democracy* (Englewood Cliffs, N.J: Prentice-Hall, 1963), pp. 195–203 and passim.

committee and subcommittee system, informal caucuses, and the very nature of the lawmaking process all serve to decentralize power. Thus, Congress's political and institutional circumstances invite presidential intrusion but also normally preclude easy or low-cost victories for the executive.

Selected Bibliography

Adler, David Gray. "The Constitution and Presidential Warmaking." *Political Science Quarterly,* 103 (Spring 1988): 1–36.

___. *The Constitution and the Termination of Treaties.* New York: Garland, 1986.

Asher, Herbert B. *Presidential Elections and American Politics.* Chicago: Dorsey, 1988.

Bailey, Thomas A. *Presidential Greatness.* New York: Appleton-Century-Crofts, 1966.

Barger, Harold M. *The Impossible Presidency.* Glenview, Ill.: Scott, Foresman, 1984.

Barnet, Richard J. *The Rockets' Red Glare.* New York: Simon & Schuster, 1990.

Barnhart, Michael, ed. *Congress and United States Foreign Policy.* Albany: State University of New York Press, 1987.

Barone, Michael, and Grant Ujifusa. *The Almanac of American Politics.* Washington, D.C.: National Journal, 1989.

Bartels, Larry. *Presidential Primaries and the Dynamics of Public Choice.* Princeton, N.J.: Princeton University Press, 1988.

Berman, Larry. *The New American Presidency.* New York: Little, Brown, 1987.

___. *The Office of Management and Budget and the Presidency, 1921–1979.* Princeton, N.J.: Princeton University Press, 1979.

Bessette, Joseph M., and Jeffrey Tulis, eds. *The Presidency in the Constitutional Order.* Baton Rouge: Louisiana State University Press, 1981.

Bickford, Charlene Bangs, and Kenneth R. Bowling. *Birth of the Nation: The First Federal Congress, 1789–1791.* New York: First Federal Congress Project, 1989.

Binkley, Wilfred E. *President and Congress.* New York: Vintage, 1962.

Bond, Jon R., and Richard Fleisher. *The President in the Legislative Arena.* Chicago: University of Chicago Press, 1990.

Bowling, Kenneth R., and Helen E. Veit, eds. *The Diary of William Maclay and Other Notes on Senate Debates.* Baltimore: Johns Hopkins University Press, 1988.

Brace, Paul, Christine B. Harrington, and Gary King, eds. *The Presidency in American Politics.* New York: New York University Press, 1989.

Brinkley, Joel, and Stephen Engelberg, eds. *Report of the Congressional*

Committees Investigating the Iran-Contra Affair. New York: Random House, 1988.

Bryce, James. *The American Commonwealth,* 2 vols. New York: Macmillan, 1891.

Buchanan, Bruce. *The Citizen's Presidency.* Washington, D.C.: CQ Press, 1987.

___. *The Presidential Experience.* Englewood Cliffs, N.J.: Prentice-Hall, 1978.

Burns, James MacGregor. *The Deadlock of Democracy.* Englewood Cliffs, N.J.: Prentice-Hall, 1963.

___. *Leadership.* New York: Harper & Row, 1978.

Caralay, Demetrios, ed. *The President's War Powers.* New York: Academy of Political Science, 1984.

Chamberlain, Lawrence. *The President, Congress, and Legislation.* New York: Columbia University Press, 1946.

Christman, Margaret C. S. *The First Federal Congress, 1789–1791.* Washington, D.C.: Smithsonian Institution Press, 1989.

Christopher, Warren. "Ceasefire between the Branches: A Compact in Foreign Affairs." *Foreign Affairs,* 60 (Summer 1982):989–1005.

Clausen, Aage R. *How Congressmen Decide.* New York: St. Martin's, 1973.

Clem, Alan L. *Congress: Powers, Processes, and Politics.* Pacific Grove, Calif.: Brooks/Cole, 1989.

Cohen, Jeffrey E. "The Impact of the Modern Presidency on Presidential Success in the U.S. Congress." *Legislative Studies Quarterly,* 7 (November 1982):515–532.

Committee on the Constitutional System. *A Bicentennial Analysis of the American Political Structure,* Washington, D.C., January 1987.

Cooper, Joseph. "Assessing Legislative Performance." *Congress and the Presidency,* 13 (Spring 1986):21–40.

Corwin, Edward S. *The President: Office and Powers.* New York: New York University Press, 1957.

Cox, Gary W., and Samuel Kernell, eds. *The Politics of Divided Government.* Boulder, Col.: Westview, 1991.

Craig, Barbara Hinkson. *The Legislative Veto.* Boulder, Colo.: Westview, 1983.

Crabb, Cecil V., Jr., and Pat M. Holt. *Invitation to Struggle: Congress, the President, and Foreign Policy.* Washington, D.C.: CQ Press, 1989.

Cronin, Thomas E., ed. *Inventing the American Presidency.* Lawrence: University Press of Kansas, 1989.

___. *The State of the Presidency.* Boston: Little, Brown, 1980.

Crotty, William, and John S. Jackson III. *Presidential Primaries and Nominations.* Washington, D.C.: CQ Press, 1985.

Crovitz, L. Gordon, and Jeremy Rabkin, eds. *The Fettered Presidency.* Washington, D.C.: American Enterprise Institute, 1989.

Davidson, Roger H., ed. "Congress and the Presidency: Invitation to Struggle." *Annals of the American Academy of Political and Social Science,* 499 (September 1988).

___, ed. *The Postreform Congress.* New York: St. Martin's, 1992.

Davidson, Roger, and Walter J. Oleszek. *Congress and Its Members.* Washington, D.C.: CQ Press, 1990.

Davis, James W. *The American Presidency.* New York: Harper & Row, 1987.

Deering, Christopher, ed. *Congressional Politics.* Chicago: Dorsey, 1989.

DeGrazia, Alfred, ed. *Congress: The First Branch of Government.* New York: Anchor, 1967.

DiClerico, Robert E., and Eric M. Uslander. *Few Are Chosen: Problems in Presidential Selection.* New York: McGraw-Hill, 1984.

Dodd, Lawrence C., and Bruce I. Oppenheimer, eds. *Congress Reconsidered.* Washington, D.C.: CQ Press, 1989.

Draper, Theodore. *A Very Thin Line: The Iran-Contra Affair.* New York: Hill & Wang, 1991.

Edwards, George C. III. *At the Margins.* New Haven, Conn.: Yale University Press, 1989.

___. *Presidential Influence in Congress.* San Francisco: Freeman, 1980.

___. *The Public Presidency.* New York: St. Martin's, 1983.

Edwards, George C. III, and Stephen J. Wayne. *Presidential Leadership.* New York: St. Martin's, 1990.

___, eds. *Studying the Presidency.* Knoxville: University of Tennessee Press, 1983.

Egger, Rowland, and Joseph P. Harris. *President and Congress.* New York: McGraw-Hill, 1963.

Farrand, Max. *The Framing of the Constitution of the United States.* New Haven, Conn.: Yale University Press, 1913.

___. *The Records of the Federal Convention of 1787,* 4 vols. New Haven, Conn.: Yale University Press, 1966.

The Federalist Papers. New York: New American Library, 1961.

Fenno, Richard F. *Congressmen in Committees.* Boston: Little, Brown, 1973.

Finer, Herman. *The Presidency.* Chicago: University of Chicago Press, 1960.

Fiorina, Morris. *Congress: Keystone of the Washington Establishment.* New Haven, Conn.: Yale University Press, 1989.

Fisher, Louis. *Constitutional Conflicts between Congress and the President.* Lawrence, Kan.: University Press of Kansas, 1991.

___. "Judicial Misjudgments about the Lawmaking Process." *Public Administration Review,* 45 (November 1985):705–11.

___. *The Politics of Shared Power.* Washington, D.C.: CQ Press, 1987.

___. *President and Congress.* New York: Free Press, 1972.

___. *Presidential Spending Power.* Princeton, N.J.: Princeton University Press, 1975.

Fisher, Louis, and Neal Devins. "How Successfully Can the States' Item

Veto Be Transferred to the President?" *Georgetown Law Journal,* 75 (October 1986):159–97.

Ford, Henry Jones. *The Rise and Growth of American Politics.* New York: Da Capo, 1967.

Franck, Thomas M., ed. *The Tethered Presidency.* New York: New York University Press, 1981.

Furlong, William L., and Margaret E. Scranton. *The Dynamics of Foreign Policymaking: The President, the Congress, and the Panama Canal Treaties.* Boulder, Colo.: Westview, 1984.

Gallagher, Hugh. "Presidents, Congress, and the Legislative Functions." In *The Presidency Reappraised,* ed. by Rexford Tugwell and Thomas Cronin. New York: Praeger, 1974, 217–233.

Galloway, George B. *History of the House of Representatives.* New York: Crowell, 1961.

Glennon, Michael J. *Constitutional Diplomacy.* Princeton, N.J.: Princeton University Press, 1990.

Goldsmith, William M. *The Growth of Presidential Power,* 3 vols. New York: Chelsea House, 1983.

Graebner, Norman A. *America as a World Power.* Wilmington, Del.: Scholarly Resources, 1984.

Greenstein, Fred I., ed. *Leadership and the Modern Presidency.* Cambridge, Mass.: Harvard University Press, 1988.

Grover, William F. *The President as Prisoner.* Albany: State University of New York Press, 1989.

Hardin, Charles M. *Presidential Power and Accountability.* Chicago: University of Chicago Press, 1974.

Hargrove, Erwin C., and Michael Nelson. *Presidents, Politics, and Policy.* New York: Knopf, 1984.

Hart, John. *The Presidential Branch.* New York: Pergamon, 1987.

Heclo, Hugh, and Lester Salamon, eds. *The Illusion of Presidential Government.* Boulder, Colo.: Westview, 1981.

Henkin, Louis. *Foreign Affairs and the Constitution.* New York: Free Press, 1972.

Hinckley, Barbara. *Congressional Elections.* Washington, D.C.: CQ Press, 1981.

___. *The Seniority System in Congress.* Bloomington: Indiana University Press, 1971.

___. *Stability and Change in Congress.* New York: Harper & Row, 1988.

Holtzman, Abraham. *Legislative Liaison.* Chicago: Rand McNally, 1970.

Hoxie, R. Gordon, ed. *The Presidency and National Security Policy.* New York: Center for the Study of the Presidency, 1984.

The Iran-Contra Puzzle. Washington, D.C.: Congressional Quarterly, 1987.

Jackson, Carlton. *Presidential Vetoes, 1792–1945.* Athens: University of Georgia Press, 1967.

Jacobson, Gary C. *The Electoral Origins of Divided Government.* Boulder, Colo.: Westview, 1990.

___. *The Politics of Congressional Elections.* New York: HarperCollins, 1992.

Janis, Irving. *Groupthink.* Boston: Houghton Mifflin, 1982.

Johannes, John R. "The President Proposes and Congress Disposes—But Not Always." *Review of Politics,* 36 (July 1974):356–370.

Johnson, Loch K. *America's Secret Power.* New York: Oxford University Press, 1989.

___. *The Making of International Agreements.* New York: New York University Press, 1984.

Jones, Charles O. *The Trusteeship Presidency.* Baton Rouge: Louisiana State University Press, 1988.

___, ed. *The Reagan Legacy.* Chatham, N.J.: Chatham House, 1988.

Jones, Gordon S., and John A. Marini, eds. *The Imperial Congress.* New York: Pharos, 1988.

Josephy, Alvin M., Jr. *On the Hill.* New York: Simon & Schuster, 1979.

Keefe, William J. *Congress and the American People.* Englewood Cliffs, N.J.: Prentice-Hall, 1988.

Kellerman, Barbara, and Ryan J. Barilleaux. *The President as World Leader.* New York: St. Martin's, 1991.

Kernell, Samuel. *Going Public.* Washington, D.C.: CQ Press, 1986.

Kessel, John H. *Presidential Parties.* Homewood, Ill.: Dorsey, 1984.

Kessler, Frank. *The Dilemmas of Presidential Leadership.* Englewood Cliffs, N.J.: Prentice-Hall, 1982.

Keynes, Edward. *Undeclared War.* University Park: Pennsylvania State University Press, 1982.

Killian, Johnny H., ed. *The Constitution of the United States of America.* Washington, D.C.: U.S. Government Printing Office, 1987.

King, Anthony, ed. *Both Ends of the Avenue.* Washington, D.C.: American Enterprise Institute, 1983.

King, Gary, and Lyn Ragsdale. *The Elusive Executive.* Washington, D.C.: CQ Press, 1988.

Kingdon, John W. *Agendas, Alternatives, and Public Policies.* Glenview, Ill.: Scott, Foresman, 1984.

___. *Congressmen's Voting Decisions.* New York: Harper & Row, 1973.

Koenig, Louis. *The Chief Executive.* New York: Harcourt Brace Jovanovich, 1986.

Koh, Harold Hongju. *The National Security Constitution.* New Haven, Conn.: Yale University Press, 1990.

Kornacki, John J., ed. *Leading Congress.* Washington, D.C.: Congressional Quarterly, 1990.

Kozak, David C., and John D. Macartney, eds. *Congress and Public Policy.* Chicago: Dorsey, 1987.

LeLoup, Lance T. *Budgetary Politics*. Brunswick, Ohio: King's Court Communications, 1988.

Lengle, James I., and Byron Shafer, eds. *Presidential Politics*. New York: St. Martin's, 1983.

Light, Paul C. *The President's Agenda*. Baltimore: Johns Hopkins University Press, 1982.

Lofgren, Charles A. "War-Making Under the Constitution." *Yale Law Journal*, 81 (March 1972):672–702.

Lowi, Theodore J. *The Personal President*. Ithaca, N.Y.: Cornell University Press, 1985.

Mann, Thomas E., ed. *A Question of Balance: The President, the Congress, and Foreign Policy*. Washington, D.C.: Brookings Institution, 1990.

Mann, Thomas E., and Norman J. Ornstein, eds. *The New Congress*. Washington, D.C.: American Enterprise Institute, 1981.

Margolis, Lawrence. *Executive Agreements and Presidential Power*. New York: Praeger, 1986.

Mason, Edward C. *The Veto Power*. Boston: Ginn, 1890.

May, Christopher N. *In the Name of War: Judicial Review and the War Powers Since 1918*. Cambridge, Mass.: Harvard University Press, 1989.

Mayhew, David R. *Congress: The Electoral Connection*. New Haven, Conn.: Yale University Press, 1974.

___. *Divided We Govern*. New Haven, Conn.: Yale University Press, 1991.

McKay, David. *Domestic Policy and Ideology*. New York: Cambridge University Press, 1989.

Mezey, Michael. *Congress, the President, and Public Policy*. Boulder, Colo.: Westview, 1989.

Milkis, Sidney M., and Michael Nelson. *The American Presidency*. Washington, D.C.: CQ Press, 1990.

Miller, Arthur S. "Separation of Powers: An Ancient Doctrine under Modern Challenge." *Administrative Law Review*, 28 (Summer 1976):299–325.

Moe, Ronald C., and Steven C. Teel. "Congress as Policy-Maker." *Political Science Quarterly*, 85 (September 1970):443–470.

Moffett, George D. III. *The Limits of Victory: The Ratification of the Panama Canal Treaties*. Ithaca, N.Y.: Cornell University Press, 1985.

Moyers, Bill. *The Secret Government*. Cabin John, Md.: Seven Locks, 1988.

Mueller, John E. *War, Presidents, and Public Opinion*. New York: Wiley, 1973.

Murray, Robert K., and Tim H. Blessing. *Greatness in the White House*. University Park: Pennsylvania State University Press, 1988.

Nathan, Richard P. *The Administrative Presidency*. New York: Wiley, 1983.

National Legal Center for the Public Interest. *Pork Barrels and Principles*. Washington, D.C.: NLCPI, 1988.

Nelson, Michael, ed. *The Presidency and the Political System*. Washington, D.C.: CQ Press, 1990.

Neustadt, Richard E. *Presidential Power and the Modern Presidents.* New York: Free Press, 1990.

Orfield, Gary. *Congressional Power: Congress and Social Change.* New York: Harcourt Brace Jovanovich, 1975.

Origins and Development of Congress. Washington, D.C.: Congressional Quarterly, 1976.

Orman, John M. *Presidential Secrecy and Deception.* Westport, Conn.: Greenwood, 1980.

Ornstein, Norman J., Thomas E. Mann, and Michael J. Malbin. *Vital Statistics on Congress.* Washington, D.C.: CQ Press, 1990.

Orren, Gary R., and Nelson Polsby, eds. *Media and Momentum.* Chatham, N.J.: Chatham House, 1987.

Ostrom, Jr., Charles W., and Dennis M. Simon. "Promise and Performance: A Dynamic Model of Presidential Popularity." *American Political Science Review,* 79 (June 1985):334–358.

Page, Benjamin I., and Mark P. Petracca. *The American Presidency.* New York: McGraw-Hill, 1983.

Parker, Glenn R. *Characteristics of Congress.* Englewood Cliffs, N.J.: Prentice-Hall, 1989.

Penner, Rudolph G., and Alan J. Abramson. *Broken Purse Strings.* Washington, D.C.: Urban Institute, 1988.

Peterson, Mark A. *Legislating Together: The White House and Capitol Hill from Eisenhower to Reagan.* Cambridge, Mass.: Harvard University Press, 1990.

Petracca, Mark P., Lonce Bailey, and Pamela Smith. "Proposals for Constitutional Reform." *Presidential Studies Quarterly,* 20 (Summer 1990):503–532.

Pfiffner, James P. *The President, the Budget, and Congress.* Boulder, Colo.: Westview, 1979.

Pious, Richard M. *The American Presidency.* New York: Basic Books, 1979.

Polsby, Nelson W. *Congress and the Presidency.* Englewood Cliffs, N.J.: Prentice-Hall, 1986.

Polsby, Nelson, and Aaron Wildavsky. *Presidential Elections.* New York: Free Press, 1988.

Pomper, Gerald. *Nominating the President.* New York: Norton, 1966.

Pyle, Christopher H., and Richard M. Pious. *The President, Congress, and the Constitution.* New York: Free Press, 1984.

Reedy, George. *The Twilight of the Presidency.* New York: New American Library, 1987.

Reveley, W. Taylor III. *War Powers of the President and Congress.* Charlottesville: University of Virginia Press, 1981.

Richardson, James D., ed. *Messages and Papers of the Presidents.* Washington, D.C.: Bureau of National Literature, 1913.

Rieselbach, Leroy N. *Congressional Reform.* Washington, D.C.: CQ Press, 1986.

Riker, William H. "The Heresthetics of Constitution-Making." *American Political Science Review,* 78 (March 1984):1–16.

Ripley, Randall B. *Congress: Process and Policy.* New York: Norton, 1988.

Ripley, Randall B., and Grace A. Franklin. *Congress, the Bureaucracy, and Public Policy.* Pacific Grove, Calif.: Brooks/Cole, 1991.

Rivers, Douglas, and Nancy L. Rose. "Passing the President's Program." *American Journal of Political Science,* 29 (May 1985):183–196.

Roberts, Charles, ed. *Has the President Too Much Power?* New York: Harper's Magazine Press, 1974.

Robinson, Donald L., ed. *Government for the Third American Century.* Boulder, Colo.: Westview, 1989.

___. *To the Best of My Ability.* New York: Norton, 1987.

___, ed. *Reforming American Government.* Boulder, Colo.: Westview, 1985.

Robinson, James A. *Congress and Foreign Policy-Making.* Homewood, Ill.: Dorsey, 1967.

Roosevelt, Theodore. *The Autobiography of Theodore Roosevelt.* New York: Scribner's, 1958.

Rossiter, Clinton. *The American Presidency.* New York: New American Library, 1960.

___. *Constitutional Dictatorship.* New York: Harcourt, Brace and World, 1948.

___. *The Supreme Court and the Commander in Chief.* Ithaca, N.Y.: Cornell University Press, 1976.

Salamon, Lester, and Michael S. Lund, eds. *The Reagan Presidency and the Governing of America.* Washington, D.C.: Urban Institute, 1984.

___. *Congress and Money.* Washington, D.C.: Urban Institute, 1980.

Schlesinger, Arthur M., Jr. *The Imperial Presidency.* Boston: Houghton Mifflin, 1973.

Schlesinger, Arthur M., Jr., and Roger Bruns, eds. *Congress Investigates: A Documented History, 1792–1974,* 5 vols. New York: Chelsea House, 1983.

Schneider, Jerrold. *Ideological Coalitions in Congress.* Westport, Conn.: Greenwood, 1979.

Schwartz, Bernard. *A Commentary on the Constitution of the United States,* 2 vols. New York: Macmillan, 1963.

Scigliano, Robert. *The Supreme Court and the Presidency.* New York: Free Press, 1971.

___. "The Framers' Congress." In *E Pluribus Unum.* Ed. by Sarah B. Thurow. Lanham, Md.: University Press of America, 1988.

Sedgwick, Jeffrey Leigh. "James Madison & the Problem of Executive Character." *Polity,* 21 (Fall 1988):5–23.

Shull, Steven A. *Domestic Policy Formation.* Westport, Conn.: Greenwood, 1983.

___. *Presidential Policy Making.* Brunswick, Ohio: King's Court Communications, 1979.

___, ed. *The Two Presidencies.* Chicago: Nelson-Hall, 1991.

Silbey, Joel H. " 'Our Successors Will Have an Easier Task': The First Congress under the Constitution, 1789–1791." *This Constitution,* 17 (Winter 1987):6–7.

Smith, Hedrick. *The Power Game.* New York: Ballantine, 1988.

Smith, Steven S., and Christopher J. Deering. *Committees in Congress.* Washington, D.C.: CQ Press, 1990.

Smyrl, Marc E. *Conflict or Codetermination? Congress, the President, and the Power to Make War.* Cambridge, Mass.: Ballinger, 1988.

Spanier, John, and Joseph Nogee, eds. *Congress, the Presidency and American Foreign Policy.* New York: Pergamon, 1981.

Spanier, John, and Eric M. Uslander. *American Foreign Policy Making and the Democratic Dilemmas.* New York: Holt, Rinehart & Winston, 1985.

Spitzer, Robert J. *The Presidency and Public Policy.* University: University of Alabama Press, 1983.

___. "Presidential Prerogative Power: The Case of the Bush Administration and Legislative Powers." *PS: Political Science and Politics,* 24 (March 1991):38–42.

___. *The Presidential Veto: Touchstone of the American Presidency.* Albany: State University of New York Press, 1988.

Squire, Peverill, ed. *The Iowa Caucuses and the Presidential Nominating Process.* Boulder, Colo.: Westview, 1989.

Story, Joseph. *Commentaries on the Constitution of the United States.* Durham, N.C.: Carolina Academic Press, 1987.

Sundquist, James L. *Constitutional Reform and Effective Governance.* Washington, D.C.: Brookings Institution, 1986.

___. *The Decline and Resurgence of Congress.* Washington, D.C.: Brookings Institution, 1981.

___. *Politics and Policy.* Washington, D.C.: Brookings Institution, 1968.

Taft, William H. *The President and His Powers.* New York: Columbia University Press, 1967.

Thach, Charles C., Jr. *The Creation of the Presidency, 1775–1789.* New York: Da Capo, 1969.

Thurber, James A., ed. *Divided Democracy.* Washington, D.C.: CQ Press, 1990.

Truman, David B., ed. *The Congress and America's Future.* Englewood Cliffs, N.J.: Prentice-Hall, 1973.

Tulis, Jeffrey. *The Rhetorical Presidency.* Princeton, N.J.: Princeton University Press, 1987.

Vogler, David J. *The Politics of Congress.* Boston: Allyn & Bacon, 1988.

Watson, Richard A. *The Presidential Contest.* Washington, D.C.: CQ Press, 1988.

Wayne, Stephen J. *The Legislative Presidency.* New York: Harper & Row, 1978.

___. *The Road to the White House.* New York: St. Martin's, 1992.

West, William F., and Joseph Cooper. "Legislative Influence v. Presidential Dominance." *Political Science Quarterly,* 104 (Winter 1989–90):581–606.

Whicker, Marcia, Raymond A. Moore, and James Pfiffner, eds. *The Presidency and the Persian Gulf War.* Lexington, Ky.: University Press of Kentucky, 1992.

White, John Kenneth. *The New Politics of Old Values.* Hanover, N.H.: University Press of New England, 1990.

White, Leonard D. *The Federalists.* New York: Macmillan, 1948.

___. *The Jacksonians.* New York: Macmillan, 1954.

___. *The Jeffersonians.* New York: Macmillan, 1951.

___. *The Republican Era.* New York: Macmillan, 1958.

Wildavsky, Aaron. *The New Politics of the Budgetary Process.* Glenview, Ill.: Scott, Foresman, 1988.

Wilson, Woodrow. *Congressional Government.* Cleveland: Meridian, 1956.

___. *Constitutional Government in the United States.* New York: Columbia University Press, 1908.

Wormuth, Francis D., and Edwin B. Firmage. *To Chain the Dog of War.* Urbana: University of Illinois Press, 1989.

Young, James S. *The Washington Community.* New York: Columbia University Press, 1966.

Zeidenstein, Harvey G. "The Reassertion of Congressional Power." *Political Science Quarterly,* 93 (Fall 1978):393–409.

Index

abortion, 217
Accountability for Intelligence Activities
    Act of 1980, 220
Acheson, Dean, 165
Adams, Henry, 34
Adams, John, 20, 24, 25
Adams, John Quincy, 25
Adler, David Gray, 200
administrative president, 129
Agriculture, Department of, 216
Allende, Salvadore, 143, 214, 219
American Bar Association, 251
Anti-Masonic party, 264
antiballistic missile system, 97
Appropriations Committee, 105, 116, 219
Arab-Israeli war of 1973, 216
Area Redevelopment Act of 1961,
    132–133
arenas of power, 127–131
Arkansas River project, 97
Armed Services Committee, 181, 202
Arms Control and Disarmament Agency,
    205
arms sales, 194, 211–214, 233
Arthur, Chester A., 33
Articles of Confederation, 1, 2–3, 5, 8,
    12, 16, 195
assassination, 30, 94, 100, 220

Baker, Howard, 205
Baker, James, 138
Balanced Budget and Emergency Deficit
    Control Act of 1985, *see* Gramm-
    Rudman-Hollings
Bas v. Tingy, 152
Bay of Pigs invasion, 219
Beal, Richard, 64–65
Benton, Thomas Hart, 30
Berman, Larry, 107
bicameralism, 122; legislative, 5, 9–10, 11
bill drafting, 42
Bill of Rights, 8
Binkley, Wilfred, 4, 23
Blaine, James G., 34

Boland, Edward, 222, 226
Boland amendments (1982–1986),
    221–225, 227
boll weevil Democrats, 60, 109, 285
Bond, Jon R., 103–104, 135, 240
Bork, Robert, 249–250
Botts, John Minor, 28, 29
Bowsher v. Synar, 111
box scores, 78–79
Boxer Rebellion, 153
Brennan, William, 200
British Bill of Rights, 2
Broder, David, 184, 256
Brooks, Jack, 121
Brownlow Committee, 106
Bryan, William Jennings, 268
Bryce, James, 33, 77, 236
Buchanan, Bruce, 63
Buchanan, James, 31, 97, 153
Buchanan, Patrick, 182
Budget and Accounting Act of 1921, 106
Budget and Impoundment Control Act of
    1974, 46, 108, 110, 120, 242, 252
budgeting, 239–240; authority, evolution,
    105–118; executive, congressional
    objections to, 107–109; legislative,
    105–107; reconciliation process,
    109; sequestering, 115
Bureau of the Budget (BOB), *see* Office
    of Management and Budget (OMB)
Burke, Aedanus, 22
Burns, James MacGregor, xxi, 92, 256,
    289
Bush, George, 40–41, 55, 59, 66, 68, 95,
    96, 111, 114, 115, 137–139,
    179–194, 215–216, 231, 232, 255,
    279; veto, 74–75
Butler, Pierce, 7, 150
Byrd, Robert, 116

cabinet, 218, 272
Caesar, Julius, 38

301